Problems from Kant

Problems from Kant

James Van Cleve

New York   Oxford

Oxford University Press

1999

Oxford University Press

Oxford   New York
Athens   Auckland   Bangkok   Bogotá   Buenos Aires   Calcutta
Cape Town   Chennai   Dar es Salaam   Delhi   Florence   Hong Kong   Istanbul
Karachi   Kuala Lumpur   Madrid   Melbourne   Mexico City   Mumbai
Nairobi   Paris   São Paulo   Singapore   Taipei   Tokyo   Toronto   Warsaw

and associated companies in
Berlin   Ibadan

Published by Oxford University Press, Inc.
198 Madison Avenue, New York, New York 10016

Oxford is a registered trademark of Oxford University Press

Library of Congress Cataloging-in-Publication Data
Van Cleve, James.
    Problems from Kant / James Van Cleve.
      p.   cm.
    Includes index
    ISBN 0—19—508322—9
      1. Kant, Immanuel, 1724–1804. Kritif der rainen Vernunft.
    2. Knowledge, Theory of.   3. Causation.   4. Reason.   I. Title.
    B2779.V33   1999
121'.092—dc21   98-26825

9 8 7 6 5 4 3 2 1

Printed in the United States of America
on acid-free paper

For My Parents

Acknowledgments

I am grateful to the following for permission to incorporate material from previously published articles:

Van Cleve, James. "Substance, Matter, and Kant's First Analogy," in *Kant–Studien*, 70. (Berlin: Walter de Grutyer & Co., 1979), pp. 149–61. Reprinted, by permission, from Walter de Grutyer & Co., Berlin.

Van Cleve, James. "Another Volley at Kant's Reply to Hume," in *Kant on Causality, Freedom, and Objectivity*, edited by William L. Harper and Ralf Meerbote. (Minneapolis: University of Minnesota Press, 1984), pp. 42–57. Reprinted, by permission, from University of Minnesota Press.

Van Cleve, James. "Putnam, Kant, and Secondary Qualities," in *Philosophical Papers,* 24. (Johannesburg: University of Witwatersrand, 1995), pp. 83–109. Reprinted, by permission, from the Editor of the Philosophical Papers.

Van Cleve, James. "Kant's First and Second Paralogisms," in *The Monist*, 69. (La Salle, Illinois: The Hegeler Institute, 1986), pp. 483–488. Copyright © 1986, *The Monist*, La Salle, IL 61301. Reprinted by permission.

Van Cleve, James. "Incongruent Counterparts and Things in Themselves," in *Proceedings: Sixth International Kant Congress*, edited by G. Funke and Th. M. Seebohm. (Washington, D.C.: University Press of America, 1989), pp. 33–45. Reprinted, by permission, from Center for Advanced Research in Phenomenology, Inc.

Van Cleve, James. "The Ideality of Time," In *Proceedings of the Eighth International Kant Congress*, edited by Hoke Robinson, vol. I. (Milwaukee: Marquette University Press, 1995), pp. 411–421. Reprinted, by permission, from Marquette University Press.

Van Cleve, James. "Reflections on Kant's Second Antinomy," Synthese, 47. (Dordrecht: Kluwer Academic Publishers, 1981), pp. 481–494. Reprinted, with kind permission, from Kluwer Academic Publishers.

Van Cleve, James. "Geometry, Transcendental Idealism, and Kant's Two Worlds," in *Minds, Ideas, and Objects*, edited by Phillip D. Cummins and Guenter Zoeller, vol. 2 of the North American Kant Society Studies in Philosophy (Atascadero, Calif.: Ridgeview, 1992), pp. 291–302.

Preface

Kant's *Critique of Pure Reason* is a critique with both positive and negative aims: its task is to "institute a tribunal which will assure to reason its lawful claims, and dismiss all groundless pretensions" (Axi). Kant seeks to determine the scope and limits of *a priori* knowledge (that is, knowledge based on reason without dependence on experience), defending such knowledge against skeptical suspicion in areas where it is legitimate and exposing its lack of credentials in areas where it is not. He argues that *a priori* knowledge (in particular, the special variety he called synthetic *a priori* knowledge) is possible in arithmetic and geometry and in the foundations of the natural sciences, but not in many areas of traditional philosophical inquiry— those concerned with the properties of the soul, the outer limits and inmost nature of the cosmos, and the existence of God. *A priori* knowledge is possible in the former areas because the objects with which our knowledge has to deal are to a significant extent the creations of our own minds; it is not possible in the latter areas because there the objects of our purported knowledge are not given to us in experience and are beyond the power of our minds to shape. Kant thus advances a novel explanation of the possibility of *a priori* knowledge, built on the supposition that things in space and time are dependent on the human mind. This is the view he calls transcendental idealism.

In the course of elaborating his theory, Kant addresses many important epistemological and metaphysical problems: the existence and nature of *a priori* knowledge, the ontological status of space, time, and matter, the role of the mind in shaping reality, the contribution of conceptualization to experience, the relation of appearances to things in themselves, the nature of the self, and arguments for the existence of God. I discuss all of these topics in this book, more or less in the same order as Kant himself. (The chief exception is the antinomy of infinite divisibility, which I discuss in chapter 6 alongside the

Transcendental Aesthetic, rather than later as part of the Transcendental Dialectic.) At times my emphasis is on making clear what Kant's problems, positions, and arguments were; at other times my emphasis is on trying to determine whether Kant was right.

On some large issues I side with Kant and against his contemporary critics. For example, I hold that there are synthetic *a priori* truths and things in themselves. On other issues I disagree with Kant and with his contemporary defenders. For example, I do not find much by way of cogent argument in the Transcendental Deduction of the Categories, and I find more of interest in the old discipline of rational psychology than in Kant's critique of it. Most of all, I do not subscribe to Kant's idealism—but unlike many contemporary interpreters, I do take it seriously, regarding it as the central strategem in his philosophy.

An argument, the logic books tell us, is something with premises and a conclusion. Yet one can read many a book purporting to expound the arguments of Kant and others of the great philosophers without being told exactly what their conclusions are or from what premises they are supposed to follow. I have done my best in this book never to discuss an argument of Kant's without making its premise-and-conclusion structure clear. Doubtless there are many readers who will disagree with my efforts, believing that arguments better representing Kant's intent or better calculated to reach his conclusions can be found. I ask of such readers only that they be as explicit as I have been about their own favored alternatives.

I began writing this book during a fellowship year at the National Humanities Center. I am grateful to the Center for its friendly and helpful staff and for the unencumbered time and pleasant space they made available to me.

I have learned about Kant from many people over the years, probably more than I can adequately acknowledge. My greatest debts to writings on Kant are undoubtedly to the two great Kant books of the 1960s, Bennett's *Kant's Analytic* and Strawson's *The Bounds of Sense*. My greatest debt to an individual is to my teacher, the late Lewis White Beck.

I am indebted to many persons for their helpful comments on one or another part of the text. I wish to thank in particular Henry Allison, Lewis White Beck, Georges Dicker, Eli Hirsch, Matthew McGrath, Trenton Merricks, Michael Pendlebury, Carl Posy, and Ernest Sosa. For research assistance in the final phases, I wish to thank Baron Reed and Timothy Chambers. I am grateful for the expert hand of Rex Welshon in preparing the index.

I should like especially to record my gratitude here to three groups of teachers: my first teachers in philosophy at the University of Iowa, my second teachers in philosophy at the University of Rochester, and my third teachers in philosophy (who are also my colleagues and students) at Brown University.

Finally, I wish to thank my parents, my wife, and my children for all that they have given me.

Contents

1. Transcendental Idealism: An Overview 3
   A. The Great Snowy Mountain 3
   B. The Copernican Revolution 5
   C. Appearances and Things in Themselves 6
   D. Virtual Objects 8
   E. Realism, Idealism, and Antirealism 12

2. Necessity, Analyticity, and the *A Priori* 15
   A. Three Distinctions 15
   B. Synthetic *A Priori* 21
   C. Quine's Attack on Analyticity 27
   D. The Hume Problem 30
   E. The Herz Problem 32

3. The Ideality of Space: Geometry 34
   A. The Argument from Geometry 34
   B. Implications for Idealism 37
   C. The Objections of Russell and Moore 37
   D. Explaining Necessity 41

4. The Ideality of Space: Incongruent Counterparts 44
   A. The Argument from Intelligibility 45
   B. The Argument from Interchangeability 45
   C. The Argument from Reducibility 47
   D. Things in Themselves as Intelligibilia 48
   E. Things in Themselves as Things Apart from Relation 49
   F. Things in Themselves as Real Existents 49

5. The Ideality of Time 52

    A. The Objection of Lambert and Mendelssohn 52

    B. Kant's Radical Response 54

    C. The Break with Cartesian Epistemology 57

    D. What Did Kant Really Believe about Time? 60

6. The Ideality of Matter 62

    A. Against Infinite Complexity 63

    B. Against Ultimate Simples 65

    C. Kant's Way Out 67

7. Experience and Objects 73

    A. Preliminaries 73

    B. An Anatomy of Experience 74

    C. The Objective Deduction 76

    D. An Outline of the Subjective Deduction 79

    E. The Unity Premise 79

    F. The Synthesis Premise 84

    G. The Category Premise 87

    H. Relation to an Object 90

    I. Strawson's Objectivity Argument 98

8. Substance and the First Analogy 105

    A. Two Concepts of Substance 105

    B. The First Analogy 106

    C. The Backdrop Argument 107

    D. From Substance$_1$ to Substance$_2$ 108

    E. The Anchoring Argument 109

    F. Two Arguments from Verifiability 111

    G. Carving Out Substances 113

    H. The Kant-Frege View 115

    I. Summary of Results to Date 117

    J. Individual Essences 118

    K. Phenomenal Substances 120

9. Causation and the Second Analogy 122

    A. Background 122

    B. Beck's Argument 125

    C. Irreversibility 125

    D. A Revision of the Argument 128

    E. Two Objections 130

    F. From Conditions of Knowing to Conditions of Being 132

10. Noumena and Things in Themselves 134

    A. The Distinction Between Phenomena and Noumena 134

    B. Classical Criticisms of the Thing in Itself 135

    C. Contemporary Criticisms of the Thing in Itself 138

D. One World or Two? 143
E. The In Itself as the Intrinsic 150
F. Isomorphism 155
G. Affection 162
H. Secondary Qualities 167

11. Problems of the Self 172
A. Is the Self a Substance? 173
B. Is the Self Simple? 175
C. Can a Self Have Emergent Properties? 179
D. Does the Self Endure? 180
E. How Many Selves? 182

12. Rational Theology 187
A. The Ontological Argument 187
B. Real Predicates 188
C. Existence and Quantifiers 189
D. Rejecting the Subject 191
E. The Modal Ontological Argument 192
F. Could There Be a Necessary Being? 194
G. A Meinongian Ontological Argument 198
H. Necessary Being and *Ens Realissimum* 200
I. The Cosmological Argument 204
J. The Principle of Sufficient Reason 207
K. The Realization of All Possibilities 208

13. Kant and Contemporary Irrealism 212
A. Putnam's Internal Realism 212
B. Is Kant an Internal Realist? 214
C. Dummett's Antirealism 217
D. Is Kant an Antirealist? 220

Appendices 226
A. Reds, Greens, and the Synthetic *A Priori* 226
B. Five Questions about Causation and Necessity 229
C. Incongruent Counterparts and Absolute Space 231
D. Unperceived Phenomena 233
E. Singularity and Immediacy 235
F. Two Concepts of Unity 238
G. Split Brains and Unity of Apperception 241
H. Synthesis and the Binding Problem 243
I. Determinism, Projection, and Imposition 244
J. Relational Predicates and Relativized Predicates 246
K. Can You Eat Your Cake Empirically and Still Have It Transcendentally? 249
L. Under a Description 252
M. Concepts of Isomorphism 253

N. A Kantian Argument Against the Correspondence Theory?   254
O. Williams Contra Lichtenberg   256

Notes   259

References   319

Index   331

Problems from Kant

1

Transcendental Idealism

An Overview

> Kant is always superbly methodical, persis-
> tent, regular and meticulous as he scales that
> great snowy mountain of thought concern-
> ing what is in the mind and what is outside
> the mind. It is, for modern climbers, one of
> the highest peaks of all.
>
> > Robert Pirsig, *Zen and the Art*
> > *of Motorcycle Maintenance*

A. The Great Snowy Mountain

"The most important and difficult function of philosophy," wrote Sir William Hamilton, is "to determine the shares to which the knowing subject and the object known may pretend in the total act of cognition." This question looms as the great snowy mountain referred to above: how much of the world owes its existence or its character to the activity of human (or other) minds, and how much would be just as it is even in the absence of minds? On this question, philosophies run the gamut from pure idealisms that ascribe everything to the knowing subject to pure realisms that ascribe everything to the object known. There are, of course, many positions in between, including most famously the doctrine (espoused by Descartes, Locke, and others) of primary and secondary qualities.

Kant gave the names 'things in themselves' and 'noumena' to those objects or aspects of reality that do not depend on human cognition; he labeled as 'appearances' or 'phenomena' those aspects that do.[1] In Kantian terminology, then, our question may be put thus: how much of the world is phenomenal and how much noumenal? Kant's own answer lies close to the idealist pole. He was not a total idealist, since he believed that the world does contain a noumenal element. But he placed many more of the world's features on the phenomenal side of the line than either Descartes or Locke. In particular, space and time (and thus nearly all of Locke's primary qualities) are for Kant merely phenomenal, space and time being "forms of intuition" rather than features of things in themselves. He also believed that certain structural features of the world (e.g., its being subject to Euclidean geometry and to deterministic causal laws) were due to the human mind. Such is the view Kant called "transcendental idealism." (See A26–28/B42–44 and *Prolegomena*, pp. 36–37.)[2]

As I interpret him, then, Kant's transcendental idealism is idealism indeed, at least regarding everything in space and time. In so taking him, however, I am running against the tide of much contemporary commentary. Reading some commentators, one can begin to wonder whether Kant's transcendental idealism has anything much to do with idealism at all. Here, for instance, is H.E. Matthews:

> To say that space and spatial objects are 'in us' . . . is not to say that they are a particular type of thing, the type of thing which exists, as sensation does, only in an individual mind. It is rather to say that thinking in spatial terms, thinking of things as having a position in space, as being extended in space, as having spatial relations to other things, etc., is a purely *human* way of thinking, determined by the nature of human experience. . . .[3]

I am not sure what positive view Matthews means to attribute to Kant, but it appears at any rate that for him, Kant does *not* make objects in space dependent on human minds.

For another instance, here is Ralph Walker:

> [T]he world of appearances [is] the world as we believe it to be on the basis of our canons of scientific procedure and theory-construction. . . . And transcendental idealism, which admits the existence of things in themselves while recognizing that our theory about the world is our theory and may not be the right one, does have the support of reflective common sense.[4]

As glossed by Walker, transcendental idealism seems to amount to little more than this: our view of the world is underdetermined by our empirical data and our methodological principles. There is nothing in this to which a realist need take exception.

A final instance is provided by Henry Allison.[5] Allison has developed an interpretation of Kant's transcendental idealism according to which its key tenets—that things in themselves are not in space and time, and that objects must conform to our knowledge of them—explicitly turn out to be tautologies. The former is a tautology because "to consider things as they are in themselves (in the Kantian sense) means precisely to consider them apart from their relation to human sensibility and its *a priori* conditions," and these conditions include space and time.[6] The latter is a tautology because "an object is now to be understood as whatever conforms to our knowledge."[7] It need hardly be said that if transcendental idealism is a tautology, it is not idealism.

When I read Kant, I cannot help thinking to the contrary that he is an honest-to-goodness idealist regarding the entire world in space and time. Compare this definition of transcendental idealism:

> By *transcendental idealism* I mean the doctrine that appearances are to be regarded as being, one and all, representations only, not things in

themselves, and that time and space are therefore only sensible forms of our intuition, not determinations given as existing by themselves, nor conditions of objects viewed as things in themselves.(A369)

One large feature of his philosophy that seems to me to be unworkable without idealism is the Copernican Revolution, to which I now turn.

B. The Copernican Revolution

In a famous passage, Kant compares his philosophy to the central thought of Copernicus:

> Hitherto it has been assumed that all our knowledge must conform to objects. But all attempts to extend our knowledge of objects by establishing something in regard to them *a priori*, by means of concepts, have, on this assumption, ended in failure. We must therefore make trial whether we may not have more success in the tasks of metaphysics, if we suppose that objects must conform to our knowledge. This would agree better with what is desired, namely, that it should be possible to have knowledge of objects *a priori*, determining something in regard to them prior to their being given. We should then be proceeding precisely on the lines of Copernicus' primary hypothesis. Failing of satisfactory progress in explaining the movements of the heavenly bodies on the supposition that they all revolved round the spectator, he tried whether he might not have better success if he made the spectator to revolve and the stars to remain at rest. (Bxvi–xvii; see also the note at Bxxii)

The pre-Copernican astronomers took the observed motions of the heavenly bodies to be their real motions (give or take a few epicycles). Copernicus, on the other hand, sought to explain the observed motions not by ascribing them to the bodies themselves as their real motions, but by supposing them to be apparent motions generated by the motion of the earthbound observer. Analogously, Kant seeks to account for many of the traits we observe in objects by supposing them to be traits at least partly due to the activity or constitution of the human spectator. He does this especially for traits that we can assign to objects *a priori*. Whenever we know *a priori* that an object O is F, O is F *because* we so apprehend it; we do not apprehend it as we do because it is that way. As Kant likes to put it, the object conforms to our knowledge rather than conversely. Such is Kant's Copernican Revolution in philosophy.

How is it possible for objects to owe any of their traits to our manner of cognizing them? The answer I find most satisfactory is this: the objects in question owe their very *existence* to being cognized by us. An object can depend on us for its *Sosein* (its being the *way* it is) only if it also depends on us for its *Sein* (its *being*, period). It is in this way that the Copernican Revolution is bound up with idealism. I say more about how this is so in the next section and elsewhere (especially in chapter 3).

Kant himself unhesitatingly draws idealist conclusions from his Copernican strategy. Immediately on the heels of the passage in which he compares himself with Copernicus, he explicitly equates objects with "the *experience* in which alone, as given objects, they can be known." And here is the moral he draws from his account in the *Prolegomena* of how we can "anticipate" or know *a priori* the geometrical properties of yet-to-be-encountered objects:

> Should any man venture to doubt that these [space and time] are determinations adhering not to things in themselves, but to their relation to our sensibility, I should be glad to know how he can find it possible to know *a priori* how their intuition will be characterized before we have any acquaintance with them and before they are presented to us. Such, however, is the case with space and time. But this is quite comprehensible as soon as both count for nothing more than formal conditions of our sensibility, while the objects count merely as phenomena. . . . (*Prolegomena*, p. 31)

He draws a similar moral from his account of how certain *a priori* concepts—the categories—can be known in advance to characterize objects of experience:

> If the objects with which our knowledge has to deal were things in themselves, we could have no *a priori* concepts of them. . . . But if, on the other hand, we have to deal only with appearances, it is not merely possible, but necessary, that certain *a priori* concepts should precede empirical knowledge of objects. For since a mere modification of our sensibility can never be met with outside us, the objects, as appearances, constitute an object which is merely in us.(A129)

The idealist implications of Kant's accounts of *a priori* knowledge and *a priori* concepts are discussed at length in chapters 3 and 7.

C. Appearances and Things in Themselves

Appearances, in Kant's vocabulary, are the objects of intuition, intuition being one species of representation.[8] They include things seen, felt, or otherwise perceived; they also include objects of inner sense or introspection, such as tickles and pains. In dozens of passages, Kant tells us that appearances have no being apart from being represented. Here is a representative sampling of such passages:

> [A]ppearances . . . must not be taken as objects capable of existing outside our power of representation.(A104)

> Appearances do not exist in themselves but only relatively to the subject in which, so far as it has senses, they inhere.(B164)

> It is a proposition which must indeed sound strange, that a thing can exist only in the representation of it, but in this case the objection falls, inasmuch as the things with which we are here concerned are not things in themselves, but appearances only, that is, representations.(A374–75; the passage occurs in a footnote attached to a sentence ending "nothing in [space] can count as real save only what is represented in it")

The objects of experience, then, are *never* given *in themselves*, but only in experience, and have no existence outside it.(A492/B521)

Kant often puts this point by saying that appearances *are* representations, as in the words I have deleted from the A104 passage above: "[A]ppearances are themselves nothing but sensible representations. . . ." When he does so, I think it is useful to keep in mind the act-object (or 'ing'-'ed') ambiguity of words like 'representation' (which is also possessed by words like *Vorstellung* in German). We should construe him as saying that appearances are representeds that have no being apart from the representing of them.

Things in themselves, by contrast, are things that exist independently of human representation or cognition. They exist whether perceived or no and have whatever properties they do independently of us. Here are some representative passages:

> [Things in themselves] exist independently of us and of our sensibility.(A369)

> . . . real in themselves, that is, outside this advance of experience.(A492/ B521)

> For if we were thinking of a thing in itself, we could indeed say that it exists in itself apart from relation to our senses and possible experience.(A493/B522)

The fundamental tenet of Kant's transcendental idealism is that things in space and time are appearances only, not things in themselves. With the contrast between appearances and things in themselves drawn as above, this amounts to the claim that things in space and time have no existence apart from being represented by us:

> [E]verything intuited in space or time, and therefore all objects of any experience possible to us, are nothing but appearances, that is, mere representations. . . . This doctrine I entitle *transcendental idealism*. The realist in the transcendental meaning of this term, treats these modifications of our sensibility as self-subsistent things, that is treats mere representations as things in themselves.(A490–91/B518–19)

> By *transcendental idealism* I mean the doctrine that appearances are to be regarded as being, one and all, representations only, not things in themselves, and that time and space are therefore only sensible forms of our intuition, not determinations given as existing by themselves, nor conditions of objects viewed as things in themselves.(A369)

Kant's idealism comes to the fore many times in the ensuing chapters.

What I have said so far in this section suggests that things in themselves and appearances are two separate types of object, one type existing independently of human cognition and the other not. This is indeed the traditional interpretation of Kant, but it is not the view now dominant among Kant scholars. The prevailing view, sometimes called the "one-world" or "double-aspect" view, holds instead that there is one set of objects and two ways of considering them. Appearances are objects as we know them; things in themselves are these same objects as they are independent of our knowledge. Moreover, what properties these objects have depends on the standpoint from which they are being considered. Considered as appearances or in relation to our sensibility, objects have spatial and temporal form; considered in themselves, they lack spatial and temporal form. That, according to the double-aspect view, is what Kant means when he says that appearances are in space and time and things in themselves are not.

The double-aspect view has always seemed to me unfathomably mysterious. How is it possible for the properties of a thing to vary according to how it is considered? As I sit typing these words, I have shoes on my feet. But consider me apart from my shoes: so considered, am I barefoot? I am inclined to say no; consider me how you will, I am not now barefoot. But perhaps I am missing the point of the "considered apart from" locution. Perhaps to say that someone is barefoot considered apart from his shoes just means this: *if* he had no shoes, he would on that assumption be barefoot. Similarly, to say that things considered apart from our forms of sensibility (space and time) are nonspatial would be to say this: *if* things had no spatial characteristics, then they would have no spatial characteristics. That is evidently what the nonspatiality of things in themselves comes to in Allison's view, mentioned above in section A: rightly understood, it is a tautology. I cannot help wondering: if transcendental idealism is a tautology, why did Kant write such a long book defending it?

Double-aspect theories do not deserve such short shrift, however, and receive a fuller hearing in the course of this book. Allison's development of it is examined and criticized in chapter 10, section D; other possible developments are considered in chapter 10, section E, and appendices K and L.

D. Virtual Objects

The two-worlds interpretation in its traditional form treats appearances as existing things distinct from, though dependent on, mental representings. This conception of appearances as distinct existents gives rise to a number of problems. For one thing, some real existents, namely, appearances, would be in space and time, a result apparently ruled out by Kant's arguments in the antinomies (as G.E. Moore pointed out).[9] For another, if appearances are entities distinct from the acts by which they are apprehended, it becomes difficult to see why they should be dependent on these acts for their existence. This difficulty is developed further below.

I recommend an interpretation of Kantian appearances that is different both from the one-world view and from the two-worlds view in its traditional form. According to this third interpretation, appearances (or phenomena) are not the same objects as noumena, considered from a specially human point of view; nor are they a second variety of objects existing alongside noumena. Instead, they are *virtual objects*. A virtual object is similar in some ways to what Brentano called an "intentional object," but it is not to be conceived as having its own special kind of being. Instead, to say that a virtual object of a certain sort (e.g., a patch of red) exists is shorthand for saying that a certain kind of representation occurs. In the case of a more complex or multifaceted virtual object (e.g., a house or a ship), to say that it exists it is to say that an entire rule-governed sequence of representations occurs or is in the offing.

My use of the term 'virtual object' is inspired by Quine's theory of virtual classes (and not, as some readers may have guessed, by computer-simulated "virtual reality"). In Quine's theory, to say that y is a member of the class {x:Fx} is only to say that y is F, "so that there remains no hint of there being such a thing as the class {x:Fx}."[10] In short, we may accord classes a nominal form of existence by ostensibly speaking of them and predicating various things of them, but we may also paraphrase away all mention of them. Virtual classes are thus a species of what Russell called "logical constructions" or "logical fictions."[11] A paradigm of a logical construction in Russell's sense is the shadow that is now creeping across my lawn: although we may truly say that there is such a shadow, so saying does not commit us ontologically to an aetherial two-dimensional entity that is literally on the move. The whole truth in what we say is exhausted by familiar facts about the sun, the lawn, and the intervening shade tree.

If Kantian appearances are virtual objects, then to say that someone is aware of an appearance of a certain sort is only to say that he is sensing or intuiting in a certain way. Ontologically, then, virtual-object theory is of a piece with adverbial theories of sensation, as developed by Ducasse and Chisholm.[12] The chief difference is that virtual-object theory admits objects back in as nominal subjects of predication. Thus, we may for convenience speak of a red object of Jones's awareness when in strictness all that is happening is that Jones is sensing redly.[13]

One advantage of construing Kantian appearances as virtual objects is that it enables us to explain how their being can depend on their being perceived. How, after all, are we to understand the relation between an object O whose *esse* is *percipi* and the corresponding act of perception, P? I see three main possibilities:

1. O and P are distinct but inseparable existents, as in many versions of the sense-datum theory that flourished from the 1920s through the 1940s: a sense datum is one thing, the sensing of it another, and the first cannot exist apart from the second.
2. O is not a normal existent at all, but an object that "intentionally inexists" in the act of perceiving it, as in the earlier views of Brentano.
3. O is a virtual object in the sense explained above, that is, a logical construction out of the states of perceivers: all talk ostensibly about O is paraphrasable away in favor of talk exclusively about P. To say what kind of object a given act of perceiving has is really to say in what *manner* the act takes place or what *kind* of act it is; it is to characterize the act intrinsically rather than relationally.

In the first case, perceiving is a relation to the existent; in the second, it is a relation to the inexistent; and in the third, it is not a relation at all. The three possibilities may be diagrammed as follows:

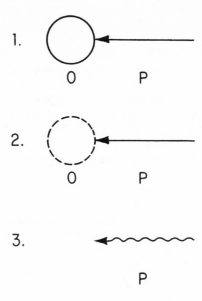

I find the first two models unsatisfactory. The first is untenable on the Humean ground that whatever items are distinct are also separable, or capable of existing apart from each other.[14] Putting the point with the help of the diagram, if I erase the act, why must I also erase the object? The first model affords no good answer to this question.[15]

The second model (unless it reduces to the third) is deeply mysterious. What is this status of "inexistence"? For the early Brentano, it was a special mode of being, "short of actuality but more than nothingness," and lasting just as long as the object is apprehended.[16] For Meinong, it was *Aussersein*, which is not supposed to be a mode of being at all: on his view, cognitive acts can put us in relation to things that do not exist in any sense however broad.[17] Brentano's view gives us the mystery of a second mode of being; Meinong's, the mystery of relations to the nonexistent. Perhaps neither mystery is insuperable, but I would prefer to avoid them if I can.

In any event, it remains unclear to me how the second model enables us to make intelligible to ourselves *esse est percipi* status. Whatever mode of being or nonbeing it is that intentional objects are supposed to have, why could they not have it even when not perceived?[18]

I believe that the third model alone gives us a satisfactory way of understanding *esse est percipi* status. In this model, an appearance cannot exist unperceived for the same reason that a waltz cannot exist undanced: in either case, for the "object" of the act to exist *is* for the act to take place in a certain way (as indicated by the undulations in the arrow).

I note that Brentano, who introduced (or revived) the notion of intentional inexistence, seems in his later writings to have moved from the second model to the third. This is suggested by the following quotations: "'There is something which is the object of thought' may be equated with 'There is something which thinks'";[19] "[i]ts *being* an object, however, is only the linguistic correlate of the person experiencing it *having* it as object. . . ."[20]

A further advantage of construing Kantian appearances as virtual objects is that it lets us explain how objects can conform to our cognition of them, as required by the Copernican Revolution. To bring this out, I now call attention to a further important feature of logical constructions. If As are logical constructions out of Bs, not only does the *existence* of any A consist in some fact's holding about the Bs, but also the possession of any *properties* by an A consists in the possession of certain properties (not necessarily the same ones) by the relevant Bs. Russell and Ayer sometimes put this by saying that every true statement about the As must be translatable into an equivalent statement just about the Bs;[21] the point is also often put by saying that the As are reducible to the Bs. But requiring translatability or reducibility is requiring more than is needed for present purposes.[22] The essential point is simply that every truth about an A must be derivable from some truths about the Bs. This point is important at a number of places in this book. Its importance just now is that it gives us a sense in which objects must "conform to our knowledge": as constructions out of our cognitive states, objects must be such that every truth about them follows from certain truths about our cognitive states.

If all objects in space and time are appearances, and if appearances are virtual objects in the sense I have explained, it follows that all objects in space and time are logical constructions out of perceivers and their states. That makes Kant a *phenomenalist*, that is, one who holds that all truths about physical things are derivable from truths about states of perceivers. Phenomenalism is now unfashionable, and so likewise is the attribution of it to Kant. Nonetheless, I show below that there are several important places in which an explicit commitment to phenomenalism plays an essential role in Kant's philosophizing. These places include the Transcendental Deduction's account of an 'object', the proof of the Second Analogy of Experience, and the solution to the Mathematical Antinomies. Unlike some phenomenalists, however, Kant is also a *noumenalist*: he believes there are some objects, the things in themselves, that resist phenomenalist reduction. If nothing else, there are the cognitive acts and agents on which phenomena depend, for these can hardly be supposed to exist only as the virtual objects of further acts.

As I have portrayed matters so far, virtual objects exist only in a manner of speaking; to say that they exist is just shorthand for saying certain things about the more basic entities out of which they are constructions. We would not quantify over virtual objects in an ontologically perspicuous language (which is why Russell sometimes calls his logical constructions "logical fictions"). But there is another conception according to which objects of the kind I am deeming "virtual" or "nominal" exist as entities in their own right. Although they exist only in virtue of certain facts about relatively more basic entities, they *do* exist, and it is legitimate to quantify over them. Such is Ernest Sosa's conception of a *supervenient entity*, which he illustrates with the paradigm of a snowball.[23] Sosa would say that when a quantity of snow is packed and rounded in a certain way, a snowball thereby comes into being: it is a genuinely new item under the sun, distinct from the snow of which it is composed, even though its existence consists entirely in the snow's being appropriately shaped. Many of the logical principles that govern virtual objects also govern supervenient entities; most important, if a supervenient entity O exists and has property F, its existing and its having F must each derive necessarily from certain properties of or relations among the more basic entities on which the existence of O supervenes. The chief difference between the two conceptions is that whereas virtual objects exist only in a manner of speaking, supervenient entities exist as "ontological emergents" over which we are free to quantify.

Why should we regard Kantian appearances as virtual objects rather than supervenient entities? In many contexts it does not much matter which way we regard them. In others, however, Kant's purposes are better served by the virtual-object approach. I note these as they come up. In the meantime, my language in this book generally favors the constructionist construal.[24]

A word is in order about the provenance of my views. For the conception of Kantian appearances as intentional objects, existing only in the representation of them, I am indebted to work by Wilfrid Sellars, Phillip Cummins, and Richard Aquila.[25] I do not know, however, whether these authors would take the further step of construing intentional objects as logical constructions out of conscious states. In Aquila's case, I suspect the answer is no; some of the things he says suggests instead a view like our model 2 above. For example, he says that the object of an intuiting might or might not exist. Suppose I am aware of a tree at t_1 that is atomized at t_2, simultaneously with the onset of a hallucination that leaves the intrinsic character of my experience unchanged. I gather Aquila would say that I am aware of the same object all along, and that it exists at t_1 but not at t_2. To say this is to quantify over objects in a way that makes them not merely virtual.

E. Realism, Idealism, and Antirealism

Realism has been defined by one author as the view that "material objects or external realities exist apart from our knowledge or consciousness of them."[26] Idealism, the main traditional rival of realism, has been defined by another as the view that "being is dependent on the knowing of it."[27] 'Knowing' as it occurs in such definitions is ambiguous, and corresponding to its two meanings are two importantly different things that can be meant by saying that reality does (or does not) depend on the knowing of it. 'Knowing' can refer to an act of awareness, acquaintance, or apprehension, whose object (if it has one) is not necessarily propositional. It can also refer, as is more common nowadays, to the knowledge of a fact or the knowledge that something is so. Knowledge in the latter sense is commonly thought to have at least three conditions: belief, truth, and evidence. Furthermore, when someone holds that a certain fact depends on being known or knowable, it is generally dependence on the third component, the evidential component, that is meant.

We may thus distinguish two principal things that might be meant by saying reality depends on being known. It could mean, on the one hand, that the constituents of reality depend for their existence on acts of awareness, on their being apprehended by a conscious mind. It could mean, on the other hand, that any facts that obtain depend for their obtaining on their being known or knowable, hence on there being evidence for them. I shall refer to these two dimensions of dependence as mind-dependence and evidence-dependence, respectively.

Note that in my usage, minds themselves are not necessarily mind-dependent. Although it is trivially true that minds would not exist unless there were minds, it does not automatically follow that they would not exist unless they were *apprehended* by minds.[28]

Mind-dependence and evidence-dependence do not necessarily go together. Entities can be mind-dependent even though facts about them are not evidence-dependent, and facts can be evidence-dependent even though the entities that figure in them are not mind-dependent. To illustrate the first of these possibilities, let us stipulate that *sensa* are entities that do not exist unless someone senses them, so they are mind-dependent. But the following facts are at least evidence-*transcendent* (i.e., there could not be *conclusive* evidence for them) and arguably also evidence-*independent* (i.e., they could obtain in the absence of *any* evidence for them, or at least in the absence of evidence sufficient for knowledge):

> A certain sensum occurs fourteen billion years after the Big Bang.
>
> A red sensum of mine is contemporaneous with a green sensum of yours.
>
> Given the round, pinkish sensa that are occurring now, if biting-sensa were to occur also, pomegranatey-tasting sensa would follow.
>
> There is a mental history containing an infinite sequence of sensa in which each red is followed by a blue and each blue by a red.
>
> Sensa of winning at Wimbledon once occurred in a dream that was never reported and is now irrecoverable in memory.

The first item might be thought not to count, since it involves a relation to something that is not a sensum. But the rest of them are about sensa exclusively, and it is arguable that each of them could be true in the absence of evidence sufficient for knowing it to be true.

To appreciate the converse possibility, evidence-dependence without mind-dependence, we need only note that some contemporary philosophers combine verificationism (there are no facts without evidence for them) with physicalism (all facts, including evidential facts, are physical facts). Quine's views on the indeterminacy of translation perhaps afford one example of this combination. Another example would be the view that there are no facts about the past unless there are current records or traces attesting to them, but that such records or traces need not involve consciousness. Indeed, preoccupation with evidence leads some philosophers into a behaviorism that effectively excludes the very existence of consciousness. So, the view that the facts in some domain are evidence-dependent does not necessarily imply that the entities that are the constituents of those facts exist only if they are apprehended by some consciousness. For one last example, this one not involving physicalism, consider a philosophy of mathematics that makes mathematical truth depend on proof without making mathematical objects depend on being apprehended.[29]

So, we have at least two things that can be meant by the dependence of reality on our knowledge of it: dependence of objects on being apprehended, and dependence of facts on there being evidence for them. Traditional idealism is the view that objects are mind-dependent; contemporary antirealism is more often the view that facts are evidence-dependent.[30] Two leading advocates of the new antirealism are Hilary Putnam and Michael Dummett, both of whom argue for a strong tie between truth and evidence. Perhaps both of them could be characterized as believing that *truth supervenes on evidence*, in the following sense: (a) nothing is ever true unless there is evidence for it, and evidence moreover of such a sort that (b) nothing could be backed by such evidence without being true. In Dummett's case, the emphasis is on clause (a); his bugaboo is truth without evidence. That is why he makes his test for realism the principle of bivalence: do you insist that one of a pair of contradictories must be true even in cases where there is no evidence for either? In Putnam's case, the emphasis is on clause (b); his bugaboo is evidence (or at any rate, ideal evidence) without truth. So, in his case, the test for realism is whether you admit that we might all be brains in vats, possessing a theory that is "epistemically ideal" but false nonetheless.[31]

Some contemporary philosophers have seen in Kant important anticipations of antirealist views. Putnam has suggested that Kant may have been the first philosopher who was not a "metaphysical realist" and has ascribed to Kant elements of the antirealist view he calls "internal realism." Meanwhile, some followers of Dummett have interpreted Kant's transcendental idealism as a species of Dummettian antirealism. The connections between Kant's ideas and those of contemporary antirealists are interesting and worth examining; I turn to that task in chapter 13. For now I will just say that on the whole I find Kant to be more an old-fashioned idealist than a new-fangled antirealist.

2

Necessity, Analyticity, and the *A Priori*

> We are in possession of certain modes of *a priori* knowledge, and even the common understanding is never without them.
>> Kant, *Critique of Pure Reason* (B3)

> Necessity and strict universality are thus sure criteria of *a priori* knowledge. (B4)

> In all theoretical sciences of reason synthetic *a priori* judgments are contained as principles. (B14)

> Now the proper problem of pure reason is contained in the question: How are *a priori* synthetic judgments possible? (B19)

A. Three Distinctions

In the introduction to the *Critique of Pure Reason* Kant draws three important distinctions: *a priori* versus empirical, necessary versus contingent, and analytic versus synthetic. Although some philosophers lump them together, we should not assume at the outset that the three distinctions divide things up in the same way. Even if it should turn out that they do, each of the distinctions must be given its own explanation.

A priori/Empirical.   Kant distinguishes *a priori* from empirical knowledge as follows:

> [K]nowledge that is thus independent of experience and even of all impressions of the senses ... is entitled *a priori*, and distinguished from the *empirical*, which has its sources *a posteriori*, that is, in experience.(B2)

The term *a priori* is in the first instance an adverb modifying verbs of cognition: person S knows proposition p *a priori* iff S knows p in a way that is independent of experience. We may then go on to define a related sense in which *a priori* is a predicate of judgments or propositions: a proposition p is *a priori* iff it is possible for someone to know p *a priori*. I leave aside the interesting question of whether it is possible for some beings to know *a priori* things that other beings cannot. (E.g., might an infinite intelligence have *a priori* knowledge of propositions about the distribution of primes in the number series that is not available to a finite intelligence?)

The notion of independence that figures in the primary definition of *a priori* must not be misunderstood. In saying that we know a given proposition independently of experience, Kant is not saying that we would still have known it even if we had never had any experience. On the contrary, he allows that experience may be requisite for the knowledge even of an *a priori* proposition in either of two ways. First, it may well be that if we had never had any experience, our cognitive faculties would never have developed to the point that we could entertain any propositions or do any thinking at all. Still, once our faculties are up and running, there are some propositions that we can know to be true without any further need of experience. That is the point of Kant's famous remark that "though all our knowledge begins with experience, it does not follow that it all arises out of experience" (B1). Second, it may be that some of the constituent concepts in a given proposition are concepts that can only be acquired through experience, such as the concept of *red* or the concept of an *event*. In that case, experience would be necessary for us to grasp the proposition or get it before our minds, but once we have framed it in our consciousness, we may be able to ascertain that it is true without any further aid from experience. Kant acknowledges this possibility when he distinguishes (within the class of *a priori* propositions) between the pure and the impure, an impure proposition being one some of whose constituent concepts are derivable only from experience (B3). He gives the example 'every alteration has a cause': the concept of an alteration (or event) is one that can be got only through experience, but the proposition as a whole Kant takes to be *a priori*. For another example (in which the *a priori* status of the proposition is less controversial), I cite 'nothing is simultaneously red and blue'. In the *Prolegomena*, Kant gives 'gold is a yellow metal' as an example of a proposition that is *a priori* (because analytic) even though it contains empirical concepts (p. 14).

The point of the previous paragraph may be made by invoking the familar tripartite analysis of knowledge. Someone knows a proposition only if (i) he believes it, (ii) it is true, and (iii) he is adequately justified in believing it. (See Kant's discussion of opining, believing, and knowing at A822/B850 for an account roughly along these lines.) Experience may be necessary in either of the two ways I have mentioned—in many cases or even in all—for the obtaining of condition (i), the belief condition of knowledge. But if experience is not necessary in a given case for the obtaining of condition (iii), the justification condition, the knowledge will still qualify as *a priori*.

The relevant points here were nicely summed up by Frege:

> [When we classify a proposition as *a priori*,] this is not a judgment about the conditions, psychological, physiological, and physical, which have made it possible for us to form the content of the proposition in our consciousness; nor is it a judgment about the way in which some other man

has come . . . to believe it to be true; rather, it is a judgment about the ultimate ground upon which rests the justification for holding it to be true.[1]

Necessary/Contingent.   The second distinction relates not to how a proposition is known, but to its manner or mode of being true. Among all the things we recognize as true, there are many that (as far as we can see) need *not* have been true—for example, that stones fall when released near the earth, or that the sun is shining as I write these lines. Such truths are contingent. There are others, however, that *had* to be true. That two and three together make five and that a thing never both has and lacks a given property are truths of this sort. They are necessary truths, the necessity of which may be characterized in any of the following ways:

p could not have been false;
p not only *is* true, but *must* be true;
the opposite of p is impossible;
p holds in every possible world.

I will not try to elucidate these notions further, as they are among the most familiar in philosophy, and I doubt that anything much can be done to explain them to anyone who does not already have a grasp of them anyway. (Such, indeed, is one ground for Quine's misgivings about necessity, discussed later.) Here I simply note that the sense of 'necessary' that is now at issue is what Plantinga calls the "broadly logical" sense.[2] It is logical as opposed to merely physical necessity (i.e., the necessity with which stones fall when released), so laws of nature are not necessary in this sense. And it is broadly logical as opposed to narrowly logical necessity, so laws of formal logic are not the *only* things that are necessary in this sense.

Though the two distinctions drawn so far differ in intension (one relating to the manner of being known and the other to the manner of being true), Kant believes they that they coincide in extension—that they divide up the field of true propositions in the same way. He believes that propositions are necessary iff they are *a priori*, and contingent iff they are empirical or *a posteriori*. As he puts it, "Necessity and strict universality are . . . sure criteria of *a priori* knowledge, and are inseparable from one another" (B4).[3] But Kant famously—and in my opinion correctly—thinks that the next distinction runs at right angles to the first two.

Analytic/Synthetic.   I come now to the distinction in this trio with which Kant is most associated. Kant's predecessors drew distinctions in the same general area as the analytic/synthetic distinction; for example, Leibniz distinguished between truths of reason and truths of fact, and Hume distinguished between relations of ideas and matters of fact. But Kant is often regarded as the first major thinker to draw the analytic/synthetic distinction in a way that exhibits it as clearly different from the necessary/contingent and *a priori*/empirical distinctions.[4]

My concern in what follows is not so much with elucidating exactly what Kant meant by the analytic/synthetic distinction as with exhibiting connections between his account of it and more recent accounts. I do not think it requires an undue amount of squinting to see Kant's distinction as essentially agreeing with its twentieth-century descendants. When Kant affirms that there are synthetic *a priori* truths and Ayer or Quine denies it, I think they are engaged in the same debate.

The Containment Characterization.   Kant gives two different accounts of the analytic/synthetic distinction, one in terms of conceptual containment and the other in terms of contradiction. The first and better known runs as follows:

> Either the predicate B belongs to the subject A, as something which is (covertly) contained in this concept A; or B lies outside the concept A, although it does indeed stand in connection with it. In the one case I entitle the judgment analytic, in the other synthetic.(A6/B10)

Note that Kant does not merely say that the predicate in an analytic judgment belongs to its *subject*, that is, to that which the judgment is about—that much is presumably the case in *any* true subject-predicate judgment. Instead, he says the predicate is contained in the *concept* of the subject. He goes on to explain that in an analytic judgment, the predicate concept is one of the "constituent concepts that have all along been thought in the subject, although confusedly," whereas a synthetic judgment has a predicate "which has not been in any wise thought in [the concept of the subject], and which no analysis could possibly extract from it" (A7/B11).[5] In another place, he equates "what I am actually thinking in my concept of a triangle" with "nothing more than the mere definition" (A718/B746). If we put these two passages together, we arrive at the result that the judgment that S is P is analytic iff the property of being P is included by definition in the concept of S. In fact, Kant would not have said this, owing to special views he held about the nature of definition.[6] But this gloss at least has the virtue of bringing out that whether a judgment is analytic or synthetic depends on what we mean by the terms used to express it.

I now turn to Kant's own examples for illustration. 'All bodies are extended' expresses an analytic judgment, because by 'body' we mean among other things an extended, impenetrable thing. The proposition we express is therefore equivalent to 'all extended and impenetrable things are extended', in which the inclusion of the predicate in the subject concept is visible to the mind's eye. 'All bodies are heavy,' on the other hand, expresses a synthetic judgment, since being heavy is not part of what we mean by 'body'. Our concept of a body allows us to acknowledge the possibility of bodies (e.g., those placed outside all gravitational fields) that do not have any heaviness at all.

Too Subjective?   It is a perennial objection to the containment account that it yields a distinction that is merely subjective and variable. What one person includes in his or her concept or definition of the metal gold may include more attributes than another does; in consequence, whether a judgment about gold is analytic or synthetic may vary from person to person. This objection was raised against Kant in his own day by J.G. Maass.[7]

It was also answered in Kant's own day. It is quite true that one person's definition of a term may include more than another's, but this turns out to be
harmless. Kant's disciple J.G. Schulze, replying to Maass, explained why:

> Now, suppose that I find, in a judgment which two philosophers express
> in the same words, that one of them connects the subject with a rich con-
> cept in which the predicate is already contained, while the other, on the
> other hand, connects it with a concept in which the predicate in ques-
> tion is not contained. I would then be entirely correct in saying that the
> judgment of the first one is analytic, and of the second one synthetic. For
> although their judgments seem to be one and the same, since they are ex-
> pressed with the same words, they are nevertheless in this case in fact
> not one but two different judgments.[8]

Schulze's point is that if it is judgments or propositions that we are classifying as analytic or synthetic, then nothing is ever analytic for one person and
synthetic for another. The fact that one person uses a more inclusive definition would only show that he or she operates with a different subject concept
and therefore frames a different judgment.

On the other hand, if it is *sentences* that we wish to classify as analytic or
synthetic, we do indeed get relativity: the same sentence may be analytic for
Smith and synthetic for Jones. But such relativity will not undermine Kant's
project in the slightest. As I argue below, there are cases in which a sentence
that is synthetic for a given person expresses a proposition that is known *a pri-*
ori by that person. Such cases still present us with the central question of the
Critique of Pure Reason, though now it needs to be phrased as follows:

> How are judgments that are known *a priori* by a given person and ex-
> pressed by sentences that are synthetic for that person possible?

That lacks the fanfare of Kant's "How are *a priori* synthetic judgments possible?" (B19), but it raises the same profound issues.

Too Narrow?   There is another common objection to Kant's containment definition that has more bite—namely, that it is too narrow. In the first place, it
applies only to judgments of subject-predicate form, whereas Kant wishes to
classify as analytic or synthetic many judgments not of that form. For example, it does not apply to existential judgments (such as 'there are lions'), which
(if we accept the dictum that existence is not a predicate) are not of subject-
predicate form. Nor does it apply to compound judgments, such as disjunctive
judgments, which need not have a single subject. In the second place, even restricting our attention to judgments of subject-predicate form, the containment
definition does not classify as analytic all the judgments that Kant himself
would wish to classify as analytic. Consider a judgment of the form 'all ABCD
is A'; under the containment definition, this will certainly count as analytic.
The equivalent contrapositive judgment, 'all non-A are non-(ABCD)', should
therefore also count as analytic, yet clearly one might think of something as
non-A without taking any thought of B, C, or D, and therefore not of non-
(ABCD).[9] Nor need non-(ABCD) be part of the definition of non-A. So, the con-

trapositive judgment is not analytic by the containment account. It is not even obvious that the containment account properly classifies as analytic those judgments in which the predicate is extractable from the concept of the subject, but only after a great many steps of definitional replacement.[10]

The Contradiction Characterization.   Fortunately, Kant has another characterization of analyticity that is less open to the charge of narrowness. There is a first hint of it at B12, where Kant speaks of extracting the predicate of extension from the concept of body "in accordance with the principle of contradiction." The role of contradiction is explicitly recognized later in the section of the *Critique of Pure Reason* entitled "The Highest Principle of All Analytic Judgments," in which Kant says that the truth of any analytic judgment "can always be adequately known in accordance with the principle of contradiction" (A151/B190). Later still, in his critique of the ontological argument for the existence of God, he says that the following feature is "found only in analytic judgments, and is indeed precisely what constitutes their analytic character": their predicates cannot be rejected without contradiction (A598/B626).

What all of this suggests is the following commonly given definition of an analytic judgment:

A is analytic iff its opposite, −A, is a contradiction.

But what is a contradiction? Many so-called contradictions are not official or formal contradictions in the hard objective sense that they have the logical form 'P & −P'.[11] If we say that a statement is analytic only if its negation is a formal contradiction, nothing will count as analytic except the law of contradiction itself ('−(P & −P)') and its instances—and they will count only with the aid of the ruling that the double negation of a contradiction is itself a contradiction. Not even that paradigm of analyticity, 'all bachelors are unmarried', has an opposite that is contradictory in the formal sense. So, what is intended in the definition above is presumably that −A either is or *implies* a formal contradiction.

Now we need to ask another question: "imply" in accordance with which rules and with the help of which auxiliary premises? *Anything* can be shown to imply a contradiction if there is no limit on what rules and premises we may use in the proof. So, which rules and premises may we use? If we look at the transformations to which we must subject the negation of 'all bachelors are unmarried' to arrive at a formal contradiction, the following answer suggests itself: we may appeal to laws of logic, and we may appeal to definitions. This gives us the following revised account:

A is analytic iff from its negation, −A, a formal contradiction may be derived, using in the derivation only laws of logic and substitutions authorized by definitions.[12]

Twentieth-Century Accounts.   What we have just arrived at is perhaps the most common twentieth-century conception of analyticity. It is equivalent to each of the following:

Frege: "If (in tracing the proof of a proposition) we come only on general logical laws and on definitions, then the truth is an analytic one."[13]

Carnap: "The first type of theorem can be deduced from the definitions alone (presupposing the axioms of logic, without which no deduction is possible at all). These we call *analytic* theorems."[14]

C.I. Lewis: "Every analytic statement is such as can be assured, finally, on grounds which include nothing beyond our accepted definitions and the principles of logic."[15]

Quine: "Statements which are analytic by general philosophical acclaim . . . fall into two classes. Those of the first class are logical truths; those of the second class can be turned into logical truths by putting synonyms for synonyms."[16]

These accounts of analyticity apply in the first instance most readily to sentences—for it is sentences that have meanings, that contain terms that can be interchanged with others having the same meaning, and so on. But we can define a related sense of 'analytic' that applies to propositions: a proposition is analytic iff any sentence expressing it would be analytic.

The resulting conception of analyticity is not open to the charge discussed above of excessive narrowness. It applies to propositions of any logical form, not just those of subject-predicate form. Moreover, it classifies as analytic propositions of the form 'all non-A are non-(ABCD)', whereas the containment definition does not. It also classifies as analytic propositions in which the predicate is extractable from the concept of the subject only after a great many steps of logical or definitional recasting.

I believe also that the resulting notion agrees tolerably well with Kant's own, at least in extension if not in intension. In any case, it is the conception I operate with in this book. If I sometimes use "the opposite implies a contradiction" as my short gloss on analyticity, the reader should remember the unstated provisos that bring the gloss into line with the Fregean conception: from the negation of the statement it must be possible to derive a formal contradiction using only definitions and laws of logic.

B. Synthetic *A Priori*

As I said above, Kant believes that his first two distinctions, *a priori*/empirical and necessary/contingent, make the same divide in the field of judgments, while the third distinction, analytic/synthetic, cuts across the field at right angles to the first two. That makes four compartments in all. Kant believes three of the four to be occupied: analytic *a priori*, synthetic *a posteriori*, and (the famous new possibility) synthetic *a priori*.[17] *A priori* knowledge is perhaps not unduly mysterious when it is of analytic truths, for it is explained in that case by whatever explains our knowledge of logic and our knowledge of our own meanings.[18] But if our *a priori* knowledge extends also to some synthetic truths, what could explain that? Disdain of having to invoke an *oculis rationis* or some other mysterious faculty led the positivists and others to maintain that *a priori* knowledge is to be had only of analytic propositions. But Kant was convinced otherwise, and that set for him the central problem of the *Critique of Pure Reason*: How are synthetic *a priori* judgments possible (B19)?

In the introduction to the *Critique*, Kant asserts that there are three important classes of synthetic *a priori* propositions: the truths of arithmetic, the truths of geometry, and certain framework principles of natural science, such as the principle that every event has a cause. (He also lists as synthetic and putatively *a priori* certain propositions of metaphysics, such as that the world had a beginning, but these turn out for him not to be *a priori* because not knowable at all.) Few agree with Kant nowadays about the synthetic *a priori* status of the propositions in these three classes. Arithmetic is generally thought to be *a priori* but (given the work of Frege, Russell, and Whitehead) not synthetic. Geometry is generally thought to be synthetic but (given the rise of non-Euclidean geometries in the nineteenth century and their subsequent incorporation into physical theory in the twentieth) not *a priori*. Nor are the framework principles of natural science generally thought to be *a priori*.

Although I cannot do justice here to the status of arithmetic and geometry, I offer below a few words in defense of what Kant has to say about a specimen from each subject matter. Then I move on to two more favorable examples of the synthetic *a priori*. Even if Kant is wrong about arithmetic and geometry at large, I believe he is emphatically right in thinking that there are synthetic *a priori* propositions.

7 + 5 = 12. '7 + 5 = 12' is Kant's well-known example of a synthetic *a priori* proposition in arithmetic. He argues for its synthetic character as follows: "[I]f we look more closely we find that the concept of the sum of 7 and 5 contains nothing save the union of the two numbers into one, and in this no thought is being taken as to what that single number may be which combines both" (B15). Here Kant is invoking the containment characterization of analyticity, and he is clearly right about the results of applying it, at least to some cases if not to this one. There are true arithmetic equalities of the form '7 + 5 = m − n', where m and n are numbers so large no human being has ever thought of them; here, of course, one may entertain the subject concept without having any thought of the predicate.[19] Nor need the concepts of m and n enter into the definition of 7 + 5, or else no concept would have a finite definition, there being infinitely many (m − n) pairs that similarly yield true equations. Thus, by the containment criterion, much of arithmetic is synthetic.

But we know that the containment criterion is too narrow, and that Kant has a better criterion in terms of contradiction. Might it be that arithmetical propositions are analytic by the superior standard? Such, of course, is precisely the contention of the logicism of Frege, Russell, and Whitehead. If they are right, there are definitions of arithmetical concepts in purely logical terms that permit the derivation of any truth of arithmetic from purely logical axioms. That would make arithmetic analytic in Kant's wider sense. But whether the logicists are right is unclear for at least two reasons. First, the status of some of their axioms (e.g., the axiom of infinity, which guarantees the existence of infinitely many objects) as purely logical is controversial. Second, Gödel's incompleteness theorem shows that there cannot be any finite and consistent set of axioms from which every arithmetical truth may be derived, thus apparently dooming the logicist project.[20]

The Straight Line Between Two Points Is the Shortest. 'The straight line between two points is the shortest' is Kant's official example of a synthetic *a priori* proposition in geometry.[21] As with the previous example, he thinks its *a
priori* status will be generally conceded. He supports its syntheticity with the
following observation: "For my concept of *straight* contains nothing of quantity, but only of quality" (B16). In an interesting discussion of the same proposition, Hume observes, "In common life 'tis establish'd as a maxim, that the
streightest way is always the shortest; which wou'd be as absurd as to say, the
shortest way is always the shortest, if our idea of a right line was not different
from that of the shortest way betwixt two points."[22]

Geometers nowadays often define a straight line in just the way Hume and
Kant say we should not: as a geodesic, or shortest line (in the space in question) between two points. That makes analytic the sentence Hume and Kant
take to express a synthetic proposition.[23] In the bargain, it threatens to undermine the *a priori* status of another of Kant's favored examples: two straight
lines cannot enclose a space. In Riemannian geometry, two lines that are geo-
desics *can* enclose a space.

Of course, if rival geometries undo the apriority of Kantian theses only by
redefining terms, they do not really undo it; they make the same sentence express a different proposition, and it need come as no surprise that the new
proposition is not *a priori*. Indeed, on first exposure to the non-Euclidean
properties of straight lines in Riemannian geometry, many students claim that
the meaning of 'straight' has been changed, in which case there is no challenge
to Kant. The impression of meaning change may be heightened when the student is told that great circles on a sphere may serve as models of straight lines.
"Those lines aren't really straight," the student may be tempted to say, "for it
is obvious that there are straighter lines, so you haven't really shown me how
Euclidean principles might fail." The standard reply to the student is that *in
the space in question*, the line really is straight, for there is no straighter. The
student is imagining a more inclusive space in which the line would not be
straight, but that is not the space that counts.

I think it is significant that to reply to the student we must use a relativized
notion of straightness, and I would like to exploit this fact in defending Kant.
For a preliminary illustration, let me switch the example from straightness to
congruence. Consider the figures a and b in the one-dimensional space of
Lineland:

. ——————   ——————   .

a   b

Are a and b congruent or not? Many writers would say no, for there is no motion in the space that will enable one to be superimposed on the other. But
Wittgenstein claimed to the contrary that a and b are in fact completely congruent. "It is quite irrelevant," he said, "that they cannot be made to coincide."[24] I agree with Wittgenstein: because there are *possible* spaces (of two or
more dimensions) in which a and b could be made to coincide, they are congruent absolutely speaking, even if they cannot be made to coincide in the limited space to which they are actually confined.[25]

In effect, we are now distinguishing two notions of congruence. The relativized notion may be defined thus: two figures are congruent *in S* iff there is

a motion in S by which the figures may be brought into coincidence. This notion must be what the writers who deny the congruence of a and b have in mind. But we may also define an absolute notion of congruence as follows: two figures are *absolutely* congruent iff there is a possible space in which they would be congruent in the relative sense. Wittgenstein's remark is defensible in light of the absolute concept.

To return now to the concept of straightness, any geodesic in a space S may be said to be straight *in S*, for no line is shorter or straighter in S. But whether a line is straight *absolutely* is a function not of the space it happens to inhabit, but of what spaces are possible, and if there are possible spaces in which a line would not be the shortest, then it is not straight in the absolute sense.[26]

We are now in a position to defend what our student says on behalf of Euclid and Kant. When she says, "Your so-called straight lines that return on themselves, enclose spaces, and behave in other non-Euclidean ways aren't really straight," she is right—the lines are not absolutely straight. The necessity of Euclid's principles as governing absolutely straight lines is not put in doubt by the fact that non-Euclidean principles govern lines that are straight relative to one or another special space. At the same time, we are not securing the necessity of Euclidean principles simply by making them analytic. That Euclid holds sway over the absolutely straight is a matter not of definition but of intuition.[27]

I pass now to two putative examples of synthetic *a priori* truths that should be less controversial than the two just discussed: 'nothing is red and green all over' and 'every cube has twelve edges'.

Nothing Is Red and Green All Over.   Nearly everyone will concede that 'nothing is red and green all over (at the same time)' expresses a necessary truth that is known *a priori*; the question is whether it is synthetic.[28] Given the account of analyticity described above, the question comes down to this: is the statement true by virtue of definitions plus logic? Anyone who says yes must answer the question: true by *what* definitions and *what* logic?

For starters, we may consider a definition that looks in part like this:

x is red =Df . . . & x is not green & . . .

A definition containing the displayed conjunct would let us derive 'nothing is both red and green' from 'nothing is both green and not green', which is a truth of logic. But what would the rest of the definition look like? How are we to fill in the blanks? Sticking with the "definition by exclusion" strategy, we would have

x is red =Df x is not blue & x is not green & . . . ,

with one conjunct for each color not overlapping redness.[29] A possible drawback of the resulting definition is that it would contain infinitely many conjuncts. Setting that problem aside, there is the following difficulty, which was raised by Arthur Pap: not all colors can be defined in this purely negative way, on pain of circularity in the total system of color definitions (for we would be defining 'x is green' as 'x is not red & . . . '). Enough of the color terms will have to be defined positively to give us some purchase on the negatives. A strong case can be made that the positive definitions will have to be *ostensive*—'to be red is to be the color of *this object*'. Now consider two colors F and G that have been defined in this ostensive way: it will be an *a priori* truth that nothing is both F and G, but nothing in the present strategy will show that such truths are analytic.

Let's try another tack. Why not define colors in terms of physical magnitudes, perhaps along the following lines:

x is red =Df x reflects light of wave length l.

x is green =Df x reflects light of wave length m.

The incompatibility of colors would then simply be a consequence of the incompatibility of certain physical magnitudes.[30]

I leave aside the objection that we understand color terms perfectly well before we know any physics, and that definitions like those above are not true to our naive understanding. The objection I wish to press is that we have only relocated our difficulty. This was pointed out by F.P. Ramsey in his review of the *Tractatus*, in which Wittgenstein had tried a similar strategy: he sought to reduce color incompatibilities to the impossibility of a particle having two velocities at once. Ramsey commented:

> But even supposing that the physicist thus provides an analysis of what we mean by 'red', Mr Wittgenstein is only reducing the difficulty to that of the *necessary* properties of space, time, and matter or the ether. He explicitly makes it depend on the *impossibility* of a particle being in two places at the same time.[31]

What we would need now is the basis in definitions and logic for saying that a particle cannot have two velocities, or that an object cannot have two different reflectance profiles, and so on.

I relegate discussion of one more strategy for deriving statements of color incompatibility from definitions and logic to appendix A.

Every Cube Has Twelve Edges.   This is a nice example for illustrating Kant's views on the epistemology of geometry.[32] Unlike many geometrical propositions, this one (which is actually a proposition of topology rather than of geometry proper) holds in Euclidean and non-Euclidean geometries alike, so there is no challenge to its apriority from non-Euclidean geometry. The question, as with the previous example, is whether it is analytic or synthetic. It is not immediately or obviously analytic, for the standard definition of 'cube' is 'regular solid (or polyhedron) with six square faces', in which there is no mention of the number of edges. How, then, do we know that the proposition is true? Most people verify it simply by visualizing a cube and counting its edges—an exercise in what Kant calls "pure intuition." If we are to exhibit the proposition as analytic, we must deduce the number of edges in a cube using just logic and any relevant definitions. Readers may wish to try their hands (or heads) at this.

Some will try to make the statement immediately analytic after all, saying that *their* definition of 'cube' *does* include the having of twelve edges. To them I say: very well, it is analytic that cubes as you define them have 12 edges. But consider now the following proposition: every cube as defined by me (in terms of six faces) is a cube as defined by you (in terms of twelve edges). That is, every regular solid with six square faces is a solid with twelve edges. I submit that this proposition may be seen to be true *a priori* as easily as the first, but it is *not* true by definition. Or if it is, that has yet to be made out. So, we may as well expend our efforts on the original statement.[33]

Here is one good try at extracting twelve edges from the original definition of a cube:[34]

1. Every cube is a polyhedron with six square faces (by definition).
2. Six separate squares have twenty-four edges, since each square (by definition) has four edges and $6 \times 4 = 24$.
3. When six squares are assembled into a cube, each edge of a square coincides with the edge of another square to form one edge of the cube, and each edge of the cube is an edge of exactly two squares (no square edge coinciding with more than one cube edge). Thus, the number of edges in the original group of squares decreases by one half.
4. Therefore, every cube has twelve edges $(24 \div 2)$. Q.E.D.

That apparently does it—at least if we may correctly assume (in opposition to Kant) that arithmetic is analytic, and that for counting purposes coincidence is as good as identity.

Even granting these assumptions, however, there is a further hitch. Where does step 3 come from? I readily concede its *truth*, for I see that things work as step 3 says when I picture squares coming together to form a cube. But unless step 3 is itself true by definition, we have not yet shown that the conclusion of the argument is analytic.

Well, perhaps step 3 is true by virtue of the definition of a polyhedron. A topology textbook offers this:

> By a *polyhedron* we mean any system of polygons arranged in such a way that (1) exactly two polygons meet (at an angle) at every edge, and (2) it is possible to get from every polygon to every other polygon by crossing edges of the polyhedron.[35]

The first clause of this definition delivers the essential part of our step 3.

That may end the argument over 'every cube has twelve edges', but there are other apparent instances of the synthetic *a priori* in the vicinity. Let's turn our attention to 'every cube has eight corners (i.e., vertices)'. That proposition is also *a priori*, but its analyticity is not brought out by any of the definitions so far considered. We could make it analytic by adding to the definition of a polyhedron a clause from which we could deduce something analogous to step 3 above: each vertex of a square coincides with two other such vertices to form one vertex of the cube, and each vertex of the cube is a vertex of exactly three squares (no square vertex coinciding with more than one cube vertex).[36] Then we could conclude that every cube has eight vertices (since six squares have twenty-four, which divided by 3 is 8).[37]

My rejoinder is by now predictable: the foregoing strategy would make analytic a statement that was formerly synthetic and whose content we knew to be true *a priori* even when the statement was synthetic. That is, we knew *a priori* that cubes in the original "thinner" sense (i.e., polyhedra with six square faces, with polyhedra defined as in the textbook definition above) have eight vertices. We can, if we like, make analytic the statement that formerly expressed what we knew about cubes, but what would that show? The knowledge was there before the analyticity. Indeed, the analytic statement does not even express our old knowledge, but a more highly articulated proposition instead.

Is It Analytic That All A Priori *Truths Are Analytic?*   The thesis that there are synthetic *a priori* truths need not be supported by examples alone. What is the status of the opposing thesis that all *a priori* truths are analytic? It is not an empirical thesis, so if true at all, it had better be analytic.[38] But is it? Defenders of the thesis have seldom risen to the challenge of demonstrating its own analyticity.[39]

C. Quine's Attack on Analyticity

Analyticity and associated notions play such a large role in Kant's philosophy that it behooves me to say something here about Quine's famous criticisms of them—even at the risk of saying little that has not been said before.

Every student of philosophy knows that Quine denies the analytic-synthetic distinction. But what exactly is it to deny a distinction? Well, what is it to *uphold* a distinction? Upholding a distinction (in robust fashion) between the As and the Bs involves maintaining each of the following: (i) there are As, (ii) there are Bs, (iii) nothing is both, (iv) nothing is neither, (v) nothing is a borderline case, (vi) nor is it otherwise indeterminate whether something is an A or a B, and finally (vii) we have a clear idea what we are talking about when we talk about As and Bs. Quine's denial of the analytic-synthetic distinction presumably involves denying one or more of (i)–(vii), but which?

I take it that Quine denies the first and the last of the theses in this sequence.[40] That is, he denies that there are any analytic statements, for reasons developed in the second part (sections 5 and 6) of "Two Dogmas of Empiricism," and he denies that we have any tolerably clear idea of what can be meant by the terms 'analytic' and 'synthetic', for reasons developed in the first part (sections 1–4) of the same article.[41]

One might wonder how these two opinions can be combined. (Compare: "I don't think anyone really knows what a hippoglub is; moreover, there aren't any.") But that difficulty can be circumvented by construing Quine's argument in the second part of "Two Dogmas" as *ad hominem*: whatever exactly 'analytic' means, believers in it associate it with a certain privileged status (irrevisability), and Quine argues that nothing has that status.

The best-known criticism from the first part of "Two Dogmas" is that the term 'analytic' is a member of a small family of terms any of which can be explained in terms of the others, but none of which can be explained from the outside. This is not an uncommon circumstance. Kant provides us with another example of it: the *chiral* family of terms, which include 'left', 'right', 'clockwise', 'counterclockwise', and names for the various points of the compass. We can give a verbal definition of 'right' if we are permitted to use other chiral terms, but we cannot define any chiral term without using other chiral terms. Does it follow that no one understands the chiral terms? Not at all, for it is possible that some of them are understood without need of any verbal definition. Kant's own view is that some of them (it does not matter which) can and must be understood ostensively, or through intuition, and may then be used to define the rest.[42]

One key member of the 'analyticity' family is 'synonymy': if we can understand the latter, we can understand 'analytic'. The notion of synonymy was implicitly involved in our characterization of analyticity above, since in a correct definition, the definiens must be synonymous with the definiendum. Now, synonymy is simply sameness of meaning; what is so problematic about that? In defense of this notion, I cite three points, all of which have been well made by Strawson or by Grice and Strawson. (1) If there is such a thing as significance, or a sentence's meaning something at all, must there not be such a thing as synonymy, or two sentences' meaning the same thing?[43] (2) Quine admits that there are cases of synonymy induced by stipulative definition or abbreviation. That is to admit that there is such a state of affairs as two expressions' having the same meaning; if so, may it not come about by other means, for example, convergence of usage?[44] (3) Quine does not think there is any unclarity about the notion of logical truth. (The logical truths are the unproblematic subclass of the class of truths that are said in "Two Dogmas" to be "analytic by general philosophical acclaim.") But the notion of logical truth already presupposes synonymy—'all banks are banks' is a logical truth only if the first occurrence of 'banks' is synonymous with the second.[45]

Quine's later writings make clear that his difficulties over synonymy stem largely from his demanding a behaviorist account of it—some way of determining from a person's linguistic responses and dispositions whether two expressions are synonymous for him or not.[46] To this might not the proper response be: so much the worse for behaviorism?

I say no more about the first part of "Two Dogmas," but turn to the second part, from which (as noted above) we may extract an argument against the existence of analytic truths. (A parallel argument could be given to discredit the notion of *a priori* truths; much of what I say below applies equally to the parallel version.) The argument I have in mind runs as follows:

1. If a statement is analytic, it is immune to revision.
2. No statement is immune to revision.
3. Therefore, no statement is analytic.

Premise 1 is implicit rather than explicit in the article; premise 2 is a direct quote.[47]

To evaluate this argument, we must begin by asking what Quine means by 'statement' and what he means by 'immune to revision'. As for 'statement', the main possibilities are obviously (a) sentence and (b) proposition.[48] As for 'im-

mune to revision', the main possibilities are (c) such that no one *could* ever re-
vise it (i.e., reject it or change one's mind about its truth value) and (d) such
that no one could ever *reasonably* reject it. These possibilities intersect to give
us four possible readings of each premise. It is my contention that there is no
combination that gives plausible readings to both premises simultaneously.

The four possible readings of the first premise are the following:

1ac: If a sentence is analytic, no one could ever reject it.
1ad: If a sentence is analytic, no one could ever reasonably reject it.
1bc: If a proposition is analytic, no one could ever reject it.[49]
1bd: If a proposition is analytic, no one could ever reasonably reject it.

The first two theses, 1ac and 1ad, have no plausibility at all. One could reject any sentence, even one that is now analytic, provided an appropriate
change in its meaning takes place first. By the same token, one could reject any
sentence reasonably, provided an appropriate change in its meaning takes
place first. If 'all bachelors are unmarried' came to mean that all triangles are
four-sided, it would be reasonable to reject it.

I am inclined to give the same verdict on the third thesis, 1bc. People do
the craziest things; couldn't any proposition whatsoever, even if analytic and
no matter how obvious, be rejected by some benighted person? Well, that is
controversial. It would be denied by Davidson, for whom ascriptions of belief
must be constrained by a principle of charity—a principle that places limits
on how much craziness there can be.[50] Here I simply note that if 1bc is to be
accepted on grounds of charity, the corresponding version of the second
premise, 2bc, which says that every proposition is such that someone might
reject it, must be rejected on the same grounds. So, there is no hope for a sound
argument against analyticity using the b–c combination.

That leaves us with the b–d combination as the only one left in the running.
That is to say, we have now to consider the argument whose premises are the
following:

1bd: If a proposition is analytic, no one could ever reasonably reject it.
2bd: Every proposition is such that it could be reasonably rejected.

Premise 1bd has more going for it than the other versions of premise 1, but I
am not sure that even this version of the premise is true. Might there not be
analytic propositions that in certain states of information it is reasonable to reject? I have in mind, for example, the negation of Cantor's naive comprehension principle, which was proved analytic by Russell's paradox, but which before the paradox came to light was arguably reasonable to reject.

(In the parallel argument against *a priori* truths, the first premise would say
that if a proposition is *a priori*, no one could ever reasonably reject it. This is
indeed a consequence of some accounts of the *a priori*, e.g., Chisholm's.[51]
However, there are other conceptions of the *a priori* that are compatible with
a thoroughgoing fallibilism, e.g., Pollock's.[52])

What I want to focus on, however, is premise 2bd, which I find highly questionable to say the least. How could it ever be reasonable to reject the proposition we now express by the sentence 'all triangles have three sides'? Or the
law of noncontradiction? Or (to take an example of an even harder-to-reject

proposition from Putnam) the proposition we now express by 'not every proposition is both true and false'? To reject *that* would not merely be to flout the law of noncontradiction; it would be to hold that every single proposition is both true and false.[53] So, it seems there are at least some propositions that could never be reasonably rejected. The only version of the "Two Dogmas" argument against analytic propositions that has any chance of succeeding fails.

D. The Hume Problem

In a well-known passage in the *Prolegomena,* Kant says, "I openly confess my recollection of David Hume was the very thing which many years ago first interrupted my dogmatic slumber and gave my investigations in the field of speculative philosophy a quite new direction" (p. 8). It is generally agreed that it is Hume's teachings on causation that Kant found so disruptive of his sleep. But *which* of Hume's teachings on causation? There are two main candidates. In the *Treatise,* Hume distinguished the following two questions:

> First, For what reason we pronounce it *necessary*, that every thing whose existence has a beginning, shou'd also have a cause?
>
> Secondly, Why we conclude, that such particular causes must *necessarily* have such particular effects? . . .[54]

In other words, he distinguished the question of the necessity or contingency of *specific causal laws* (e.g., that fire causes smoke) from the question of the necessity or contingency of the *general causal maxim* (i.e., the principle that every event has a cause). These questions are independent of each other. (For a discussion of this, see appendix B.) As he is standardly interpreted, however, Hume's position is that they are to be answered in the same way: specific laws are not necessary, and neither is the general maxim.[55]

Which of these two negative theses about causation roused Kant from his slumber? Despite a few misleading indications from Kant that point toward the first, Norman Kemp Smith has made a convincing case that it was the second.[56] Ample support for Kemp Smith occurs in the following passage:

> That sunlight should melt wax and yet also harden clay, no understanding, [Hume] pointed out, can discover from the concepts which we previously possessed of these things, much less infer them according to a law. Only experience is able to teach us such a law. . . . If, . . . [however], wax, which was formerly hard, melts, I can know *a priori* that *something* must have preceded . . . upon which the melting has followed according to a fixed law, although *a priori*, independently of experience, I could not determine, *in any specific manner*, either the cause from the effect, or the effect from the cause. Hume was therefore in error in inferring from the contingency of our determination *in accordance with the law* the contingency of the *law* itself. (A766/B794)

Taking "the law itself" to refer to the general maxim and bearing in mind that for Kant the empirical coincides with the contingent, we learn four things from this passage. (i) Kant distinguished the question of the necessity or contingency of specific causal laws from the question of the necessity or contingency of the general causal maxim.[57] (ii) He accused Hume (whether fairly or not) of erroneously inferring from the contingency of specific laws the contingency of the general maxim. (iii) He agreed with Hume that specific causal laws are contingent. (iv) In opposition to Hume, he held that the general causal maxim is necessary.

The real point of contention between Kant and Hume, then, was the modal and epistemic status of the general causal maxim. Kemp Smith has suggested that it was through pondering Hume's views on this principle that Kant was led to formulate the central question of the *Critique of Pure Reason*.[58]

We can see how this might have come about by looking at Hume's argument against the apriority of the maxim, which occurs in *Treatise* I.3.iii. Taking a few liberties, we may reconstruct the argument as follows:[59]

1. If a proposition is *a priori*, its denial implies a contradiction.
2. If a proposition implies a contradiction, it is inconceivable.
3. The denial of the causal maxim is conceivable.
4. Therefore, the denial of the causal maxim does not imply a contradiction (from 2 and 3).
5. Therefore, the causal maxim is not *a priori* (from 1 and 4).

We may add to this that the causal maxim is not knowable empirically, either. As a universal proposition (*every* event has a cause), it outruns what experience could ever establish. (Even its individual instances lie beyond the power of experience to verify, for they, too, are implicitly universal: an event E has a cause only if there is some event C such that *whenever* a C-type event occurs, an E-type event follows.) So, if Hume is right, the causal maxim is not knowable at all—a result that Kant thought would be disastrous for science and knowledge. Such is the problem Hume posed for Kant.

The reconstruction above may not be entirely true to Hume, for reasons discussed below. Nonetheless, setting the argument out as I have lets me show how Hume's challenge generates the central problem of the *Critique of Pure Reason*. In Kantian terminology, the short way to say that the denial of a proposition p implies a contradiction is 'p is analytic'. From Kant's point of view, therefore, the argument amounts to this: the causal maxim is not *a priori* because it is not analytic (step 4), and only the analytic is *a priori* (step 1). A similar argument, Kant perceived, would show that not even mathematics is *a priori*—an assertion from which Hume's "good sense would have saved him" (B20). This is why the category of synthetic *a priori* judgments was so important for Kant: if they are possible, the Humean argument above can be evaded.

I believe the argument 1–5 is a plausible reconstruction of how Hume's argument may have struck Kant;[60] I believe it is also usefully pedagogically as a lead-in to the central question of the *Critique of Pure Reason*. To be fair to Hume, however, I note two alternative ways in which his argument might be construed.

First, some scholars have questioned whether Hume was committed after all to denying the existence of synthetic *a priori* propositions. Perhaps when he speaks of a proposition p "implying a contradiction," he does not mean that p by itself (or p augmented only by definitions) logically implies a contradiction, but rather that p in conjunction with one or more self-evident or intuitively certain premises logically implies a contradiction. If the admissible extra premises may include propositions not certified by logic and definitions alone, premise 1 above would not imply that only the analytic is *a priori*.[61]

Second, Gary Rosenkrantz has pointed out to me that premises 1 and 2 in the argument above could be telescoped into the single premise *if a proposition is* a priori, *its denial is inconceivable*. This premise is capable of standing on its own, without need of defense using 'implies a contradiction' as a middle term,[62] and it combines with premise 3 to yield the original conclusion. There is no need in the resulting argument to rely on the questionable assumption that only the analytic is *a priori*.

So much by way of defense Hume; I end here with a criticism of him. On a closer look at *Treatise* I.iii.3, it is not entirely clear that he says the denial of the causal maxim is conceivable. What he says appears rather to be this: for any event e and any supposed cause of it c, we can separate the ideas of e and c in the imagination; that is, we can imagine or conceive e to happen without its being preceded by c. Invoking Hume's principle that whatever is conceivable is possible, we could then conclude that for any events e and c, it is possible that e occurs without being caused by c. But that is not yet to show that an event e might occur without *any* cause; it is only to show that for any particular cause c, e might occur without being caused *by c*.[63] So, perhaps in the end Hume offers cogent reasons only for denying the necessity of specific causal laws, not for denying the necessity of the general maxim.

E. The Herz Problem

Believing that some synthetic propositions are known *a priori* makes Kant a *judgment rationalist* as textbooks define that term. He is also a *concept rationalist*, for he tells us that "*a priori* origin is manifest in certain concepts no less than in judgments" (B5). More precisely, he believes that there are concepts that are *a priori* in the sense that they are not abstracted from experience (or compounded in Lockean fashion out of concepts so abstracted) but that are applicable to objects of experience nonetheless. The most famous of these are his twelve categories, of which the concepts of substance and causation are the most important.

In his Inaugural Dissertation of 1770, Kant had distinguished two sources of representations, sensibility and intelligence.[64] Through the former we have empirical representations, which are caused to arise in us by our encounters with objects; through the latter we have *a priori* representations, which are not caused by any such encounters. The *a priori* representations include several of the concepts that later figure in Kant's list of categories—possibility, necessity, existence, substance, and cause. He had also held in the Dissertation that the representations of sensibility are only representations of things as they appear, whereas the representations of intelligence are representations of things as they are.

The status of such *a priori* concepts came not long thereafter to seem very puzzling to Kant. In a letter to his former pupil Marcus Herz in 1772,[65] he asked how it is possible for representations to represent or refer to objects if (i) the objects do not cause the representations (as happens with empirical concepts) and (ii) the representations do not cause the objects (as happens, Kant says, "when divine cognitions are conceived as the archetypes of all things"). Our *a priori* representations stand in no causal relation, either active or passive, to their putative objects, so how do we know that they *have* objects? Indeed, what could their having objects possibly amount to? As he put it in the *Nachlass*: how can "that which is merely an offspring of my own brain . . . be related to an object as its representation?"[66]

Notice the assumption that Kant is apparently making here: a concept can have the Fs for its denotation only if there is a causal connection between Fs and our employment of the concept. This is an assumption that is also found in some important contemporary writing on reference and intentionality—for example, in the work of Putnam and Fodor.[67]

The problem suggested to Kant by his remembrance of Hume—how are synthetic *a priori* judgments possible?—may be rephrased as follows: how is judgment rationalism possible? In similar fashion, the problem posed by Kant in his letter to Herz may be rephrased this way: how is concept rationalism possible? How, in other words, is it possible for there to be *a priori* concepts with nonempty denotation—concepts that were not derived from experience but that have application to the objects of experience nonetheless?[68]

The answer Kant eventually worked out to the Herz problem is contained in his Transcendental Deduction of the Categories, to which I devote chapter 7. The gist of it is that the categories, though not derived from experience, help to make it possible: their "objective validity" or applicability to objects is necessary if experience is to take place at all. As he puts it in the *Prolegomena*, "they do not derive from experience, but experience derives from them" (p. 60).

3

The Ideality of Space

Geometry

> If the object (the triangle) were something in itself, apart from any relation to you, the subject, how could you say that what necessarily exist in you as subjective conditions for the construction of a triangle, must of necessity belong to the triangle itself?
>
> Kant, *Critique of Pure Reason* (A48/B65)

The sentence above expresses the gist of the "argument from geometry" for Kant's transcendental idealism. It also expresses the gist of the Copernican Revolution in his philosophy. It thus expresses one of Kant's deepest philosophical insights—or errors, if one takes a less favorable view of it.

In this chapter I (A) expound the argument from geometry, (B) show that a genuinely idealist interpretation of transcendental idealism is needed to make sense of the argument, (C) discuss a famous criticism to which the argument is susceptible, and (D) show that a similar criticism is applicable to views advanced within the past century as alternatives to Kant's.

A. The Argument from Geometry

The argument from geometry occurs in three main passages in Kant's writings: (i) in section 3 of the Transcendental Aesthetic, "Transcendental Exposition of the Concept of Space," which was added in the B edition; (ii) in sections 7–12 and the ensuing remark 1 of the *Prolegomena*; and (iii) in a passage of the Transcendental Aesthetic running from A46/B64 to A49/B66. Note that the last of these passages occurs in A as well as B, so it is not correct to maintain, as some scholars do, that the argument from geometry does not occur in the first edition of the *Critique*.

Relying mainly on the third of these passages (which contains the quotation with which this chapter begins), I offer the following reconstruction of the argument from geometry:

1. We cannot construct any cubes with more than eight corners (or, any polygons that do not have at least three sides, etc.).
2. Therefore, there cannot *be* any cubes with more than eight corners.
3. The inference from 1 to 2 must be legitimate—otherwise, there would be no accounting for our knowledge of geometrical truths such as 2.
4. But the inference from 1 to 2 would *not* be legitimate if cubes were things in themselves.
5. Therefore, cubes are not things in themselves, but only appearances.

I now present a series of comments to throw further light on the argument.

(a) "Construction" is Kant's technical term for visualizing, or exhibiting to oneself through "pure intuition," spatial figures such as triangles and cubes (see A713/B741). To say that we cannot construct a cube with nine corners is simply to say that we cannot visualize such a cube—that when we try to put together in our imagination a cube with more than eight corners, we see that the thing cannot be done.

(b) The conclusion of the argument may be generalized beyond cubes to all spatial figures. One possible justification for thus generalizing it would be that any spatial figure whatever is potentially an object of geometrical knowledge on our part, so a similar argument could be repeated for an arbitrary spatial figure. On the other hand, there are no doubt many spatial figures so complicated that they defy construction, so it would be safer to offer the argument only for simple figures and to extend it to the rest by means of a "sauce for the goose, sauce for the gander" principle. It is hardly likely that octagons should be appearances while chiliagons are things in themselves.

(c) Steps 1 and 2 function in the argument not so much as asserted premises as propositions about which further assertions are made in 3 and 4. The premises proper are just 3 (up to the dash) and 4; they are all we need to generate the conclusion.

(d) What follows the dash in 3 is a compressed "transcendental argument" for accepting what precedes it, an argument from the existence of knowledge to its necessary conditions. Spelled out, the argument has two steps: (i) if the inference from 1 to 2 were *not* legitimate, I could not know that no cube anywhere has nine corners, but (ii) I *do* know this. (Compare Kant's two requirements for a "transcendental exposition" at A25/B40: the knowledge in question must "really flow from the concept," and it must be "possible *only* on a given mode of explaining the concept.")

(e) Having established that the validity of the inference from 1 to 2 is a necessary condition of our having geometrical knowledge, Kant goes on to ask what, in turn, is necessary for this inference to be valid. When we make this inference, we are in a fashion inferring from subjective to objective necessity—from a necessity governing our modes of construction to a necessity governing objects. What authorizes such an inference? Kant's answer, expressed in premise 4, is that it is only legitimate on condition that the objects are *not* things in themselves.

To clarify the argument further, I now consider two possible objections to it. First, there are many who will repudiate construction or visualization as a source of geometrical knowledge. They may maintain instead that geometrical truths are known because they are analytic (as is arguably the case with the axioms common to the various Euclidean and non-Euclidean geometries) or because they are part of an overall theory that is confirmed by empirical tests (as is nowadays generally believed to be the case with the propositions peculiar to a given geometry). This objection would undermine the case for premise 3. We thus see why it is a crucial presupposition of Kant's argument that geometrical truths—some of them, at least—be both synthetic and *a priori*. For the sake of argument, I assume in the rest of this chapter that he is right about this. (I argue in chapter 2, section B, that he is indeed right about the proposition I have chosen for my example, even if not about geometry at large.)

The second objection (and the one I focus on) is directed rather at premise 4: why does the legitimacy of the 1–2 inference preclude the possibility that some things in themselves are cubical? Could it not be the case that the laws of geometry govern not only the constructions that are possible for human beings, but also the configurations that are possible among things in themselves? Perhaps (as Kant sometimes charges) that would be an implausible preestablished harmony, but what rules it out?

This objection is closely related to the perennial "neglected alternative" objection, raised against Kant by Maass and Pistorius in his own day and doubtless by students in every generation since. Kant assumed that space was a *mere* form of intuition, that it was *only* our way of viewing appearances. But why could it not be *both* a form of intuition *and* a form of things as they are in themselves?[1] That is the neglected alternative. Furthermore, if the neglected alternative were our actual situation, why could appearances and things in themselves not be governed by the same geometrical laws?

These are good questions. I shall now show that under my interpretation of the argument from geometry, Kant has answers to them.

I begin with a concession to the objection. The inference from 1 to 2 might well be *truth-preserving* even if some cubes were things in themselves. That is to say, the same geometrical laws might govern the cubes we construct and cubes in general, including cubes in themselves. Our question, however, is under what conditions the 1–2 inference would be *necessarily valid*—not just contingently truth-preserving.[2] Kant maintains that the inference would not be valid in the required sense if cubes were things in themselves.[3]

To appreciate the plausibility of Kant's contention, ask yourself what further assumption would be needed to get from 1 to 2. The assumption that immediately suggests itself is this: cubes, and spatial figures generally, *exist only in the construction of them*. That is why the constraints on what we can construct are also constraints on all spatial objects: such objects exist only in being constructed.[4]

The thesis I have just enunciated cannot be attributed to Kant as it stands; we need to add two qualifications. First, a cube need not be constructed (exhibited in pure intuition) in order to exist; it can also exist in virtue of being perceived (exhibited in empirical intuition). This qualification does not affect the argument from geometry, since in Kant's view empirical intuition and pure intuition are governed by the same constraints.[5] Second, Kant is at times willing to allow that things in space exist even if not *actually* intuited; it suffices that they *would* be intuited under certain conditions.[6] This qualification need not affect the argument, either, since it will still reach its conclusion as long as we have appropriate rules for attributing properties to unintuited objects. One such rule might be this: cubes have feature F if anyone who intuited a cube would thereby intuit a figure as having F.[7] In what follows, I ignore the second qualification and the complications it requires in Kant's argument.

B. Implications for Idealism

I now pause to take stock. I have contended that premise 4 of the argument from geometry is quite compelling if the contrast between appearances and things in themselves is understood in the manner I have suggested. When it is so understood, the conclusion of the argument is precisely transcendental idealism as I am expounding it in this book: things in space are appearances, that is, things that exist only in being apprehended; they are not things in themselves, that is, things that exist independent of human apprehension. So, the "neglected alternative" has now been ruled out. It is not absent-mindedly neglected, but deliberately and forcefully rejected, on the strength of an argument that embodies the central strategy of Kant's philosophy.[8]

This strategy, of course, is none other than the Copernican Revolution. Kant explains one application of it in the following passage:

> If intuition must conform to the constitution of the objects, I do not see how we could know anything of the latter *a priori*; but if the object (as object of the senses) must conform to our faculty of intuition, I have no difficulty in conceiving such a possibility. (Bxvii)

Now, what manner of objects must conform to our faculty of intuition? I answer, only such objects as owe their very existence to being intuited. There are both textual and philosophical reasons for this answer. For a textual reason, I cite the sentence immediately following the one I have just quoted, in which Kant equates "objects" and "the *experience* in which alone, as given objects, they can be known."[9] For a philosophical reason, I submit that it is inexplicable why objects should depend on us for being the *way* they are if they do not also depend on us for their *being*, period. To put it in a slogan, objects cannot depend on us for their *Sosein* unless they also depend on us for their *Sein*.[10]

C. The Objections of Russell and Moore

The argument from geometry, as reconstructed above, is apparently vulnerable to a famous objection by Russell. Kant's argument starts from a premise about human cognitive capabilities—about what is and is not within our power to construct or visualize. It is natural to assume that it is a contingent matter that our powers are what they are in this regard. From this presumably contingent starting point, Kant goes on to make a claim about what must necessarily hold of all spatial figures. The stage is now set for Russell's objection. He illustrates it with an example from arithmetic, but it is clearly applicable to geometry as well, as my bracketed additions indicate:

Apart from minor grounds on which Kant's philosophy may be criticized, there is one main objection which seems fatal to any attempt to deal with the problem of *a priori* knowledge [necessary truth] by his method. The thing to be accounted for is our certainty [the necessity] that the facts must always conform to logic [geometry] and arithmetic. To say that logic [geometry] and arithmetic are contributed by us does not account for this. Our nature is as much a fact of the existing world as anything, and there can be no certainty [necessity] that it will remain constant. It might happen, if Kant is right, that to-morrow our nature would so change as to make two and two become five [cubes have nine corners]. This possibility seems never to have occurred to him.[11]

Russell's complaint echoes a remark by G.E. Moore, made about the same time:

[I]t never seems to have occurred to [Kant] to ask how we can know that *all* men's minds are so constituted as *always* to act in a certain way.[12]

As I discuss further below, however, Moore's point is somewhat different from Russell's.

Russell seems to be arguing as follows. According to Kant, the necessary truths of arithmetic and geometry owe their necessity to our cognitive constitution—for example, to the fact that we can only apprehend cubes as being eight-cornered. But it is contingent that we have the constitution we do—our nature might change, or it might have been different originally even if for some reason it cannot change. Hence, the laws of arithmetic and geometry are not necessary after all—if our constitution had been different, those laws would have been false and other laws would have held in their place. But that is absurd, as Kant should be among the first to acknowledge.

A possible defense of Kant can be mounted as follows.[13] In giving the necessary truths of geometry a contingent grounding in our form of intuition, Kant is not denying that these truths are necessary after all; he is only denying that they are *necessarily* necessary. In other words, he is denying the characteristic axiom of the modal system S4, $\Box p \to \Box\Box p$. He may still hold that the laws of arithmetic and geometry are necessary truths in *our* world, even if in some other worlds (in which forms of intuition are different) they are not necessary.

According to the suggestion I am now pursuing, what emerges from Russell's observation is only the following supposedly harmless argument. First, we have the Kantian premise that if a proposition of geometry is necessary, that is only because it is a deliverance of our form of intuition. This premise I symbolize as follows, using '$\Box$' for necessity, '$\Diamond$' for possibility, '$\to$' for material implication, and '$\Rightarrow$' for strict implication or entailment:

1. $(p)(\Box p \to [\Box p \Rightarrow Fp])$

Call this the Dependency Premise. Next, add the presumed fact that it is contingent (hence, possibly false) that any given proposition *is* delivered by our form of intuition:

2. $(p)\Diamond -Fp$

Call this the Contingency Premise. Now we reason as follows. Let p be any geometrical truth. We have:

3. $\Box p$

From 3 and 1 we may infer:

4. $\Box p \Rightarrow Fp$

Now, it is an uncontroversial theorem of modal logic that if one proposition entails another and the second is possibly false, so is the first.[14] Thus, from 2 and 4 we derive

5. $\Diamond -\Box p$

or, equivalently,

6. $-\Box\Box p$.

In this version of the argument, we do not reach the conclusion that the propositions of arithmetic and geometry are not necessary after all; we only reach the conclusion that they are not *necessarily* necessary. And this is a conclusion that some people are quite prepared to live with.

The issue before us may be illuminated by reference to the controversy surrounding one of the more notorious doctrines of Descartes, the *creation of the eternal truths*:[15]

> The mathematical truths which you call eternal have been laid down by God and depend on Him entirely no less than the rest of his creatures [do]. . . . [I]t is God who has laid down these laws in nature just as a king lays down laws in his kingdom.[16]

Some scholars (e.g., Frankfurt[17]) have concluded from passages such as these that for Descartes there really are no such things as necessary truths. But others (e.g., Geach and Curley[18]) have proposed instead that Descartes is committed only to the less radical view that the truths that are necessary in our world are not necessary in all worlds. If we substitute 'God wills that $\Box p$' for 'Fp' in the symbolic argument above, we get an argument for this less radical conclusion. Necessary truths are necessary only because God wills them to be so; it is contingent that he so wills; therefore, any necessary truth is only contingently necessary.

It must be said, of course, that the idea of the contingently necessary strikes many people as absurd. Anyone so minded, as I am myself, will adopt the S4 axiom $\Box p \rightarrow \Box\Box p$ as a principle constitutive of necessity, and once that axiom is in place, the position attributed to Descartes by Geach and Curley collapses into a denial of necessity altogether. But I do not propose to debate the merits of the S4 principle here. Instead, I show below that a slightly modified form of the argument above leads *directly* (without invoking S4) to the result that there is no necessity.

The modified argument is just like the original argument, except that it uses the following strengthened form of the Dependency Premise:

1. $(p)(\Box p \rightarrow [p \Rightarrow Fp])$

The original Dependency Premise said that if a proposition is necessary, it owes its necessity to factor F; this one says that if a proposition is necessary, it owes its *truth* to factor F. I submit that if the original Dependency Premise is plausible for a chosen factor F, so is the corresponding version of the Strengthened Dependency Premise. If we say with Descartes that the Pythagorean Theorem is necessary only because it was established by God, we should also say that it is *true* only because it was established by God. To believe otherwise is to attribute to God a queer form of omnipotence that holds sway over truths of the form '$\Box p$' but not over truths generally. And similarly in other cases. For example, proponents of the linguistic theory of logical necessity should say (and did say) that necessary truths are *true* in virtue of meanings. Returning to Kant, if we say that the propositions of geometry owe their necessity to our cognitive constitution, we should also say that they owe their *truth* to our constitution.

With this premise granted, the rest of the argument can proceed by the same logic as before, but substituting p for $\Box p$ from line 4 onward:

1. $(p)(\Box p \rightarrow [p \Rightarrow Fp])$ (Strengthened Dependency Premise)
2. $(p)\Diamond -Fp$ (Contingency Premise)
3. $\Box p$ (assumption for reductio)
4. $p \Rightarrow Fp$ (from 3 and 1)
5. $\Diamond -p$ (from 4, 2, and the same modal principle as before)
6. $-\Box p$ (from 5)

Russell drew the correct conclusion after all: if Kant is right, the propositions of arithmetic and geometry lose their necessity. If our nature changed drastically enough, we could wake up tomorrow and find that cubes have nine corners or that $2 + 2 = 5$.

But would Kant really admit that our nature could thus change, or that it might have been different originally? Is he committed, as I have been supposing, to the Contingency Premise? Here are two passages that suggest that the answer is yes:

> We cannot judge in regard to the intuition of other thinking beings, whether they are bound by the same conditions as those which limit our intuition and which for us are universally valid. (A27/B43)

> This peculiarity of our understanding, that it can produce *a priori* unity of apperception solely by means of the categories, and only by such and so many, is as little capable of further explanation as why we have just these and no other functions of judgment, or why space and time are the only forms of our possible intuition. (B145–46)

These remarks strongly suggest that it is a brute contingency that we have the forms of intuition that we do.[19]

At the same time, however, the context of the passages makes clear that what Kant is entertaining is the possibility of beings whose form of intuition is not spatial at all—not of beings whose form of intuition is spatial but non-Euclidean. Perhaps it would be open to him to maintain that a spatial form of intuition is necessarily a Euclidean form, or that *we* are essentially Euclidean creatures, whatever may be possible for others. I do not believe such a stance would be out of the question. It may initially seem that any proposition beginning 'I am of such a nature that . . . ' and continuing in some detail is bound to be contingent, but when the proposition is of the form 'I am of such a nature that I *cannot* do such and such' (e.g., visualize a cube with nine corners), it is a modal proposition, and thus arguably noncontingent.[20] So, let us try the hypothesis that Kant would reject the Contingency Premise. Can he evade Russell's objection by maintaining that human beings are of necessity so constituted as to intuit in Euclidean fashion?

It is at this stage that the objection of Moore comes into play. Let me quote it this time at greater length:

> [T]his proposition, that our minds are so constituted as always to produce the same appearances, is itself a universal synthetic proposition. . . . But how can any of us know this? Obviously, it is a question which requires an answer just as much as any of those which Kant set out to answer; and yet he never even attempts to answer it: it never seems to have occurred to him to ask how we can know that *all* men's minds are so constituted as *always* to act in a certain way. And once this question is raised, I think the whole plausibility of his argument disappears.[21]

In my reconstruction above of the argument from geometry, I represented Kant as saying we have knowledge of any geometrical proposition only because we can validly infer it from a premise about our own cognitive relation to that proposition. If such an inference is to give us knowledge of its conclusion, it is presumably required that we have knowledge of the premise. So, Moore's challenge to Kant—how could we possibly have knowledge of the premise?—seems quite fair.[22]

Putting the objections of Russell and Moore together, we obtain a dilemma: that our form of intuition is Euclidean is either necessary or contingent. If it is contingent, then geometrical truth depends on a contingency of human nature, and its necessity is thereby abolished. If it is necessary, the question arises as to how we are to obtain knowledge of *this* necessity (as presumably we must, if we are to base geometrical knowledge on it). Kant's theory does not account for knowledge of necessary facts about our own nature. Therefore, Kant must renounce either the existence of necessary truths or his explanation of how we come to know them.

D. Explaining Necessity

I do not know how to get Kant out of the difficulty raised by Russell. It is worth pointing out, however, that it is by no means a difficulty for Kant alone. I have already shown that Descartes's theory of the creation of the eternal truths falls into the same difficulty. The leading theory of necessary truth in the twentieth century—that all necessary truth is a matter of convention—is also open to the same difficulty, since it is contingent that our conventions are what they are.[23] In this section I air the suspicion that the problem here is quite general—that *any* theory that tries to *explain* necessity (as opposed to accepting it as ultimate) is bound to fail.

There are actually two problems I discuss. The first is the threat of vacuity or triviality in any purported explanation of necessity, as suggested in the following remark by Quine:

> [A]ny sentence logically implies the logical truths. Trivially, then, the logical truths are true by virtue of any circumstances you care to name—language, the world, anything.[24]

We can expand this point to cover not only the logical truths but also necessary truths generally. The idea would be that in virtue of the modal theorem $\Box p \rightarrow (q \Rightarrow p)$ (one of the so-called "paradoxes of strict implication"), any proposition that is necessarily true is entailed by, and thus arguably true in virtue of, any fact you care to mention. If we have the S4 axiom $\Box p \rightarrow \Box\Box p$ at our disposal, we can go a step further. That axiom combines with the theorem above to yield the theorem $\Box p \rightarrow (q \Rightarrow \Box p)$.[25] That is, if p is necessary, its being necessary is entailed by any fact you care to mention. So, we could say that $2 + 2 = 4$ is a necessary truth because Quine thought of it while brushing his teeth.

On further reflection, however, I think it can be seen that we are not really driven into saying such things. It is true that for any necessary truth p, any feature F of p we cite will be a feature such that p's having F entails its being necessary. But that is not yet to say that p is necessary *in virtue of* its having F. To make such an "in virtue of" claim is to say more, namely, that F is a feature such that (necessarily) *any* proposition that had F would also be necessary. That is not true if F is the property of being thought of by Quine while he brushes his teeth; nor is it obvious that there is any such F that is not already a modal property.

The second problem I discuss is a dilemma that has been raised by Simon Blackburn.[26] Suppose we offer an explanation of the form '$\Box p$ because Fp'. Fp will be either necessary or contingent. If it is contingent, "the original necessity has not been explained . . . so much as undermined." If it is necessary, we are left with a "bad residual 'must'." All we are doing is explaining some necessities in terms of others, which is unsatisfying.

The first horn of the dilemma is very nearly the problem I discussed above in connection with Russell. For this horn to be lethally sharp, it must be p and not just $\Box p$ that holds because Fp; further, the 'because' must express a relation of dependency. With these provisos, the first horn is indeed fatal to necessity.

What is dangerous about the second horn? Blackburn's worry is apparently that our explanation (if it is not simply circular) will be incomplete: if we are invoking necessities in our explanans, then we are not explaining necessity *tout court*. If this is the problem, I think it may be possible to get around it. To say that F is possessed necessarily by p is not yet to say that F is itself a modal property; for all that has been said, F might be some property expressible in modal-free vocabulary (unlike, say, 'true in all possible worlds'), and in that case it could be a suitable property for an illuminating explanation of necessity. We would not simply be explaining some necessities in terms of others, for although our explanans would *possess* necessity, it would not *invoke* it. (Compare: if we wanted an explanation of how anything whatever could be reasonable, we should not object if someone proffered an explanans that was itself reasonable.) So, it may be that the second horn of Blackburn's dilemma is one we can safely grasp.[27]

At the same time, however, I must confess that I have not the slightest idea what nonmodal property might serve to guarantee the presence of necessity in whatever had it. To me, the prospects for a general explanation of necessity look quite dim. So, I conclude this chapter with the following backhanded defense of Kant: it may be that one can do better than he did only by not trying at all.

4

The Ideality of Space

Incongruent Counterparts

> Those who cannot yet rid themselves of the
> notion that space and time are actual quali-
> ties inherent in things in themselves may ex-
> ercise their acumen on the following para-
> dox. When they have in vain attempted its
> solution and are free from prejudices at least
> for a few moments, they will suspect that the
> degradation of space and time to mere forms
> of our sensuous intuition may perhaps be
> well founded.
>
> Kant, *Prolegomena to Any Future
> Metaphysics* (sec. 13)

Incongruent counterparts are objects that are perfectly similar except for being
mirror images of each other, such as left and right human hands. Kant was evidently the first major thinker to notice the philosophical significance of such
objects. He called them "counterparts" because they are alike in every intrinsic spatial respect,[1] "incongruent" because, despite their similarity, one could
never be put in the place of the other. The left glove, as Kant points out, will
not fit the right hand.

Kant called on incongruent counterparts during the course of his career to
establish three very different conclusions. In an essay published in 1768, he
cited them as proving that space is absolute (existing in its own right and independent of matter), thus vindicating Newton against Leibniz.[2] In the
Inaugural Dissertation of 1770, he cited them as proving that our knowledge
of space and spatial configurations is by way of intuition, not concept.[3] Finally,
in the *Prolegomena* of 1783, he cited them as proving that space is ideal, belonging only to our form of intuition and not to things in themselves.[4] I have
dealt at length with Kant's first two uses of incongruent counterparts elsewhere[5] and will not do so here (but, for a brief recap of the 1768 argument, see
appendix C). In this chapter I discuss Kant's third use of incongruent counterparts—the so-called paradox that he offers in proof of idealism. I consider
three different reconstructions of Kant's argument and three associated con-

ceptions of things in themselves, seeking to determine which conception of them affords the best argument.

A. The Argument from Intelligibility

Norman Kemp Smith interprets the argument given in Kant's *Prolegomena* along the following lines:[6]

1. The difference between two incongruent counterparts cannot be known conceptually. (A purely conceptual description of a hand will not determine whether it is left or right.)
2. Things in themselves *can* be adequately known conceptually—all their features can be captured by purely conceptual descriptions.
3. Therefore, objects like left and right hands are not things in themselves.

From this conclusion we may presumably generalize and say *no* spatial objects are things in themselves.[7]

The argument above is not explicit in the *Prolegomena*. The materials for it are rather to be found in the Inaugural Dissertation, where Kant does indeed assert each of the premises and the conclusion. Curiously, however, he does not assemble them all into one argument; he asserts the conclusion on independent grounds, and the only lesson he draws from the facts about incongruent counterparts is that our knowledge of space is intuitive rather than conceptual.

Could the argument above be the argument Kant meant to give in the *Prolegomena*? The first premise is indeed there, and there is a hint of the second in Kant's use of the phrase "things as they are in themselves *and as some pure understanding would know them*" (emphasis mine). It is extremely puzzling, however, to find Kant using such an argument in 1783. As Kemp Smith notes, the second premise is pre-Critical. It amounts to saying that things in themselves are noumena in the positive sense (things adequately knowable by nonsensible means), not just in the negative sense (things not adequately knowable by sensible means), and this is a doctrine Kant rejects in the *Critique of Pure Reason* (at least as far as human beings are concerned).[8] Kemp Smith thus concludes that the argument is a remnant of a repudiated view, taking this to explain why there is no trace of the argument in the second edition of the *Critique* in 1787.

B. The Argument from Interchangeability

What is the "paradox" about incongruent counterparts? Kant states it as follows:

> If two things are quite equal in all respects as much as can be ascertained by all means possible, quantitatively and qualitatively, it must follow that the one can in all cases and in all circumstances replace the other, and this substitution would not occasion the least perceptible difference. This is in fact true of plane figures in geometry; but some spherical figures [e.g., spherical triangles in opposite hemispheres with an arc of the

equator as common base and corresponding sides equal] exhibit, notwith-standing complete internal agreement, such a difference in their exter-nal relation that the one figure cannot be put in the place of the other. (*Prolegomena*, p. 33)

Let me use "internally alike" to abbreviate Kant's "quite equal in all respects as much as can be ascertained by all means possible, quantitatively and qual-itatively" (i.e., alike in all nonrelational respects) and "interchangeable" to ab-breviate his "the one can in all cases and in all circumstances replace the other." The paradox can then be stated more compactly as follows:

1. Things that are internally alike must be interchangeable.
2. Some spatial figures are internally alike but *not* interchangeable.

This is indeed a paradox, since as they stand 1 and 2 contradict each other. What is the way out?

According to Kant, we must first of all recognize that the first premise is true only with a qualification; it must be rewritten as

1'. Things *in themselves* that are internally alike must be interchange-able.

This restores consistency—*provided* we do not shrink from drawing the con-clusion that now follows:

3. Some spatial figures are not things in themselves.

This is just the conclusion Kant draws: the figures in question are not things in themselves, but only "appearances, whose possibility rests upon the rela-tion of certain things unknown in themselves to something else, namely to our sensibility" (*Prolegomena*, p. 33). As before, we may presumably extend the result to all spatial configurations.

My objection to this argument is that the first premise seems perfectly plau-sible *without* the qualification. If that is so, the only way to avoid contradiction is to deny the *second* premise. This would mean either denying that incongru-ent counterparts are internally alike or holding that they are interchangeable after all. I mention below a supporting ground for each option.[9]

(i) Suppose we take seriously the idea of *absolute direction*. That is, sup-pose we maintain that having a part lying in a certain direction from another part does not tacitly involve a relation to something outside the whole.[10] Then it would be false that incongruent counterparts are internally alike: Kant's spherical triangles would differ in that the direction from middle to largest to smallest angle would be clockwise in one and counterclockwise in the other.

(ii) Suppose we take seriously the idea of a *fourth spatial dimension*. Then it would be false that incongruent counterparts are noninterchangeable: al-though we cannot interchange spherical triangles in *our* space, spaces would be possible in which they *could* be interchanged.[11] One could resist this ob-jection to the second premise by holding that 'interchangeable' must mean 'in-terchangeable in the *actual* space', but then the *first* premise would become questionable.

C. The Argument from Reducibility

According to Jill Buroker, the gist of Kant's incongruent counterparts argument is that "the nature of space is incompatible with the analysis of relations."[12] I agree completely as to gist but would like to give a different account of the details. Here, then, is a third reconstruction of Kant's argument:

1. Incongruent counterparts (e.g., Kant's two spherical triangles) are different in virtue of their differing relations to space as a whole. (Thus, triangle 1 bears R to space and triangle 2 does not.)
2. All relations among things in themselves are reducible to nonrelational characters (qualities) of the relata.
3. Therefore, if space and figures within it are things in themselves, triangle 1 must differ internally from triangle 2.
4. But, in fact, triangle 1 does *not* differ internally from triangle 2.
5. Therefore, space itself and figures within it are not things in themselves.[13]

Now for a series of comments to elucidate the argument.

(a) The premise that comes to the fore in this version of the argument is the *reducibility of relations* among things in themselves. It is a merit of Buroker's discussion to bring out the importance of this Leibnizian element in Kant's philosophy. Kant does not explicitly state this premise in the *Prolegomena* argument, but he does endorse it at least implicitly elsewhere. It underlies two of his assumptions in the "Amphiboly" section of the *Critique of Pure Reason*: things in themselves cannot have their nature exhausted by relations, and they cannot differ numerically without also differing qualitatively.[14]

(b) Strictly speaking, it is not the *reducibility* of relations that is needed in the argument above, but only their *supervenience*. That is, a relational fact aRb need not be *equivalent* to any conjunction Fa & Gb, but there must be some such conjunction that *entails* it. I shall nonetheless stick with the language of reducibility in what follows.

(c) In accordance with the reducibility principle, if we have

triangle 1 bears R to space & triangle 2 does not,

we must also have (for some nonrelational features F and G)

triangle 1 is F & space is G & −(triangle 2 is F & space is G),

which implies

triangle 1 is F & triangle 2 is not F.

Thus, the triangles must differ internally. This is the justification for step 3 above.

(d) Note that the first premise in the argument above is the conclusion of Kant's 1768 argument: the difference between incongruent counterparts is a difference in their relations to space itself. This bears out Buroker's contention that Kant's later arguments incorporate, rather than contradict, his earlier conclusion.[15]

(e) But note as well that it would not have been necessary for Kant to make space a term of relations in the argument. He could simply have noted that the relation of incongruent counterparthood, a relation holding directly between the triangles, is an irreducible relation. If relations among things in themselves must be reducible, it would then follow that the triangles are not things in themselves. Thus, I disagree with Buroker's view that if Kant's conclusion of 1768 were denied, the 1783 version of his argument would be undercut.[16]

(f) Moreover, once armed with the reducibility principle, Kant need not have resorted to anything so recondite as incongruent counterparts to make his point, for spatial relations quite generally fail to be reducible (or "internal," in one leading sense of that term). Take, for example, the relation of *distance*: there is nothing about my pen and my ruler taken separately that would enable anyone to deduce that they are now six inches apart. So, Kant could simply have argued thus: all relations among things in themselves are reducible; distance is not a reducible relation; therefore, nothing in the field of the distant-from relation (which is to say, nothing in space) is a thing in itself.

(g) The big question raised by this interpretation of the argument is this: why should Kant have thought that the Leibnizian reducibility principle holds for things in themselves but not for appearances? In the sections that follow, I consider three possible answers to this question, each invoking a different conception of the contrast between appearances and things in themselves.

D. Things in Themselves as Intelligibilia

The first answer is given by the following syllogism:

1. Intelligible entities (entities adequately knowable by the intellect alone) can stand in none but reducible relations.
2. Things in themselves are intelligible entities.
3. Therefore, things in themselves can stand in none but reducible relations.

Appearances, as sensible entities, would not fall under the major premise.

This answer to our question (which seems in places to be Buroker's[17]) is unsatisfying for two reasons. First, the minor premise is the Dissertation doctrine all over again, so we are thrown back to the argument from intelligibility. Is there an answer to our question the *Critical* Kant can give? Second, why should even the pre-Critical Kant have thought the major premise true? That is, why should he have thought irreducible relations a bar to intelligibility? To use James's famous figure, why may the life of the intellect not include flights as well as perchings?

I note in this connection that according to some philosophers, the nature of a number is exhausted by its relations to other numbers.[18] Yet numbers are intelligible entities *par excellence*.

E. Things in Themselves as Things Apart from Relation

In some contexts, Kant's phrase "in itself" seems to contrast with "in relation to other things (or to us)." If we understand the phrase in this way, the unknowability of things in themselves is no longer the utter unknowability of things of a special kind but rather the unknowability in certain respects (namely, nonrelational respects) of things in general.[19] The way is then open for holding that what present themselves to our senses are the very things that are unknowable "in themselves"; what is denied us is not any access whatever to these things but merely knowledge of their nonrelational or qualitative aspects. In support of such an interpretation one might cite the following passage:

> Now a thing in itself cannot be known through mere relations; and we may therefore conclude that since outer sense gives us nothing but mere relations, this sense can contain in its representation only the relation of an object to the subject, and not the inner properties of the object in itself. (B67)

I discuss the merits of this interpretation of the 'in itself' at greater length in chapter 10, section E. For now, I discuss only its usefulness in answering our present question—why Kant thought the reducibility principle holds for things in themselves. The idea would be that if 'in itself' means 'apart from relation', it becomes a tautology to say that things in themselves stand in no relations (or at any rate, none but reducible relations, which in a sense are nothing in addition to the relata and their qualities).

But there is clearly a fallacy in this attempt to derive the reducibility principle. 'No knowledge of things in themselves' may mean 'no knowledge of things apart from relation', but we cannot infer from this that 'things in themselves' means 'things apart from relation'. Or, if we do, we have no right to assume that there *are* any things in themselves; that would be to make an illicit shift from 'in itself' as adverb to 'in itself' as adjective.[20]

F. Things in Themselves as Real Existents

According to the interpretation of transcendental idealism I am advocating, Kant's distinction between things in themselves and appearances is the distinction between things having genuine independent existence and things existing merely as intentional objects. As Wilfrid Sellars has put the matter, it is the distinction between things that have formal reality and things that merely have objective reality (in the medieval and Cartesian senses of these terms).[21] The idea is that to be a thing in itself is to exist *simpliciter*, whereas to be an appearance is to exist only as a content of thought or awareness. Let us see what light this interpretation throws on the incongruent counterparts argument.

It is useful to begin with a little paradox. Consider the following principle:

1. A genuinely existent entity must be *fully determinate*—that is, one predicate out of every possible pair of contradictorily opposed predicates must belong to it.

To me this principle seems self-evident.[22] Kant endorses it at A573/B601, and I believe it also underlies his assumption in section 7 of his chapter on the antinomies that the spatiotemporal world, if it existed as a thing in itself, would have to be either finite or infinite.

So far, so good, but now let us confront our principle with the following recalcitrant fact:

2. The dragon I dreamt of last night was *not* fully determinate. It had teeth, but no definite number of them.

The paradox is that 1 and 2 both seem true, yet seem to conflict. The solution is obvious: 1 and 2 do *not* conflict but can both be true provided the following is also true:

3. The dragon I dreamt of was not a genuinely existent entity.

The dragon existed only in the dreaming of it and therefore falls outside the intended scope of the determinacy principle.

Now what I suggest is that Kant's incongruent counterparts argument should be viewed as paralleling the argument 1–3:

1'. Genuinely existent entities must stand in none but reducible relations.
2'. Spatial figures stand in some irreducible relations.
3'. Therefore, spatial figures are not genuinely existent entities.

On the suggested interpretation of things in themselves, this is exactly what the argument from incongruent counterparts amounts to. To verify this, please refer back to comment (e) of section C. If you think 3' a most un-Kantian conclusion, please read on.

One thing I wish to suggest with the parallel argument about the dream entities is the following possibility: Kant does not regard the reducibility principle as holding for things in themselves in virtue of some special feature they possess, but instead simply regards it as holding for existents as such. Like the determinacy principle, it is intended as a general logical or ontological principle. That being so, the more pressing half of our question is not why things in themselves must be subject to the reducibility principle, but why appearances are exempt from it.[23]

At one level the answer is that appearances, as things merely having intentional being, do not really exist and hence are not there to be exceptions to any principle. But that cannot be the whole story. There is an important sense in which spatial items *do* exist (they are "empirically real," as Kant insists), and we must inquire how items with their ontological status can be exempt from laws governing the *an sich*.

My answer to this question has two parts. First, *things that exist only in relation to consciousness are logical constructions out of conscious states*. This, of course, is the conception of intentional objects as virtual objects that I set forth in chapter 1. I think this conception is both plausible in its own right and plausibly attributable to Kant. If we do not adopt this conception, we must evidently suppose that intentional being or objective reality is a separate ontological status, a second way of being in the world, and it has always been hard to understand what such a status could amount to. Moreover, that Kant himself thinks of intentional objects as constructions is strongly suggested by many of his remarks about "objects" in the Transcendental Deduction and elsewhere,[24] as discussed in chapter 7.

Second, *if As are logical constructions out of Bs, As need not obey all the same laws as Bs, however self-evident these laws may be.* Here is an example: matrices are logical constructions out of ordinary numbers; ordinary multiplication is commutative, but matrix multiplication is not.

Putting the two italicized principles together, we see that intentionalia need not obey all the same laws as the realia out of which they are constructed. (I assume that conscious states are realia, for otherwise we embark on an endless regress of constructions out of constructions.) For an illustration, let us return to the dragon of my dream. The dragon is a logical construction out of dream states; this explains not only how it is possible for the dragon to have no existence outside the dream, but also how it is possible for it to be indeterminate. The construction is governed by the following rule: if 'p' states a fact about the dragon internal to the dream, then p iff Dp (i.e., one dreams that p).[25] Now, since reality is determinate, we must have either Dp or $-$Dp, but we need not have either Dp or D($-$p). It follows that the dragon may be indeterminate: there need not be a correct answer to the question, "Did it have more than 100 teeth?"

Lest the dream example mislead, I must enter two caveats. I do not mean to suggest that appearances in general have for Kant exactly the same status as dream objects. They do not: an empirically real beast has relations to the rest of our experience that the dragon does not.[26] But appearances in general are nonetheless *like* dream objects in that they exist only in relation to consciousness. Nor do I mean to suggest that the basis in realia for any fact about appearances must always consist in a subject's apprehending that very fact. To take one of Kant's famous examples, the basis for saying that opposite sides of a house exist simultaneously is not that anyone perceives them as existing simultaneously; it is rather that the perceptions of the sides individually can be obtained in any order. (See A192–93/B237–38; this example is discussed further in chapter 9.)

I have not addressed the question of how the reducibility principle in particular might fail for appearances, but I hope I have at least made it clear how appearances might fail to obey laws that are deemed valid for things in themselves. I hope also to have shown how the conception of things in themselves and appearances as real beings and intentional beings, respectively, makes sense of the incongruent counterparts argument for idealism.

5

The Ideality of Time

[The view that time is unreal] seems self-refuting in something of the way in which . . .
the view that evil is an illusion is self-refuting: that is, if there is no evil, the illusion
that there is evil is certainly evil. . . . Clearly,
even if the world is static, our apprehension
of it changes.

Michael Dummett,
Truth and Other Enigmas

A. The Objection of Lambert and Mendelssohn

Kant maintains that time, no less than space, is transcendentally ideal:

> This, then is what constitutes the *transcendental ideality* of time. What
> we mean by this phrase is that if we abstract from the subjective condi-
> tions of sensible intuition, time is nothing, and cannot be ascribed to the
> objects in themselves. . . . (A36/B52)

His reasons are in good measure parallel to his reasons in the case of space. If
time were transcendentally real, antinomies would threaten; moreover, there
would be no accounting for our *a priori* knowledge of the structure of time.[1]

But the ideality of time has always been a good deal harder to accept than
the ideality of space. Kant opens section 7 of the Transcendental Aesthetic
with an acknowledgment of this fact:

> Against this theory, which admits the empirical reality of time, but denies
> its absolute and transcendental reality, I have heard men of intelligence so
> unanimously voicing an objection, that I must suppose it to occur spon-
> taneously to every reader to whom this way of thinking is unfamiliar.

The "men of intelligence" to whom Kant refers include, among others, Lambert
and Mendelssohn, both of whom had communicated versions of the objection
to him in response to his Inaugural Dissertation. What is the objection?

The objection is this. Alterations are real, this being proved by change of our own representations—even if all outer appearances, together with their alterations, be denied. Now alterations are possible only in time, and time is therefore something real. (A36–37/B53–54)

According to an interesting suggestion by Lorne Falkenstein,[2] Lambert and Mendelssohn had actually raised significantly different objections to Kant. Here is what Lambert wrote to Kant:

I think, though, that even an idealist must grant at least that changes really exist and occur in his representations, for example, their beginning and ending. Thus time cannot be regarded as something unreal.[3]

And here is Mendelssohn:

[W]e have to grant the reality of succession in a representing creature and in its alterations. . . .[4]

Note that Lambert speaks only of changes in our representations, whereas Mendelssohn speaks of changes in the states of a representer or self. I take it that Mendelssohn's claim goes further at least in this way: changes in representations could occur even in a Humean bundle, whereas changes in the states of a self could occur only if there *is* a self. Falkenstein suggests that the Mendelssohn objection is more damaging to Kant's view, since it contends for changes in a real object, namely, the self. He also maintains that Kant has made things too easy on himself by reporting the objection only in Lambert's form.[5]

I disagree on both points. To take the second first, I do not think Kant presents only the Lambert version of the objection. The objection as Kant states it above can be cast into the following argument:

1. Our own representations change.
2a. If our own representations change, alterations occur.
2b. If alterations occur, time is real.
3. Therefore, time is real.

The Mendelssohnian version of the objection is strongly suggested by Kant's use of the terms 'change' (*Wechsel*) and 'alteration' (*Veränderung*). It is a safe assumption that Kant is using these words here in the same technical senses he explains later in connection with the First Analogy (see A187/B230–31, which I discuss further in chapter 8, section B). If so, a *change* in a representation is its coming into being or going out of being, and an *alteration* in something is its entering or leaving a state. According to the First Analogy, nothing ever changes unless something alters, and Kant is apparently invoking that thesis here: if representations change, he says, alteration is real. What could the alteration correlative with the change of a representation be, except an alteration in the representer or self? So, even though Kant makes no mention of the self in his passage, it seems to me that he is implicitly presenting the objection in its Mendelssohnian form.

Independent of that, however, I would still disagree with the claim that the objection Kant has taken on is the easier of the two to deal with. It seems to me that even the Lambert version of the objection poses a challenge to Kant's transcendental idealism that is quite stiff. We can arrive at Lambert's version simply by telescoping premises 2a and 2b:

1. Our own representations change.
2. If our own representations change, time is real.
3. Therefore, time is real.

In this version, the first premise and the conclusion are the same as before; the only difference is that premise 2 is left to stand on its own, without the support of 2a and 2b. But it *does* stand quite well on its own: surely, if any representations come into or go out of existence, time must be real![6] Thus, I find the Lambert version fully as cogent as Mendelssohn's; it reaches the same conclusion (that time is real) from premises no less demanding of our assent.[7]

One point needs to be made clear before I go further. The question of whether time is real is not the question (debated by Newton and Leibniz) of whether time is an entity in its own right; it is simply the question of whether any items genuinely stand in temporal relations. Newton and Leibniz agreed that they do; Lambert and Mendelssohn feared that Kant was maintaining otherwise.

B. Kant's Radical Response

I turn now to Kant's response to the argument:

> There is no difficulty in meeting this objection. I grant the whole argument. Certainly time is something real, namely, the real form of inner intuition. It has therefore subjective reality in repect of inner experience; that is, I really have the representation of time and of my determinations in it.(A37/B54)

Does he really "grant the whole argument"? Far from it! He grants its conclusion in words only. What is at issue, as we just noted, is whether any items really stand in temporal relations. What Kant appears to concede is something far less than this—namely, that things are *represented* as being in time. For dramatic confirmation of this, we need only look at the footnote Kant includes on the same page:

> I can indeed say that my representations follow one another; but this is *only* to say that we are conscious of them *as* in a time sequence, that is, in conformity with the form of inner sense. Time is not, therefore, something in itself, nor is it an objective determination inherent in things. (emphasis mine)

Kant here appears to be taking a radical line indeed—that no items whatever stand in temporal relations, not even our own mental episodes. Contrast this with the more moderate line that would deny the temporality of things in themselves (considered as beings of one sort) while affirming the temporality of appearances or representations (considered as real beings or happenings of another, perhaps mental, sort). The moderate line would indeed "grant the whole argument"; the radical line does not.

Kant had already intimated the radical line in an unfamous portion of his famous letter to Herz:

> [T]he form of the inner sensibility does give me the appearance of changes. I do not deny that changes are real, any more than I deny that bodies are real, even though by *real* I only mean that something real corresponds to the appearance. I can't even say that the inner appearance changes, for how would I observe this change if it doesn't appear to my inner sense?[8]

Note the implicit distinction between the appearance of change (which the first sentence admits) and change of appearance (which the third sentence denies). Rather than "granting the whole argument," Kant is rejecting its first premise, that our representations change.

For further illustration of the radical line, consider the following view, which is advocated by some physicists as an alleged consequence of Special Relativity:

> Time exists only as one dimension of a static four-dimensional manifold. The appearance of change is an illusion due to the fact that the searchlight of human consciousness illuminates portions of the manifold successively.

This view (which has been aptly characterized as "the fallacy of the animated Minkowski diagram"[9]) invites the obvious objection that if the searchlight of consciousness *successively* illuminates various scenes, there is change after all, one episode of consciousness being succeeded by another. The "radical" view I am tentatively ascribing to Kant is what you get if you make the physicist's picture consistent, that is, if you refuse to admit any succession even among states of consciousness. Instead, you say there is consciousness of succession, but no succession of conscious states.[10]

Could the radical view possibly be true? And could it really have been what Kant intended? These are the questions I address in the remainder of this chapter.

Kant certainly allows that there are experiences symbolizable as 'e(aPb)', that is, experiences or representations of one state a as preceding or giving way to another state b. Let us assume that this much is possible only if there are representations of a and b separately, ea and eb.[11] What Kant must deny, if he takes the radical line, is that there are facts symbolizable as 'eaPeb', that is, facts of one experience preceding another, for that would involve temporal relations as genuinely holding between some items in the universe. The relation P (along with all other temporal relations) must occur exclusively as an experiential content—only *within* experiences and not *between* them, if I may so put it.

Some philosophers have argued that any such view is impossible—that time is one feature of the world (perhaps even the only one) that cannot occur merely as content. A good representative of this viewpoint is D.H. Mellor:

[P]erceptions of temporal order need temporally ordered perceptions. No other property or relation has to be thus embodied in perceptions of it: perceptions of shape and colour, for example, need not themselves be correspondingly shaped or coloured. This sharing by a perception of the property thereby perceived is peculiar to time, and fundamental enough in my view to define it.[12]

On Mellor's view, e(aPb) can occur only in virtue of the fact that eaPeb—the experience of succession requires a succession of experiences.

I think Mellor regards this as self-evident, but some of his remarks also suggest an argument for it. The argument consists of the following chain of implications: e(aPb) occurs → ea is recollected in eb → ea affects eb → eaPeb.[13] Kant would have to find fault with at least one link in this chain, but I am not at all sure which it would be.[14]

Daniel Dennett has explicitly challenged Mellor's contention that e(aPb), the representation of a as preceding b, can be accomplished only by means of a representation of a preceding a representation of b.[15] For two reasons, however, I do not think Dennett's challenge to Mellor can be enlisted in defense of the radical Kantian line. In the first place, Dennett would regard the mere *judgment* that aPb as a case of representing aPb, whereas the representations of aPb we are concerned with here are *experiential*. In the second place, Dennett does not dispute that e(aPb) must be accomplished by means of representings of a and of b that occur in *some* temporal order—he only disputes that the order represented must be the *same* as the order of the representings. He leaves untouched the claim that representations of temporal order require temporally ordered representations.

Another interesting suggestion linking the experience symbolized by 'e(aPb)' with the fact stated by 'eaPeb' has been advanced by John Foster.[16] Foster undertakes to construct the order *of* experiences (mental time, as he calls it) out of the order displayed *in* experiences (phenomenal time, as he calls it). His analysis thus runs in the opposite direction from Mellor's, but it threatens to deliver equally un-Kantian results. The basic principle of his construction is roughly the following: if e is an experience whose content is abc (i.e., an experience of a preceding b and b preceding c) and f is an experience whose content is bcd, then e begins before f. If this principle is taken at face value, it implies that whenever there is an experience of succession, there is also a succession of experiences, and that, once more, would put the radical view beyond the pale.[17]

This much is clear: in opposition to Mellor and Foster, the radical Kant would have to deny that either e(aPb) or eaPeb is analyzable in such a manner as to make occurrences of the first entail the second. He would have to take e(aPb) as *sui generis*, or, if analyzable at all, analyzable in terms of some *non*temporal relation holding between ea and eb. In the latter case, we would have

e(aPb) occurs iff eaReb,

where R is wholly nontemporal.[18] Compare: the experience of a stone as being next to a twig plausibly involves there being an experience of a stone, an experience of a twig, and a relation between the experiences—but presumably not a relation of spatial adjacency.

Is this a possible position—that the experience of succession should be rooted in something wholly nontemporal? Here is a consideration that may soften us up for the possibility of it. A succession of experiences is by no means *sufficient* for the experience of succession, since each experience might be forgotten before the next one begins. Even if we add (as Mellor does) that one experience be recollected in the next, we do not thereby obtain the experience of succession, as shown by the example of the clock hand whose motion is inferred but not seen. To obtain the experience of succession, something more must still be added.[19] Is it possible that what must be added is no mere ingredient in the total phenomenon, but rather the phenomenon itself? If so, we would lose any basis for saying that the experience of succession is possible only through a succession of experiences. Though we may boggle at accepting the radical view, we have yet to uncover a knockdown argument against it.

C. The Break with Cartesian Epistemology

The objections to the radical ideality of time canvassed above are ontological— they proceed from consideration of what the experience e(aPb) would have to be grounded in, that is, what facts it would take to make it true that such experiences occur. I turn now to an epistemological objection, which was raised by Kant himself. Kant's attempted answer is of considerable interest, as it involves making a significant break with the Cartesian tradition.

Here is the key passage:

> But the reason why this objection [i.e., the Lambert objection to the ideality of time] is so unanimously urged, and that too by those who have nothing very convincing to say against the doctrine of the ideality of space, is this. They have no expectation of being able to prove apodeictically the absolute reality of space; for they are confronted by idealism, which teaches that the reality of outer objects does not allow of strict proof. On the other hand, the reality of the object of our inner sense (the reality of myself and my state) is, [they argue,] immediately evident through consciousness. The former may be merely an illusion; the latter is, on their view, undeniably something real. . . .

I pause here to note that Kant's parenthetical ("the reality of myself and my state") shows that he is thinking here of Mendelssohn and not just of Lambert. He continues:

> What they have failed, however, to recognise is that both are in the same position; in neither case can their reality as representations be questioned, and in both cases they belong only to appearance. . . . (A38–39/ B54–55)

As Kant here recognizes, Cartesian doctrine about knowledge of our inner states would doom the radical position. For Descartes, inner sense presents us with "things as they are in themselves" in two senses:

(i) in presenting us with our own mental states, inner sense presents us with *an sich* existing items, and

(ii) in presenting them as standing in temporal relations to one another, it presents them as they really (and not just apparently) are.

Thesis (ii) is a corollary of more general Cartesian doctrine about the infallibility of our awareness of our mental states.[20] Putting (i) and (ii) together, we get the result that any case of e(aPb) in which a and b are mental states is a case in which one *an sich* existing item genuinely precedes another.[21] But cases of the latter sort are just what the radical line excludes.

The upholder of the radical line must therefore deny either (i) or (ii). Presumably Kant is denying at least one of them when he says that the objects of inner sense "belong only to appearance."[22] But does he deny (i), (ii), or both?

One possibility would be to deny (ii) while retaining (i). On this alternative, we are aware of our own mental states and are thereby aware of items existing *an sich*, but we misperceive them as successive. This would be like McTaggart's view. There are hints of it in the startling footnote already cited and in the following remark as well:

> If without this condition of sensibility I could intuit myself, or be intuited by another being, the very same determinations which we now represent to ourselves as alterations would yield knowledge into which the representation of time, and therefore also of alteration, would in no way enter. (A37/B54)

There is a large textual obstacle, however, to taking the combination of (i) without (ii) as Kant's settled position. Thesis (i) implies that some objects of (inner) intuition are things in themselves, which contradicts his frequently repeated assertion that nothing we intuit is a thing in itself.

Another possibility would be to deny (i) while keeping (ii). On this alternative, the items we are aware of as successive really are successive, but they are not items existing *an sich*: they are only appearances, that is, items that exist only in being represented.[23] This raises two interesting difficulties—one that affects the denial of (i) all by itself and another that affects the denial of (i) in combination with the affirmation of (ii).[24] Let us begin with the trouble for the combination.

In the proposed combination, there are items a and b of which it is true that a precedes b, but the items in question are mere appearances or intentionalia, items that exist only in being apprehended.[25] Is there anything problematic about this for Kant? I think the answer depends on precisely what ontological status we assign to items that exist only in being apprehended. In chapter 1, section D, I distinguish two main alternatives: on the one hand, appearances may be regarded as supervenient entities; on the other, they may be regarded as virtual objects or logical fictions. If appearances are supervenient entities, they do genuinely exist and can be quantified over, but they are dependent entities, existing only if appropriate cognitive acts by perceivers take place. If appearances are logical fictions, they exist only in a manner of speaking; we may say, if we like, that they exist, but this means no more than that the cognitive acts just referred to are taking place and are suitably related to other cognitive acts. I now argue that the radical line can be sustained only if we construe appearances in the latter of these two ways.

If one appearance precedes or gives way to another, it goes out of existence as the second comes into existence; that is to say, both of them change in Kant's technical sense. Now, it is usually taken as analytic of the notion of supervenience that if As supervene on Bs, there cannot be change or alteration in any As without change or alteration in the underlying Bs. It follows that if appearances are supervenient entities (supervening on perceivers and their states), there cannot be a change in any appearance without a change or alteration in some perceiver. That, of course, would concede the day to Lambert and Mendelssohn. So, the combination of (ii) without (i)—admitting that the relation of succession is exemplified, but insisting that its relata are only appearances—does not preserve the radical line if appearances are supervenient entities.

If appearances are logical fictions, however, it may be possible for Kant to sustain the radical line. 'An appearance of the moon came into being' could have for its truthmaker some fact about perceivers not involving change or alteration—for example, that a certain perceiver had an experience as of the moon rising over the horizon. That such facts do not indeed involve any alteration was the possibility left moot in the preceding section. One may open up further to that possibility by reflecting that growth or change in a fictional character must have some basis in what the author has written, but not necessarily in any *alteration* in the text. Virtual objects can change or alter in the temporal dimension in virtue of the founding objects' varying in some other dimension.

The upshot so far is that Kant could adhere to the radical line while admitting that there is change of and succession among appearances, provided the appearances are treated as logical fictions. Change in a fiction, unlike change in a supervenient entity, is not change in any existing object; nor does it presuppose change or alteration in any existing object. (At the same time, however, it must be conceded that the change and succession thus accommodated are fairly nominal.)

I turn now to the difficulty that affects the denial of (i) all by itself. To deny (i) is to deny that inner sense presents us with any items that exist in themselves; instead, it presents us with appearances only. Inner sense is usually defined as the sense that has for its objects inner states, or states of the self, and these presumably include all states of apprehension or cognition. In denying (i), therefore, Kant would be saying this: states of apprehending are not items that exist in themselves, which means in turn that they are items that exist only in being apprehended. Thus is generated an infinite regress: each mental state exists only in virtue of being apprehended by another mental state, which in turn owes its existence to being apprehended by a further mental state, and so on forever, without anything to anchor the series. This is a truly disastrous outcome.[26]

It may seem now that Kant is caught in an inescapable dilemma. If he affirms Cartesian thesis (i), he goes against his repeated insistence that we have no intuition of things in themselves. If he denies it, he generates an absurd infinite regress of higher order states of apprehension. Is there any way out?

Perhaps there is. Here is how Cartesian thesis (i) was formulated above: in presenting us with our own mental states, inner sense presents us with *an sich* existing items. We may represent this as the conjunction of two separate bits of information:

(ia) inner sense presents us with our own mental states, and
(ib) our own mental states are *an sich* existing items.

The disastrous regress I have pointed out arises if Kant denies (ib). But perhaps he could deny (i) by denying (ia) and letting (ib) stand. In that case, he would slip between the horns of the dilemma presented above.

Denying (ia) (that inner sense has our own states for its objects) would fit in with the parallelism Kant sometimes claims for inner and outer sense. External items in themselves affect us so as to produce intuitions or cognitions whose objects are not those very items, but appearances. The appearances are mind-dependent and spatial; the affecting external items not. Similarly, our own cognitive states, which are internal items in themselves, affect us so as to produce further cognitive states, whose objects are appearances "of" the original states rather than those states themselves. The appearances are mind-dependent and temporal; the internal affecting items are not. The appearances will have to be construed as logical fictions, in the manner noted above; such is the price for holding fast to the radical line.

D. What Did Kant Really Believe about Time?

Did Kant really adhere to the radical line? This is a question on which I find it difficult to reach a final verdict. Some aspects of Kant's philosophy require us to answer it yes, but other equally important facets require us to answer it no.

In favor of yes, there is first of all section 7 itself, which has been the focus here. As I have shown, much of what Kant offers in response to the Lambert-Mendelssohn objection—for example, the footnote at A37/B54 and the repudiation of Cartesian epistemology—would be unmotivated unless he were trying to make room for the radical view.[27] Second, there is the requirement that transcendental idealism about time be parallel to transcendental idealism about space. The ideality of space does not allow that there is a special class of items that are spatial in themselves after all. Finally, there is G.E. Moore's point that the First Antinomy, if sound, would show that no items whatsoever (not even representings) can be situated in time.[28] If representings were in time, there would have to be either a temporally first representing or a beginningless series of them, and either alternative is subject to the difficulties Kant raises in the Antinomy.

In favor of no, one can point to many important sections of the *Critique of Pure Reason* where Kant explicitly affirms that our representations (i.e., representings) succeed one another in time. The argument of the Second Analogy is based on the observation that our representations are always successive, though their objects may or may not be. The Refutation of Idealism seeks to elicit the necessary conditions our determining the temporal order of our own mental states. The solution to the Mathematical Antinomies depends on the fact that our representations are successive, for it is only in successions extending into the future that Kant finds room for the idea of the potential infinite.[29] We could try to reconstrue all of this in terms of the mere appearance of succession, but I think the results of doing so would nearly defy comprehension.

6

The Ideality of Matter

Each of these three sects [partisans of points,
advocates of atoms, and believers in infinite
complexity], when they only attack, tri-
umphs, ruins, and destroys; but in its turn,
it is destroyed and sunk when it is on the de-
fensive.

Pierre Bayle, "Zeno of Elea,"
Historical and Critical Dictionary

The First and Second Antinomies, together known as the Mathematical
Antinomies, are advanced by Kant as a *reductio ad absurdum* of transcendental realism and thereby a proof of his own transcendental idealism. The
First Antinomy is concerned with the extent of the world in space and time;
the Second, with the composition of matter. In this chapter I focus on the
Second Antinomy, though much of what I say applies to the First Antinomy
as well. In chapter 13 I say something explicitly about the First Antinomy and
the structure of the Antinomies generally.

What is the mereological structure of matter, or of extended substances? Does
each bit of matter contain parts within parts ad infinitum, or do we eventually
reach simple parts, that is to say, parts that have no parts themselves? In the latter case, are the simple parts extended or extensionless? Depending on how we
answer these questions, we arrive at one of the following three views, which
seem to exhaust the possibilities: either (1) matter is infinitely complex, every
part containing further parts, or (2a) it is composed of extended simple parts,
or (2b) it is composed of unextended simple parts. Which view is correct?

Pierre Bayle observed that anyone who embraces any of these three alternatives does so not because of its own attractiveness but because of the re-
pugnance of the other two. In this circumstance alone there is nothing unto-
ward; arguments from elimination can be entirely cogent. (As Holmes was
fond of pointing out to Dr. Watson, when you have eliminated the impossible,
whatever remains, however improbable, must be the truth.) The trouble in the
present connection is that according to a long line of philosophers (including
Zeno, Bayle, and Leibniz in addition to Kant), *all three* views may be eliminated as impossible. If this is indeed the case, what is to be done?

The moral drawn by all the philosophers I have mentioned is that matter is ideal—that it belongs only to appearance, not to reality.[1] Thus Kant, having refuted to his satisfaction both the alternative of simple parts (the Thesis of the Second Antinomy) and that of infinite complexity (the Antithesis), bills the result as indirect proof of transcendental idealism: "[all things in space] are nothing but appearances . . . which, in the manner in which they are represented, as extended beings, . . . have no independent existence outside our thoughts" (A490/B518). In the following two sections I expound and evaluate Kant's arguments against the classical alternatives, treating together as Kant does the two of Bayle's three "sects" that believe in simples. In the final section of this chapter I discuss Kant's solution to the Antinomy and the role played in it by transcendental idealism.

A. Against Infinite Complexity

The Thesis of the Second Antinomy is that every composite substance is made up of simple parts.[2] Kant's argument for this is really an argument against the idea that a substance could be infinitely complex. It may be set out in five steps as follows (compare A434−36/B462−64).

(1) No substance can be annihilated by totally decomposing it.

By 'totally decomposing' a substance I mean bringing it about that no two parts of it that formerly composed a larger whole any longer do so, and by 'annihilating' a substance I mean destroying it so completely that no part of it whatsoever remains.

(2) Every infinitely complex substance is such that if it were totally decomposed, it *would* be annihilated.

This premise can be seen to be true on logical grounds alone. If an infinitely complex substance were totally decomposed, no simple part would remain, since *ex hypothesi* there are none; nor would any composite part remain, since the decomposition is supposed to be *total*. Thus, no part whatsoever would remain.

(3) Therefore, either no substance is infinitely complex, or no infinitely complex substance can be totally decomposed.

This follows from (1) and (2).

(4) Every composite substance (hence, every infinitely complex substance) can be totally decomposed.

In support of this premise Kant appeals to the following principle: "[C]omposition, as applied to substances, is only an accidental relation" (A435/B463). I take this to mean that any substances that are so related as to compose a larger whole could exist without composing that whole.

(5) Therefore, no substance is infinitely complex.

This is what was to be demonstrated, and it follows from (3) and (4).

I turn now to evaluation of the argument. It contains three premises, of which I said (2) was true on logical grounds alone; that leaves (1) and (4) to consider.

Premise (4) says that any composite substance can be totally decomposed, in support of which Kant asserts that composition is an accidental relation. Suppose we interpret this to mean that given any parts p_1 through p_n that compose a certain whole, it would be possible for p_1 through p_n all to exist without composing that whole. In this case, (4) clearly does not follow, for the supporting principle implies only that a whole can be broken up into any *finite* number of parts that formerly composed it, and this does not imply that it can be *totally* decomposed—unless one already assumes, question-beggingly, that the number of parts must be finite. Suppose, then, that we give the supporting principle this stronger formulation: given any set of parts, finite or infinite in number, that compose a given whole, it would be possible for the members of the set all to exist without composing that whole. Now I maintain that even in this case, (4) does not follow. Perhaps the easiest way to see this is to note the invalidity of the contrapositive inference: from the supposition that there are substances that cannot be totally decomposed, it does not follow that there are things that stand in the composition relation essentially. If anyone thinks otherwise, I suspect it is due to the mistaken belief that if a substance cannot be totally decomposed, this can only be because there is some composite part of it that cannot even be partially decomposed.

The question remains of whether (4) is true despite its not following from the reason Kant gives for it. I contend that we cannot decide this question unless we have already reached a decision about infinite complexity, in which case there is a kind of circularity in Kant's argument. To see this, let us ask what verdict we would pass on (4) if we had not already rejected the possibility of infinite complexity. In that case (supposing we have no reason to believe that composite substances as such must be totally decomposable) we would have to ask separately whether a substance can be totally decomposed if it is infinitely complex. Assume for the moment that decomposition takes place in a series of steps, rather than all at one stroke. In that case the total decomposition of an infinitely complex substance will be an infinite task—a task involving the completion of an infinite series of steps that began at some time. It may be doubted for this reason alone whether total decomposition is possible. Suppose, however, that we have no qualms about infinite tasks.[3] In that case we will not have grounds for doubt about (4), but we *will* have grounds for doubt about (1). Premise (1) says that no substance can be annihilated by total decomposition, but if some substances are infinitely complex and infinite tasks are possible, this will be false. The upshot is that depending on what we have decided about infinite tasks, either (1) or (4) will be such that we cannot decide about it unless we have already decided about infinite complexity.

Suppose we seek to avoid this dilemma by saying that total decomposition takes place at a single stroke. There is to begin with the difficulty that it is no longer clear that we are talking about *decomposition*, for how is the total decomposition of an infinitely complex substance at a single stroke to be distinguished from its annihilation outright? But waiving this problem, a similar dilemma still arises: the total decomposition of an infinitely complex substance is either possible or not; if it is not possible, then (4) is false if there are infinitely complex substances; and if it is possible, then (1) is false if there are infinitely complex substances.

I hope it is clear that my objection to Kant's argument is not merely that its premises do jointly entail its conclusion. That is true of any valid argument, and validity is no vice. My complaint is rather that at least one of the premises will be such that one could not reasonably assert it unless one already knew that the conclusion was true. That is no mere upshot of validity, and it *is* a vice.

B. Against Ultimate Simples

I turn now to the Antithesis, which claims that no composite substance is made up of simple parts. Kant's argument for this (see A434–37/B462–65) may be set out in three steps as follows.

(1) Every part of a composite substance occupies a space.

By 'occupying' a space Kant means *filling* it, as opposed to merely falling within it.[4] This premise therefore rules out the possibility that composite substances are composed of unextended simple parts, or what Bayle called mathematical points. His reason for ruling it out is not that there could not be such entities as points,[5] but rather that such entities could never "fill space through their mere aggregation" (A440/B468). The basic intuition here was forcibly expressed by Bayle: "[P]ersons of the slightest depth can comprehend with complete certainty, if they give the matter a little attention, that several nonentities of extension joined together will never make up an extension."[6]

(2) Whatever occupies a space is composite.

This premise rules out the possibility of extended simple parts, or what Bayle called physical points or atoms. In support of it Kant appeals to two auxiliary premises: (a) whatever occupies a space has as many parts as the space it occupies, and (b) every space has parts. The basic intuition was again put nicely by Bayle: "[E]very extension, no matter how small it may be, has a right and a left side."[7]

(3) Therefore, every part of a composite substance is itself composite.

This follows from (1) and (2) and implies the Antithesis position that no composite substance is made up of simple parts.

Let us now pass judgment on the premises, beginning with the case against extended simples. It comes down to this: anything extended, no matter how small, must have a left and a right half. This intuition can be reinforced by the following argument: (i) anything extended, no matter how small, could be made to be red on one side and green on the other; (ii) a thing can be both red and green only if one part is red and another part is green; and (iii) by giving a thing two colors you do not make it have parts that it lacked before. It follows that anything extended has parts.

But a proponent of extended simples might not find subpremise (ii) compelling. He might maintain that a thing can have a plurality of colors without having a plurality of parts: it can be *partly red* and *partly green*, where these properties are not to be analyzed in terms of having a part that is wholly red and another part that is wholly green. Perhaps in this way one could avoid having to quantify over undetached parts of things.[8]

Now for the case against unextended simples. It rests on the intuition that out of extensionless elements an extended aggregate will never arise. But this, too, can be challenged. There are two possibilities to be considered, depending on whether one takes the number of elements to be finite or infinite.

The idea that an extended whole could be composed of finitely many unextended elements is generally thought plausible only in conjunction with the hypothesis, advanced by Boscovich as early as 1745 and by Kant himself in 1756,[9] that each of the elements is a center of repulsive force. According to this conception, none of the elements fills any space, but each of them exerts a force that prevents anything else from entering its sphere of influence.

Points endowed with force may constitute an impenetrable field, but I do not see how a finite number of them can constitute an extended object. A region populated by a scattered colony of Boscovichian points is a region of which no subregion, however small, is filled, and if no subregion of a given region is filled, it is surely incorrect to say that the region contains anything that is *extended*. What Boscovichian points give us is the *appearance* of extension, not extension itself.[10]

I turn, then, to the second possibility—that an extended whole is composed of infinitely many unextended elements. In this connection, Adolf Grünbaum has shown that according to the modern theory of dimension, the union of a nondenumerable infinity of unit sets containing one point each (and thus having dimension zero) can itself have dimension greater than zero.[11] But the relevance of these set-theoretic considerations may be doubted. To derive from them the result that an extended whole or material thing can be composed entirely of unextended points, we would evidently have to assume that material things are identical with sets of points. But things are not *sets* of anything— things are concrete; sets are abstract. Moreover, even if a thing were a set of some kind, why should it be the set of its points, rather than the set containing its top half and its bottom half, or any of the indefinitely many other sets whose members add up to the whole?[12]

It is not necessary to identify things with sets, however, to show that an extended whole may be composed entirely of unextended points. Suppose S is a set of points. Then the members of S will compose an extended whole—will fill a volume V—provided that (i) every subregion of V, no matter how small, contains at least one member of S, and (ii) every member of S falls within some subregion of V.[13] These conditions can be fulfilled if S contains a *nondenumerable* infinity of points—a conception that became available only in the century after Kant.

The intuition of Kant and Bayle was therefore mistaken: extensionless elements *can* compose an extended whole, provided you have enough of them and they are suitably deployed. If there is to be any doubt about this alternative, I think it should concern the availability of the materials, since I find it hard to believe that points could exist otherwise than as logical constructions out of larger three-dimensional objects. But I shall not pursue this issue here.

C. Kant's Way Out

Let us put aside the criticisms I have just canvassed and assume that Kant's arguments against Thesis and Antithesis are sound. In that case, we have ruled out both simple parts and infinite complexity; yet on the face of it, these seem to be the only alternatives. How can this be? In this section I examine Kant's solution to this conundrum.

He begins by pointing out that two opposed propositions need not exhaust the alternatives if both of them "presuppose an inadmissible condition." In such a case they will be contraries, not contradictories, and both of them "will fall to the ground, inasmuch as the condition, under which alone either of them can be maintained, itself falls" (A503/B531). He gives as an example the propositions 'this has a smell that is good' and 'this has a smell that is not good', both of which presuppose the condition that the thing in question has a smell.

Kant's solution, then, involves the claim that the antinomial alternatives are really contraries, not contradictories, so we need not choose between them after all. But if this is so, what is the "inadmissible condition" that they both presuppose?

One possible answer is suggested by the logical forms of Thesis and Antithesis. In Kant's formulation, one is an A-proposition (*every* composite substance is made up of simple parts) and the other an E-proposition (*no* composite substance is made up of simple parts). Both would be false if some composite substances were made up of simple parts and others were not. In this case the "presupposed inadmissible condition" would be that all matter is the same in structure.

But this solution cannot be taken seriously. No one would maintain that some hunks of matter are composed of simples while others are infinitely complex. Moreover, Kant's arguments (if sound) show that it is impossible for *any* hunk of matter to be composed of simples and also impossible for *any* hunk of matter to be infinitely complex.

A second possible answer comes to mind when we recall that the logic of Kant's day treated universal propositions as having existential import. Thus, Kant would regard both Thesis and Antithesis as presupposing the condition that matter exists. If this condition is regarded as inadmissible, no choice between simple parts and infinite complexity need be made. This would give us a neat way to avoid the antinomial alternatives—but it would also make most of the details of the solution Kant proposes otiose.

This brings us to what Kant himself identifies as the presupposed inadmissible condition. It is not that matter exists, but rather that matter exists *as a thing in itself* or, as Kant also puts it, is transcendentally real (see A504/B532). What this means is that matter exists independent of human perceivers. Kant's transcendental idealism maintains to the contrary that matter exists only in being perceived.

Let us grant, then, that matter exists, if only in the sense allowed by transcendental idealism. Now, regarding any bit of matter M, there seem to be just two alternatives:

(1) every part of M has further parts, or

(2) some part of M has no further parts.

Alternative (1) is what the Antithesis would say about M; (2) is what the Thesis would say about M; and if we are not denying the existence of M altogether, it would appear that we must choose between them. How does Kant think the choice can be avoided?

Before I try to answer this question, I must note that Kant generally presents the alternatives in different terms. He thinks of the Thesis of the Antinomy as the "finite" alternative and of the Antithesis as the "infinite" alternative. There is some justification for this. Let us say that a series is a *part series beginning with* M if and only if (i) its first member is M, (ii) each subsequent member is a part of its predecessor, and (iii) its last member, if any, has no parts. Then, (1) and (2) above are respectively equivalent to

(1') every part series beginning with M is nonterminating, and

(2') some part series beginning with M is terminating.

Since a part series must be finite if terminating and infinite if nonterminating, there is, as I have said, some justification for Kant's way of construing the alternatives.[14]

Our problem now is that (1') and (2') appear to be just as exhaustive as (1) and (2); how does Kant think we can avoid having to choose between them? It is here that transcendental idealism comes into play. Kant would have us shift our attention from the various part series beginning with an object M to the series of perceptions we would have as we successively perceived smaller and smaller parts of M. Following Strawson, I call a series of the first sort an *explored* series and a series of the second sort an *exploring* series.[15] Now, one way of understanding transcendental idealism is this: the explored series and the exploring series are not merely correlated, but *identical*. This would make Kant's idealism a form of ontological phenomenalism. The members of the explored series come into being only as we encounter them in the exploring series; they exist, as Kant likes to put it, "only in the empirical regress" (A505/ B533). Thus, a given explored series will be finite or infinite according to whether the identical exploring series is finite or infinite, and Kant thinks that an exploring series will be neither.

But how can this be? An exploring series is a series of perceptions, and a series of perceptions must surely either come to an end or not. How does Kant think that by identifying parts with our perceptions of them he can avoid the disjunction: finite or infinite?

One answer has been suggested by Strawson, who attributes to Kant a form of verificationism.[16] According to the form in question, if it would be impossible to discover empirically that a thing has a given characteristic, then it is senseless to suppose that it does have that characteristic. To apply this doctrine to Kant's problem, we must maintain that whether a given perception series comes to an end or not cannot be discovered empirically. We cannot know that every member will have a successor, nor can we know of any member that it will *not* have a successor. So, a perception series cannot sensibly be said to be either finite or infinite.

It should be noted that this strategy involves giving up the principle of bivalence. It admits that the alternatives "finite" and "infinite" are logically contradictory, but denies that at least one member of a pair of contradictories must be true.

Whatever the merits of this solution, I think it is clear for three reasons that it is not Kant's. The first reason is that verificationism makes transcendental idealism, which Kant calls "the key" (A490/B518) to the solution of the Antinomies, superfluous. For if we are going to be verificationists about the exploring series, we might just as well be verificationists about the explored series, considered now as a distinct series existing in its own right. We could say that although matter exists independent of our perceptions, no part series is either finite or infinite, because we could never know which.[17]

The second reason for doubting that Kant is a verificationist emerges from his attitude toward traditional metaphysics. He thinks that the various topics he discusses in the Transcendental Dialectic—for example, God, freedom, and immortality—are topics on which no knowledge is possible on either side. But he does not think that regarding these topics there is no *sense* on either side. His avowed purpose is to "deny *knowledge* in order to make room for *faith*" (Bxxx), and there is hardly room for faith in what is demonstrably lacking in sense.

The third reason for doubting that Kant is a verificationist is that he nowhere says the antinomial alternatives are devoid of sense. Instead, he says they are contraries, and that both of them are *false* (A504/B532; A528/B556). This contention receives no support from Strawson-style verificationism and is, in fact, positively incompatible with it.[18]

Kant's reasons for thinking that a series of perceptions can be neither finite nor infinite must be sought elsewhere. We find the clearest clue to his thought in the section entitled "Critical Solution of the Cosmological Conflict of Reason with Itself" (A497–502/B525–30). Here Kant tells us that the Antinomy arises because both warring parties accept an argument of the following general pattern:

Major Premise: If something conditioned is given (exists), then the entire series of its conditions is given (exists)—that is, its own conditions exist, as well as any conditions of those conditions, and so on.

Minor Premise: Something conditioned exists.

Conclusion: The entire series of its conditions exists.

Any whole is "conditioned," its conditions being its parts. Thus, in application to the Second Antinomy the conclusion would tell us that all the members of any part series beginning with a given whole exist, and it would be left to the two warring parties to argue whether their number is finite or infinite.

Kant's reaction to this argument is as follows. If matter existed as thing in itself, the major premise would be true, and we would indeed have to take sides with one of the two warring parties. But if matter exists merely as appearance, having no being apart from our perceptions, then the major premise is false. We cannot say that all the members of a given part series exist, for they come into being only as we perceive them—that is to say, successively, rather than all at once.

The crux of Kant's solution to the Antinomy is thus the contention that the series whose magnitude is in dispute is a *successive* series, and the role of transcendental idealism is to underwrite this claim.[19] This is made clear in the following passage:

> The synthesis of the conditioned with its conditions (and the whole series of the latter) does not [in the case of things in themselves] carry with it any limitation through time or any concept of succession. The empirical synthesis, on the other hand, that is, the series of the conditions in appearance, . . . is necessarily successive, the members of the series being given only as following upon one another in time; and I have therefore, in this case, no right to assume the absolute *totality* of the synthesis and of the series thereby represented. (A500/B528)

We find confirmation of this strategy in the *Metaphysical Foundations of Natural Science*, where Kant says that the inference from the infinite divisibility of matter to an actual infinity of parts would be valid if matter existed as a thing in itself, but not if matter is "actual only by its being given in representation."[20]

The question remains, however, why Kant should have thought that a successive series extending into the future, unlike a series whose members coexist, must be neither finite nor infinite. Some of his remarks suggest the following answer (compare A517–20/B545–48). We cannot say that an exploring series is infinite, for no matter how long we have been embarked on it, it will not be true that infinitely many perceptions have occurred. Nor can we say that an exploring series is finite, for in that case it would terminate in a "limiting" member, but no such member is possible.

Neither of these considerations warrants the conclusion Kant wishes to draw from it. Consider first his reason for denying the infinitude of a series. I grant for the sake of argument that if someone starts having perceptions now and never stops, it will never be true that he has had infinitely many perceptions.[21] Still, it does not follow that the series of his perceptions is not infinite, for if he starts now and never stops, he *will have* infinitely many perceptions. It is true that he will never *have had* infinitely many perceptions, but this is irrelevant.[22] The series of his perceptions is infinite for the same reason that the series of integers is infinite: none is the last.[23]

Consider now the reason for denying finitude. By a "limiting" member of a perception series Kant evidently means a member beyond which it is not possible to go; perhaps he has in mind something like a *minimum visible*. I grant for the sake of argument that there can be no such member. Still, to grant this is only to grant that there can be no member that *must* be the last, and from this it does not follow that there can be no member that is *in fact* the last. If some member is in fact the last (e.g., because the perceiver eventually turns his attention elsewhere), the series will be finite.

The solution to the Antinomy I have been criticizing seems to me to be the one Kant probably had in mind, but there is one more solution I wish to consider. The solution just discussed identifies the explored series with the exploring series and seeks to show that the latter can be neither finite nor infinite. The solution now to be proposed concedes the finitude of the exploring series but denies that the finitude of the explored series follows. This will obviously require an interpretation of transcendental idealism other than the one I have been operating with so far in this chapter. That interpretation treats transcendental idealism as a version of *ontological* phenomenalism, according to which material things are identical with certain of our perceptions. But there are occasional hints in Kant that transcendental idealism should rather be construed as a version of *analytical* phenomenalism, according to which truths purportedly about material things are necessarily equivalent to truths solely about our perceptions.[24] Consider, for example, the following passage:

> That there may be inhabitants in the moon, although no one has ever perceived them, must certainly be admitted. This, however, only means that in the possible advance of experience we may encounter them. (A493/B521)

This does not identify the lunar creatures with any perceptions, but suggests that facts about them are to be analyzed in terms of what perceptions "may" occur.

The advantage of this interpretation of transcendental idealism is that it enables us to deny that the finitude of the explored series follows from that of the exploring series. If a given exploring series comes to an end, we may still say that there are yet more parts in the object of our exploration, provided that the exploring series *could* be prolonged—that is, provided that there are possible circumstances under which it *would* contain further members. One may even wish to say that an explored series is finite only if there is some stage in any associated exploring series beyond which it is not possible to go—in other words, only if there is a limiting member in the sense discussed above.

But what ground does this strategy provide for denying the *in*finitude of the explored series? I conjecture that Kant may have made the following mistake: having construed finitude in the explored series as

(i) for some m, it is not possible to go beyond m

(where the variables range over members of the exploring series), he construed infinitude as the negation of (i), that is,

(ii) for every m, it is possible to go beyond m,

but then confused the latter with

(iii) it is possible, for every m, to go (have gone?) beyond m,

which, as I have shown, he would have rejected as involving the possibility of a completed infinity.

There is one more point to be made in connection with the analytical phenomenalist interpretation of transcendental idealism. According to this interpretation, matter is a logical construction out of perceivers and their perceptions. Now, if As are logical constructions out of Bs, there is no guarantee that every sentence purportedly about As will have a sufficient truth condition statable in sentences about Bs;[25] the concept of an A may not be fully determinate. Perhaps for this reason Thesis and Antithesis might both fail to have a truth value. But I doubt that Kant had anything quite like this in mind, for as I have already remarked, he says that Thesis and Antithesis are both *false*.

In summary, Kant's idealism does not really provide him with a legitimate way of avoiding the Baylean alternatives, but it is possible to see why he thought it did.

7

Experience and Objects

The proof proceeds by showing that experience itself, and therefore the object of experience, would be impossible without a connection of this kind [in accordance with the
categories].

Kant, *Critique of Pure Reason*
(A783/B811)

A. Preliminaries

The heart of the *Critique of Pure Reason* is the Transcendental Deduction of
the Categories, Kant's attempt to show that the concepts of substance and causation and the other *a priori* concepts on his list of twelve are exemplified in
the world we experience, or, as he puts it, are "objectively valid." In the
course of the Deduction he also argues for another conclusion that has been
of much interest to contemporary philosophers, namely, that the validity of
the categories enables our representations to be parlayed into knowledge of
objects distinct from ourselves. This additional thesis has led many to hope
that the Transcendental Deduction may furnish us with (or at least make an
important contribution toward) a refutation of skepticism about the external
world.[1]

Kant's argumentative strategy is a paradigm instance of what is nowadays
often called "transcendental proof": he argues that if the categories were *not*
objectively valid, experience would be impossible. Such arguments from the
possibility of experience immediately prompt the question: *in what sense of
'experience'?* That term, one of the most multivocal in philosophy, is by no
means exempt from ambiguity in the *Critique of Pure Reason*. In the first paragraph of the introduction to the work, Kant uses 'experience' in two different
senses without calling the reader's attention to the fact. The experience with
which all our knowledge is said to begin is "the raw material of the sensible
impressions"; experience in this sense is then said to be worked up by the understanding into "that knowledge of objects which is entitled experience"
(B1). The same ambiguity runs throughout the work.

C.I. Lewis distinguishes two senses of 'experience' that seem to correspond
to those of Kant's opening paragraph. According to Lewis:

The datum of our philosophic study is not the "buzzing, blooming confusion" on which the infant first opens his eyes, not the thin experience
of immediate sensation, but the thick experience of everyday life.[2]

Again:

It is indeed the thick experience of the world of things, not the thin given
of immediacy, which constitutes the datum for philosophic reflection.
We do not see patches of color, but trees and houses; we hear, not indescribable sound, but voices and violins.[3]

It turns out that on Lewis's view just as on Kant's, thick experience is the product of subjecting thin experience to conceptual interpretation so as to yield
knowledge of objects.

In Lewis's terms, our question of one paragraph back may be put thus: for
which variety of experience is the validity of the categories a necessary condition, thick or thin? Insofar as we look to Kant for a satisfactory reply to
Hume's skepticism about the external world, we may hope that the answer is
"thin." Hume will hardly be refuted if the categories are only shown necessary
for a kind of experience whose existence he doubted, namely, knowledge of
objects. But Hume did not doubt that he was spectator to a play of impressions
(or at any rate, that there *was* a play of impressions), so if the categories can be
shown necessary even for this, he will be refuted indeed.

Our question should really be split into two. First, for what kind of experience did Kant aim to show that the validity of the categories is a necessary condition? Second, did he succeed? In this chapter I am concerned with both questions. I also examine an attempt by Strawson to construct a transcendental
proof that improves on Kant's own.

B. An Anatomy of Experience

Our first task must be to refine our original classification of experience into
thick and thin. 'Experience' may be used to designate episodes of any of the
following sorts, which I have listed more or less in order of increasing complexity:

(e1) having *sensations*
(e2) having sensations and *being conscious* of them
(e3) having *intuitions*
(e4) having intuitions and *conceptualizing* them (bringing them under
      concepts)
(e5) having intuitions and conceptualizing them by means of *physical-
      object* concepts
(e6) having intuitions and conceptualizing them as *mine*
(e7) having intuitions and *making judgments* about them
(e8) having intuitions and *knowing* propositions about them

The "thinnest" sense of 'experience' on our list is (e1), the mere having of
sensations. With (e2) we add that the sensations be attended with consciousness. This is a genuine further step for Kant, for he holds, with Leibniz, that

there can be representations of which the subject is not aware. This is clear both from his scattered remarks about the sensory states of animals[4] and from his classificatory scheme at A320/B376, which makes "representation with consciousness" subordinate to the genus "representation."[5]

Having intuitions, (e3), goes beyond having sensations in two ways. First, a sensation "relates solely to the subject as the modification of its state" (A320/ B376), whereas an intuition purports to be *of* something distinct from itself— it has an intentional object. Second, sensations are punctiform, or lacking in extensive magnitude, whereas intuitions are subject to our forms of intuition, space and time.[6]

The grades of experience from (e2) on are all grades of conscious experience. With (e2), this is because it is stipulated that the sensations be states *of* which we are conscious. With (e3), it is because an intuition is a state *by* which we are conscious of something else—its intentional object. Perhaps in addition (e3) experience will involve consciousness of the intuition itself or whatever sensations are ingredients in it.

With (e4) we add the requirement that our intuitions be brought under concepts. (I do not necessarily mean by this that the intuition itself, as opposed to its object, is taken to instantiate whatever concept is brought to bear.) Many philosophers would say that this is not an *additional* requirement at all, because in their view the use of concepts is necessarily involved in any consciousness whatever.[7] Indeed, many would cite Kant himself as the authority for this view, quoting his dictum "intuitions without concepts are blind" (A51/ B75).[8] I will say more about the meaning of the dictum below. For now I simply note that if all consciousness is conceptual consciousness, a transcendental deduction that showed Kant's categories to be necessary for conceptual consciousness would also show them to be necessary for consciousness *überhaupt*.

One form that conceptual experience might take is (e5). I say *might* take, but others have said *must* take. One such is Lewis, who holds in *Mind and the World Order* that the "given" can only be interpreted by means of concepts pertaining to physical objects. Another is Quine, who holds that it is a mistake to seek a "sub-basement of conceptualization" deeper than the level of physical things.[9] I refer to experience that involves the exercise of physical-object concepts as *objectual experience*, saving the term 'objective' for experience that is both objectual and veridical. Then we can put the Lewis-Quine view thus: all conceptual experience is objectual experience. Other philosophers (e.g., Strawson) hold the weaker view that although not all conceptual experience need be objectual, none can be conceptual unless *some* is objectual. In other words, conceptual experience in general presupposes objectual experience in general. I discuss Strawson's views in more detail in the final section of this chapter.

Another form that conceptual experience might take, and in the opinion of some, must take, is (e6). To conceptualize an intuition as one's own is to conceptualize it as belonging to a certain self and is therefore to be self-conscious in the central meaning of the phrase.[10] Some philosophers maintain that every episode of conceptual consciousness must be accompanied by (or included within) an episode of self-consciousness; some hold the weaker view that conceptual consciousness can occur only in a being who is at least sometimes self-conscious; and some hold that the ability to have objectual experience and the ability to have self-conscious experience are mutually entailing.[11] Below I return to this topic, too, in connection with Strawson's views.

With (e7) we make explicit the requirement that our intuitions be judged. According to Kant, this requirement has been with us implicitly ever since (e4). As Kant puts it, "The only use which the understanding can make of these concepts is to judge by means of them" (A68/B93). If this is right, (e7) is already implied by (e4).[12] One could, of course, make further subdivisions under (e7) according to the types of concepts employed in the judgment: physical-object concepts, concepts of the self, and so on.

Our last entry, (e8), is simply (e7) plus truth, justification, and whatever else is required for knowledge.

When Kant says that the objective validity of the categories is a necessary condition of experience, which of (e1) through (e8) is he talking about? On this question commentators run the gamut. Near one extreme, Norman Kemp Smith and R.P. Wolff maintain that the validity of the categories is necessary even for (e2), the bare consciousness of representations.[13] At the other extreme, C.I. Lewis, D.P. Dryer, and Paul Guyer maintain that the validity of the categories is necessary only for (e8), propositional knowledge.[14] In between, Rolf George holds that the categories are necessary for (e3), having intuitions, since it is only through the offices of the categories that representations acquire intentionality or aboutness;[15] P.F. Strawson holds that the categories are necessary for (e4), conceptual experience;[16] H.J. Paton and S. Körner hold that they are necessary for (e5), objectual experience;[17] and Jonathan Bennett holds that they are necessary for (e6), self-conscious experience.[18] Insofar as some of the types of experience on our list imply or involve others, it is to be expected that some of our commentators hold more than one of the theses just identified.

In the preceding section I said that if the categories are shown necessary only for thick experience, we obtain no leverage against a skeptic. But now that I have distinguished several grades of thick experience, we can see that this claim is true only regarding the thickest of them, (e8). The experiences of the other types are all wholly internal states, episodes within a subject's own mind whose occurrence not even a skeptic should doubt. If the validity of the categories could be shown to be necessary for experience in any of these senses— and if such validity were in turn sufficient to convert our experience into "knowledge of objects"—philosophy's long-sought refutation of skepticism would be in hand.

C. The Objective Deduction

Kant tells us in the preface to the *Critique of Pure Reason* that the Transcendental Deduction has two sides, one objective and the other subjective. The first side is concerned with the objective validity of the categories and with how much we can know apart from experience; the other side is concerned with the question "how is the faculty of thought itself possible?" (Axvi–xvii). We might say that the first line of inquiry belongs to epistemology and the second to cognitive science. Kant tells us that only the first is essential to his purposes, but I shall provide reason to question his assessment before I am done. In this section I show how much is accomplished by the so-called "Objective Deduction."

The heart of the Objective Deduction occurs at A92–93, section 14 of the *Critique*, in a passage that Kant said should "suffice by itself" as a deduction of the categories (Axvi–xvii). The argument consists of two premises and a conclusion. The first premise is stated twice:

> There are two conditions under which alone the knowledge of an object is possible: first, *intuition*, through which it is given . . . ; secondly, *concept*, through which an object is thought corresponding to this intuition. (A92–93/B125)

> Now all experience does indeed contain, in addition to the intuition of the senses through which something is given, a *concept* of an object as being thereby given. (A93/B126)

Note that Kant here uses 'experience' and 'knowledge of an object' interchangeably;[19] I comment on the significance of this further below. The second premise and the conclusion are contained in the following sentence:

> [The categories] relate of necessity and *a priori* to objects of experience, for the reason that only by means of them can any object whatsoever of experience be thought. (A93/B126)

Paraphrasing somewhat, we may put the argument as follows:

1. The experience of an object has both an intuitional and a conceptual component.
2. The conceptual component can occur only if categories apply to the object.
3. Therefore, categories apply to all objects of experience.

Kant affirms the second premise because he believes that to use any concepts is to judge and that all judging requires the application of categories. The latter claim is the burden of the Metaphysical Deduction of the Categories, discussion of which I postpone until section G.

The fact that Kant uses 'experience' and 'knowledge of an object' interchangeably may tempt one to conclude that the sense of 'experience' at work in the Objective Deduction is (e8). That conclusion would be premature, however, since Kant often uses the term 'knowledge' where the term 'belief' would do as well or better. For example, he defines 'truth' as conformity of knowledge with its object; if by 'knowledge' he meant justified true belief, this definition would be circular. Moreover, it is clear that the present argument turns on no features of knowledge by which it is distinguished from objectual experience. What he appears to mean by 'knowledge' is the sort of thing twentieth-century philosophers have called 'perceptual taking' or 'ostensible seeing'—for example, ostensibly seeing this red item to be an apple.[20] All Kant assumes about such episodes is that they have both an intuitional component (e.g., sensing an expanse of red) and a conceptual component (e.g., believing that the concept *apple* applies to what one is experiencing). It does not seem to matter to the argument whether the belief is either justified or true. The sense of 'experience' that figures in the argument, therefore, is not (e8), but only (e5).

I say that Kant has (e5) in mind because he speaks of concepts by which one "thinks an object." But given the result of the Metaphysical Deduction, even an episode of subsuming an intuition under a sensory-quality concept like *red* would have to involve categories. Therefore, by means of the present argument Kant could also arrive at the stronger conclusion that categories must apply to all objects of experience in sense (e4).

But the present argument will *not* show that categories are required for experience in any thinner sense. As of this point in the *Critique*, there is nothing to rule out the possibility that we might be conscious of (or by means of) unconceptualized and uncategorized intuitions. Indeed, just two paragraphs before the passage containing the argument we have considered (in the penultimate paragraph of section 13), Kant emphatically asserts that there *could* be uncategorized intuitions:

> The categories of the understanding . . . do not represent the conditions under which objects are given to intuition. . . . For appearances can certainly be given in intuition independently of functions of the understanding. . . . Intuition stands in no need whatsoever of the functions of thought. (A89–91/B122–23)

This paragraph has disturbed many commentators. Some, including Kemp Smith and Wolff, have condemned it as inconsistent with what they take to be Kant's later doctrine that the categories are indispensable for all consciousness whatsoever. According to Wolff, Kant's view is that "sense-datum languages and the uninterpreted given, those foundation-stones of contemporary phenomenalism, are sheer impossibilities."[21]

Wolff presents a series of four passages in which he claims Kant gradually moves away from the position of section 13, coming around finally to the position that the categories are essential for all (human) consciousness whatsoever.[22] The first three passages he cites are suggestive, but not in Wolff's opinion conclusive. For example, in the second of them Kant says that "appearances might, indeed, constitute intuition without thought, but not knowledge; and consequently would be for us as good as nothing" (A111). Wolff observes: "With the tantalizing phrase, 'as good as nothing,' he pulls back from the flat statement that the perceptions would not enter consciousness."[23] But the fourth passage is supposed to be a clincher:

> It is only because I ascribe all perceptions to one consciousness . . . that I can say of all perceptions [*kann ich bei allen Wahrnehmungen sagen*] that I am conscious of them. (A122)

Since Kant argues later that perceptions can be ascribed to one consciousness only if the categories apply to them, Wolff takes this passage to imply that the categories are necessary even for our consciousness of perceptions.

But perhaps not even this passage is conclusive. For one thing, the difference between *being* conscious of perceptions and *saying* that you are may be significant. For another, the conditions necessary for consciousness of *all* perceptions (as a collective) may go beyond those that are necessary for consciousness of perceptions *individually*. I return to this second distinction in section E.

For a passage that *is* conclusive, however, we have not far to seek. A few pages beyond the last passage quoted is this:

> For only by means of [categories] can appearances belong to knowledge *or even to our consciousness*, and so to ourselves. (A125, emphasis mine)

Kant has now evidently repudiated the position of section 13, declaring that consciousness without the categories is impossible after all.

Whether reconcilable with section 13 or not, Kant's new position is at any rate not established by the Objective Deduction of section 14. That argument, as I have shown, establishes at most the necessity of the categories for *conceptual* experience. To find an argument that the categories are necessary for consciousness as such, we must look to the Subjective Deduction—which therefore turns out to be essential to Kant's purposes after all.

D. An Outline of the Subjective Deduction

Paton compared the region of the *Critique* we are about to enter to the Great Arabian Desert. It is more aptly compared to a tropical jungle; the interpreter's main task must be to clear away the undergrowth that obscures the main path of argument. When this is done, the Subjective Deduction stands forth as three premises and a conclusion:

1. *The Unity Premise*: All representations of which I am conscious have *unity of apperception*.
2. *The Synthesis Premise*: Representations can have such unity only if they have been *synthesized*.
3. *The Category Premise*: Synthesis requires the application of Kant's *categories*.
4. *Conclusion*: The categories apply to all representations of which I am conscious.

This argument reaches the stronger conclusion advertised above. I now discuss and evaluate each of the premises.

E. The Unity Premise

The starting point of the Transcendental Deduction (which I identify henceforth with the Subjective Deduction) is the principle of the transcendental unity of apperception, also known as the transcendental unity of consciousness. Kant tells us that this principle is "the highest principle in the whole sphere of human knowledge" (B135).

The phrase 'transcendental unity of apperception' names both a *property* and a *principle*—a principle attributing the property to certain collections of representations. It does not, despite the impression conveyed by some writers, name an entity or an agent. Below I demonstrate first what the property is and then what the principle is.

As a preliminary approach to discovering what property is expressed by the above phrase, I consider the meanings of the constituent terms separately. First, we may say that a collection of items has *unity* if and only if there is some item to which all the items bear a common relation. Thus, a collection of children may have unity in virtue of their all having the same parent, a collection of properties may have unity in virtue of their all being exemplified by the same object, and so on. It would be hard to think of a collection that did *not* have unity in this very general sense.

Unity of *apperception*, however, is a much more exclusive affair. Kant uses 'apperception' in the same sense as Leibniz, who defines it in the following passage:

> Thus it is well to distinguish between *perception*, which is the inner state of the monad representing external things, and *apperception*, which is *consciousness*, or the reflective knowledge of this inner state. . . .[24]

In other words, apperception is an act of consciousness that apprehends one or more of the subject's own perceptive states. Unity of apperception, accordingly, would be the property possessed by a collection of representations if and only if there is some one act of apperception that apprehends them all.

Finally, Kant explains the term 'transcendental' in the following passage:

> The unity of this apperception I likewise entitle the *transcendental* unity of self-consciousness, in order to indicate the possibility of *a priori* knowledge arising from it. (B132)

This agrees with Kant's official definition of 'transcendental' at A56−57/B80−81.[25] One should not assume that the unity of apperception is *transcendent*, that is, not empirically accessible.

Now let us approach the unity of apperception from a different angle, starting from the following well-known formulation:

> It must be possible for the 'I think' to accompany all my representations. (B131)

This is how Kant formulates the principle, but I am still concerned only with the property. The first thing that must be realized about the sentence just quoted is that Kant means more than "it must be possible for *each* of my representations to be accompanied by an 'I think'." The 'I think' must attach to my representations *conjointly*. The following passage makes this clear:

> [Unity of apperception] comes about, not simply through my accompanying *each* representation with consciousness, but only in so far as I *conjoin* one representation with another, and am conscious of the synthesis of them. (B133, first emphasis mine)[26]

Elsewhere Kant characterizes the *lack* of unity of apperception as follows:

The given representations would not have *in common* the act of apperception 'I think', and so could not be apprehended *together* in one self-consciousness. (B137, emphasis mine)

The key idea, then, is *compresence to consciousness* or *cognitive togetherness*. I shall speak of representations that have this feature as being *U-related*.

But how exactly are we to understand this relation? Let us consider several possible ways of explicating it. In the list that follows, 'S' ranges over conscious subjects, 'R' over relations, 'r1' and 'r2' over representations, and 't' over times. 'A' stands for a relation of acquaintance or awareness. For simplicity I pretend that only two representations are involved.

(u1) $(\exists S)(SAr1)$ & $(\exists S)(SAr2)$.
(u2) $(\exists S)(SAr1$ & $SAr2)$.
(u3) $(\exists S)(\exists t)$ $(SAr1$ at t & $SAr2$ at t$)$.
(u4) $(\exists S)(SA \{r1 + r2\})$.
(u5) $(\exists S)(\exists R)(SAr1$ & $SAr2$ & S judges that $r1Rr2)$.
(u6) $(\exists S)(S$ judges that $(\exists x)(xAr1$ & $xAr2))$.
(u7) $(\exists S)(S$ judges that $(\exists x)(xAr1$ & $xAr2$ & $x = S$ himself$))$.
(u8) $(\exists S)(\exists R)(S$ judges that $(\exists x)(x$ judges $r1Rr2$ & $x = S$ himself$))$.

Which of these best explicates the U-relation?[27] We may scratch (u1) from the list immediately, since it does not guarantee that one and the same subject is aware of r1 and r2. This, of course, is the point of William James's famous example:

Take a sentence of a dozen words, and take twelve men and tell to each one word. Then stand the men in a row or jam them in a bunch and let each think of his word as intently as he will; nowhere will there be a consciousness of the whole sentence.[28]

But we do not yet remove the shortcoming if we merely stipulate that one and the same subject be aware of the various representations, as in (u2). Wolff contrasts James's case with one in which one man reads out the entire sentence, but if this one man forgets each word as he comes to the next, the words will not be compresent to one consciousness.[29] Nor can we secure the desired state of affairs merely by requiring that our single subject be aware of the various representations at the same time, as in (u3). If my attention were absorbed in a painting, I might be simultaneously aware of marks on the canvas and sounds in the background without being aware of them *together*. The analogy with belief is instructive here: I can believe each of two propositions at the same time without believing their conjunction.[30]

To symbolize the togetherness that is not yet necessarily present in any of (u1)–(u3), I have had recourse in (u4) to braces enclosing 'r1' and 'r2'. (I have used "+" rather than "&" because r1 and r2 need not be propositions.[31]) But can anything further be said by way of explaining what this togetherness amounts to? One can give examples of the sort of thing that is intended: tasting the tart along with the sweet in a sip of lemonade, hearing voices against a background of music, or being aware of hearing a clap of thunder simultaneously with seeing a flash of lightning. But I find it difficult to give any kind of analysis of such togetherness. The trouble is that although various conditions can be specified that are *sufficient* for it, none of these seems to be *necessary*. I would say, for example, that each of (u5) through (u8) is sufficient, but none is necessary. Let us consider only (u5), since if it is not necessary the others will not be. If I am aware of two spots of color and judge one to be to the left of the other, then I am surely aware of them together, but I might be aware of them together even if I did not judge them to be related in this or any other way.[32] Or, to take an example that involves a manifold of concepts rather than a manifold of intuitions, consider what happens when I hold the complex concept *even prime number* before my mind: I am aware of the constituent concepts together, but I do not judge them to be related.

Passing now to the remaining items in the list, (u6) requires the subject to judge not simply that his representations are related but that they are *co-apprehended*, (u7) requires him to judge that it is *he himself* who co-apprehends them, and (u8) requires him to judge not merely that he co-apprehends them but that he connects them in a judgment.

The relation between (u6) and (u7) calls for comment. (u6) merely says that the subject judges that someone or something co-apprehends certain representations; (u7) says that he judges that *he himself* co-apprehends them—in other words, that he makes a judgment he would express by saying "*I* apprehend r1 and *I* apprehend r2." The peculiarities of such first-person judgments have been penetratingly discussed in recent years by Castañeda and Chisholm among others.[33] On the face of it, 'I'-judgments certainly seem to say something more than '($\exists$x)'-judgments. But it may be Kant's view that they do not: his frequent remarks to the effect that 'I' stands for no intuition, that it is an empty representation, and the like, may perhaps be taken to suggest that 'I' is a disguised description or quantifier.[34] It may be Kant's view that knowing that two representations are co-apprehended (that there is an x who apprehends them both) is all anyone can do by way of knowing that he himself apprehends them.[35]

Let us return to the question of which of (u1)-(u8) should be taken as explicating the U-relation. I have already dismissed the first three as inadequate. I have suggested that (u4) is the weakest formula that captures the idea of cognitive togetherness, but Kant may have thought that more yet is involved in the U-relation. To determine what he had in mind, we must answer two questions. First, what is the meaning of the '*I think*' that is supposed to accompany our representations? Should we take it (1) in a broad Cartesian sense covering all acts of consciousness, or (2) in a narrower sense covering only acts of judging? Second, what does it mean for an 'I think' to *accompany* a representation r? Does it just mean (a) that an 'I think' attaches to the representation externally, that is, that the proposition 'I think (something regarding) r' is true? Or does it mean (b) that an 'I think' accompanies r on the stage of consciousness, that is, that I am aware of or entertain the proposition 'I think (something regarding) r'? If the right combination of answers is (1a), then (u4) is the minimal U-relation. If the right combination is (2a), (u5) is the minimal U-relation. If it is (1b), then (u6) or (more likely) (u7) is suggested. (I note here that awareness of awareness as attaching jointly to r1 and r2 is awareness of a state of affairs; hence, even though the "inner" awareness may be nonpropositional acquaintance, the "outer" awareness is judgmental.) Finally, if the right combination is (2b), we get something like (u8). These results are displayed in the following matrix:

	(a) 'I think' accompanies r = 'I think r' is true	(b) 'I think' accompanies r = 'I think r' is an object of awareness
(1) I think = I am aware	(u4)	(u6) or (u7)
(2) I think = I judge	(u5)	(u8)

I postpone the choice among these alternatives until I have said something about the *principle* of unity of apperception.

The principle of the unity of apperception attributes U-relatedness (whichever of the foregoing that turns out to be) to the representations in certain classes. The next task is to determine *which* classes—in other words, to determine the *scope* of the unity principle. I focus on the official formulation again: "It must be possible for the 'I think' to accompany all my representations." What does Kant mean by "*my* representations"? Does he really mean to speak of *all* my representations? And why does he only say that it must be *possible* for the 'I think' to accompany them?

The obvious answer to the first question is that for a representation to be mine is for it to be *owned by me*—for it to be a representation in my mental history, not someone else's. But that, of course, is only a *nominal* answer—it does not tell us in what such ownership by a single person consists. In C.D. Broad's terms, it does not tell us what constitutes the *unity of mind*.[36]

Following Broad,[37] we may divide theories of the unity of mind into two types: (1) center theories, according to which representations belong to the same mind if and only if they bear a common relation to some one item (e.g., a Cartesian ego or a material body), and (2) system theories, according to which representations belong to the same mind if and only if they bear certain relations (e.g., memory, causation) to one another. Which type of theory does Kant hold?

We can be led to answer this question either way, depending on what portion of Kant's text we are looking at. As I discuss in chapter 11, Kant certainly believed in a noumenal self, and this, one might think, provides him with just what he needs for a center theory. At the same time, however, there are places in Kant's philosophy, including especially the Transcendental Deduction, that strongly suggest a system theory. One clue that points in this direction is his contention that the principle of the unity of apperception is *analytic* (B135, B138). A good explanation for this contention would be this: he thinks that the relation that unites diverse representations into one mind is *none other than unity of apperception*. In other words, unity of mind is to be accounted for in terms of unity of apperception. The principle that all my representations are U-related would therefore be analytic because I could mean nothing else in calling them mine.[38]

To implement this suggestion, we would need a way of understanding the U-relation distinct from all eight canvassed above. Each of those explications *presupposes* a center of consciousness with its quantifier '∃S', and could not for that reason legitimately be used in constructing a system theory. I explore the prospects for analyzing unity of mind in terms of a centerless U-relation in appendix F.

I turn now to the second of the three questions above: does Kant really mean to say that *all* my representations (throughout my history) are U-related, each with every other? That would be enormously implausible no matter how we understand the U-relation. Does he mean only that all the representations occurring in a given temporal slice of my history are U-related? Even that is implausible, for among the representations occurring in me at a given time, there may be some that are not U-related to each other in any sense stronger than (u3).

We have probably just arrived at the answer to our third question, for it was very likely considerations such as these that led Kant to introduce the qualification about possibility. My representations need not all be actually U-related, but it must be *possible* for them to be so related.[39]

But there is a danger that if we weaken the unity premise in this fashion, it will no longer be capable of doing the work required of it in the Transcendental Deduction. Kant wants to argue that representations can be U-related only if they are synthesized in accordance with the categories. From this he wants to conclude that all my representations (or all representations of which I am conscious) are subject to the categories. But this conclusion is warranted only if all my representations are *actually* U-related. If they are only *possibly* U-related, all he can conclude is that they are *possibly* subject to the categories. And that is not enough.

I propose, therefore, that we weaken the Unity Premise not by limiting its claim to one of mere possibility, but by further narrowing its scope. There are various ways in which we could do this. One that would suffice for the purposes of the Deduction is this: given any representation of which I am conscious, there is another with which it is U-related. I find this quite plausible, especially if the unity relation is no stronger than (u4).

F. The Synthesis Premise

The version of the Unity Premise we have settled on says that every representation of which I am conscious (or perhaps more strongly, every representation owned by me) is U-related to some other representation. The Synthesis Premise says that representations can be U-related only if they have been *synthesized*. Here are two of Kant's formulations of this premise:

> The principle of the necessary unity of apperception . . . reveals the necessity of a synthesis of the manifold given in intuition. (B135)

> For without such combination [synthesis] . . . the given representations would not have in common the act of apprehension 'I think', and so could not be apprehended together in one self-consciousness. (B137)

To see what this means, we have to find out what Kant means by 'synthesis'. Here is one of his clearest definitions of it:

By *synthesis* in its most general sense, I understand the act of putting different representations together, and of grasping what is manifold in them in one [act of] knowledge. (A77/B103)

In the same place he speaks of synthesis as an act whereby a manifold is "gone through in a certain way, taken up, and connected."

Given only this much information, we might be led to believe that the Synthesis Premise is an analytic truth. For we might think that when we substitute defining terms for defined terms in Kant's formulation, we come up with something like this:

If a number of representations are U-related (apprehended together in one act), then they are synthesized (apprehended together in one act).

As we read further, however, it becomes clear that the Synthesis Premise is by no means trivial, obvious, or analytic. To say that a collection of representations has been synthesized is not merely to say that they are apprehended together in one act; it is to say how they *got* that way. And on Kant's view, they can get that way only as the result of a special three-step procedure, set forth in A98–104, which I now describe.

First, there is the Synthesis of Apprehension in Intuition, which consists of apprehending the representations to be unified *separately* and *successively*. Second, there is the Synthesis of Reproduction in Imagination, which consists of forming and retaining memory-images of each of the representations apprehended in the first phase. Finally, there is the Synthesis of Recognition in a Concept, which consists of surveying the images generated during the second phase and seeing what they all add up to. The whole procedure may be illustrated by the adventures of a curious flea on the back of an elephant. First, it makes a complete circuit of the beast, successively apprehending its various parts; all the while it forms and retains memory-images of the parts thus apprehended; finally it looks these over and exclaims, "Trunk, tusks, tail—by Jove, it's an elephant!"

The example is of necessity oversimplified. The representations I have assumed as inputs (e.g., the representation of a trunk) would on Kant's view themselves have to be outputs of a prior threefold synthesis. Indeed, the representation of even the tiniest spatial extent or temporal duration would on his view have to be achieved by synthesis:

All intuitions are extensive magnitudes. . . . I entitle a magnitude extensive when the representation of the parts makes possible, and therefore necessarily precedes, the representation of the whole. I cannot represent to myself a line, however small, without drawing it in thought, that is, generating from a point all its parts one after another. (A162–63/B202–3)

Kant holds that the only way to obtain a representation of something with a plurality of parts or phases is to obtain a representation of each part and then synthesize these representations.[40]

It should be apparent by now that the Synthesis Premise is not an analytic truth. Indeed, in my opinion, it is not a truth at all. I present three objections to it.

The first is phenomenological. When I imagine a line, I am aware of at least some of its parts together. In Kant's view, this can come about only through synthesizing those parts (or one's representations of them). "We cannot think a line without *drawing* it in thought, or a circle without *describing* it" (B154). But when I imagine a line, I am aware of no such successive generation; I simply plop the whole line down at once.[41]

The second objection is also phenomenological and is based on an example found in discussions of the "specious present." Consider how I know that the minute hand of a clock is moving: I don't *see* it move, but I apprehend successively its various positions, remember what these were, and finally conclude that the hand has moved. Kant's doctrine of the threefold synthesis is a fairly accurate account of what goes on in this case. But now consider how I know that the *second* hand is moving. Nothing like synthesis seems to be involved; I simply *see* it move. But for Kant the second must be a case of synthesis no less than the first. His view simply does not accommodate the enormous phenomenological difference between the two cases.

Some may find these phenomenological objections irrelevant, insisting that we must posit acts of synthesis to account for what we are aware of even if we are not aware of synthesis itself. Indeed, Kant himself characterizes synthesis as "a blind but indispensable function of the soul, without which we should have no knowledge whatsoever, but of which we are scarcely ever conscious" (A78/B103). I therefore present a third objection that is dialectical rather than phenomenological. Kant holds that we cannot apprehend the parts of a manifold straight off in one act. Instead, we must apprehend the parts successively, retain memory images of them, and see what they all add up to. But how are we supposed to survey these images? A manifold of images presents the same problem we had to begin with. Either we must perform a threefold synthesis on *it*, in which case we are off on an infinite regress, or we can take it in all at once, in which case we could have done likewise with the original manifold.

The objection as I just stated it may saddle Kant with an unduly imagistic theory of remembering,[42] but a similar objection would arise even if Kant did not hold an image theory. Suppose the second "moment" in synthesis consisted entirely of propositional memory: remembering that first you saw a patch of gray, then a patch of white, and so on. You would still need to hold together the various concepts in each proposition and the various propositions in one conjunctive proposition, and this presents the original problem of a One knowing a Many.[43]

In my view, the only solution to these difficulties is to recognize with William James that "whatever things are thought in relation are thought from the outset in a unity."[44] The key phrase here is *from the outset*—there must not be any question of having first to go through, take up, and connect. For more that is relevant to this point, see appendix H.

What could have led Kant to his seemingly impossible position? Perhaps he was influenced by a model of perception according to which sensory receptors can deliver only punctiform inputs, and these only successively. But this would not explain his insistence that even a manifold of representations of *inner sense* must be synthesized. Or perhaps he combined the idea that awareness of things together must be awareness of them as related with the

British Empiricists' idea that relations are never simply given but are only generated by acts of the mind. In either case, I wish I understood better why the underlying ideas had such a powerful hold on him.

G. The Category Premise

As I have been interpreting it so far, Kant's main argument in the Transcendental Deduction may be represented as a chain of implications containing the following links: consciousness → U-relatedness → synthesis → categories. The last implication corresponds to the Category Premise, which affirms that all synthesis requires the application of categories. Kant argues for this premise by inserting another link into the chain: synthesis → judging → categories. That is, he maintains

    (i) that synthesis either involves or is akin to judging, and
    (ii) that judging requires the application of categories.

What is the basis for claim (i)? Unfortunately, the passages in which Kant discusses the relation of synthesis to judging are as individually dense as they are collectively rare. Here is one of them:

> The same function which gives unity to the various representations *in a judgment* also gives unity to the mere synthesis of various representations *in an intuition.* (A79/B104−5)

Three interpretations of this passage seem possible: (a) synthesis is *identical* with judging, (b) synthesis is not identical with judging but *involves* it, and (c) synthesis neither is nor involves judging but belongs to the same genus as judging (viz., *function*) and is subject to the same categorial requirements as the other members of the genus.[45] Kant's description of the three moments in synthesis suggests interpretation (b), since the third moment, Recognition in a Concept, is plainly an episode of judging. For our purposes, however, it is not necessary to decide among these interpretations, since they all imply that if judging requires the application of categories, so likewise does synthesis.

Some passages in Kant suggest that the problematic doctrine of synthesis could be bypassed. In section 19 of the B Deduction he proposes to define judging as "nothing but the manner in which given modes of knowledge [*Erkenntnisse*] are brought to the objective unity of apperception" (B141). Again, in the *Prolegomena* he says, "The union of representations in one consciousness is judging" (p. 52). With these definitions, Kant could argue from the U-relatedness of representations directly to their being connected in a judgment; the intervening link of synthesis could be dropped.

The trouble with this shortcut is that the proposed definition of judging is simply unacceptable. One half of it is plausible—if representations are connected in a judgment, then they are U-related. But the converse half, which is what the bypass argument would need, is not plausible at all. If in response to the request, "Think of your favorite color and your favorite number," I hold the color blue and the number two before my mind, these concepts will be U-related, but not connected in any judgment.

Admittedly, if we adopt (u5) or any of the stronger explications of the U-relation, the counterexample I have just given is ruled out. Indeed, if we adopt any of those explications, we have a second way of bypassing the doctrine of synthesis: U-related representations would automatically be connected in a judgment, not in virtue of the definition of 'judgment' but in virtue of the definition of 'U-related'. But the gain here would be offset by a loss elsewhere, since (as I discussed in section E) under the stronger explications of the U-relation the Unity Premise is itself implausible.

I turn now to claim (ii)—the claim that all judging requires the application of categories. If we do not bypass the doctrine of synthesis, claim (ii) is needed to support the Category Premise; if we do bypass the doctrine of synthesis, claim (ii) takes the place of the Category Premise. Either way, the claim is essential to the overall success of the Transcendental Deduction.

Establishing claim (ii) is the burden of the Metaphysical Deduction of the Categories. This means that the Metaphysical Deduction is more important to Kant's purposes than some commentators are willing to allow. A common view divides the labor of the two deductions this way: the Metaphysical Deduction is concerned with the *discovery* of the categories and the Transcendental Deduction with their *validation*;[46] again, the Metaphysical Deduction is concerned with "determining the list of the categories" and the Transcendental Deduction with establishing their "objective validity."[47] This view may tempt one to think that the Transcendental Deduction could demonstrate, without the aid of the Metaphysical Deduction, that *some* set of categories is valid and that the job of the Metaphysical Deduction is only to determine *which* set it is. What this view overlooks is that the Metaphysical Deduction must establish that *some* set of categories (even if not Kant's in particular) is indispensable to judging.

The nub of Kant's case for (ii) is that unless it were true, judging could not be distinguished from the mere association of ideas. If I think of redness on an occasion when I am thinking of apples, I do not thereby make any judgment; a judgment comes about only insofar as I bind the associated concepts together, for example, into the judgment 'some apples are red'. Kant thinks that the categories are precisely those concepts that are needed to bind other concepts together into judgments. In Dryer's apt phrase, they are *connective concepts*.[48] Corresponding to each of the twelve forms of judgment Kant recognizes, there is supposed to be a unique category that is required for connecting concepts in a judgment of that type. Since any judgment will exemplify at least four of the twelve forms, any judgment will mobilize at least four of the categories.[49]

Most criticisms of the Metaphysical Deduction focus on its shortcomings as an attempt to elicit Kant's twelve categories in particular.[50] I wish to make a more radical criticism: it fails to show that *any categories at all* are required for judging. Let us look more closely at the fundamental strategem of the Metaphysical Deduction, namely, that categories are just those concepts that enable other concepts or representations to be connected in judgments. It should be clear that the mere "superaddition" (to use a word from the *Prolegomena*, p. 49) of a category to a nonjudgmental cluster of representations—for example, the intuition of this apple, and the concept of red—is not sufficient to yield a judgment. For the result of such superaddition might simply be a *larger* nonjudgmental cluster—for example, the intuition of this apple, the category of inherence, and the concept of red. To make a judgment, you must *do* something with all the concepts in the cluster. Indeed, on Kant's view, you must *subsume* the original representations under the superadded category.[51] But if acts of subsumption must be introduced, what work is left for the category to do? Why can't you subsume some intuitions or concepts *directly* under other concepts, without dragging in the categories? Kant is faced with the following dilemma: without the act of subsumption, you have not got a judgment; with it, you do not need a category.[52]

The more or less Bradleyan lesson to be drawn so far is that judging as such does not require the use of special concepts, contrary to the central strategem of the Metaphysical Deduction. It remains open to Kant, of course, to maintain that judgments of certain types (specified in terms of their contents) cannot be made without using certain associated concepts. Indeed, this is obviously true. You cannot make causal judgments without using the concept of causation, or apodeictic judgments without using the concept of necessity, and so on. But Kant has not shown that we cannot judge at all without making judgments of these specific types.[53]

I pass now to what I regard as the really fundamental criticism of the Category Premise, and one that has not received the attention it deserves. Even if Kant could show that some of his categories must be employed in any judgment we make (and that all of them must be employed on some occasion or other), this would not be enough for his purposes. For that result in conjunction with the rest of the Transcendental Deduction would yield no conclusion stronger than this: all my representations are connected in judgments that use Kant's categories. But Kant wants to show that the categories are *objectively valid*—that they actually apply to objects of experience.[54] To reach this conclusion he needs the further premise that any categories used in judging are *actually exemplified* by the items judged about. But we have only to state this premise to see how implausible it is. If I judge that the shining of the sun has caused the warming of the stone, there is no guarantee that the category of cause applies to the events connected in my judgment—*for my judgment may not be true.*

I fear that some may have overlooked this obvious point because of the easy verbal slide from 'we must apply categories' to 'categories must apply'. One may slip without noticing it from one to the other, but between the two there is no small distance. It is the distance between our using a category and its being instantiated, or between our making a judgment and its being true.

I fear that others may have overlooked the present point because of the loose practice, common among commentators, of saying that "the categories" are necessary for this or that (e.g., making judgments). *What about* the categories is necessary—their existence, their being used by us, their being instantiated by objects, or what? One who does not sufficiently articulate the necessary condition may too quickly acquiesce in the necessity of "the categories" without realizing that the necessity of *their being instantiated*—which of course is Kant's *demonstrandum*—has not been demonstrated at all.

Kant could get around the present objection by qualifying the needed extra premise thus: any categories used in making *true* judgments must apply to or be instantiated by the items judged about. But if we make this change here, we must make a correlative change elsewhere in the Deduction to preserve its validity as a whole. We must now say (in the Synthesis Premise) that a necessary condition of our representations being U-related is not simply our having synthesized them, but our having synthesized them by means of true judgments. This is a claim for which Kant has advanced no argument whatever.

To summarize our results to this point, Kant's aim in the Transcendental Deduction is to show that the validity of the categories is necessary for experience in sense (e2). He fails in this aim because the Synthesis and Category premises are neither intrinsically plausible nor adequately supported by argument.

H. Relation to an Object

In my discussion of the Transcendental Deduction so far I have said little about a topic that looms large: the relation of representations to an object. Here is a more complete map of the Transcendental Deduction than I provided before, showing the place of this important topographical feature in Kant's jungle:

I am conscious of representations A through Z.

$1\downarrow$

A–Z are subject to the unity of apperception.

$7\nearrow 8\nearrow$ $2\searrow 4\searrow$

A–Z relate to an object. $\overset{5}{\underset{6}{\rightleftarrows}}$ A–Z have been synthesized.

$9\searrow$ $3\nearrow$ (Synthesis is subject to the same categorial requirements as judging.)

A–Z are subject to the categories.

The conditionals corresponding to arrows 1, 2, and 3 are the premises I singled out in section D as constituting the main moves of the Transcendental Deduction. But in the course of his argument, Kant affirms many other conditionals as well, which are also indicated in the chart.[55] In particular, he claims a three-way equivalence among the characteristics of having unity of apperception, having been synthesized, and being related to an object. What this "relation to an object" (*die Beziehung auf einen Gegenstand*) amounts to is the topic of the present section.

Two Senses of 'Object'. I introduce this topic with a passage in which Descartes explains what he means by 'idea':

> Hence the idea of the sun will be the sun itself existing in the mind, not indeed formally, as it exists in the sky, but objectively, i.e. in the way in which objects are wont to exist in the mind. . . .[56]

Here Descartes distinguishes two modes of being and two correlative senses in which items can be objects for a mind. Merely by being thought of, an item is an object in one sense and is said to have "objective reality" in a now-misleading use of the phrase. Corresponding to objects in this first sense, there may or may not be items that have "formal reality," such as the sun existing in the sky; such items are objects in a second sense.

Consider now the following passage from Kant:

> Everything, every representation even, in so far as we are conscious of it, may be called object. But it is a question for deeper enquiry what the word 'object' ought to signify in respect of appearances when these are viewed not in so far as they are (as representations) objects, but only in so far as they stand for an object. (A189–90/B234–35)

Here Kant is drawing a distinction that is at least superficially similar to Descartes's. An item counts as an object in one sense simply in virtue of the fact that there is consciousness of it, and an object in this first sense may or may not "stand for" or have corresponding to it an object in a further sense.[57] It is an important side-task of the Transcendental Deduction to elucidate this second sense.[58]

Using traditional terminology, we could call objects in the first sense immanent objects and objects in the second sense transcendent objects. Alternatively, we could speak of objects internal and external to representational states. But both terminologies are potentially misleading in the Kantian context, so I shall speak simply of objects$_1$ and objects$_2$.[59]

Objects$_1$ are internal accusatives or intentional objects that have no being outside being represented or intuited; they are virtual objects in the sense I discussed in section D of chapter 1.[60] Examples of objects$_1$ are such rudimentary phenomenal individuals as patches of color and stretches of sound. They have both intensive and extensive magnitude and may be either outer (i.e., spatial) or inner (i.e., merely temporal). Examples of objects$_2$ (whose ontological status I discuss below) are material things like houses and ships and perhaps also empirical selves.

The Reductive Account of Objects. What is Kant's view about the ontological status of objects$_2$? And what does it mean for a representation to be related to one? For the time being I shall drop the subscript, letting it be understood that objects$_2$ are what we are concerned with.[61]

Kant addresses these questions in a series of paragraphs in the first-edition Deduction, beginning by posing the problem as follows:

At this point we must make clear to ourselves what we mean by the expression 'an object of representations'. . . . What, then, is to be understood when we speak of an object corresponding to, and consequently also distinct from, our knowledge? (A104)

The first answer he considers is that such an object must be conceived of "only as something in general = x" (A104) or, as he puts it a few pages later (A109), as the "transcendental object = x"—a phrase we might naturally take to refer to a thing in itself.[62] But Kant rejects any suggestion that the objects corresponding to our representations are things in themselves. His reason seems to be that if the objects were things in themselves, we could never know, as he assumes we sometimes do, that our representations are indeed related to objects.

Kant moves a step closer to a positive characterization of objects by noting the role they play in our cognitive lives: "[T]he object is viewed as that which prevents our cognitions [*Erkenntnisse*] from being haphazard and arbitrary" (A104). If a red, round apple lies on the table before me, the course of my experience will not be a matter of "anything goes"; rather, experiences of grasping and turning will be followed by further experiences of redness and roundness, experiences of lifting and biting by experiences of crispness and tartness, and so on.

The final move in this series is, in effect, to let objects be *defined* by their role. To say that there is an apple before me is *equivalent* to saying that I am having certain sorts of experiences (intuitions), and that if I (or other observers similarly placed) were to perform certain actions, they would have further experiences of predictable sorts. As C.I. Lewis said in putting forth a similar view:

[I]f I should bite this, it would taste sweet; if I should pinch it, it would feel moderately soft; if I should eat it, it would digest and not poison me; if I should turn it over, I should perceive another rounded surface much like this. . . . These and a hundred other such hypothetical propositions constitute my knowledge of the apple in my hand.[63]

Passages to this effect are scattered through both editions of the Transcendental Deduction. Here are two, one from each edition, that I find particularly telling:

[T]his object is no more than that something, the concept of which expresses such a necessity of synthesis. (A106)

[A]n *object* is that in the concept of which the manifold of a given intuition is united. (B137)[64]

In both passages Kant defines an object as something *the concept of which* plays a certain role. The conditions of such a definition may be fulfilled even if objects do not exist as entities alongside or outside representational manifolds; as long as the constituents of the manifold are suitably related or unified, it will *follow* that there is an object to which these representations are related. It will follow because there being such an object is nothing more than the holding of such relations among representations. To put the point in

Russellian terms, what Kant is giving us is a contextual definition—not a definition that gives us anything with which to equate objects (or any referent for the term 'object'), but a definition that tells us how to understand phrases such as 'relates to an object' (as predicated of a representation) or 'is united as prescribed by the concept of an object' (as predicated of a group of representations).

Here is another passage that makes the point as explicitly as one could like. This one occurs not in the Transcendental Deduction but in the discussion of the Second Analogy of Experience, following up on the "question for deeper enquiry" I quoted above from A189–90/B234–35:

> How, then, does it come about that we posit an object for these representations, and so, in addition to their subjective reality, as modifications, ascribe to them some mysterious kind of objective reality? . . . If we enquire what new character *relation to an object* confers upon our representations, what dignity they thereby acquire, we find that it results only in subjecting the representations to a rule, and so in necessitating us to connect them in some one specific manner; and conversely [*umgekehrt*], that only in so far as our representations are necessitated in a certain order as regards their time-relations do they acquire objective meaning. (A197/B242)[65]

In other words, what it is for representations to have "relation to an object" *just is* for them to stand in certain relations to one another.[66]

Kant is here giving us a reductive analysis of relation to an object. He is following a strategy that was later advocated by Bertrand Russell: "Whenever possible, substitute constructions out of known entities for inferences to unknown entities."[67] When we posit an object corresponding to one of our representations, we are not believing in an unknown something = x; we are believing in a larger fabric of representations connected with each other and with the original in accordance with certain rules.

Objects (i.e., objects$_2$) thus turn out to be logical constructions at one remove: they are constructions out of objects$_1$, which are themselves constructions out of representations (in the 'ing' sense, i.e., representings). But since the relation 'is a construction out of' is transitive, we may equally well say that objects$_2$ (which comprise houses, ships, and all the furniture of the earth) are constructions out of representations. In other words, Kant is a phenomenalist, like Berkeley before him and Russell, Ayer, and Lewis after him. Insofar as his phenomenalism is of the analytical rather than the ontological variety (objects being logical constructions out of representations rather than being identical with them or having them as parts), the resemblances are greater in the later direction.

The reductive account of objects may be seen as fulfilling the second strategy Kant identifies in his letter to Herz and as consummating the Copernican Revolution. The second strategy requires that representations make their objects possible; the Copernican Revolution calls for objects to conform to our knowledge rather than conversely. In the "objective" version of the Transcendental Deduction discussed above in section C, it may have seemed that Kant was offering us only a cheap substitute for this—representations (and in particular the categories) there seemed required only to make *cognition* of objects possible, not the objects themselves. But now we have a more robust sense in which the objects themselves are "made possible" by the categories: their existence is constituted by the occurrence of representations in certain patterns, patterns prescribed (as we are about to see) in large part by the categories.

We find confirmation of what I have just said at B138. Kant tells us there that what he is expounding "is not merely a condition that I myself require in knowing an object, but is a condition under which every intuition must stand in order *to become an object for me.*"[68] If 'intuition' has its 'ing' sense here, the phrase he italicized should rather be put thus: in order to *have* an object for me. In any case, I take him to be saying that his concern is not epistemological, but ontological: not with the conditions of obtaining knowledge of pre-existing objects, but with the question of what it is for objects to exist at all.

Objects, Unity, and Rules.   Kant does not merely claim that relation to an object is constituted by certain relations holding exclusively among representations; he also claims that the interrepresentational relations in question are the very relations in virtue of which representations have unity of apperception:[69]

> [T]he unity which the object makes necessary can be nothing else than the formal unity of consciousness in the synthesis of the manifold of representations. (A105)

> Now all unification of representations demands unity of consciousness in the synthesis of them. Consequently it is the unity of consciousness that alone constitutes the relation of representations to an object. . . . (B137)

How plausible is this contention that relation to an object and unity of apperception go together? To my mind, it is not plausible at all.[70] Could not *any* collection of representations, no matter how chaotic or phantasmagorical, have unity of apperception just in virtue of being cognized together?

At this point some will remind us that for Kant unity of apperception comes about only insofar as I synthesize my representations, and that synthesis is guided by rules. Will the fact that representations enjoying unity of apperception have been synthesized according to rules guarantee that they have relation to an object?

Here it may be useful to distinguish two conceptions of rules. On the first conception, rules are regularities to which representations *might or might not* conform, and such conformance (when it occurs) is definitive of 'relation to an object'. On the second conception, rules are imperatives that I follow in my dealings with a manifold, and my representations are related to one another in object-constituting ways because *I see to it* that they are so related. The first conception fits nicely with Beck's metaphor of the net and with the "analytic" construal of Kant's transcendental idealism that Bennett and Strawson recommend. The second conception goes well with Beck's metaphor of the dam and with the "genetic" construal of transcendental idealism that Bennett and Strawson deplore.[71]

On the first conception of rules, Kant's reductive account of relation to an object is not without epistemological or antiskeptical benefits. That representations have relation to an object is more easily ascertained on this account than it would be if such relation were relation to some X altogether different from representations.[72] Still, there is no assurance that any representations *will* be related to an object, or that such relation automatically goes along with the unity of apperception.

On the second conception of rules, any representations of which I am conscious are bound to be related to objects because I see to it that this is the case. Incredible as it is, this sometimes seems to be Kant's view. This side of Kant finds expression in passages such as the following:

> [T]he order and regularity in the appearances, which we entitle *nature*, we ourselves introduce. We could never find them in appearances, had not we ourselves, or the nature of our mind, set them there. (A125)

The counterpart of this claim in the B deduction occurs in section 15, where Kant tells us that "combination" or relatedness is never given through the senses but must be brought about by acts of the understanding. I see this section as designed to pave the way for the incredible view by laying down that awareness of any items as related (by any relation whatever) is possible only if the subject himself has put them in that relation. This is a theme that was later sounded with a vengeance by T.H. Green.[73]

I turn now to important issues connected with our topic that have been raised by Rolf George and Lewis White Beck.

Objectivity or Intentionality?   I have been assuming so far that Kant's concern with "relation to an object" is a concern with what one might call objectivity or veridicality—with the difference between there being a sun merely in one's mind and there being a sun in the sky. Rolf George has suggested that Kant's concern is rather with intentionality or aboutness, and thus with the relation or purported relation to an object that occurs even in cases of nonveridical experience.[74] George classifies Kant (along with Condillac and Reid among others) as a *sensationist*. According to sensationism, all of our knowledge begins with sensations, and sensations are nonintentional states—they do not even have objects$_1$. An account is therefore required of the mechanisms that engender intentionality, that is, the reference of mental states to items beyond themselves. In the terms Kant uses at A320/B376, we need an account of how we pass from mere sensation ("which relates solely to the subject as the modification of its state") to *Erkenntnis*, rendered here and elsewhere by Kemp Smith as "knowledge." But if one thinks of knowledge as justified true belief, that translation is bound to mislead. Kant's concern, according to George, is not with what differentiates true from false or justified from unjustified belief; it is with what differentiates a state of mind making ostensible reference to an object from a state making no such reference. He therefore proposes that a better translation of *Erkenntnis* would be "reference" (or, as I might also suggest, "referential cognition").

In the positive account George outlines, reference to objects is an affair not of sensibility alone but of the understanding. He attributes to Kant a mentalistic version of Frege's principle that it is only in the context of a sentence that words have meaning: it is only by being embodied in judgments that representations come to have reference. This interpretation of Kant makes possible an interesting and plausible reading of Kant's famous dictum "intuitions without concepts are blind" (A51/B75). A minimal reading of the dictum would be that it is only propositionally structured knowledge that requires the collaboration of intuition and concept; this leaves it open that intuitions without concepts could still constitute some kind of nonjudgmental awareness. A radical reading would be that intuitions without concepts do not even constitute qualitatively differentiated states of consciousness—they are "as good as nothing," presenting us with a blank or at best a blur. George's reading falls between these extremes: without the exercise of concepts in judgments, intuitions would be blind in the sense that they are not directed on objects. They would not be intuitions in Kant's official sense at all.[75]

I believe that George's interpretation has much to recommend it, and that many sections of the *Critique* take on a new look when viewed in its light. For example, recall the section 14 version of the Transcendental Deduction, in which Kant seeks to elicit the conditions of "knowledge of objects." I took Kant to be concerned there with the conditions of experience in the sense of (e5)—roughly, perceptual takings. For George, however, conceptualization is not something that gets added to intuition to yield richer states of perceptual taking; it is something without which intuitions would lack intentionality and therefore not be intuitions at all. Kant's topic in section 14 must therefore, according to George, be the conditions of experience in sense (e3).

Nonetheless, I am not convinced that Kant's concern with "relation to an object" is concern with intentionality rather than objectivity. I raise two reasons for doubt, each suggested by a different feature of the passage quoted near the beginning of this section. Here is the passage again:

Everything, every representation even, in so far as we are conscious of it, may be called object. But it is a question for deeper enquiry what the word 'object' ought to signify in respect of appearances when these are viewed not in so far as they are (as representations) objects, but only in so far as they stand for an object. (A189–90/B234–35)

On George's interpretation, Kant's project is to tell us something about the basis of intentionality in general. But notice that in this passage Kant is taking for granted the notion of a representation's *being* an object. A representation can *be* an object only if another state *has* it as an object, that is to say, only if another state has intentionality.[76] So, it looks as though when Kant formulates his "question for deeper inquiry," he is already taking the notion of intentionality for granted. His concern can at most be with reference to external objects and not with reference *überhaupt*.[77]

The second feature of the passage to which I call attention is its context. The passage occurs at the beginning of the Second Analogy as a prelude to Kant's puzzle about the house whose sides are seen successively. The representations we obtain as we walk around the house occur successively, but we do not wish to say that the four walls themselves exist successively. We distinguish, in other words, between the order of our representations and the order "in the object," and it is *this* meaning of 'object' that Kant wishes to elucidate. That suggests to me a concern with objectivity, not with mere intentionality.

It must be said that relation to an object in George's sense of intentionality would be an excellent starting point for a transcendental argument. Relation to an object in the sense of objectivity would be an excellent conclusion. Or would such an argument prove too much?

Did the Sage Have No Dreams?   Suppose Kant holds that the employment of his categories is (i) necessary for our being conscious of representations and (ii) sufficient for our having objective experience—experience in which our representations "relate to an object." From these two theses it follows that there is no stretch of conscious experience that is not object-related experience. That apparent conclusion gave rise to a question asked by C.I. Lewis and to an essay by Lewis White Beck with the same title: "Did the sage of Königsberg have no dreams?"[78] It appears, in other words, that the Transcendental Deduction is guilty of proving too much.

To avoid the overly strong conclusion, we must deny either claim (i) or claim (ii). I have noted that according to some interpreters, Kant thinks his categories necessary not for bare consciousness but for thicker, richer varieties of experience. However, as long as they are necessary for anything weaker than (e8), Lewis's question will retain its bite. So, we must deny or weaken claim (ii). Here are three possible ways of doing so:

(1) Let the relation to an object conferred by the categories be mere intentionality or purported reference, not necessarily successful reference.

(2) Let the object to which a representation is related be something less than a full-fledged material object—perhaps an object$_1$ or perhaps the empirical self.

(3) Let the relation be produced not in all but only in some cases.

The first alternative is the view of George that I have just discussed, though it is not advanced by him in connection with the present problem. The second two alternatives both figure in Beck's answer to Lewis's question, as may be seen from the following:

Kant [maintains] that L-experience [Lockean experience or "the raw material of sensible impressions"] is possible only if K-experience [Kantian experience or "knowledge of objects"] is possible; but that there is L-experience (such as dreams and wild sense-data) which is not taken up into K-experience. What is not so taken up nevertheless belongs to the consciousness which must contain veridical representations of objects, and may be seen as modifications of my mind and thus as contributing to knowledge of the self as phenomenon of the inner sense.[79]

A weakening of claim (ii) along any of dimensions (1)–(3) would enable us to sidestep Lewis's question. However, any weakening will leave us with the following question: does anything remain in the Transcendental Deduction that is of interest as an argument against skepticism? Can the Deduction reach a conclusion that is antiskeptical, as many have hoped, yet not absurdly strong, as Lewis feared?

The third of our weakenings is the only one that leaves a Transcendental Deduction with much antiskeptical import. It would allow us the following conclusion: any conscious being must be in cognitive contact with objects$_2$ at least some of the time. That would be a significant result, though not one that entirely banishes skepticism, for the skeptic may still maintain that we never know on which occasions we are so lucky. Compare: critics of Descartes's skeptical reflections in the First Meditation sometimes argue that dreaming experience in general presupposes waking experience in general, making it impossible that one's whole life should be a dream. But that leaves undisturbed the skeptical contention that one can never know at any given time whether one is then awake or dreaming.

In the next section, I examine a notable recent attempt to extract antiskeptical results (more or less in line with our third weakening) from the Transcendental Deduction.

I. Strawson's Objectivity Argument

Strawson has offered a reconstruction of the Transcendental Deduction that has the following attractive features: it offers us the conclusion that we are experiencers of an objective world, and it does so without relying on the aspects of Kant's Deduction so often found objectionable—his implausible theorizing about synthesis and the artificial trappings of the Metaphysical Deduction. Strawson offers his argument as part of his general program of disentangling analytical arguments from "the imaginary subject of transcendental psychology." It will be worth our while to see whether a cogent argument emerges from Strawson's efforts.

Strawson's argument is a commentary on the relations among three theses: the thesis of the conceptualizability of experience (CE), the thesis of the unity of consciousness (UC), and the objectivity thesis (OT). His bottom line is that CE entails UC and that UC entails OT.[80] CE, the conceptualizability thesis, is the thesis that an item can be experienced only if it is brought under a concept, made the topic of a judgment, or recognized as having some general character—these three conditions being equivalent (pp. 25, 72, and 244; parenthetical page references in the rest of this section are to Strawson's *The Bounds of Sense*). This principle is analytic of what I have been calling thick experience—the grades from (e4) up. For Strawson it is likewise analytic: it is a "standard-setting definition of what is to count as 'experience'" (p. 25).

Kant, of course, would agree with CE. He may even, as I have shown, subscribe to a stronger, synthetic version of CE: nonconceptual modes of consciousness, besides not deserving the title 'experience', would be "nothing to us" if they occurred at all.

UC, the thesis of the unity of consciousness, is the thesis that any series of diverse elements constituting the experience of a single subject S must be such that it is possible for S (a) to know that there is a subject to whom all the elements belong or, as Strawson sometimes also puts it, (b) to ascribe all the elements to himself as his own experiences (pp. 24, 93–94, and 98). Ending (a) corresponds roughly to my (u6), (b) roughly to (u7).[81] The differences between the two turn out not to matter for Strawson's argument. What turns out to be crucial is a requirement not highlighted in (u6) or (u7): that the elements be conceptualized *as experiences*, regardless of whether they are ascribed to oneself as in (b), or merely to a single subject as in (a), or even to nothing at all.

The objectivity thesis, OT, is the thesis that any series of diverse elements constituting the experience of a single subject S must contain such unity as to make them experience of an objective world. Experience of an objective world is explicated by Strawson as involving the following four features:

(i) it is experience of objects that are distinct from the experience of them (p. 24);

(ii) it is experience of objects that are topics of objectively valid judgements, that is, judgements that are true or false independent of the occurrence of whatever experiences issue in the judgements (pp. 24 and 73);

(iii) it is experience of objects that can be other than they seem (pp. 101 and 107); and

(iv) it is experience of objects such that the temporal order of the objects can be other than the temporal order of the experiences of them (p. 98).

Strawson seems to regard the four conditions I have collected and numbered as more or less equivalent or coming together as a package deal. Some of them do clearly entail others; for example, (iv) obviously entails (i). But I do not think they are all equivalent. To cite just one instance to the contrary, (ii) does not entail (i), since a judgement can have truth conditions that transcend the occurrence of any experiences even if the objects it is about just are experiences. Consider, for example, the subjunctive judgment that if experience e1 were to occur, experience e2 would follow. I leave it to the reader to work out the remaining logical relations among the four conditions.

The four conditions admit of both a phenomenalist and a realist interpretation. I believe that Kant would accept all four, but only under a phenomenalist interpretation. For example, he would certainly agree that much experience is objective in sense (ii), insofar as the truth of the judgment 'there is a house on the hill' is not entailed by the particular experiences that lead me to make it; nonetheless, he would regard its truth as supervening on a more inclusive body of truth about the other experiences available or forthcoming to me and to others. In a similar vein, he accepts objectivity in sense (iv), but only because he operates with a phenomenalist analysis of objective time order: 'the sides of the house are simultaneous, though the experiences of them are successive' means 'the experiences of the sides are obtainable in any order'. (This is part of Kant's argument for the Second Analogy of Experience, the topic of chapter 9.) He can even accept condition (i), insofar as virtual objects, as constructions out of experiences, are not identical with any experiences.[82] But Strawson intends his objectivity thesis to have a realist interpretation. This is clear (among other places) from page 91, where he says that the objects of which he speaks are not only distinct from the experiences of them, but are also irreducible to any patterns of experiences. This is one reason why his argument promises to deliver a more exciting conclusion than Kant's.

I can now state Strawson's argument. In overall outline it is very simple:

1. CE implies UC.
2. UC implies OT.
3. CE is true.
4. Therefore, OT is true.

Most interpretations of the Transcendental Deduction, including the one I have offered above, take the unity of consciousness as Kant's starting point and the conceptualizability of experience (in a nonanalytic version) as one of the conclusions derived from it. Strawson reverses this direction of derivation, making CE the deeper premise. "What features," he asks, "can we find to be necessarily involved in any coherent conception of experience solely in virtue of the fact that the particular items of which we become aware must fall under (be brought under) general concepts?" (p. 72).

The burden of Strawson's case consists in the subsidiary arguments for the entailments claimed in premises 1 and 2, to which I now turn.

From UC to OT. Strawson begins by arguing that UC implies OT, bringing CE into the picture only later. He argues for this implication by arguing for its contrapositive: by considering a putative variety of experience (sense-datum experience, as he calls it) that would violate OT and arguing that such experience would also violate UC.[83]

The key feature of a sense-datum experience, as far as Strawson's argument goes, is that it violates the first condition of objectivity: in a sense-datum experience there is no distinction between object and act, between the datum itself and our awareness of it.[84] As Strawson puts it, just as the *esse* of sense data is their *percipi*, "so their *percipi* seems to be nothing but their *esse*" (p. 100). How, then, he goes on to ask, could a collection of sense data have unity of consciousness? There could be no act of awareness by which they are all apprehended, for there are no acts over and above the objects at all. In other words, we cannot depict a sense-datum experience as follows

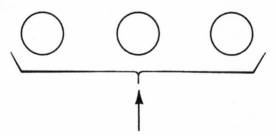

because the act gets "absorbed" into the object. Instead, it seems that we can have only

which looks very much like a disconnected heap.[85]

Strawson also argues in a similar vein that there is a "deeper level of difficulty" with the hypothesis that experiences are exclusively of the sense-datum sort (pp. 100–1); namely, they would violate CE. The reason is apparently the same as before: if there is no awareness over and above the object, then *a fortiori* there is no conceptualizing awareness.[86]

To Strawson's argument as so far presented, there is a natural objection. Sense-datum theorists need not be seen as collapsing the act into the object; they may be construed instead as collapsing the object into the act. It is not that any possible awareness of the datum gets sucked into the datum, as into a black hole; it is rather that the object is nothing apart from the awareness, in the sense that its existence consists in the act's occurring in a certain way. (Compare the discussion on virtual objects in chapter 1, section D.) The diagram, therefore, should not be of circles without arrows, but of arrows without circles. And once that is granted, what prevents us from adding further arrows to the picture, directed on the original arrows either individually or in sheaves?

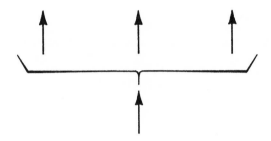

In other words, what prevents us from admitting apperception alongside perception, and with it the potentiality for unity of apperception? The same suggestion would enable us to deal with the "deeper difficulty" about CE, since the added acts could be acts of conceptualization.

Strawson is aware of the possibility I have just raised. Indeed, it seems to be precisely what he exploits in his argument that CE implies UC, to which I now turn.

From CE to UC.   The argument that CE implies UC must be extracted from a passage as cryptic as any to be found in Kant. Speaking of the difficulty of satisfying the requirements of CE in a sense-datum experience (how can you have the duality of recognition and item recognized if act and object collapse?), Strawson writes as follows:

The way out [of the difficulty just mentioned] is to acknowledge that the recognitional component, necessary to experience, can be present in experience only because of the *possibility* of referring different experiences to one identical subject of them all. Recognition implies the *potential* acknowledgement of the experience into which recognition enters as being one's own, as sharing with others this relation to the identical self. It

> is the fact that this potentiality is implicit in recognition which saves the recognitional component in a particular experience from absorption into the item recognized . . . even when that item cannot be conceived of as having an existence independent of the particular experience of it. (p. 101)

What Strawson is getting at seems to be something along the following lines.[87] A train of experience that consisted exclusively of sense data could not satisfy CE, for (as claimed in the argument from UC to OT) there is no awareness of sense data over and above the data themselves. *A fortiori*, there is no conceptualizing awareness of sense data. This is evidently what Strawson means when he says that the conceptual or recognitional component, if the items to be conceptualized are sense data, would get "absorbed" into the items to be recognized. So, we must *add* something to a train of sense data to obtain experience of which CE is true—but what? Strawson's answer is that it is nothing short of "the *possibility* of referring different experiences to one identical subject of them all" and the "*potential* acknowledgement of the experience into which recognition enters as being one's own. . . ."

One puzzling thing about this passage is why the mere *possibility* of acknowledging an experience as one's own should enable the recognitional element in experience to be reinstated. As Rorty notes, "[O]ne would think that this possibility must be actualized."[88] I therefore henceforth ignore Strawson's qualifications about possibility and potentiality. His argument may then be encapsulated as follows. Wherever there is experience satisfying the demands of CE, there is a duality of item recognized and the recognition of it. If an experience *has* no object distinct from itself (as Strawson takes to be the case with sense-datum experience), it must therefore *be* an object for an act distinct from itself. This further act must recognize the experience as an experience bound up with others in the history of a single self; we thus satisfy the requirement of CE (as imposed on a sense-datum experience) only by meeting the further requirements of UC.

If this is Strawson's argument, I have three critical observations to make. First, Strawson has not given us a *general* argument from CE to UC, but only a more limited argument from CE *as applied to sense-datum experience* to UC. More accurately, what he has offered is an argument that a sense-datum experience can be part of a larger whole of experience satisfying CE only if the larger whole satisfies UC. The argument does not show that *objectual* experience could satisfy CE only by satisfying UC. For example, if the objects being experienced and conceptualized were houses and trees, they would obviously not have to be conceptualized as experiences and therefore not as experiences of a single subject, and so on. But perhaps Strawson's more limited result will suffice for his purposes. Assuming that sense-datum experience is what any experience falling short of objectivity would amount to, he has shown that CE & −OT entails UC, which still combines with his other premises to yield the following valid argument: (1') CE & −OT → UC, (2) UC → OT, (3) CE, therefore (4) OT.[89]

Second, even if we restrict our attention to sense-datum experience, why must the added stratum of conceptualization classify the component experiences as experiences belonging to one subject, or even as experiences at all? The items to be conceptualized *are* experiences, to be sure, but why must they be conceptualized *as* experiences?[90] Why can't an experience be judged to be of a certain qualitative sort ('this is blue' or 'this hurts'), or to be similar to another experience, or to have preceded another experience, without any thought to the effect that experiences are what these episodes are? In effect, I am raising the possibility of consciousness without self-consciousness, even if the latter is construed not as consciousness of a self, but simply as consciousness of experiences conceptualized as such. It seems to me that Strawson has simply not made out his case that sense-datum experience could meet the demands of CE only by meeting those of UC.[91]

Third, it has now become clear that we need a new argument for the implication from UC to OT. The original argument was the "absorption" argument—the argument that the elements of an OT-violating sense-datum experience would absorb into themselves any acts of awareness whereby unity of consciousness could be constituted or recognized. But now, it appears, Strawson has acknowledged that such unity could be constituted or recognized by superadded acts of higher order awareness. (It is only the first-order acts that get absorbed.) So, how now do we make the case for objectivity?

The Final Argument.   The answer is to be found in an argumentative passage on pages 107–8 that seems to displace the original argument from UC to OT. Here is the heart of it:[92]

> For "This is how things are (have been) experienced *by me* as being" presupposes "This is how things are (have been) *experienced* as being"; and the latter in turn presupposes a distinction, though not (usually) an opposition, between "This is how things are experienced as being" and "Thus and so is how they are." (p. 108)

The I-thought 'it is *I* who had experiences a, b, and c' thus turns out to be a dispensable thought for Strawson; what is important is only a weaker thought contained within it, namely, that a, b, and c are all experiences. To this Strawson adds that for anyone to understand what it is for a, b, and c to be experiences, he must grasp the distinction between seeming and being and thus have the concept of items that are objective in the sense of condition (iii). The argument from UC to OT thus finally boils down to this:

1. If UC is true, any experiencing subject knows what an experience is.
2. Anyone who knows what an experience is grasps the distinction between seeming and being.
3. To grasp that distinction is to have the concept of an objective item.
4. Therefore, if UC is true, any experiencing subject has the concept of an objective item.

Now I take stock. Is not the conclusion much weaker than we were originally led to hope? We were promised an argument for the objectivity thesis—for the thesis that any experience worthy of the name (satisfying CE and thus, according to Strawson, UC) must be experience of an objective world. I initially took this to imply that there *are* objective items—items that can exist unperceived, that can be other than they seem, that can have an order different from the order of the experiences of them, and so on. It now appears that Strawson has shown much less: any experiencer must *have the concept* of an objective world, or must conceive of some of his experiences as being experiences of objective items.[93] As far as I can see, Strawson has done nothing to show that any of the objectivity conditions (i)–(iv) are actually satisfied. He has shown only that subjects of experience must believe them to be satisfied or, more weakly yet, have the concepts requisite for such belief. Is that not much less than we were promised? To put the point in Kant's terms, Strawson may have answered the *quid facti* (what concepts must experiencers operate with?), but not the *quid juris* (do these concepts have legitimate application?).

The gap I am now complaining about is precisely the gap that Barry Stroud has complained about in transcendental arguments generally: they only show that if we are to have experience (or meaningful discourse or whatever), then we must have certain concepts or beliefs—not that the concepts must be instantiated or that the beliefs must be true.[94] Stroud goes on to suggest that the gap could be closed by invoking the following verificationist principle: if we genuinely possess a certain concept, if a given notion makes sense to us, then it must be possible for us to know that it applies or know that it does not apply (by way of knowing that criteria for its application are, or are not, fulfilled). He observes finally that once we have adopted such verificationism, we may employ it to refute skepticism directly, without need of transcendental arguments, since if a skeptic says that we cannot know whether there are objective particulars, he denies a precondition of the meaningfulness of his own thesis.

To what Stroud has said, I add this: the external-world skepticism that is refutable if verificationism be true is only what Kant calls problematic idealism, the thesis that the existence of objects outside us in space is doubtful and indemonstrable. Dogmatic idealism, which holds the existence of objects outside us in space to be false and impossible, is untouched: the dogmatic idealist could say it is false that we cannot know whether there are objective particulars, for we can know that there are not.[95] So, with or without verificationism, Strawson's objectivity argument does not prove the existence of an objective world.

Let me end by noting that what Kant says in one place about the concept of a cause seems equally apposite regarding the concept of an objective particular:

> [If the concept of cause rested only on subjective necessity] I would not then be able to say that the effect is connected with the cause in the object, that is to say, necessarily, but only that I am so constituted that I cannot think this representation otherwise than as thus connected. This is exactly what the sceptic most desires. (B168)

8

Substance and the First Analogy

> All appearances contain the permanent (substance) as the object itself, and the transitory as its mere determination, that is, as a way in which the object exists.
>
> Kant, *Critique of Pure Reason* (A182)

The stretch of the *Critique of Pure Reason* containing Kant's proofs of the First and Second Analogies of Experience has been hailed as "one of the great passages in modern philosophy."[1] This chapter and the next are devoted to the exposition and critical assessment of Kant's proofs.

A. Two Concepts of Substance

Kant defines 'substance' as that which can exist only as subject, never as predicate (see B149 and B288). Here, of course, the terms 'subject' and 'predicate' mark an ontological distinction between kinds of entity, not a grammatical distinction between types of linguistic item, so we might (in first approximation) restate his definition by saying that a substance is a bearer of properties that cannot itself be borne by anything. This is a perennial definition of substance, to be found in Aristotle, Descartes, and Leibniz before Kant and in Russell and McTaggart after him.[2] For a closer approximation, I believe we must understand Kant's definition in such a way that we exclude from the category of substance not only *properties* (items exemplified by other things), but also what Spinoza called *modes* (items whose existence consists in the exemplifying of properties by other things). A good example of a mode is my fist, which bears properties without itself being a property, but which neither Kant nor Spinoza would classify as a substance. The reason is that the existence of my fist consists in my hand's being closed; it is a thing whose existence consists in the exemplifying of properties by something else. Such things, though not "adjectives" (i.e., properties), have an adjectival rather than a substantival mode of being.[3]

Kant thinks that the definition of substance so far given (that which exists only as subject, never as predicate) does not enable us to apply the notion in experience, for we are "ignorant of any conditions under which this logical pre-eminence may belong to anything" (A243/B301). For us to be able to apply the category, it must be *schematized*, or provided with a rule that lays down empirical conditions for its application. The schematizing rules for the categories all have the general form 'apply C to x iff x has T', where T (the schema) is some temporal characteristic. For example, Kant schematizes the category of cause (the unschematized concept of which is simply the concept of a ground) by means of the rule 'apply the concept of cause to x iff there is an event y such that x precedes y and events of x's type are always followed by events of y's type' (A144/B183, A243/B301). The rule for substance is 'apply the concept of substance to x iff x is permanent, that is, exists throughout the whole of time' (A143/B183, A241/B300).

Kant's theory of schematism prompts the following question: is the schema for a category meant to *replace* its original definition, or to *supplement* it? I take the answer to be the latter.[4] If that is right, the schematized category of substance is the concept of something that is *both* (i) an ultimate subject and (ii) an everlasting thing.

Following Bennett, I henceforth use 'substance$_1$' to mean something that exists only as subject and 'substance$_2$' to mean something that exists at all times.[5] The schematized category of substance will then be the concept of something that is both a substance$_1$ and a substance$_2$; I shall designate this conjunctive notion by 'substance' without subscript.

B. The First Analogy

To each of Kant's categories there is supposed to correspond a synthetic and *a priori* "Principle of Pure Understanding" that employs that category. The principle employing the category of substance is the First Analogy of Experience, which Kant states in the B edition as follows: "In all change of appearances substance is permanent; its quantum in nature is neither increased nor diminished" (B224). Unfortunately, this formulation is defective in two ways. If the principle employs the schematized category, the first clause is analytic, not synthetic as it is supposed to be.[6] Moreover, the second clause appears to conflate the First Analogy with the principle of the conservation of matter, a principle Kant argues for in the *Metaphysical Foundations of Natural Science*, but not in the *Critique of Pure Reason*.[7]

We get a better statement of the First Analogy in the summary paragraph Kant inserted in B at the beginning of the Second Analogy:

> The preceding principle has shown that all appearances of succession in time are one and all only *alterations*, that is, a successive being and not-being of the determinations of substance which abides. . . . All change (succession) of appearances is merely alteration.

To understand what Kant is saying here, we need to pay attention to his technical use of the terms 'alteration' and 'change'.[8] A helpful explanation occurs in the following passage:

> Alteration is a way of existing which follows upon another way of existing of the same subject. All that alters persists, and only its *state*

changes. Since this change thus concerns only the determinations, which can cease to be or begin to be, we can say, using what may seem a somewhat paradoxical expression, that only the permanent (substance) is altered, and that the transitory suffers no alteration but only a *change*, inasmuch as certain determinations cease to be and others begin to be. (A187/B230–31; see also A32/B48)

Thus, to change is to come into being or go out of being, and to alter is to acquire or lose a property. Kant would say that when an autumn leaf turns from green to gold, the colors change and the leaf alters. Similarly, when I open my clenched fingers, my fist changes (ceases to be) while my hand alters (acquires a new configuration).

I may now give a brief and exact formulation of the First Analogy:

1A. For any x, if x changes, there is a y such that (i) y is a substance and (ii) x's change is an alteration in (or of) y.

Thus, the ceasing to be of the fist is the opening up of the hand, and so it is with all other changes.[9] For short, all change is alteration of substance.

C. The Backdrop Argument

How is the First Analogy to be proved? I begin by discussing the Backdrop Argument,[10] which occurs in the opening paragraph of the First Analogy section in B. Never having been able to make much headway with this argument, I do not attempt a complete reconstruction of it. Instead, I quote a few relevant lines of it and then note three criticisms to which it seems vulnerable:

All appearances are in time; and in it alone, as substratum . . . can either coexistence or succession be represented. . . . Now time cannot by itself be perceived. Consequently there must be found in the objects of perception, that is in the appearances, the substratum which represents time in general; and all change or coexistence must, in being apprehended, be perceived in this substratum, and through relation of the appearances to it. But the substratum of all that is real, that is, of all that belongs to the existence of things, is *substance*; and all that belongs to existence can be thought only as a determination of substance. (B224–25)

The leading idea is that we need substance as a backdrop against which changes are perceived.

Now for the criticisms. First, Kant rejects time itself as the backdrop on the ground that it is not perceivable, but his own best candidate for substance is not perceivable either. We do not perceive the matter that undergoes transformation from wood to ashes or from caterpillar to butterfly; we only conceive of it.

Second, granting the need for a backdrop, why must it be permanent? This is the question on which critical discussion of the Backdrop Argument has tended to focus. Coming to Kant's aid on this point, Allison and Walsh have contended that if there were no permanent things, there would be "a rupture in the unity of time."[11] I take the unity of time to consist in this: all events belong to one connected temporal order, which means that any two events are such that either one begins before the other or they are simultaneous. I cannot myself see any reason why the absence of permanent things would lead to the disunity of time. You might as well say that unless there were some omnipresent or all-pervading object (the ether, perhaps), there would be a rupture in the unity of space—two items in space that were not spatially related to each other.

Third, even granting the need for a permanent backdrop, why would changes have to be alterations *in it*? This is a lacuna in Kant's argument that has gone largely unnoticed. What the argument proves at most is that every change takes place *against* the backdrop of something permanent, but it does not prove that any change is an alteration *in* that permanent something, or even that it is an alteration in anything at all.

Let the sun be hung as permanent backdrop in the sky: things under the sun are still free to pop into and out of existence as they please, violating the maxims *gigni de nihilo nihil* and *in nihilum nil posse reverti*. Yet it is clear that Kant wants the First Analogy to vindicate these ancient principles (see A186/B229). For this purpose, the Backdrop Argument is seriously wanting.

D. From Substance$_1$ to Substance$_2$

By what other argument might the First Analogy be proved? I propose to answer this question by focusing first on the relation between 1A and the apparently weaker thesis 1A':[12]

> 1A'. For any x, if x changes, there is a y such that (i) y is a substance$_1$, and (ii) x's change is an alteration in (or of) y.

This proposition is *prima facie* weaker than 1A, since there is no stipulation that the thing that alters be a substance (with its built-in implication of permanence). I express 1A' briefly by saying all change is alteration of substance$_1$.

Some commentators (e.g., Bennett[13] and Dryer[14]) concede 1A' to Kant but go on to object that the move from there to 1A is a *non sequitur*. They claim that change need be alteration only of something relatively enduring, not of something absolutely permanent.[15] But I now argue to the contrary that if we concede 1A' to Kant, we give him everything that is needed to establish 1A.

In the argument that follows, I use the following principle, which relates the conditions of a thing's existing to the conditions of its beginning or ceasing to exist:

> *Principle P*: If x's existence consists in y's having some property, then x's coming into or going out of existence consists either in (i) y's acquiring or losing that property or (ii) y's coming into or going out of existence with the property. (E.g., if the existence of a fist consists in a hand's being closed, then its ceasing to be is either the opening of the hand or the hand's ceasing to be.) Conversely, if x's coming into or going out of existence consists in y's acquiring or losing a property, x must be adjectival upon y; it must be either a property of y[16] or something whose existence consists in y's having some property.

Principle P follows from two truisms: (i) if it is necessary that x exists iff y has F, then it is necessary that x comes to exist iff it comes to be that y has F; and (ii) it comes to be that y has F iff either y acquires F or y comes into being already in possession of F. Similarly for ceasing to be, *mutatis mutandis*.

Now for the promised argument from 1A' to 1A:

1. For any x, if x changes, there is a y such that (i) y is a substance$_1$, and (ii) x's change is an alteration of y. (This is 1A', our premise.) Let y* be the item that alters in some arbitrary case of change. What must be shown is that y* is not merely a substance$_1$ (which is true *ex hypothesi*) but also a substance$_2$ and thus a substance.

2. Assume y* is *not* a substance$_2$, that is, that at some time it changes (= comes into or goes out of being).

3. For some z, z is a substance$_1$ and y*'s change is an alteration in z. (This follows from 2 and a reapplication of 1.)

4. For some z, y* is adjectival on z. (This follows from 3 and the converse half of Principle P.)

5. y* is not a substance$_1$ after all. (This follows from 4 but contradicts 1. Hence, 2 is false.)

6. y* is a substance$_2$ (from 2–5 by reductio).

7. For any x, if x changes, there is a y such that (i) y is a substance and (ii) x's change is an alteration in y (from 1–6).

From the premise that all change is alteration of substance$_1$, it is thus easy to derive the conclusion that all change is alteration of substance$_2$ and therefore of substance.[17] I turn now to examination of the premise.

E. The Anchoring Argument

And how might we argue for the premise? I propose now to examine the relationship between 1A' and something apparently weaker yet, namely, 1A":

1A". For any x, if x changes, there is a y such that x's change is an alteration in y.

For short, all change is alteration of *something or other*. We now no longer stipulate that the something even be a substance$_1$.[18]

On the face of it, 1A" makes a weaker and more plausible claim than 1A'. Consider the ceasing to be of my fist that occurs when I unclench my fingers: that change is an alteration of my hand, but perhaps my hand is not a substance$_1$ any more than my fist is; perhaps it is only a certain organic arrangement of flesh and bone. Perhaps flesh and bone are not substances$_1$, either, but only modes of their constitutent particles; and so on.

And so on, but how far? Our purported example of an alteration that is not an alteration of substance$_1$ points immediately to a premise that, if added to 1A", would yield 1A'. As the reader will guess, the premise is this: there cannot be infinitely descending chains of modes, chains nowhere anchored in substances$_1$. If this is granted, we can show after all that all change is alteration of substance$_1$.

Suppose x is a mode of y and y in turn of z. That means that x's existence consists in y's being F and that y's existence (as well as its being F) consists in z's being G. By a kind of transitivity that is plainly operative here, x's existence will consist in z's being G. By the first half of principle P above, x's ceasing to exist will therefore consist either in z's ceasing to exist or in its ceasing to be G. That is, x's ceasing to exist will be an alteration (or perhaps a change) not only in its immediate substratum, y, but also in its proximate substratum, z, as well as in whatever substrata lie further down. If somewhere in the downward series there must be a substance$_1$ (which is what the new premise tells us), it will follow that every change in x is an alteration or a change in this substance$_1$. But a substance$_1$ cannot change, for its change (by 1A″) would have to be an alteration, and there is nothing further down for its alteration to be an alteration *of*. Therefore, every change in x must be an alteration in some substance$_1$. Q.E.D.

One refinement is needed in the argument just given. What we really need to exclude is not an *infinite* downward series of modes, but an *ungrounded* series of modes, one not anchored anywhere in substances$_1$. An infinite series of modes would be all right, provided its members were grounded in something outside the series. To see the formal possibility of this, consider that a line may be composed of shorter lines and these of still shorter ones *ad infinitum*, while at the same time every line in the series is composed of points.[19] In analogous fashion, there could be modes that were adjectival on further modes *ad infinitum*, as long as every mode in the series was also adjectival on a substance$_1$. I may sometimes speak of the groundedness assumption as an antiregress assumption, but bear in mind that ungroundedness, not infinity per se, is what it excludes.

What now are the credentials of the grounding assumption? I think the issue turns in part on whether one regards modes as mere logical constructions, existing only in a manner of speaking, or as supervenient entities, existing robustly even though dependently on other entities. In the former case, modes without substances$_1$ would be out of the question indeed—they would be constructions without materials, or fictions without realities. In the latter case, we are invited to contemplate infinite downward chains of dependence of entities that are real each step of the way. This may still boggle the mind, but is not so clearly out of the question.[20]

What is Kant's own attitude toward our antiregress assumption? Is there any basis in his philosophy for accepting it? I mention one basis that he *cannot* have. Suppose one held that (a) adjectival entities are always adjectival on the parts of the matter composing them, and (b) there cannot be parts within parts forever without there being ultimate parts. It would follow that there cannot be modes of modes forever without there being ultimate subjects, or substances$_1$. In his discussion of the Second Antinomy, however, Kant denies the need for ultimate parts of matter. He thus rejects premise (b) of the argument just stated. Moreover, the fact that he accepts ungroundedness in the series of parts may make one wonder whether he would or could insist on groundedness in the series of modes.[21]

On the other hand, some of his remarks suggest that he would indeed insist on groundedness in the series of modes. He speaks of accidents or determinations as "way[s] in which the existence of a substance is positively determined" (A187/B230); he also says that "accidents could not exist outside one another, in the absence of substance" (A435/B463). These certainly suggest a principle of "no modes without substances$_1$."

There is even one passage that hints at an argument similar to the argument of the present section:

> How are we to conclude directly from the action to the *permanence* of that which acts? . . . [A]ccording to the principle of causality actions are always the first ground of all change of appearances, and cannot therefore be found in a subject which itself changes, because in that case other actions and another subject would be required to determine this change. (A205/B250)

Kant is here rejecting a regress, but I am not sure whether it is a regress to deeper substances (as in the Anchoring Argument) or a regress to "lateral" substances (as in the causal regress that theories of immanent or agent causation seek to cut off).

F. Two Arguments from Verifiability

I have shown that Kant can prove 1A if he uses 1A′ as a premise, and that 1A′ may itself be derived from the weaker 1A″ together with an antiregress assumption. But how about 1A″? What reasons can be given for accepting it?

Kant's only attempt to establish anything like 1A″ that I can find occurs in the following passage:

> A coming to be or ceasing to be that is not simply a determination of the permanent but is absolute, can never be a possible perception. For this permanent is what alone makes possible the representation of the transition from one state to another, and from not-being to being. These transitions can be empirically known only as changing determinations of that which is permanent. If we assume that something absolutely begins to be, we must have a point of time in which it was not. But to what are we to attach this point, if not to that which already exists? For a preceding empty time is not an object of perception. But if we connect the coming to be with things which previously existed, and which persist in existence up to the moment of this coming to be, this latter must be simply a determination of what is permanent in that which precedes it. (A188/B231)

This argument seems to involve the following steps. (1) Suppose we know by perception that a thing x has come into being (or gone out of being, in which case a parallel argument could be given). (2) This requires us to perceive that x exists at some time t2 and also to have perceived that x did not exist at an earlier time t1. (3) Since we cannot perceive an empty time, there must be something else, y, that existed at t1. (4) x must be a "determination" of y (a property of y or something whose existence consists in y's having some property). Therefore, (5) x's coming into being is an alteration in y.

I am not concerned just now with Kant's claim in the passage that y must be permanent. I am concerned rather with the rationale for step 4, which appears simply to be a *non sequitur*. Why must x be a "determination" at all, and why in any case of y or anything existing at t1?[22] Kant gives us scarcely a clue. I consider four proposals for plugging the gap, two in this section and two more in sections G and H.

The first proposal, which was suggested to me by a discussion of Dryer's,[23] runs as follows. To know by perception that an item has come into being, we must know that at an earlier time it did not exist. That is, we must have knowledge of a negative empirical proposition. The possibility of such knowledge has sometimes perplexed philosophers. According to one view, we can know a negative empirical proposition (e.g., that this is not green) only via inference from a positive proposition (e.g., that this is red) together with a principle of incompatibility (e.g., that whatever is red is not green). Now suppose that what needs accounting for is our knowledge that a particular state of hotness did not exist at t1. What would be the requisite positive proposition? *Coldness existed at t1* will not do, since it is perfectly compatible with *hotness existed at t1*. To get incompatibility, it might be claimed, we need for our positive proposition something like *coldness existed as a property of object O at t1*. This would enable us to know by inference that hotness did not exist as a property of O at t1. If we also knew that hotness did exist as a property of O at t2, we would know that a particular state of hotness had come into being. But then O would have altered, from being cold to being hot. The general conclusion might be drawn that we can know by perception that something has come into being only if the coming into being is an alteration in something else.

One difficulty with the foregoing argument is that the positive propositions need not be of the form 'x existed as a property of y'; they could be of the form 'x existed in place p'. Another difficulty is that, as Russell suggests, some negative empirical propositions may be epistemologically basic and thus in no need of derivation from positive propositions.[24] Russell's candidates for negative-yet-basic status include such propositions as 'I am not now perceiving hotness', which could serve as evidence for the nonexistence of hotness in the vicinity of the perceiver.

However, the routes to negative knowledge just indicated do not take us as far as we want to go. To know that an item has just come into being, we must know that it did not exist *anywhere* a moment ago—not merely that it did not exist in the place where it now is or that it did not exist in the vicinity of the perceiver—for we must be able to rule out the possibility that the newly perceived item has *moved* to its present location.

This consideration naturally brings me to the second proposal for filling the gap in Kant's argument. Arthur Melnick has suggested that, in the passage I quoted near the beginning of this section, Kant may have wished to argue as follows:[25]

1. It is empirically verifiable that S2 came into being at t2 only if it is empirically verifiable that S2 did not exist anywhere at t1.
2. It is empirically verifiable that S2 did not exist anywhere at t2 only if for some S1, there is a law implying that if S2 existed anywhere at t1, it existed where S1 existed.
3. If there is such a law, then S1 and S2 are connected as states of a single object (Melnick says 'substance').
4. Therefore, it is empirically verifiable that S2 came into being at t2 only if its coming into being is an alteration in something else.

I find premises 2 and 3 in this argument dubious. The idea behind premise 2 is that in order to know that S2 did not exist anywhere at t1, we would have to have performed the impossible task of scanning the entire universe—unless there were a law limiting the number of places we would have to look. But why must the law tie S2 to another item or kind of item? Why not simply a law saying that items of S2's kind are never subject to rapid transport? That would limit our area of search to the neighborhood of S2 at t2. As for premise 3, there is a law implying that if an infant existed anywhere just before its birth, it existed where its mother did, but it is by no means obvious that mother and child are connected as states of a single thing.

Thus, neither of our proposals yields a convincing argument. But that is not their only drawback: even if successful, they would establish something too weak for Kant's purposes. Both arguments are attempts to show that a necessary condition of someone's *perceiving* or *verifying* that a change has occurred is that the change be an alteration. To show this would be to show that all perceived or verified changes are alterations. Coupled with the antiregress assumption of the preceding section, this would imply further that all perceived changes are alterations in substances$_1$. Call this proposition 1A'*. To see that 1A'* is too weak for Kant's purposes, go back to the argument I presented for 1A. In step 3 of that argument, it was inferred that if y* (the subject of an alteration underlying some change) ever itself changes, its change must be an alteration. That inference is sanctioned by 1A', but not by 1A'*. With only 1A'* to rely on, we would have to know that y*'s change was *perceived* before we could conclude it was an alteration. But are there not unperceived changes, for example, changes that occurred in the remote past or in quantum particles too tiny to see? We thus see that the substitution of 1A'* for 1A' opens up a gap in the argument. There is nothing to rule out the creation or annihilation of a substance$_1$ as long as it happens when no one is looking.

Perhaps you will say I am forgetting that Kant is an idealist, who believes that everything that happens supervenes on human perceivers and their states, and for whom any change is therefore a perceived or verifiable change. No, I am not forgetting that, but the objector is forgetting the distinction I drew in chapter 1, section E, between mind-dependence and knowledge-dependence. To say that all changes are parasitic on changes in the states of human perceivers is not automatically to imply that all changes are perceived or verifiable.

G. Carving Out Substances

In this section and the next I consider two more proposals for plugging the gap in Kant's argument for 1A'', one implicit and the other explicit in Bennett's treatment of the First Analogy. The gap, recall, is this: given that x came into being at t2 and that y existed through the interval spanning t1 and t2, why must we assume (as Kant does) that x is a mode of y and that x's change is consequently an alteration in y?

The first answer is simple and bold: we are free to carve the world into things and properties in any way we like. What to treat as a property or mode and what to treat as a substance$_1$ is not forced upon us by the facts themselves, but is a matter wholly up to us. If this is so, then we are free to regard any change as an alteration, as long as something existed before or after the change for it to be an alteration of.

I do not know whether Bennett actually subscribes to the view I have just stated, but I find a hint of it in his tale of the porcelain pig that vanishes without a detectable trace.[26] He says we *could* treat the pig as adjectival on its surroundings (the air, the bystanders, etc.) and its change therefore as an alteration, though he demurs at saying we *should* do so. Whatever Bennett's position may be, a view like this has been commended to my attention by Felicia Ackerman.[27]

If the carve-it-as-you-like-it view is right, many of the philosophical problems discussed in this book are really pseudo-problems. Take, for example, the issues of absolute versus relational space and of the relative priority of matter and space. You can have space be adjectival on matter (Leibniz), matter adjectival on space (Spinoza), neither adjectival on anything (Newton), or both adjectival on some third thing (Kant, who makes both adjectival on minds from 1770 on). All the views are equally tenable.

The carve-it-as-you-like-it view prompts a number of questions. Are there any limits on permissible ways of partitioning the world into substance and mode? Can we treat item x as a mode of anything we please, or must its subject at least exist at the same place? How about at the same time—could everything that exists now be a mode of a substance$_1$ that existed only several centuries ago? Do we even need substances$_1$ at all, or might we make everything a mode—either because we have modes of modes all the way down, or because we have modes without subjects on the model of 'it is raining'?

Assuming that we do accord at least one item the status of substance$_1$, we are free under the carve-it-as-you-like-it view to select any item and make that one the *only* subject. Thus, we can be cheap monists: we can say that JVC is the only substance, and that everything else is adjectival on him. To say that the Eiffel Tower is part of the universe along with JVC is only to say that JVC eiffeltowerizes.

Here is a dilemma for cheap monism: 'JVC eiffeltowerizes' is either mere shorthand for something whose logical form is 'JVC bears R to the Eiffel Tower', or else 'eiffeltowerizes' is a semantically unstructured predicate whose meaning is not a function of the meanings of its syntactical constituents. In the former case, we are countenancing the Eiffel Tower in our ontology alongside JVC after all, even though our terminology disguises the fact. In the latter case, how are we to account for the easily recognized validity of inferences such as that from 'JVC eiffeltowerizes' to 'JVC towerizes'? Its logical form is 'a is F; therefore, a is G'—not one of the generally accredited patterns.

Arguments like that of the last paragraph have some currency in recent philosophy, and I do not go into full-scale evaluation of them here. I simply note that a good Kantian would not find the second horn difficult or dangerous to grasp. She already countenances lots of synthetic *a priori* principles and inferences that are not sanctioned solely by the logical or semantic structures of antecedent and consequent or premise and conclusion. So, 'whatever eiffeltowerizes also towerizes' might be just one more synthetic *a priori* truth.[28]

I do not attempt to settle here the question of whether the carve-it-as-you-like-it view is tenable. Instead I pass to the question of whether the view can really be put to good use in Kant's behalf. The principle lets us treat any item as a mode and any change as an alteration; we can therefore make 1A″ come out true.[29] But recall that 1A″ was of interest to us as a lemma to secure 1A′, that every change is an alteration of substance$_1$, and recall that Kant defines substance$_1$ as that which is always subject and never predicate. I am not sure that the concept of a substance$_1$ has application anymore if *everything* is treatable as a mode. Wouldn't that mean that nothing is a substance$_1$, absolutely speaking?[30]

The current defense of Kant admittedly fits with one strain of his thought—that certain features not belonging to reality *an sich* do nonetheless belong to the phenomenal world, precisely because we conceptualize or construct the world in the way we do. That, of course, is a characteristically idealist pattern: certain constraints on how things can be are up to us rather than being up to the world. At the same time, however, the defense runs counter to another important strain in Kant's thought—that certain ways of doing things (of experiencing or conceiving) are necessary and nonoptional, that we could not have experience at all if we operated otherwise. For all the present defense shows, we do not have to believe in substances$_1$ or substances$_2$—we could be Buddhists or Heracliteans. So, I think Kant should decline the assistance I have offered him in this section.

H. The Kant-Frege View

Bennett offers a deep and interesting reason for holding that all changes are alterations: the so-called Kant-Frege view, according to which existence statements are properly made only with quantifiers and have to be expressible in the form '∃xFx'.[31] In connection with the ontological argument in chapter 12, I examine the credentials of this thesis and the reasons for ascribing it to Kant. My concern in this section is only with its logical consequences.

Here is the gist of what Bennett has to say:

> It has not been widely noticed that the Kant-Frege view entails that there is no legitimate way of reporting the occurrence of an absolute existence-change [i.e., an existence-change that is not merely an alteration on the part of something else].
>
> Dependent existence-changes are all right. The birth of a blush, say, can be reported in the form (−Fa at t1 and Fa at t2)—John was not blushing at t1 and was blushing at t2. . . .
>
> But how can we state in Fregean form that a hydrogen atom, say, absolutely went out of existence between t1 and t2?[32]

Our best try, Bennett thinks, would be to say

(*)   ∃x(Hx at t1 & Lx at t1 & −Lx at t2),

where L is some essential or unlosable property, for example, location. His objection to (*) is that it is incomplete unless we also *say* that L is an essential property, that is, that any hydrogen atom necessarily has L at every time at which it exists:

> There's the rub: how, in Fregean form, are we to capture 'it exists'? I think it cannot be done, and so I do seriously regard the Kant-Frege view as constituting a logical objection to the notion of an absolute existence-change.[33]

I don't think Bennett has quite put his finger on the problem posed by the Kant-Frege view. Note to begin with that if there were a problem about how to say 'it exists', it would equally be a problem for the reporting of *dependent* existence-changes. That John was blushing one moment and not the next does not entail that any blush went out of existence unless we make further assumptions—for example, that blushes cannot exist unblushed and cannot pass from one face to another (as a "wave" moves through the spectators at a baseball game). We need to *say* that a particular blush b is essentially such that it exists only if John blushes—and for that we need 'it exists' again.

What is the problem about 'it exists'? Contrary to what Bennett's remarks may suggest, there is none in *expressing* it. There is a standard way of saying 'x exists' with quantifiers, namely, '$\exists y(y = x)$'. ['$\exists F(Fx)$' would also do, on the assumption that only what exists has properties.[34]] Given this way of expressing existence, we can go on to say what it is for L to be an essential property of Hs:

(D) $(x)(Hx \rightarrow \Box[\exists y(y = x)$ only if $Lx])$

So, the problem is not one of expressibility. (Existence is a *logical* predicate, as Kant says.) The problem, if there is one, is that some of the things we might say using the notion of existence are *false*. Thus, (*) above, given the assumption that L is essential in the sense defined, turns out to imply

(**) $\exists x(Hx$ at t1 & Lx at t1 & $-\exists y[y = x]$ at t2).

In standard quantification theory, the third conjunct is false, since it contradicts the theorem $(x)\exists y(y = x)$, that is, that everything exists. As I show further below, that is part of the truth in Kant's claim that existence is not a *real* predicate.

The moral to be drawn so far is at least this: we cannot truly say that anything ceases to exist through *its* losing a property essential to it, for nothing ever loses an unlosable property. We can say, however, that x ceases to exist through the loss *by something else* of a property essential to the existence of x, as the blush ceases to exist when John stops blushing. And if that is the only way to report existence-changes, Bennett is right: the Kant-Frege view makes all ceasing to be alteration.

But the proper moral is more radical than the preceding paragraph allows; we have not yet gone as far as we need to go to comply with the Kant-Frege view. Suppose we say the blush exists if and only if John blushes; add to this that John is no longer blushing, and it follows that the blush no longer exists. *But that is false*, for reasons already noted: in standard quantification theory we cannot say of anything that it does not exist without implying '$\exists x(x$ does not exist)', and this formula is contradictory given the Kant-Frege view. To avoid this problem,[35] we have to say 'the blush does not exist' does not really report the aftermath of an existence-change but is *mere shorthand* for 'John is not blushing'. Compare: we can accept 'the average plumber has 3.2 children' as true, provided it is shorthand for 'the number of plumber's children divided by the number of plumbers is 3.2', but the sentence does *not* express a truth if taken literally as saying of a certain subject that it has a fractional number of children. Similarly, we can accept 'the blush no longer exists' as true if it is shorthand for 'John is no longer blushing', but not if we take it literally as saying of a certain subject that it no longer exists.

The more radical conclusion to which we are now driven has two significant corollaries. (1) 'All change is alteration' should not be taken to mean 'there are changes, but they all consist in alterations'; instead it must mean 'really, there are no changes; what we describe as such are only alterations'. (2) Correlatively, items such as blushes become logical constructions, rather than supervenient entities: a blush isn't a new entity that bursts on the scene when John blushes; it is just a fictitious reification of what happens to John's face. Talk of it is a *façon de parler*.

These points are noteworthy because they have larger consequences when combined with results reached above. In section D, I showed that 1A (all changes are alterations of substances) may be derived from 1A' (all changes are alterations of substances$_1$). In section E, I showed that 1A' may be derived in turn from 1A" (all changes are alterations of something or other) together with the assumption that there cannot be a regress of entities adjectival on other entities *ad infinitum*. I also observed in section E that the antiregress assumption is compelling indeed if adjectival entities are accorded the status of mere logical constructions. I have shown in the present section that Bennett makes a strong case for holding that the Kant-Frege view rules out absolute existence-changes, thus implying the truth of 1A". I have also shown just now that if the Kant-Frege view rules out absolute existence-changes, it also forces us to regard adjectival entities as constructions—*thus underwriting the antiregress assumption*. So, it appears that if the Kant-Frege view is correct, it yields everything we need to establish the First Analogy.

I. Summary of Results to Date

The results to this point may be summarized in the following diagram.

1A: Every change is an alteration of some substance.

↑

1A': Every change is an alteration of some substance$_1$.

↑

| 1A": Every change is an alteration of some entity or other. | The antiregress assumption: There cannot be a series of modes not grounded in any substance$_1$. |

The Kant-Frege view:
To say that something exists is to say that some concept is instantiated.

Reading down from the top, we trace our route in sections D, E, and H, beginning with 1A, proceeding to the apparently weaker theses 1A′ and 1A″, and ending with the Kant-Frege view. But along the way I argued for entailments corresponding to all the upward arrows. Consequently, reading up from the bottom, we have a cogent argument for the full-strength First Analogy.

J. Individual Essences

There is one entailment in the foregoing chart that may merit further scrutiny, the one represented by the lower lefthand arrow and purportedly established by Bennett's argument that the Kant-Frege view rules out absolute existence-changes. Is there any way around Bennett's argument?

Recall that according to Bennett, there is a problem with the following attempt to report the annihilation of a hydrogen atom in Fregean style:

(*) $\exists x (Hx$ at t1 & Lx at t1 & $-Lx$ at t2)

Here it is to be understood that L is a property essential to Hs, say, location. The problem as I developed it above is that (*) together with D implies the falsehood that something to which L is essential lacks L at t2.[36] We might try to avoid this problem by making a slight change in the quantificational structure of (*):

(#) $\exists x (Hx$ at t1 & Lx at t1) & $-\exists x (Lx)$ at t2

Given that L is essential to Hs, (#) implies as desired that an H existed at t1 that no longer exists at t2, and it does this without implying the falsehood just noted. It does, however, imply another falsehood—that at t2 nothing whatever is located. To avoid the new problem, let's make a second modification: keep the logical form of (#), but replace reference to the shareable essence L with reference to an *individual* essence, S:

($) $\exists x (Hx$ at t1 & Sx at t1) & $-\exists x (Sx$ at t2)

An individual essence of an item x (sometimes also known as a haecceity or "thisness") is a property necessarily possessed by x if it exists and *not* possessable by anything *other* than x.[37] The third conjunct, $-\exists x (Sx)$, now merely denies the existence of a single individual; it is not the sweeping falsehood as before in $-\exists x (Lx)$.

Now that we have had recourse to individual essences, it is no longer necessary to retain the clause 'Hx' above. The report of annihilation simplifies to

(%) $\exists x (Sx$ at t1) & $-\exists x (Sx$ at t2).

It may seem that (%) does everything we want: (i) it *does* imply that something went out of existence, (ii) it does *not* represent this existence-change as an alteration in something else, and (iii) it does *not* imply any of the falsehoods that foiled our earlier attempts. If so, the Kant-Frege argument against absolute existence-changes would break down, or at least require bolstering.

One way of bolstering it would be to add a premise denying that there *are* any such properties as individual essences. The existence of such properties is, after all, controversial, and both Kant and Frege have reasons for excluding them. For Frege, the reasons have to do with his thesis that every proper name has the sense of some definite description. For Kant, the reasons have to do with his view that only intuitions, not concepts, are *singular* representations— that is to say, representations that specify their objects uniquely.[38] So, the attempted end run around the Kant-Frege argument suggested above could be blocked by adding an antihaecceities assumption.

On further reflection, however, it becomes apparent that the Kant-Frege argument goes through even if we *admit* haecceities, for (%) cannot really have all of features (i), (ii), and (iii). If 'S' expresses an individual essence (say, Socrateity), then (%) does indeed have feature (i): it implies that Socrates has gone out of existence. But recall the radical moral reached above in the discussion of John's blush: any statement to the effect that something (e.g., a blush) has gone out of existence is false unless construed as shorthand for saying that something else (e.g., a face) has altered. The reasons for saying this are no less compelling when we are dealing with something apparently so substantial and unblushlike as Socrates. So, (%) cannot have features (ii) and (iii) both: if, in implying that Socrates went out of existence, it manages not to imply a falsehood, that can only be because his going out of existence is really an alteration.

What could the alteration be an alteration *of*? I see two main alternatives. (1) We could construe Socrateity as the property of being so arranged as to constitute our nominal Socrates and let the transition from $\exists x(Sx)$ to $-\exists x(Sx)$ be an alteration in the matter of which our Socrates is composed. That, of course, would be very much in line with what Kant says must really be going on. (2) We could do away with matter altogether and let the transition from $\exists x(Sx)$ to $-\exists x(Sx)$ be an alteration in the form or property of Socrateity itself: first it is instantiated and then not. On this alternative, being instantiated would be a monadic property of the form, not a relation of it to any matter. We would thus arrive at a pure Platonic ontology in which (to put it paradoxically) forms are the only substances.[39]

Frege does not explicitly adopt any such purely Platonic ontology—when a concept is instantiated, he speaks of an object falling under it, which sounds like a relational view of instantiation. But a monadic view of instantiation may be implicit in the reasons he has for saying that existence-statements are about concepts, not objects. There is also a hint of the Platonic view in the phrasing I have used from Bennett: to say that something exists is to say that some concept is instantiated. If it is *only* to say that some concept is instantiated, then concepts are the true substances.

Our Platonic alternative, (2), thus preserves the letter of 'all change is alteration', leaving the Kant-Frege argument unchallenged. It even preserves the letter of 'all change is alteration of substance.' But it is not Kantian in spirit. Kant was no Platonist; for him, properties are not substances, but ways in which substances exist. Alternative (1) is therefore the truer from a Kantian perspective.

K. Phenomenal Substances

It is time to confront Kant with a problem. I believe the argument just given is a reasonable argument for the First Analogy—reasonable, at any rate, for someone who is not a transcendental idealist. But it may not be an argument that establishes what Kant wants it to, given that he *is* a transcendental idealist.

For Kant, the entire world in space and time is a world of appearances, and according to the interpretation advanced in this book, appearances are virtual objects. Virtual objects are logical constructions out of perceivers, and perceivers are noumenal beings. But logical constructions are precisely modes and not substances—they are adjectival on the entities out of which they are constructions. So, it appears that for Kant, nothing in the world of space and time qualifies as a substance, and there can be no hope of establishing the First Analogy in its intended sphere. Genuine substances, it now appears, are to be found only in the noumenal realm.

There are several passages in which Kant himself seems to acknowledge what I have just said. At A277/B333 he says, "Matter is *substantia phaenomenon*," and at A265/B322 he says the same of substances in space. Baumgarten's *Metaphysica*, which Kant used as a text in his courses and from which he took much of his terminology, defines *phaenomenon substantiatum* as an accident taken to be a substance.[40] It thus appears that Kant himself realized that everything in the phenomenal world really has the status of accident or mode. One piece of confirmation comes at A360, where he says that matter, being a species of representations, reduces to "determinations" of the thinking self, in which case its mode of being is adjectival rather than substantival. Karl Ameriks has collected several other passages (some from Kant's lectures) in which Kant says or implies that true substances are to be found not among appearances, but only among things in themselves.[41]

It also appears that the demands of the argument charted out in section I could be met by noumenal substances. I require there that modes must ultimately be modes of substances, hence that changes must ultimately be alterations in substances; this requirement is adequately met by noumenal substances. So, what can Kant do to argue for phenomenal substances?

There are actually two problems that need to be distinguished here: (1) how even to *define* phenomenal substances, given that, strictly speaking, everything in the phenomenal world is a mode, and (2) how to *prove* that there must be phenomenal substances so defined.

I mention here two solutions to the definition problem. First, it could be that the schema for a category is meant after all not to enrich its meaning but to replace it (contrary to what I said in section A). In that case, we should drop the requirement that a phenomenal substance be a substance$_1$ or a nonadjectival being; it need only be a permanent being or substance$_2$. (Of course, the permanence must be carefully understood. To achieve a representation of permanence, we do not need a permanent representation, as Kant notes at Bxli.) Several passages suggest this. A242–43/B300–1 says we cannot apply pure categories, but only the categories as schematized. Kant's wording here implies a conjunctive treatment: "If I leave out permanence (which is existence in all time), nothing remains in the concept of substance save only the logical representation of . . . something which can exist only as subject and never as predicate." But at the same time, if schematizing is to facilitate application, it seems that the schema must replace the original meaning. If I do not know how to apply 'exists only as subject', how can I apply the conjunction 'exists only as subject & exists at all times'? Adding the schema as a second conjunct would not help at all unless it renders the first conjunct superfluous.

A second approach, which I like better, takes a leaf from Descartes's definitions of substance. According to Descartes's official definition of a substance, it is "a thing which exists in such a way as to depend on no other thing for its existence." Descartes confesses that by this definition, there is strictly speaking only one substance, namely, God, and that the term cannot be applied univocally to God and his creatures. Yet he wants to apply the term also to things other than God, so he introduces a secondary sense of the term 'substance': a created substance is something that needs only the concurrence of God to exist and does not depend on any other created thing.[42] Perhaps Kant could say in similar fashion that a substance$_1$ strictly speaking is something that is not adjectival on anything else, whereas a phenomenal substance is something that is not adjectival on any other phenomenal being. A snowball, being adjectival upon a suitably shaped quantity of snow, would not count as a phenomenal substance, but the matter of which it is composed arguably would.

So much for making sense of the notion of a phenomenal substance; the task remains of arguing that there must be such things. Here I think Kant is in trouble. The best Kantian argument I could assemble for the existence of substances (the argument charted in section I) is not an argument for phenomenal substances in particular. The antiregress assumption it invokes could be satisfied by the existence of those noumenal substances on which all phenomena are adjectival.

If Kant wants to show that there are items deserving the name of substance in the phenomenal world, he needs an argument better than the best I have identified in this chapter. In the absence of such an argument, perhaps the import of the First Analogy must be more like that of the Third Antinomy. Perhaps substance, like freedom, is something to be found only in the noumenal world.

9

Causation and the Second Analogy

> [W]e derived the principle that everything
> that happens has a cause from the condition
> under which alone a concept of happening
> in general is objectively possible—namely,
> by showing that the determination of an
> event in time, and therefore the event as be-
> longing to experience, would be impossible
> save as standing under such a dynamical
> rule.
>
> Kant, *Critique of Pure Reason*,
> (A788/B816)

The Second Analogy of Experience is the principle that every event has a cause or, as Kant also puts it, "everything that happens, that is, begins to be, presupposes something upon which it follows according to a rule" (A189). It was Hume's doubting of this principle that aroused Kant from his dogmatic slumber, and it is Kant's attempt to prove the principle that constitutes the core of his reply to Hume. There have been many attempts to reconstruct and defend Kant's proof, but in my opinion none of them is successful.[1] In this chapter I offer a critique of the best such reconstruction known to me—that of Lewis White Beck in his "Six Short Pieces on the Second Analogy of Experience."[2]

A. Background

What Hume doubted and Kant sought to demonstrate is the principle

(a) every event has a cause.

To this end Kant tried to show

(b) we can *know* that an event has occurred only if we also know that it had a cause.

In the first five sections of this chapter, I discuss Kant's attempt, as aided by Beck, to prove (b). In the last section, I take up the question of whether a proof of (b) would amount to a proof of (a).

Kant defines an *event* (or alteration) as a transition from one to another of two "opposite" or contrary states of a substance; in his words, it is "a successive being and not-being of the determinations of substance" (B232). Here I use Beck's notation '[AB]' to symbolize an event, 'A' and 'B' standing for two opposite states in one and the same substance.

When we perceive an event [AB] we have a perception or representation of A followed by a perception or representation of B; again following Beck, I here symbolize such a sequence of perceptions as '$[A_rB_r]$'.

Having a sequence of perceptions, though necessary for knowing through perception that an event [AB] has occurred, is not *sufficient* for it, since the perception of an unchanging object may also involve a sequence of perceptions. To cite Kant's famous example, as I walk around a house I see its sides successively, but that "the manifold of the house is also itself successive . . . is what no one will grant" (A190/B235). This fact is the starting point of Kant's proof. He argues that when we have a perception sequence we can know there is an event corresponding to it only if we also know that the event had a cause.

The fact that the external reality corresponding to a succession of perceptions may itself be nonsuccessive, though unproblematic for common sense, was deeply puzzling to Kant. The reason lies in his transcendental idealism. As I have been interpreting it, transcendental idealism is a variety of phenomenalism. Kant explains it as follows: "By transcendental idealism I mean the doctrine that appearances are to be regarded as being, one and all, representations only, not things in themselves" (A369). For 'appearance' in this context we can substitute 'empirical object'—the term is meant to cover houses, ships, and all the furniture of the earth. Now, what does it mean to say that objects are "only representations?" In chapter 6, section C, I distinguished two possibilities. On the one hand, objects may be *literally composed* of representations, as in Berkeley and Hume; on the other hand, they may be *logically constructed* from representations, as in Ayer and Lewis. In the latter case, objects are not identified with patterns of representations, but any statement about objects is held to be logically equivalent to some statement solely about representations. As before, I will call the former doctrine *ontological* phenomenalism and the latter *analytical* phenomenalism.[3]

The *Critique of Pure Reason* contains many explicit statements of ontological phenomenalism. For example, Kant says that an object like a house is a *sum* of representations (A191/B236) and that matter is a *species* of representations (A370). But we also find occasional implicit statements of analytical phenomenalism, such as the following:

If we enquire what new character *relation to an object* confers upon our representations, what dignity they thereby acquire, we find that it results only in subjecting the representations to a rule, and so in necessitating us to connect them in some one specific manner; and conversely, that only in so far as our representations are necessitated in a certain order as regards their time-relations do they acquire objective meaning. (A197/B243)

In other words, to say that there is an object corresponding to our representations is only to say that our representations are related appropriately to one another.

Kant himself seems not to have been clearly aware of the difference between the two phenomenalisms, and he sometimes operates with ontological phenomenalism when analytical phenomenalism would serve his purposes better. This is especially so in the third paragraph in B of the proof of the Second Analogy, the place in which Kant first makes his point about successive apprehension of a nonsuccessive manifold. Most of this paragraph is laden with ontological phenomenalism. Kant says that objects (or appearances) *are* representations and even tends (here as elsewhere in the proof of the Second Analogy) to use the terms 'appearance' and 'representation' interchangeably. But if there is no distinction between appearances and representations, neither can there be a distinction between the *order* of appearances and the *order* of representations. One could not say that the sides of the house, though seen successively, exist simultaneously, and the opening wedge of Kant's argument would thus be lost.

Kant worries about this, putting the problem to himself as follows: "What, then, am I to understand by the question: how the manifold may be connected in the appearance itself, which yet is nothing in itself?" (A191/B236). To bring out the paradox here, I would give this question the following gloss:[4] how can the manifold of appearances be ordered otherwise than the manifold of representations, given that the manifold of appearances is *nothing apart from* the manifold of representations? The answer he comes up with is this:

> Appearance, in contradistinction to the representations of apprehension, can be represented as an object distinct from them only if it stands under a rule which distinguishes it from every other apprehension and necessitates some one particular mode of connection of the manifold. (A197/B243)

We can see this as a step toward analytical phenomenalism, but Kant never breaks completely free of ontological phenomenalism.[5]

Had Kant more clearly seen that transcendental idealism could take the form of analytical phenomenalism, his problem would not have been so intractable. He could have reformulated it as follows: how can the fact that a manifold consisting of A and B is nonsuccessive be expressed in statements about representations A_r and B_r, given that A_r and B_r are successive? To this question his ensuing paragraphs suggest the following answer: to say that A and B were simultaneous even though the corresponding perceptions A_r and B_r were successive is to say that A_r and B_r could have been obtained in the opposite order, whereas to say that A and B were successive is to say that A_r and B_r could *not* have been obtained in the opposite order.[6] To use a term common in the secondary literature, a manifold consisting of A and B is simultaneous if the sequence $[A_r B_r]$ is *reversible*, and successive otherwise.[7]

If this were Kant's solution to the puzzle, the task remaining would be to argue that if a perception sequence $[A_r B_r]$ is irreversible, the corresponding event [AB] that is constructed out of it has a cause. It would then follow that all events constructed out of perception sequences—which, if analytical phenomenalism is true, is to say *all* events—have causes. The trouble is that it is notoriously difficult to find a valid argument leading from '$[A_r B_r]$ is irreversible' to '[AB] had a cause'.[8]

It is at this point that Beck comes to Kant's rescue. He interprets Kant as an analytical phenomenalist[9] but does not reconstruct his argument along the lines suggested by the above two paragraphs. That is, he does not think that succession "in the object" can be defined in terms of the irreversibility of perceptions, or that Kant argues directly from '[A_rB_r] is irreversible' to '[AB] had a cause'. What further ingredients he thinks must be added to the argument we see in the next section.

B. Beck's Argument

So that we may have it before us, I here reproduce Beck's reconstructed argument verbatim:[10]

1. That the state A in the object precedes the state B in the object (that is to say, that the objective event symbolized as [AB] occurs) is a sufficient condition, given perceptual isomorphism,[11] for the irreversibility of the sequence of the perceptual representations of the states A and B. (The sequence of representations is symbolized as [A_rB_r].)
2. But knowledge of [A_rB_r]-irreversibly is not a sufficient condition for knowledge that [AB] occurs, and a fortiori not a sufficient condition for knowledge that [AB]-irreversibly occurs. For:
    (i) it could be the case that A and B are coexistent but such as to be always perceived in the order [A_rB_r], which is interpreted as [A_rB_r]-irreversibly; or
    (ii) it could be the case that B precedes A, if perceptual isomorphism fails.
3. In order to know, or to have good reason to believe, that [AB] occurs, given knowledge of [A_rB_r]-irreversibly, I must know or have good reason to believe both that:
    (i) A and B are opposite states of a substance (B233), in order to rule out 2(i); and
    (ii) [AB]-irreversibly, in order to rule out 2(ii).
4. Knowledge of, or a sufficient reason to believe, 3(i) is sufficient reason to know or justifiably believe that there is an event (a change of states of an object) but not sufficient reason to know or believe that the event is [AB] and not [BA] (B233).
5. But I know, or have sufficient reason to believe, that [AB] occurs.
6. Therefore I know, or have sufficient reason to believe, that [AB]-irreversibly occurs (3(ii)).
7. [AB]-irreversibly is the schema of causation.
8. Therefore to know, or to have sufficient reason to believe, that [AB] occurs, I must know, or have sufficient reason to believe, that A is, or contains, a causal condition of B.

C. Irreversibility

To appraise this argument, we must determine the meaning of its middle term, 'irreversible'. It seems to me that three distinct meanings of this term figure in Beck's writings, one of them having to do with what must be true on a *given* occasion and the other two with what must be true on *any* occasion.

The first sense of 'irreversible', which I shall call irreversibility$_1$, is illustrated by Kant's example of seeing a ship move downstream. First, I have a perception of a ship at a place higher in the stream, then a perception of the ship at a place lower in the stream. On *another* occasion I might have perceptions similar to these in the reverse order: there is nothing to prevent my seeing a ship moving backward upstream. But on *this* occasion, given that I was watching a ship move downstream, I could not have had similar perceptions in the reverse order. The order of my perceptions was "bound down" or determined by the order of the positions of the ship. This determination is a *causal* affair—the movement of the ship caused me to have my perceptions in the order I did. More generally, let us say that a sequence [XY] is irreversible$_1$ if and only if something causes X and Y to occur in the order they do.[12]

The second sense of 'irreversible', which I shall call irreversibility$_2$, characterizes any sequence that not only must occur in a given order on a given occasion, but also must occur in the same order on *any* occasion. We may define this sense as follows: a sequence [XY] is irreversible$_2$ if and only if no token of Y's type ever immediately precedes or occurs at the same time as a token of X's type. This can be abbreviated to 'never Y before X'.[13]

The third sense of 'irreversible', which I shall call irreversibility$_3$, characterizes any sequence of which the first member must be followed by the second on all occasions when the first occurs. We may define this sense as follows: a sequence [XY] is irreversible$_3$ if and only if every token of X's type is immediately followed by a token of Y's type. This can be abbreviated to 'always Y after X'.

Irreversibility$_2$ and irreversibility$_3$ are logically distinct notions. A sequence can be irreversible$_2$ without being irreversible$_3$, as is the sequence [being a plum, being a prune]: nothing is ever a prune before it is a plum, but something can be a plum without ever being a prune. Conversely, a sequence can be irreversible$_3$ without being irreversible$_2$, as is the sequence [running fast, breathing hard]: running fast is always followed by breathing hard, but breathing hard may in turn be followed by more running fast.

Each of these senses figures at one place or another in Beck's "Six Short Pieces." His official definition of 'irreversible' gives it the meaning of 'irreversible$_2$':

When we speak of an irreversible sequence we mean the following: any R' not distinguishably different from R1 except that we are conscious of it at a different time, and any R" not distinguishably different from R2 except that we are conscious of it at a different time, are in the same temporal relationship to each other that R1 and R2 were.[14]

In other words, the sequence [R1R2] is irreversible if and only if no tokens of the same types as R1 and R2 ever occur in an order different from that in which R1 and R2 occurred. It follows that if R1 precedes R2 irreversibly, R2 never occurs before R1.

The definiens of Beck's definition does not imply that R1 and R2 are irreversible$_3$. It does, of course, imply that on any occasion when a token of R1's type and a token of R2's type *both* occur, the R1-token must be followed by the

R2-token; but it leaves open the possibility that an Rl-token may occur on some occasion when no R2-token occurs at all.

A second meaning of 'irreversible' is demanded by Beck's premise 7, which says that irreversibility is the schema of causation. This cannot be true unless what is intended is irreversibility$_3$, for Kant tells us that the concept of cause is schematized as "the real upon which, whenever posited, something else always follows" (A144/B183). In other words, the schema for causation is 'always Y after X', which is irreversibility$_3$.

Irreversibility$_2$ is neither necessary nor sufficient for causation. It is not necessary, for a clap of thunder can be followed by a bolt of lightning perfectly similar to the one that caused it. Nor is it sufficient, for as I have already shown, it is not sufficient for irreversibility$_3$.

It is also worth noting that irreversibility$_1$ is not sufficient for causation. To say that [XY] is irreversible$_1$ is to say that something caused X and Y to occur in the order they did, but this does not imply that X is the cause of Y. To think otherwise would be to commit the fallacy Lovejoy attributed to Kant and labeled as "one of the most spectacular examples of the *non-sequitur* which are to be found in the history of philosophy."[15]

A third meaning of 'irreversible' is demanded by Beck's premise 1, which says that A's preceding B is sufficient (given perceptual isomorphism) for [A$_r$B$_r$]'s being irreversible. This would not be true if the sense of 'irreversible' were that of 'irreversible$_2$', as Beck points out.[16] If A$_r$ and B$_r$ are perceptions of successive positions of the ship moving downstream, I might have perceptions of the same types in the opposite order on another occasion. Nor would the premise be true if the sense of 'irreversible' were that of 'irreversible$_3$', for the same reason and others besides (e.g., on another occasion the ship might stay put, or I might look away before it moves downstream). If there is any sense in which [A$_r$B$_r$] is irreversible, it can only be irreversibility$_1$ (more specifically, irreversibility$_{1'}$—see n. 12): A$_r$ and B$_r$ are caused to occur in the order they do by the movement of the ship. That this is what Beck has in mind is confirmed by his putting in the proviso about perceptual isomorphism, which is "the condition that there be no relevant difference in the modes of causal dependence of A$_r$ on A and of B$_r$ on B."[17]

The suggestion that [A$_r$B$_r$] is irreversible$_{1'}$ is problematic, however, if Kant is an analytical phenomenalist. The idea that external objects and events may cause internal perceptions is acceptable enough if we are realists, maintaining an ontological distinction between physical objects or events on the one hand and perceptions on the other. But what becomes of it if physical objects and events are reduced to perceptions? I maintain that it is no longer tenable. Nothing can be *both* a logical construction out of perceptions *and* a cause of those same perceptions. To see this, remember that for an analytical phenomenalist the statement 'there is a ship in the stream' must be equivalent to some such statement as 'anyone who looked toward the stream would have ship-perceptions'. (This is only a crude first approximation, but for the point at hand it will suffice.) Now, can the fact expressed by the latter statement together with S's looking toward the stream be a *cause* of S's having ship-perceptions? No, for the alleged cause *logically entails* the alleged effect. But as Kant and Hume both insist, particular causal connections are logically contingent. (I return to the question of what causes our perceptions in chapter 10, section G.)

Let me sum up. The sense of 'irreversible' captured by Beck's definition is irreversibility$_2$, the sense required for the truth of premise 7 is irreversibility$_3$, and the sense required for the truth of premise 1 is irreversibility$_1$ (although if I am right this is at the cost of inconsistency with a phenomenalist interpretation of Kant).

One might fear that this multiplicity of meanings would issue in a fallacy of equivocation, but fortunately it does not. Neither the definition nor premise 1 is essential to Beck's argument. The definition does not occur in the same article as the one setting forth the reconstruction we are considering, and it need not be presupposed in the argument. Nor is premise 1 essential to the argument, for it is not needed in the derivation of any subsequent step. In fact, the conclusion of the argument follows from premises 3(ii) and 7 alone, the other premises serving mainly to support or clarify premise 3.[18] The crucial question, therefore, is what sense of 'irreversible' is required to make 3(ii) true.

Premise 3(ii) says that the only way to rule out B's having preceded A is to know that [AB] is irreversible. If this premise is to connect with premise 7, 'irreversible' must have the meaning of 'irreversible$_3$'. But is the premise true when so construed? I think not, for we could rule out the alternative [BA] if we knew 'never B before A', that is, that [AB] was irreversible$_2$, and I have already shown that a sequence can be irreversible$_2$ without being irreversible$_3$.

Although knowing [AB] to be irreversible$_2$ would thus be sufficient to let us rule out [BA], it is not necessary. Consider the ship again: it can move upstream as well as down, so if knowing the order of its positions to be irreversible$_2$ were necessary for knowing that it had moved, we could never know that it had moved.

If there is any sense in which the order of the ship's positions is irreversible, I think it must be irreversibility$_1$: something causes the ship successively to occupy positions upstream and downstream. Moreover, if we *knew* this, we would be in a position to rule out the possibility that the ship had been downstream first. So, perhaps there is some hope for 3(ii) if we interpret it in terms of irreversibility$_1$. The trouble is that 3(ii) would then seem not to connect with premise 7, as it must if any conclusion is validly to be drawn. But this problem may be dispelled, as I show at the end of the next section.

D. A Revision of the Argument

The conclusion reached by Beck's argument is that in order to know an event [AB] has occurred, we must know that A is, or contains, a causal condition of B. In this section I argue that this conclusion has implications Kant did not want. I then offer a revised conclusion and ask whether Beck's argument can be made to yield that one instead.

Let me begin by noting that the qualification expressed by the phrase "or contains" is of vital importance, for without it the conclusion would have absurd consequences. Recall that in any sequence [AB] that constitutes an event, A and B are *opposite* states of the same substance. Examples of sequences that meet this condition are [ship at p1, ship at p2] and [air particles still, air particles thundering]. Now consider the unqualified claim that we cannot know any such sequence to have occurred unless we know that the first member caused the second. If this were true, ships could not remain stationary, or the sky long silent. Schopenhauer charged Kant with proving the absurd result that all sequence is consequence, every *post hoc* a *propter hoc.*[19] We do not have *that* result here, but we do have the almost equally absurd result that all sequence of *opposites* is consequence.[20]

This absurdity is avoided by Beck's qualification: to know that [AB] has occurred, one must know that A is, *or contains*, a causal condition of B.[21] The still sky as such does not cause thunder but may contain lightning, which does. What does 'contain' mean here? I think at a minimum it must mean this: one state contains another just in case it is *co-instantiated* with it. In this sense any state of a substance would contain all other states the substance is in at the same time. Beck's conclusion would thus amount to this: to know that an event [AB] has occurred in a substance S, we must know that some state of S simultaneous with A caused it to enter state B.

In other words, to know that a substance has come to be in a certain state, we must know that its coming to be in that state was caused by an *earlier* state of the *same* substance. But this goes beyond what Kant himself wanted in two ways. First, it rules out *simultaneous* causation, for if the cause of the onset of B is simultaneous with A, the cause precedes the effect. But according to Kant, "the great majority of efficient natural causes are simultaneous with their effects" (A203/B248).[22] Second, it rules out *transeunt* causation—the causing of an alteration in one substance by an alteration in some other substance. But Kant wished to allow for this, too, as the Third Analogy and two of his examples in connection with the Second (the stove's heating the room, the ball's indenting the cushion) make clear.[23]

To accommodate Kant on these points, we may reformulate the conclusion as follows: to know that an event [AB] has occurred, we must know that it was caused by some other event [CD]. Here we are not ruling out simultaneous causation, for although A is followed by B, the cause of this transition may be another transition that is simultaneous with it.[24] Nor are we ruling out transeunt causation, for it is left unspecified whether the substance in which [CD] occurs is the same as or different from the substance in which [AB] occurs. Finally, we are steering clear of Schopenhauer's objection, for what we require of [AB] is that it be a *caused* sequence, not a *causal* one.

If we make this change in the conclusion, we have to adjust premise 3(ii) accordingly. The new premise, 3(ii)′, is this: to rule out the possibility that B precedes A, we must know that some event [CD] causes A to give way to B. We can put this by saying that we must know that [AB] is irreversible$_1$. The problem with this, as I showed at the end of the preceding section, is that 3(ii)′ would then apparently not mesh with premise 7, which must be put in terms of irreversibility$_3$ (now to be understood as suggested in n. 21). *But notice that we can also put 3(ii)′ in terms of irreversibility$_3$:* to say that [AB] is irreversible$_1$ is to say that there occurred some event [CD] such that the sequence [[CD][AB]] is irreversible$_3$. If we put 3(ii)′ this way, it meshes with premise 7 after all and yields the conclusion of Beck's argument as now reformulated.

Now we have a valid argument for the Second Analogy. It remains to consider whether 3(ii)' is true.

E. Two Objections

Here I discuss two objections to 3(ii)'. To set the stage for the first, let me show what 3(ii)' would say about a typical situation of the sort to which it is supposed to apply. Suppose I have a perception of a certain piece of litmus paper as blue, followed by a perception of it as red. Since red and blue are opposites, I can know that an event has occurred, but Beck would maintain that I cannot yet know *which* event it was, a turning blue or a turning red. To know that what took place was, say, a turning red, I must, according to 3(ii)', know that some other event occurred that caused a transition from blue to red.[25] But I do not need to know what this other event was; as Kant puts it, the cause of the perceived event may be "indeterminate" (A199/B244; see also A766/B794). Indeed, to hold otherwise would be to hold the absurd view that no one can ever know that an event has occurred without knowing what caused it.

The difficulty I want to raise is that it is hard to see how the absurd view is to be avoided without giving up 3(ii)' altogether, for how am I supposed to acquire the bare existential knowledge that *something* caused a turning red? How can I know that the something, whatever it was, was such as to cause a turning red rather than a turning blue? There seem to be only two answers: either (i) I know *what* the cause was—for example, that it was a dipping in acid, or (ii) I know *independently* that what I witnessed was a turning red and infer from this that something caused a turning red. But (i) gives us the absurd view we are trying to avoid, and if (ii) is true, knowing an event to be caused is not a condition of knowing it to occur, contrary to 3(ii)'.

The difficulty may be restated generally as follows. Since merely knowing of the *existence* of a cause would not settle whether what I witnessed was [AB] or [BA], knowing which of these two occurred cannot reasonably be held to require knowledge of *some* cause unless it is also held to require knowledge of *what* cause. But it is admitted that I can sometimes know that a given event has occurred without knowing what caused it; therefore, it should also be admitted that I can sometimes know that a given event has occurred without knowing that *anything* caused it.

The second objection I discuss here was raised by Lovejoy, who claimed that one can sometimes *just see* that an event is occurring.[26] If an object undergoes an alteration within your specious present, you do not first see A, then see B, then infer that the object has altered; you just see the transition from A to B. "There is therefore no occasion," Lovejoy concluded, "for appealing to anything so remote from immediate experience as the Principle of Sufficient Reason" as a criterion for distinguishing perceptions of events from perceptions of nonevents.[27]

Although Beck does not address himself specifically to Lovejoy on this point, it is clear from his reconstruction and from his reply to Murphy what he would say. He would concede that one can know on the basis of "just seeing" a transition that *an* event has occurred, but deny that one can know *which* event it was. Knowing which event occurred requires knowing (i) in what or-

der the opposite states occurred and (ii) in what *object* the transition took place, but neither these things is *schlicht gegeben*. Beck cites the possible failure of perceptual isomorphism to show that (i) is not immediately known[28] and the illusion of the moving train on the next track to show that (ii) is not immediately known.[29]

I consider first the question about the *order* in which a transition takes place. Is "just seeing" enough to determine this, or must we invoke causation in some way? Here I think both sides are partly right and partly wrong. Beck is right in pointing out that "just seeing" a transition from A to B is no *guarantee* that A really did precede B, but Lovejoy is right in maintaining that "just seeing" such a transition can be *reason enough to believe* that A preceded B and may thus amount in favorable cases to knowing that it did. An example will bear this out.

Suppose I see an apple fall from a tree. How do I know that the apple traveled from branch to earth rather than vice versa? It may be proposed that I know this only because I know that it is characteristic of apples not to fall upward.[30] But how do I know this fact about the behavior of apples? Presumably it is through induction from past experience; I have seen many apples falling earthward but none rising skyward on their own. But how do I know that all of the apples I saw falling were really falling and not rising? The doubt that appeal to the law is supposed to remove attaches equally to the particular cases from which the law must be extrapolated. There is thus a vicious circle here: knowledge of particular happenings (e.g., that this apple just fell downward) is held to depend on knowledge of general laws (e.g., that apples never fall upward), which in turn can only be derived from knowledge of other particular happenings of the same type. To avoid the circle, it must be allowed that seeing an apple fall downward stands on its own as *prima facie* evidence that the apple really did fall downward. It is not *conclusive* evidence; that is why it can on occasion be overridden by appeal to laws. But unless it were at least *prima facie* evidence, the laws themselves could never get established. In short, knowledge of laws can function negatively in such matters to correct the evidence of the senses, but need not function positively to corroborate it. Because of this, it is wrong to suggest that "just seeing" a transition from A to B always yields knowledge that A has given way to B, but equally wrong to suggest that it never does.

Now consider the question about the *object* in which a transition takes place. Is "just seeing" enough to determine this, or must we invoke causation in some way? The answer, I think, is that we do sometimes need to invoke causation, but not always, and when we do, it need not be in the way that 3(ii)' requires. Suppose that as I am sitting in a boat on a lake at night, I "just see" two lights on the shore gradually appear to move apart. The apparent motion of the lights has three possible explanations: (i) one or the other or both of the lights has really moved; (ii) neither light has moved, but my boat has, giving rise to a parallax effect; (iii) nothing has moved—the whole thing was a dream or a hallucination. Let us assume that we can rule out the last alternative without appeal to causation. (Kant, unlike Wolff, did not think the Second Analogy was needed to distinguish reality from dreams.) How am I to decide between the first two alternatives? Well, one way is to check to see whether my boat is still moored; if it is, I can conclude that one of the lights has moved. Now I would be relying here to be sure on knowledge of causes—for example, the knowledge that a moored boat does not drift. But I would not have to know that the motion I impute to the *lights* had a cause. In general, even if knowing in which object an event occurred requires having some causal knowledge, it does not require knowing that the *event in question* had a cause.

Moreover, I would maintain that in at least some cases I can know in which object an event occurred without having *any* causal knowledge. Notice that in the last example the causal knowledge that came into play was knowledge of specific causal connections. I could not have known that my boat had remained motionless merely by knowing that *something* had caused it to stay put, for such knowledge would be parasitic either on more specific knowledge of the cause or on independent knowledge of the effect. Now, knowledge of specific causal connections is based on induction from repeated pairings of previously known events.[31] On pain of infinite regress, therefore, some events must be known to occur independently of any knowledge of specific causal connections.[32] But since knowledge of specific causal connections would be required if *any* causal knowledge were, we may conclude that there must be some events that are known to occur independent of *any* causal knowledge.

Among such events are events in the mind of the observer. If I have a perception of A followed by a perception of B, it may be that I cannot know without invoking causation that an event [AB] has occurred in some external object. But at least I can know that the event $[A_r B_r]$ has occurred in *me*—that I have undergone a transition from seeing A and not seeing B to seeing B and not seeing A.[33] Surely no knowledge of causes, specific or general, is required here.[34]

To sum up, 3(ii)' is too stringent in its requirements. Knowing that an event [AB] has occurred may in some cases require knowing about particular causal relationships but does not in all cases require knowing that [AB] had some cause or other.

F. From Conditions of Knowing to Conditions of Being

I said at the outset of this chapter that Kant tries to prove (a) that every event has a cause by proving (b) that we can *know* that an event has occurred only if we know (or would be correct in thinking) that it had a cause. I have expressed doubts about the key premise in Beck's attempt to prove (b). The most I think one could hope to show along the lines of (b) is this: every event that is known to occur must have either causes *or effects*. This would be because (i) those events known to occur *indirectly* (on the basis of inference from other events) must be lawfully connected (either as cause or as effect) with those other events, and (ii) those events known to occur *directly* (on the basis of observation or remembered observation) must, as part of what it means to be observed, have effects in the mind of the observer. But I do not see how it could be proved that every event that is known to occur must have a *cause*.

Suppose, however, that this *could* be proved: how far would that go toward establishing (a)? That is the question I discuss here.

We are confronted initially with the following apparent gap between (a) and (b): (a) implies that *every* event has a cause, (b) only that every event *known to occur* has a cause. My complaint here is not that the argument fails to show that *noumenal* events have causes; it was never supposed to show that. The problem is rather that there are *phenomenal* events of which we have no knowledge, as (b) itself may be used to show: if I know that event e has occurred, (b) guarantees that e has some phenomenal cause f, but f may be an event that no one knows to have occurred. (Here, of course, we must distinguish between 'we know that e was caused by some event f' and 'some event f is such that we know e was caused by it'.) What guarantees that f has a cause?

A possible answer here is that (i) every phenomenal event, if not known, is at least *knowable*, and (ii) by showing that a necessary condition of an event's being known to occur is that it have a cause, one shows precisely that all *knowable* events have causes. Let us examine each of these contentions.

The inference embodied in contention (ii) may leave us uneasy, for it bears an uncomfortable resemblance to the obviously invalid inference from 'a necessary condition of a sound's being heard is that it strike an eardrum' to 'all audible sounds strike eardrums'. If there is a relevant difference between the two arguments, what is it?

I think the difference is this: a tree that falls in the forest with no one around to hear it makes a sound that is audible in the sense that if any normal hearers *were* present they *would* hear it. The absence of a necessary condition for its being heard—there being eardrums nearby—does not make it inaudible, for if any hearers were present this necessary condition would be instated. An event that occurs without a cause, on the other hand, cannot be said to be knowable in the parallel sense that if any observers *were* present it *would* be known. This is because the condition lacking for its being known—its having a cause— would not be instated merely by the presence of observers. Having a cause, unlike striking an eardrum, is a trait that something has throughout its duration or not at all,[35] independent of the comings and goings of observers.

Let us grant, then, that showing (b) would show that all knowable events have causes. Must we also grant (i), that all phenomenal events are (in the same sense) knowable? It might be thought that to this question analytical phenomenalism dictates the answer yes. Analytical phenomenalists have traditionally maintained that to say an unobserved event has occurred is to say that under certain realizable conditions it *would* have been observed, thus implying that all phenomenal events are at least observable.[36] The catch is that to be observable is not yet to be knowable, since as Beck's argument on Kant's behalf makes clear, witnessing an event is not always sufficient for knowing that an event has occurred. So, there does not seem to be any guarantee that all phenomenal events are knowable.[37]

In conclusion, there remains a gap between (a) and (b). Showing (b) would show that all knowable events have causes, but not that all phenomenal events have causes.

10

Noumena and Things in Themselves

> Without the thing in itself, I could not enter
> the Kantian philosophy; with it, I could not
> remain.
>> Loosely attributable to F.H. Jacobi

> With the thing in itself, I could not enter
> postmodern philosophy; without it, I could
> not remain.
>> A disenchanted student

A. The Distinction Between Phenomena and Noumena

For Kant, things in themselves are things that exist independent of human cognition; they do not depend on human beings either for their existence or for their being the way they are. Appearances, on the other hand, are things that exist only in being apprehended, and they do owe at least some of their features to the character of our cognitive apparatus.

'Noumena' and 'phenomena' are alternative terms for marking this distinction. Etymologically, a phenomenon is something that appears to the senses, and a noumenon is an entity knowable by *nous* or pure intelligence. In his Inaugural Dissertation, Kant subscribed to the rationalist creed that things in themselves are noumena in just this sense. In the *Critique of Pure Reason*, he officially renounces this belief, even though remnants of it remain. He now distinguishes two senses of the term 'noumenon'—a positive sense, in which a noumenon would be an entity knowable by nonsensible means, and a negative sense, in which a noumenon is something not knowable by sensible means. (For the distinction between the positive and the negative senses of 'noumenon', see B307–9.) He writes that we are entitled to regard things in themselves as noumena in the negative sense only. So, in its positive sense, the term 'noumenon' is not even coextensive with the term 'thing in itself'; in the negative sense, 'noumenon' may be coextensive with 'thing in itself' but is not synonymous with it. Despite all this, Kant and those who write about him often use 'noumena' and 'things in themselves' as interchangeable terms. So do I unless I give notice to the contrary.

Some of Kant's major views about noumena and phenomena may be listed as follows. (1) There certainly is a noumenal element in the world; otherwise, "we should be landed in the absurd conclusion that there can be appearance without anything that appears" (Bxxvii). (2) The noumenal element in some way affects us, giving rise to the representations through which phenomena are presented and constituted. (See, e.g., A190/B235 and *Prolegomena*, pp. 61–62.) (3) More of the world's features fall on the phenomenal side of the line than either Descartes or Locke believed. In particular, space and time (and thus nearly all of Locke's primary qualities) are merely phenomenal, space and time being "forms of intuition" rather than features of things in themselves. This, of course, is the heart of Kant's transcendental idealism. (See A26–28/B42–44 and *Prolegomena*, pp. 36–37.) (4) Things in themselves are unknowable by human beings. (See A30/B45 and A44/B62.) We can have knowledge only concerning what is given in intuition, and things in themselves are not thus given.

It is not surprising that this combination of views has struck many of Kant's readers as highly problematic. If things in themselves are unknowable, as claimed in point 4, how can Kant be in a position to affirm that they are outside of space and time, as claimed in point 3 or, indeed, that they exist at all, as claimed in point 1? Moreover, if things in themselves are nonspatial and nontemporal, what sense can we make of the supposition that they cause our representations? Point 2 thus seems jeopardized by point 3. Indeed, is it not Kant's own teaching that the categories, including causation, have no application to anything but phenomena? These are perennial sore spots in Kant's philosophy, responsible for inducing some of his successors to do away with the thing in itself. Hence the remark often attributed to F.H. Jacobi that begins this chapter.

I do not think that Kant's philosophy—or philosophy in general—is improved by jettisoning the thing in itself. In the next two sections, I say what I can by way of rebutting or mitigating some of the objections to it.

B. Classical Criticisms of the Thing in Itself

In this section I discuss two criticisms of the thing in itself that go back to Kant's own day, one stemming from the professed unknowability of things in themselves and the other from the problem of noumenal causation.

The Unknowability of Things in Themselves. The seriousness of the first difficulty is often overestimated. It is sometimes presented as though Kant falls into an outright contradiction—he says there can be no knowledge of things in themselves, then proceeds to make an impressive number of claims about them. If this is indeed what Kant does, he is open to reproach but not to a charge of contradiction. What he is guilty of is rather pragmatic paradox, the sort that is involved in any assertion of the form 'p, but I do not know that p'. Such an assertion is self-enfeebling (as someone has said), but not self-refuting. A wholesale skeptic who says we know nothing must admit that he does not know his own view to be correct, but that is not to say he contradicts himself.

Matters would be worse if Kant had claimed that talk of things in themselves must be lacking in *sense*. Such a view is sometimes attributed to Kant (notably by Bennett and Strawson[1]), but he does not on the whole espouse it. Perhaps some interpreters attribute a "noumena are nonsense" doctrine to Kant because they combine what he does often say (there can be no knowledge of things in themselves) with verificationist doctrine of their own (whereof one cannot know, thereof one may not sensibly speak—or think). The latter cannot be Kant's considered view, however, for he says he has "found it necessary to deny *knowledge* in order to make room for *faith*" (Bxxx). There is no room for faith in what is demonstrably lacking in sense.

In any case, the most charitable way to interpret Kant is to assume that when he says "there can be no knowledge of things in themselves" he is indulging in hyperbole. He must have thought at the very least that the laws of logic apply to them. And did he not think that the nonspatiality and nontemporality of things in themselves could be proved by philosophical arguments? I have examined three such arguments in this book: the argument from geometry, the argument from incongruent counterparts, and the argument from the Mathematical Antinomies. Though I found something to question in each of these arguments, Kant himself must have thought they were arguments whereby we come to know some truths about things in themselves.

So, the "unknowability of things in themselves" must be taken as subject to qualification. At the very least, we can know *analytic* truths about them. Perhaps we can also know certain *negative* facts about them, such as their nonspatiality. And I discuss in sections E and F the possibility that we can have knowledge of certain *relational* or *structural* features of things in themselves— that what we must be ignorant of is just their *intrinsic* nature.

We have yet to address the question why Kant saw fit to affirm the existence of things in themselves in the first place. The arguments for the nonspatiality of things in themselves could perhaps all be taken hypothetically—as showing us that *if* there were things in themselves, they could not be spatial or temporal. Why assume that there are things in themselves at all? One can cite at least three Kantian motives. First, he wants to account for the given or brute elements in our experience, to allow for the fact that the world is not entirely of our own making. As J.N. Findlay likes to say, experience is not a free composition, but a translation into the diction of space and time.[2] I explore this theme further in section F. Second, there is Kant's moral philosophy. He believes that the demands of morality are demands on free rational agents, and that the freedom presupposed by morality can be found only in a noumenal world. This theme looms largest in writings of Kant not considered here, but is visible in the first *Critique* in his discussion of the Third Antinomy. Finally, Kant wanted to distinguish his philosophy from that of Berkeley, and he thought the thing in itself was one important distinguishing feature. This motive for positing things in themselves is especially prominent in the *Prolegomena* (see especially remarks II and III at the end of the first part).

None of the preceding motives amounts to a proof. There is, however, one absolutely compelling reason for believing in the existence of things in themselves, already adumbrated in chapter 5. The distinction between appearances and things in themselves (as I am interpreting it) is the distinction between virtual objects and real objects—between things that exist only as objects of human apprehension and things that exist independent of such acts. If there were no things in themselves, everything would be a virtual object—that is to say, everything would owe its existence to being apprehended by a mind, or at least by a cognitive act (if one countenances the possibility of acts without agents). But what about these minds or acts? Do they owe their existence to being apprehended? Presumably not, since in that case there would be either an absurd infinite regress to ever higher acts or else an impossible feat of existential bootstrapping, some items pulling themselves into existence by virtue of their own self-apprehension.[3] Even if literal self-apprehension were deemed possible (as in some Indian philosophies), we would have to accord to "both" terms of the relation the status of existence *an sich*, for a mere content cannot do any apprehending.

I must confess that this way of proving the existence of things in themselves does not show that there are things distinct from our own selves or other conscious beings. For all that it shows, the world of things in themselves might consist entirely of Berkeleyan spirits or Leibnizian monads. But perhaps this is as it should be; though he rankled at comparisons with Berkeley, Kant would probably have acknowledged that Leibniz's monadology presents one possible model of what noumenal reality is like.

Noumenal Causation.   This is the problem that occasioned Jacobi's famous gibe, loosely quoted above. What he actually said was, "Without this presupposition [of affection by the thing in itself] I could not enter into the system, and with this presupposition I could not remain there."[4]

Here there are two separate difficulties to be considered. (1) Kant insists repeatedly that the categories have no application except to objects of experience, which are all phenomenal. So, how can he speak of things in themselves as causing our representations? (2) Things in themselves are nonspatial and nontemporal. What sense can we make of a nonspatial, and especially of a nontemporal, cause?

Kant's philosophy contains an escape clause for dealing with the first difficulty. Recall the distinction between the pure and the schematized categories. The schematized categories all have temporal conditions of applicability; for example, an event C causes an event E in accordance with the schematized category only if C is followed by E and all other events of the same type as C are followed by events of the same type as E. The schematized categories obviously cannot apply to any items that lie outside of space and time, as noumena are said to do. But perhaps Kant can allow that the *pure* categories have application to noumena. The pure category of causation is the concept of something whose existence is the ground or explanation for the existence of something else. Noumena might be the grounds of our representations (and in the Third Antinomy, of our actions) even if they are not the (schematized) causes.[5]

Indeed, there is reason to think that Kant not only may, but also must, hold that some of the pure categories have application to noumena. Consider the pure category of substance, that is, the concept of a substance$_1$, or an item having a nonadjectival mode of being. I showed in section K of chapter 8 that, strictly speaking, this concept does not apply to any phenomenon, since phenomena, as virtual objects, are adjectival on other things. But it is arguable that the concept must apply to something, on pain of an endless downward regress of modes. It must therefore apply to something noumenal.

I should also point out that if Kant's official line in the Metaphysical Deduction is to be believed, we cannot make judgments (or at least not true judgments) about anything whatever except by bringing the judged-about matters under the pure categories. An upholder of Kant's system must therefore either admit that the pure categories do apply to things in themselves, or else maintain that *things in themselves are never the subject matters of any true judgments.* But the sentence I just italicized expresses a negative and universal judgment; if the sentence is true, the corresponding pure categories must have application to things in themselves.

The upshot so far is that Kant is free to talk of things in themselves as causes, as long as causation is understood abstractly as the relation of ground to consequent, a relation that can hold between nontemporal items. But this throws us right into the second difficulty distinguished above, which I cannot do as much to alleviate. How are we to conceive of a grounding relation that holds among nontemporal realities? Our grasp of such a relation must be analogical at best. I do not say that such a relation is unintelligible or incoherent, but I do find it difficult to comprehend. If in the end we reject the idea that nonspatial and nontemporal things in themselves stand in causal relations, I would counsel that we not give up the very idea of things in themselves, or the idea that they affect us; we should give up instead the idea that things in themselves are outside space and time. That would leave open the possibility that tables and chairs and stars and electrons are things in themselves.

C. Contemporary Criticisms of the Thing in Itself

The thing in itself is the *bête noir* of much contemporary philosophy. In this section I consider a sampling of the arguments and complaints against it. The arguments to be canvassed are not all directed against things in themselves in exactly the same sense; which notion is at issue must be allowed to emerge in each case. For the most part, however, the arguments are directed against the idea of things whose existence and character are independent of our knowledge, language, or conceptual scheme. They are not necessarily directed against things in themselves in Kant's sense, which are simply things whose *esse* is not *percipi*.

First Argument: Things in Themselves Are Unknowable. I leave aside for now the question of whether unknowability is a vice and simply consider whether things in themselves are guilty as charged. I often encounter an argument that runs like this: "We can know something about an object only insofar as we stand in some cognitive relation to it; therefore, we cannot know anything about how objects are apart from our cognitive relation to them, that is, about how they are in themselves."

The premise of this argument may be symbolized thus:

P.   (F)(o)(SKFo → SRo)

That is, we know an object to have a feature F only if we bear some cognitive relation R to the object. Now, how should we symbolize the conclusion? That depends on whether the phrase "apart from our relation to them" is meant to modify "know" or "how objects are." If it modifies "know," the appropriate symbolization would be

C1.   −(∃F)(∃o)(SKFo & −SRo)

C1 has the merit of following from the premise, but it is not an exciting result. It only says we never know anything about an object o while not standing in R to it, which allows that *what* we know about o may hold of it even when we do *not* stand in R to it and might, indeed, have held of it even if we had *never* stood in R to it.

If "apart from R" modifies "how objects are," the likely symbolizations of the conclusion are

C2.   −(∃F)(∃o)(SKFo & Fo even if −SRo)

and (putting the second conjunct in the scope of the knowledge operator)

C3.   −(∃F)(∃o)[SK(Fo & Fo even if −SRo)]

C2 and C3 are reasonable renditions of 'we do not know how any object is in itself,' and both are theses with some bite. But neither thesis follows from the premise.

Second Argument: Things in Themselves Are Ineffable, Indescribable, and so on.   By way of characterizing what he takes Kant to have meant by the noumenal world, H.E. Matthews writes as follows:

> We might contrast the world as we describe it, using our conceptual framework, with the world that we thus describe, the world to which our concepts are applied. The latter world would be *ex hypothesi* indescribable, and, in a sense, unthinkable.[6]

A few simple substitutions should suffice to show what is wrong with this kind of reasoning:

> We might contrast the football as we kick it, using our skeletal framework, with the ball that we thus kick, the ball to which our foot is applied. The latter ball would be *ex hypothesi* unkickable, and, in a sense, untouchable.

The fallacy here is structurally the same as that by which some thinkers are led to believe in bare particulars or propertiless substrata, to which indeed noumenal items are sometimes assimilated. Without noticing that their conclusion contradicts their premise, such thinkers reason, "A substance can have no qualities, because it is that which *has* the qualities."[7]

Third Argument: Talk of a Noumenal World Is Self-Defeating.   The noumenal world is sometimes conceived (as in the remarks by Matthews above) as that to which we apply our concepts, that of which we seek to give adequate descriptions in our theories, and that by which these theories are made true or false. Though a noumenal world in this sense may seem indispensable, it is apparently repudiated by Nelson Goodman, who maintains that there is no such thing as a world apart from our various "versions" of it (our world-descriptions, world-depictions, and the like). Goodman is moved by the following considerations among others:

> If I ask about the world, you can offer to tell me how it is under one or more frames of reference; but if I insist that you tell me how it is apart from all frames, what can you say? We are confined to ways of describing whatever is described. Our universe, so to speak, consists of these ways rather than of a world or of worlds.[8]

> Talk of unstructured content or an unconceptualized given or a substratum without properties is self-defeating; for the talk imposes structure, conceptualizes, ascribes properties. . . . We can have words without a world but no world without words or other symbols.[9]

I believe that Goodman here perpetrates a fallacy very much of a piece with one of Berkeley's more notorious arguments. At one point, Berkeley says that he is willing to rest the entire case for his immaterialism on the following point:

> But, say you, surely there is nothing easier than to imagine trees, for instance, in a park, or books existing in a closet, and nobody by to perceive them. I answer you may so, there is no difficulty in it; but what is all this, I beseech you, more than framing in your mind certain ideas which you call books and trees, and at the same time omitting to frame the idea of anyone that may perceive them? But do not you yourself perceive or think of them all the while? This therefore is nothing to the purpose; it only shows you have the power of imagining or forming ideas in your mind; but it does not show that you can conceive it possible the objects of your thought may exist without the mind. To make out this, it is necessary that you conceive them existing unconceived or unthought of, which is a manifest repugnancy.[10]

> Is it not as great a contradiction to talk of *conceiving* a thing which is *unconceived*?[11]

Berkeley's argument has been plausibly diagnosed as resting on an illicit quantifier shift.[12] There is indeed a contradiction in "conceiving of something existing unconceived" if this means conceiving of *some particular thing* that is unconceived, a state of affairs we may symbolize as '∃x(Cx & −Cx)'. But there is no contradiction in conceiving of there being *something or other* that exists unconceived, which we may symbolize as 'C(∃x-Cx)'.[13] Berkeley has evidently confused the second with the first, putting his quantifier on the wrong side of the 'C' operator. If Goodman thinks there is something self-defeating in speaking of that which is unspoken of, or self-contradictory in conceiving of material for conceptualization that exists independent of being conceptualized, he is making the same mistake as Berkeley.

One should also protest Goodman's lumping together of the unconceptualized given and the featureless substratum. To treat these indifferently is to equate 'has no properties ascribed to it' with 'has no properties'—an absurd assimilation of the undescribed to the nondescript.

Fourth Argument: The Noumenal World Is Impoverished, Indeterminate, and so on.   This is a recurrent theme in the postrealist writings of Hilary Putnam. Here is a representative passage:

> Any sentence that changes truth value on passing from one correct theory to another correct theory—an equivalent description—will express only a *theory-relative* property of the world. . . . The fact is, so many properties of 'the world'—starting with just the categorical ones, such as cardinality, particulars or universals, etc.—turn out to be 'theory relative' that 'the world' ends up as a *mere* 'thing in itself'. If one cannot say how 'the world' is, theory-independently, then talk of theories as descriptions of 'the world' is empty.[14]

By Putnam's definition, a property P is *theory-relative* iff there are equivalent theories that differ as to whether P is instantiated. The "equivalence" of which he speaks is *epistemic* equivalence: equivalent theories are theories that are epistemically equal in the sense that every empirical datum explained by one is explained by the other and every theoretical virtue (simplicity and so forth) possessed by one is possessed in equal degree by the other. Putnam cites several examples of pairs of theories that he takes to be logically incompatible yet epistemically equivalent, such as field theory versus action-at-a-distance theory and theories that treat points as primitive entities versus theories that treat points as logical constructions (e.g., sets of nested volumes *à la* Whitehead). If Putnam is right in assessing these pairs of rivals as equivalent, then the properties of *being a point* and *being a field* will count as theory-relative.

We may now reconstruct Putnam's argument as follows:

1. A thing in itself has property P only if P is not theory-relative.[15]
2. A great many properties are theory-relative, so many, in fact, that a thing that had *only* properties that are *not* theory-relative would be drastically impoverished (indeterminate, nondescript, etc.)
3. Therefore, things in themselves are drastically impoverished (indeterminate, nondescript, etc.).

Having reached this point, one could go on to say that things in themselves do not exist (because nothing could be nondescript, etc.) or that they are not worth bothering about, so the noumenal world is (in Rorty's phrase) a world well lost.

To this argument there are two possible lines of response. The first, which Putnam calls "soft-core" realism, admits the first premise but challenges the second. It agrees that no theory-relative properties can be ascribed to objects in the noumenal world, but tries to recover enough properties underlying the theory-relative properties to give the noumenal world some character. One variant of this strategy has been advocated by C.I. Lewis:

> If relative to R, A is X, and relative to S, A is Y, neither X nor Y is an absolute predicate of A. But "A is X relative to R" and "A is Y relative to S," are absolute truths. Moreover they may be truths about the independent nature of A. Generally speaking, if A had no independent character, it would not be X relative to R or Y relative to S. These relative (or relational) characters, X and Y, are partial but absolutely valid revelations of the nature of A.[16]

A related strategy has been propounded by Max Born, taking up Einstein's notion of an invariant.[17] In the special theory of relativity, whether two events are simultaneous is not the absolute affair it is commonsensically taken to be; two events can be simultaneous in one frame of reference and nonsimultaneous in another, with neither frame being privileged. Similarly, the mass of an object can vary from frame to frame. It is possible, however, to extract certain invariants (e.g., the spacetime interval between two events and the rest mass of an object) that are constant from frame to frame. Knowing these, we can calculate time relations and masses in any frame. Einstein's procedure has suggested to some a general program: always seek out the invariants underlying whatever properties vary from one frame or perspective to another.

Putnam tells us that he formerly subscribed to this approach (at least to the extent of saying that it is a property of the world itself that it "admits of these different mappings")[18] but he gave it up once he realized that how the world is to be carved into objects is one of the theory-relative matters. In my opinion, Putnam's rejection is premature and the soft-core approach is worth pursuing. I do not discuss the matter further here, however, since I believe there is also much to be said for the other line of response.

The other line, which Putnam calls *hard-core* realism, denies the first premise above. It says that noumenal objects may possess a certain property *despite* its being theory-relative. This amounts to saying that one or the other of the "equally correct" theories *gets things wrong*. (Or perhaps they both do, if the theories are logical contraries rather than contradictories, and the truth is captured by some third theory.) Hard-core realism is too hard a position for some philosophers to be comfortable with. It offends against the following principle, which is implicit in much contemporary antirealism: there can be no difference in *truth value* (between two theories, worldviews, or the like) unless there is also some difference in the *evidence* for them. (I here use 'evidence' broadly to cover any epistemic virtue that a theory may possess.) If two theories are evidentially on a par, it simply will not do (according to this principle) to suggest that reality itself makes one true and the other false.

But why won't it do? What is so compelling about the principle "no difference in truth value without a difference in evidential value"? I maintain that this principle is actually self-refuting. It does not *look* self-refuting, for unlike more obvious examples of principles that refute themselves, such as the principle that all generalizations are false, it does not at first sight appear to make any claim about itself. But further reflection shows that it makes a claim about itself after all. One way to see this is to rewrite it in accordance with the logic of supervenience. 'There is never a difference in A-properties without a difference in B-properties' is equivalent to 'Whenever anything has a given A-property, it also has a B-property that suffices for the having of that A-property.'[19] The principle "no difference in truth value without a difference in evidential value" therefore has the following corollary: if a statement is true, there is evidence for it that suffices for its being true, in the sense that any statement backed by similar evidence will also be true. Now, what truth-sufficing evidence is there for the "no difference" principle itself? I submit that there is none. The principle turns out to be self-refuting in much the same way as the logical positivists' criterion of meaningfulness: it fails to satisfy the requirements it seeks to impose on other views.[20] So, we need not be timid about venturing to suggest that noumenal reality may favor one of two competing but equivalent theories over the other. In other words, we may be hard-core realists.

D. One World or Two?

It is no longer the fashion to treat Kant's philosophy as a philosophy that posits two worlds, one phenomenal and the other noumenal. Commenting on Kant's distinction between appearances and things in themselves, Michael Devitt writes as follows:

> It is tempting to equate an appearance with the foundationalist's sense datum, taking the thing-in-itself as the unknowable external cause of this mental entity. Kant's writing often encourages this temptation. Nevertheless, scholars seem generally agreed—and have convinced me—that this two-worlds interpretation is wrong. What Kant intends is the following influential, but rather mysterious, one-world view.
>
> An appearance is not a mental sense datum but an external object *as we know it*. In contrast the thing-in-itself is the object *independent of our knowledge of it*; it is not a second object and does not, indeed could not, cause an appearance, for causation has its place only in the phenomenal world. Appearances are familiar objects like stones, trees, and cats. . . .[21]

Devitt does not identify the scholars who have convinced him that the two-worlds interpretation is wrong, but there are many to whom the credit might belong. Here are some representative quotations from opponents of the two-worlds view:

Graham Bird: "Such phrases [e.g., 'transcendental objects and empirical objects'] should be understood to refer not to two different kinds of entity, but instead to two different ways of talking about one and the same thing."[22]

D.P. Dryer: "Kant . . . points out that the distinction between a thing as it presents itself to the senses [an appearance] and that thing as it is in itself is not a distinction between two different things. It is rather a distinction between two ways in which the same thing is regarded—between considering it as it stands in a certain relation, namely, as presented to the senses, and considering it apart from that relation."[23]

H.E. Matthews: "To talk about 'appearance' is rather to talk about things from a particular point of view, namely, as they are experienced by human beings. . . . If this interpretation is correct, then 'things in themselves' will not be things located, like Locke's 'substance', as it were, 'behind' the things we perceive, but will be the very same things that we perceive, but considered from some other point of view than that of human experience."[24]

Others who should be mentioned in this connection are H.J. Paton, Lewis White Beck, Gerold Prauss, and Henry Allison.[25]

Devitt is right about at least one thing: the one-world (or double-aspect) view is influential. I believe he is also right about something else: it is mysterious! But I do not agree that it provides the best interpretation of Kant's thought.

Evaluating the Textual Evidence.   There is no denying that in many passages Kant uses language strongly suggestive of the one-world view. Here is a well-known passage from the preface to the B edition:

> [Our Critique shows to be necessary a distinction] between things as objects of experience and those same things as things in themselves. . . . [T]he object is to be taken *in a twofold sense*, namely as appearance and as thing in itself; if the deduction of the concepts of understanding is valid, and the principle of causality therefore applies only to things taken in the former sense, namely, in so far as they are objects of experience—these same objects, taken in the other sense, not being subject to the principle—then there is no contradiction in supposing that one and the same will is, in the appearance, that is, in its visible acts, necessarily subject to the law of nature, and so far *not free*, while yet, as belonging to a thing in itself, it is not subject to that law, and is therefore *free*. (Bxxvii–xxviii; this is one of the chief texts cited by Allison)

We can also cite passages from the Transcendental Aesthetic:

> We cannot say that all things are in time, [but we can say that] all things as appearances, that is, as objects of sensible intuition, are in time. . . . (A35/B51)

> [T]his object as *appearance* is to be distinguished from itself as object *in itself.* (B69)

From the section on phenomena and noumena:

> The understanding, when it entitles an object in a certain relation mere phenomenon, at the same time forms, apart from that relation, a representation of an *object in itself.* (B306)

And from the Paralogisms:

> [It may be that] the very same being which, as outer appearance, is extended, is (in itself) internally a subject, and is not composite, but is simple and thinks. (A360)

I would like to suggest that the linguistic evidence is not decisive in favor of the double-aspect interpretation. For one thing, there are also many passages in which Kant uses language equally suggestive of a two-worlds view; more on that shortly. But my present point is that writers sometimes use double-aspect language to express what is plainly a double-object view. Witness the following notorious passage from Locke:

> Whatsoever the Mind perceives in itself, or is the immediate object of Perception, Thought, or Understanding, that I call *Idea*; and the Power to produce any Idea in our mind, I call *Quality* of the Subject wherein that power is. Thus a Snow-ball having the power to produce in us the Ideas of *White, Cold,* and *Round,* the Powers to produce those *Ideas* in us, as they are in the Snow-ball, I call *Qualities*; and as they are Sensations, or Perceptions, in our Understandings, I call them *Ideas*: which *Ideas*, if I speak of sometimes, as in the things themselves, I would be understood to mean those Qualities in the Objects which produce them in us.[26]

The purpose of this passage is to draw a distinction between ideas and qualities, ideas being in the mind and qualities in bodies. Yet in the very course of drawing the distinction, Locke uses the pronoun "they" in a way that suggests that the same items that are in bodies are also in minds. That, of course, runs counter to the whole point of the passage. We can only suppose that the second occurrence of "they" is a sort of metalinguistic pronoun. Under this construal, 'Xs as they are Ys are F, and Xs as they are Zs are not F' means 'Xs, in the sense of the term "X" in which Xs are Ys, are F; but Xs, in the sense of the term "X" in which Xs are Zs, are not F'. Here there is no suggestion that the same things are F (qua being Ys) and not F (qua being Zs).

Here is another instance of the same phenomenon, coming this time from Berkeley:

> Hylas: You must distinguish, Philonous, between sound as it is perceived by us, and as it is in itself; or (which is the same thing) between the sound we immediately perceive and that which exists without us. The former indeed is a particular kind of sensation, but the latter is merely a vibrative or undulatory motion in the air.[27]

Here again we have the "as" locution and a pronoun apparently picking out the same thing in two different settings: sound as it is in itself and as *it* is perceived by us. Yet nothing could be clearer than that Hylas is distinguishing two different entities, physical vibrations and mental sensations. The "as" locution is merely a rhetorical device and the pronoun is metalinguistic.

My point in citing these passages, of course, is to raise the possibility that for Kant, too, double-aspect language is a rhetorical device for expressing what is actually a double-object view. Thus, to return to the Bxxvii passage with which this subsection began, my suggestion is that when Kant uses the phrase "these same objects," he really means "these same-sounding 'objects'" (if I may echo his phrase "the same-sounding 'I'" from A363). I would paraphrase his point as follows: objects, in the sense of that term in which it refers to appearances, are subject to the law of causality; but objects, in the sense of that term in which it refers to things in themselves and their actions, are exempt from that law. This reading of the passage is confirmed by Kant's saying, within the very paragraph we are looking at, that "the object is to be taken *in a twofold sense.*" Objects don't have senses—words do.

The second reason that textual evidence cannot be decisive in favor of the one-world view is that Kant often uses language at least equally suggestive of a two-worlds view. For example, he speaks of "that which is alone given to us, namely, their [objects'] appearance" (A43) as though appearances constitute a separate realm. And at times he expressly repudiates the notion of a single domain of objects to which we have two modes of access:

> [T]he concept of appearances . . . justifies the division of objects into *phenomena* and *noumena*, and so of the world into a world of the senses and a world of the understanding . . . , and indeed in such manner that the distinction does not refer merely to the logical form of our knowledge of one and the same thing, according as it is indistinct or distinct, but to the difference in the manner in which the two worlds can be first given to our knowledge, and in accordance with this difference, to the manner in which they themselves are generically distinct from one another. (A249; see also A43–44/B60–62)

Kant is here opposing the Leibnizian view that through our sensibility we achieve representations, but confused ones, of things in themselves. On the contrary, he says, "[W]e do not apprehend them in any fashion whatsoever" (A44/B62). How is one to develop a one-world view in a way that does not run afoul of Kant's opposition to Leibniz's doctrine of the two modes of access?

The fact of the matter is that Kant's language as it bears on the issue of one world versus two is a puzzling mix. It points sometimes in one direction, sometimes in the other—sometimes even within a single sentence.[28] The interpretive controversy may better be settled by seeing which view is more philosophically satisfactory. I turn, therefore, to some logical and metaphysical difficulties in which I believe the double-aspect view entangles us.

Difficulties for the One-World View.   One of the leading proponents of a one-world interpretation of Kant in recent years has been Henry Allison. In developing my criticisms of the one-world view, I take Allison's rendition of it as my main focus.

According to Allison, things may be considered either in relation to the conditions (both sensible and intellectual) of our knowing them, or apart from such conditions. To consider things in the former way is to consider them as they appear; to consider them in the latter way is to consider them as they are in themselves.[29] When Kant says that appearances have spatial attributes but things in themselves do not, his meaning is therefore this: considered in relation to our form of sensibility, things have spatial attributes, but considered "in themselves" or apart from our sensibility, they—these same things—do not.[30]

A similar theme is sounded by Devitt. He says that as things in themselves, external objects exist independent of human cognition, but as known by us, these same objects exist only because (to a degree) we create them:

External objects exist objectively [i.e., independently of human cognition] only as things-in-themselves. As we know them—i.e. as familiar objects—they exist partly in virtue of our imposition of concepts and a spatio-temporal setting. To a degree we *create* the world we live in.[31]

Now, how can the same things be both spatial and nonspatial? How can they be both dependent on human cognition and not thus dependent? They cannot, of course, on pain of contradiction. That is where the modifying phrases come in: "considered in relation to our sensibility" versus "considered in themselves," "as known by us" versus "as things in themselves." These phrases are supposed to block what would otherwise be a contradiction. But how exactly do they do it? How, in general, do modifiers remove a contradiction? In my opinion, this is a question that Allison and other one-worlders have not adequately addressed.

It is useful for our purposes that David Lewis has addressed just this question in another connection. He distinguishes three ways, exemplified by the following three models, in which modifiers remove contradictions.[32]

First model: 'Square on the third floor, round on the fourth'. Here it is really different things (different segments of the same building) that have the contrary predicates.[33]

Second model: 'Honest according to the *News*, crooked according to the *Times*'. Here different papers tell different stories, and at least one of them gets things wrong.

Third model: 'Tall compared to Ed, short compared to Fred'. Here different relations are borne to different individuals. What would be a contradiction if we were dealing with a one-place predicate expressing a monadic property is no longer a contradiction once the predicate is properly understood as a two-place predicate expressing a relational property.

Let us see which of these models best enables us to understand the one-world view.

First model: This is no good. Following this approach, we would need to find different entities to bear the contradictory properties of spatiality and nonspatiality. That, of course, would be to revert to a two-worlds view, which is the very thing the view under discussion is designed to avoid.

Second model: This is no good, either. One of the ways of considering things would have to be *erroneous*, whereas it is essential to Allison's view that the two ways be equally correct.

Third model: This is the best bet. Spatial predicates, such as 'square' and 'triangular', must turn out for Allison not to express intrinsic properties, contrary to what we would initially suppose. Nothing is square *simpliciter*, but only square in relation to perceivers endowed with our form of sensibility.

The resulting view may perhaps be compared with the "objective relativism" espoused by Whitehead, McGilvary, and others several decades ago.[34] The table *is* square when viewed from above, and it *is* trapezoidal when viewed from the end. The one-world view is like this, but more radical: the table has shape when considered in relation to our form of sensibility, but no shape at all (because no spatial attributes) when considered apart from this relation. Allison never actually says this, but if I am right, it is an implication of the most plausible way of elaborating his position.

Let us ponder this further. The locution 'x is F in relation to y' suggests that F is an intrinsic property of x that it somehow bears only in relation to y. That would be puzzling. If Lewis is right, what we really have is not a y-relative intrinsic property of x, but a relation *between* x and y.[35] Thus, the correct understanding of 'Ed is tall in relation to Fred' is simply 'Ed is taller than Fred.' Similarly, the correct understanding of 'x is cubical in relation to us' would be 'x cubifies us' or some such—our language lacks a natural term for this relation, because we do not normally think of shape as a relation at all. But that is what it evidently becomes on Allison's view.

Is it intelligible to suppose that shapes are disguised relations rather than intrinsic properties? "If we know what shape is," Lewis writes, "we know that it is a property, not a relation."[36] He is objecting to the view that shape is a relation between objects and times, but the same point would obviously hold with just as much force against the view that shape is a relation between objects and perceivers. So, it seems to me that there is room for doubt about the intelligibility of what the one-world view would have us say on this score.

But perhaps I am being too hasty. In defense of shape as a relation, one might appeal to an analogy with weight as it is conceived in Newtonian physics.[37] Before Newton, weight might have seemed a paradigm case of a nonrelational property. "If we know what weight is," we can even imagine a philosopher saying, "we know that it is a property, not a relation." Yet a relation is precisely what we now know it to be, since the same object has different weights on different planets and can be assigned no weight at all except in relation to a place of weighing. If weight is a disguised relation, why not shape?

I do not think this suggestion can be conclusively ruled out. Perhaps we can never know for sure that a property we regard as monadic is not really relational, or more generally, that a relation we regard as having n places does not really have $n + 1$. Nonetheless, there is a significant difference between the cases of weight and shape. We can understand the relation to which our pre-Newtonian notion of weight gives way: it is roughly the relation of being-pulled-to-a-certain-extent-by. By contrast, I do not believe we have any notion at all of whatever relation is supposed to supersede our conception of shape as intrinsic.

Perhaps it will be suggested that there is really no mystery about what the relation is: it is the relation of *appearing to us to have such-and-such a shape*. We are familiar enough with the idea that a table that is not trapezoidal in itself may appear trapezoidal from certain perspectives; why not go further and say that an object that is not spatial in itself may nonetheless appear to us to be spatial, that is, may affect us with experiences as of a spatial object?

I have nothing to say against this suggestion by itself. I wish only to point out that it is incompatible with the version of the one-world theory I am now discussing. It amounts to giving up on the disguised relation model and going back to the mistaken newspaper model. It is saying (to use Allison's words) that "things only *seem to us* to be spatial," which implies that "our consciousness of a world of objects extended and located in space is somehow illusory."[38] Such an "illusion thesis" is one of the very things Allison's version of the one-world theory is designed to avoid.[39] That is why it is important for Allison to say, not that things *appear* spatial to us, but that they *are* spatial *in relation to* us.

Suppose we now set aside any doubts there may be about the tenability of extension, shape, and other spatial properties as relations to us.[40] Further objections to the "two ways of considering" view will emerge when we ask what becomes of some of Kant's characteristic doctrines when they are recast as that view would require.

In the section of the *Critique of Pure Reason* entitled "The Amphiboly of Concepts of Reflection," Kant presents his critique of the system of Leibniz. His main contention is that many of Leibniz's best-known principles, though valid if their sphere of application is things in themselves, are not valid regarding appearances.[41] The principles in question include the following:

(a) complexes must be composed of simples;
(b) relations must be grounded in qualities;
(c) objects that are indiscernible must be identical.[42]

A two-worlder will simply say that these principles hold for one set of objects but not for the other. A one-worlder must say instead that the principles hold for objects considered apart from our sensibility but fail when the objects are considered in relation to our sensibility. To take principle (a) as an example, objects considered in themselves must be composed of simples, but these same objects considered in relation to our sensibility need not be composed of simples. But how can that be? How can the mereological structure of an object be one thing in a certain relation and another thing apart from that relation?

With principle (b), the reducibility of relations, matters get more perplexing yet. Consider the relation of cubifying us that (according to one-worlders) must supersede our notion of intrinsic shape. Is this relation grounded in intrinsic features of its relata or not? For a one-worlder, the answer is *no* when the relata are considered in relation to us, but *yes* when they are considered apart from us. Does this mean that the dyadic relation 'x cubifies us' is grounded whereas the triadic relation 'x cubifies us in relation to us (or our form of sensibility)' is not grounded? And is the latter relation perhaps grounded after all if we consider its three terms alone, not in relation to our sensibility again as a fourth? I find myself at a loss to know what one-worlders are to make of all this.

Consider finally principle (c)—the identity of indiscernibles. Here we have a special difficulty. Kant says that the sharing of all qualities would be sufficient for identity in the case of things in themselves, but not in the case of appearances (see A263–64/B319–20 and A271–72/B327–28). Things in themselves that are qualitatively identical must be numerically identical, but appearances (e.g., two raindrops) that are qualitatively identical need *not* be numerically identical. (They may be differentiated by sheer difference of position.) Here is what the one-worlder must evidently make of this: objects A and B may be identical with each other if considered in themselves but diverse from one another if considered in relation to our form of sensibility. In short, A and B may be the same thing in itself, but different appearances—one thing or two, depending on how considered. I find this result absurd,[43] and I cannot believe that Kant ever meant to embrace it.[44] Let shape and other spatial properties become relative if you must, but please, not identity and diversity!

A Qualified Two-Worlds View.   I end this section with a note on the sense in which the virtual-object theory of appearances gives us a two-worlds view. It does *not* give us a dualism of two sorts of existent, such as would be involved in a sense-datum theory of appearances. I hold that appearances are intentionalia and that intentionalia are logical constructions out of states of perceivers. It follows that appearances do not, strictly speaking, form a second class of existents alongside things in themselves, since they are only constructions out of noumenal beings and their states. My interpretation is nonetheless dualistic in the following sense: the distinction between appearances and things in themselves is a distinction between two separate universes of discourse—not between two ways of discoursing about the same class of objects.

If there is a sense in which I believe in one world only, it is not a world containing objects that are things in themselves or appearances depending on how one considers them. It is, instead, a world whose *only* denizens are things in themselves.

E. The In Itself as the Intrinsic

In some contexts, Kant's phrase 'in itself' seems to contrast with 'in relation to other things' and especially with 'in relation to us'. If we understand the phrase in this way, the much-decried unknowability of things in themselves is no longer the utter unknowability of things on the noumenal side of the great divide; it is rather the unknowability in certain respects (viz., nonrelational or intrinsic respects)[45] of things in general. The way is then open for holding that the things presented to us in ordinary perception are the very things that are unknowable "in themselves"; what is denied to us is not any access whatever to these things, but only knowledge of their intrinsic or nonrelational features. It naturally goes along with this to hold that the phrase 'knowledge of things as they appear' contrasts not with 'knowledge of how they *really* are' but with 'knowledge of how they *intrinsically* are'. In knowing how things appear, we know genuine facts about them; they are just not facts about how the things are 'in themselves'.

The foregoing reflections provide us with another way in which we might develop a one-world reading of Kant. Knowledge of things as they are in themselves and knowledge of things as they appear would not be knowledge of truths about objects in two separate domains; instead, they would be knowledge, respectively, of nonrelational facts and of relational facts about the same objects.[46]

The possibility of reading Kant in this way was first suggested to me by the chapter of C.I. Lewis's *Mind and the World Order* entitled "The Relativity of Knowledge and the Independence of the Real." There Lewis develops the idea that even if all our knowledge about things is knowledge about how they are related to perceivers, it is nonetheless genuine knowledge about mind-independent things.[47] Subsequently, I have encountered intimations or variations of the same idea in several other authors, including John Stuart Mill, D.P. Dryer, and Hilary Putnam.[48] In this section I focus on the views of Mill and Putnam.

Here is how Mill formulates the doctrine he calls the "Relativity of Knowledge":

> [T]hat all the attributes which we ascribe to objects, consist in their having the power of exciting one or another variety of sensation in our minds; that to us the properties of an object have this and no other meaning. . . . This is the doctrine of the Relativity of Knowledge to the knowing mind. . . .[49]

Mill attributed versions of this doctrine to Berkeley, Hume, Kant, James Mill, Spencer, and various other philosophers of the eighteenth and nineteenth centuries. He distinguished two main forms of it: a phenomenalist form, which reduces the object to a complex of sensations, and a noumenalist form, according to which the object "must be *something* 'in itself,' but all that we know it to be is merely relative to us, consisting in the power of affecting us in certain ways. . . ."[50] Not surprisingly, it is the noumenal form of the doctrine that Mill attributed to Kant.

A view in some ways similar to Mill's Relativity of Knowledge, but more radical, has been attributed to Kant by Putnam. Putnam writes, "I suggest that (as a first approximation) the way to read Kant is as saying that what Locke said about secondary qualities is true of *all* qualities. . . .[51] He goes on to explain:

> If *all properties are secondary*, what follows? It follows that *everything* we say about an object is of the form: it is such as to affect *us* in such-and-such a way. *Nothing at all* we say about any object describes the object as it is 'in itself', independently of its effect on *us*. . . .[52]

So, Putnam is attributing to Kant the view that all properties are secondary qualities in Locke's sense; that is, they are powers to affect our minds in certain ways.[53] In remarks elsewhere on the same theme, he says that secondary qualities in this sense are not intrinsic properties:

> These are not 'intrinsic properties' of the external things we ascribe them to, but rather (in the case of external things) dispositions to affect us in certain ways. . . .[54]

Thus, for Putnam's Kant, none of the properties possessed by external things are intrinsic properties.

In what sense do the "powers to affect us" spoken of by Locke, Mill, and Putnam fail to be intrinsic properties of the objects that have them? Here it may be useful to distinguish two senses of the term 'intrinsic' and a test associated with each. In the first sense, 'intrinsic property' contrasts with 'relational property'. A good test for whether a property P is intrinsic in this sense is *Kant's test*: could an object that was all alone in the universe have P? I call this Kant's test because Kant used it to show that a hand's being right or left is not a matter of how it is related to other objects. If the only created thing were a human hand, he maintained, it would still be a right hand or a left hand. (For more on this, see appendix C.) In this first sense, it seems that powers or dispositions may qualify as intrinsic. If a cube of sugar had the dispositional property of being soluble in water, we would not take this property away simply by destroying everything else (including all the water) in its universe.

But there is another sense in which the passive power to dissolve in water (or the active power to affect human beings in a certain way) is *not* intrinsic. This is brought out by *Moore's test*: P is intrinsic if and only if "when anything possesses it, that same thing or anything exactly like it would *necessarily* or *must* always, under all circumstances, possess it in exactly the same degree."[55] By this test, the sugar cube's solubility in water is not intrinsic, since a cube just like it might fail to dissolve in water in a universe in which the characteristics of water (or perhaps the laws of nature) were different. So, although sugar's solubility in water is intrinsic in one sense—it does not depend on the *existence* of anything else—it is extrinsic in another: it is not determined solely by how the sugar is 'in itself'.

Returning now to the theses attributed to Kant by Mill and Putnam, we may note the way in which Putnam's thesis is the more radical of the two. Mill's Kant holds that the only properties *we know of* in external (i.e., noumenal) things are dispositions or powers to affect us; Putnam's Kant holds that the only properties *there are* in external things are such dispositions.[56]

The Putnam view (as I call the view Putnam attributes to Kant) thus invites an objection that the Mill view does not—it would be disputed by philosophers who hold that dispositional properties must have a categorical basis.[57] Locke himself is one such philosopher: his secondary qualities are "Powers to produce various Sensations in us by their *primary Qualities*."[58] Locke's view, otherwise put, is that dispositional properties supervene on nondispositional properties. If that is true, it is of course out of the question that all the properties of any object should be dispositional.

Besides this Lockean reason for rejecting the view that all properties of external things are dispositional, there is also the following Leibnizian reason: if there are analyzable properties, there must also be simple properties. Given that dispositional properties are all analyzable (in first approximation, by conditionals of the form 'if x were placed in circumstances C, it would as a result exhibit behavior B'), it follows that not all properties are dispositional.

Does Kant subscribe to the Putnam view despite the foregoing objections to it? I think not. Recall that he holds that relations among things in themselves must be grounded in their nonrelational properties. Here are two representative passages:[59]

> If I think to myself merely things in general, the difference in their outer relations cannot constitute a difference in the things themselves; on the contrary, it presupposes this difference. (A280/B336)

If [I confine myself to the concept of a thing in general], I can abstract from all outer relation, and there must still be left a concept of something which signifies no relation, but inner determinations only. (A283/B339)[60]

I suspect that when he speaks of differences in outer relations, he means to cover not merely differences in the actual relatings of the things, but also differences in whatever powers they have that are manifestable in such relatings. If so, he would hold that the properties of things in themselves cannot be exhausted by their powers to affect us.

I turn now to the more qualified view stated by Mill, that the only properties *we know of* in external things are their powers to affect us. Even the qualified view is controversial. It was explicitly rejected by Thomas Reid, who maintained that in knowing an object to be extended or solid or square, we know how the object is 'in itself' and not merely (or perhaps even not at all) what sensations it produces in us.[61] My present concern, however, is not with the truth of the view, but with whether it is to be found in Kant. Here is one passage in which he may seem to be espousing it:

[E]verything in our knowledge which belongs to intuition . . . contains nothing but mere relations; namely, of locations in an intuition (extension), of change of location (motion), and of laws according to which this change is determined (moving forces). What it is that is present in this or that location, or what it is that is operative in the things themselves apart from change of location, is not given through intuition. Now a thing in itself cannot be known through mere relations; and we may therefore conclude that since outer sense gives us nothing but mere relations, this sense can contain in its representation only the relation of an object to the subject, and not the inner properties of the object in itself. (B67)

The passage is actually rather confusing. Kant begins by saying that the only properties we intuit in outer objects are relations to *other objects*; he ends by saying that the only properties we intuit in outer objects are relations to *the subject*. I consider two interpretations of the passage, one emphasizing relations to the subject and the other emphasizing relations to other objects.

According to the first interpretation, Kant is saying that although objects certainly do (or may well) *have* some "inner" or intrinsic properties, the only properties of objects *we know of* are how they are actually affecting us (relations) or how they are capable of affecting us (dispositions to have relations). This is very like the Mill view. On this interpretation, Kant offers the following syllogism:

Syllogism 1
1. All we know about objects through outer sense is what relations they stand in (to us?).
2. To know how an object is in itself is to know how it is in nonrelational respects.
3. Therefore, we do not know through outer sense how objects are in themselves.

If we read Kant's passage as containing syllogism 1, it expresses the Millian view: our ignorance of how things are in themselves is ignorance of their intrinsic properties. In the bargain, it permits a one-world interpretation of Kant's philosophy: the objects that present themselves to our senses are not appearances, considered as entities distinct from things in themselves, but "the very Things" (as Mill said). What we know of these things is only how they are related to us (how they appear to us), but it is nonetheless the things themselves about which we have this knowledge.

Although syllogism 1 is a possible reading of our passage, it is not the only one, nor in my opinion the best. I now offer an alternative reading in which the emphasis is not on "relations to us" but on "relations to other objects." More significantly, the first premise makes a claim not about which properties we know about, but about which properties things *have*.[62] On this reading, the passage puts forth the following syllogism, which is very different from syllogism 1:

Syllogism 2
1. The only properties had by objects of outer sense are relational properties.
2. A thing in itself cannot have relational properties only.
3. Therefore, objects of outer sense are not things in themselves (but only appearances).

Syllogism 2 commits Kant to a two-worlds view: appearances are one class of entity and things in themselves another. The point of the argument is that objects of outer sense (bodies, things in space) belong to the former class and not to the latter. So much the worse, some will say, for reading the passage as containing syllogism 2. But there are three strong reasons for thinking that syllogism 2 is exactly what Kant intended.

First, Kant says he is offering the argument at B67 in "confirmation of th[e] theory of the ideality of both outer and inner sense, and therefore of all objects of the senses, as mere appearances." Given that a Kantian appearance is an item that exists only in being represented,[63] the conclusion of syllogism 2 is precisely idealism regarding the objects of outer sense. (He deals with inner sense in the ensuing sentences.) Interpreted as syllogism 2, therefore, the argument lives up to its billing. But if the conclusion of the argument were merely that we lack knowledge of the nonrelational properties of things, as in syllogism 1, what would that have to do with idealism?

Second, syllogism 2 fits better with the views Kant expresses elsewhere about the status of relations. I have already referred above (especially in chapter 4 in connection with the *Prolegomena* argument from incongruent counterparts) to Leibniz's principle that relations supervene on nonrelational properties of the things related. Kant's position, most explicitly stated in the Amphiboly section of the *Critique of Pure Reason*, is that this principle *holds for things in themselves*, but *not for appearances*. The fact that it holds for things in themselves delivers the second premise of syllogism 2; the fact that it does not hold for appearances accommodates the first. (Syllogism 2 is indeed very much of a piece with the *Prolegomena* argument concerning incongruent counterparts—one invokes the Amphiboly doctrine to prove the ideality of matter and the other invokes it to prove the ideality of spatial figures.)

Third, syllogism 2 fits better with other passages in which Kant recurs to the "outer sense gives us nothing but relations" theme. Here are two such passages:

> Matter as mere object of the external senses has no other determinations than those of external relations in space. . . . [64]

> All our concepts of matter contain nothing but the mere representation of outer relationships (for that is all that can be represented in space).[65]

In each of these passages, Kant is attempting to prove that changes in an object's state of motion require an external cause; toward this end he denies that there are any suitable internal causes. So, his point in the two sentences just quoted must be that bodies do not *have* inner states (as in the first premise of syllogism 2), not simply that we are not cognizant of them (as in the first premise of syllogism 1).

I now summarize my conclusions about the B67 passage. On the first interpretation of it, Kant holds that all properties we know of in external things are relations to us (or dispositions to have such relations), as in Mill's doctrine of the Relativity of Knowledge. This would be congenial to a one-world view in which 'in itself' connotes mainly the intrinsic. But I have favored a second interpretation, according to which Kant holds that all properties whatsoever of bodies are relations, either among their own parts or to other things. From this he concludes (given his view that things in themselves must have a nonrelational nature) that bodies are only appearances, not things in themselves. Thus, the passage provides one more confirmation of Kant's commitment to two worlds.

F. Isomorphism

A main motive for postulating a world of things in themselves has always been that we ourselves are not the sole determiners of all that we experience. The fact that I am now seeing squirrels and heaps of leaves rather than camels and sand dunes is presumably a function not only of my own cognitive apparatus, but also of what sorts of mind-independent objects are now in my vicinity. As J.N. Findlay likes to say, experience is not a free composition, but a constrained translation.[66]

Kant holds that the *matter* of appearances (the element corresponding to sensation) is given to us *a posteriori*, or impressed on us from without. It is due to the causal or affective powers of objects around us. The *form* of appearances, on the other hand, "must lie ready for the sensations a priori in the mind" (A20/B34); it is something that we ourselves contribute. Does this mean that we ourselves are responsible for *all* the spatial and temporal features of the objects we experience, including even their shapes and relative locations? That seems scarcely credible.

According to many commentators, Kant would be the first to agree. H.J. Paton writes as follows:

> Because of the nature of our mind things must appear to us as spatial and temporal; but it is because of the character of the thing-in-itself that we see one object as round and another as square.[67]

C.D. Broad makes a similar suggestion. What accounts for my seeing A as round and at one place and B as square and at another place? Is the difference in my perceptions due solely to the initiative of my own mind, or is it due directly to some nonspatial difference in the ingredient sensations and indirectly to some nonspatial difference in the things in themselves that give rise to the sensations? Rejecting the first alternative as incredible, Broad says the second would be the "least unsatisfactory" alternative for Kant to hold.[68]

J.N. Findlay has carried this theme further yet. The noumenal world that we postulate to explain the nonarbitrariness of our experience must be *isomorphic* to the phenomenal world:

> Kant believed that there were relations among Things-in-themselves that corresponded one for one, and in their logical properties, to the spatiotemporal order of phenomena. . . .[69]

That the noumenal world and the phenomenal world share the same structure is a central theme of Findlay's book. He even chooses for his epigraph the following remark from Wittgenstein's *Tractatus*:

> A gramophone record, the musical idea, the written notes, and the sound-waves, all stand to one another in the same internal relation of depicting that holds between language and the world. They are all constructed according to a common logical pattern.[70]

In this section, I discuss two potential difficulties for the idea of an isomorphism between the phenomenal and the noumenal orders. I presuppose, of course, that there *are* two orders—not simply a single order that may be considered in two ways.[71] The first alleged difficulty is that the claim of isomorphism is too weak to be of any interest—that under closer inspection, it collapses into a near triviality. The second is that the claim of isomorphism is too strong—if not too strong to be true, at least strong enough to conflict with official Kantian doctrine. Believers in the consistency of Kant's philosophy will trust that at most one of these difficulties proves to be genuine.

Too Weak?   The first charge, that isomorphism is a vacuous notion, was leveled by M.H.A. Newman against views espoused for a time by Bertrand Russell.[72] According to Russell, we are acquainted only with our own percepts and can know nothing directly of the physical world. We are entitled to posit a physical world, however, and to suppose that there is a systematic isomorphism between physical objects or events and our own percepts. To this, Newman and subsequent critics objected that such isomorphism is guaranteed to exist under almost any assumptions about what the physical world is like, so the claim of isomorphism carries almost no information.[73]

To illustrate the difficulty, I must first set forth a precise account of the idea of isomorphism, or sameness of structure, as it figured in Russell's philosophy. Two sets A and B are said to have the same structure with respect to a function f and two relations R and R* exemplified in A and B if and only if the following conditions hold: (i) f is a function setting up a one-to-one correspondence between members of A and members of B, and (ii) whenever the relation R holds between two members x and y of A, the relation R* holds between their correlates in B, and conversely; that is to say, xRy iff f(x)R*f(y). To say that two sets have the same structure without qualification is then simply to say that *some* correlating function f and *some* relations R and R* exist with respect to which the sets have the same structure in the sense defined above.

What Russell's critics pointed out is this: *any* two sets will have the same structure in the sense just defined, provided only that they have the same cardinality; sameness of structure in the unqualified sense thus turns out to add nothing to sameness of cardinality.[74] Sameness of cardinality (equinumerosity) by definition implies the existence of a function satisfying clause (i), and whenever clause (i) is satisfied, we are assured of finding relations that satisfy clause (ii). We can go even further: if f and a relation R exemplified in A are specified in advance, we can always find a relation R* exemplified in B such that the sets are isomorphic with respect to f, R, and R*. Let R be any set of ordered pairs in set A; the relation R* can then simply be the set of corresponding pairs in B, that is, the set containing a pair [f(x),f(y)] iff [x,y] is in the extension of R. To illustrate, consider the relation R of adjacency among stops in the London subway system. A handful of pennies tossed randomly on a countertop is guaranteed to have the same structure as the subway system, as long as there are as many pennies as there are stops. Correlate pennies and stations one to one in any way you please, then let the relation R* be the set of ordered pairs that contains [f(x),f(y)] iff x and y are adjacent stations.

It is important to be clear about what is trivial and what is not in a claim of isomorphism between equinumerous sets. What is trivial is the claim of isomorphism without qualification—that is, the bare existential statement that there are *some* relations R and R* exemplified in the sets under which they are the same in structure. It may be far from trivial (and a matter of great interest or importance) that two sets are isomorphic with respect to a given pair of *specified* relations. In a properly played melody, for example, whenever two notes in the score are such that one is higher on the staff than the other, the corresponding notes in the melody are such that one is higher in pitch than the other. There is nothing trivial about that, or musicianship would be much easier than it is. Again, it is by no means trivial to say that two cities are *n* miles apart on the earth if and only if their corresponding dots are *n* inches apart on a certain map. What would be trivial is only the bare existential statement that the earth and the map (each considered as sets of points) are isomorphic in *some* way, for that is likewise true of the earth and a candy wrapper.

Newman's observation made trouble for Russell only because Russell had held that *all* we can assert about the physical world is its sameness of structure (in the unqualified sense) to the world of our percepts—that there are *some* relations with respect to which they are isomorphic. Had Russell been prepared to *identify* the relations under which the isomorphism holds, there would have been no problem of triviality. He may have thought we could not identify them because he held that we are acquainted only with relations among our percepts, not with relations among physical things.[75]

Let me now show how these points apply to the hypothesis of noumenal-phenomenal isomorphism in Kant. Some readers will want to point out immediately that for Kant we cannot even get as far as one-to-one correspondence between phenomena and noumena, because we cannot say whether things in themselves are one or many. Perhaps there is only one undivided noumenon, in which case there certainly cannot be any correlation of noumena with elements of the phenomenal manifold. To this we can make the following reply: perhaps, indeed, there is only one noumenal object, but there will surely be a plurality of facts involving this noumenal object. The needed correlation could then hold between phenomenal objects and noumenal facts. Compare for a moment the relation of the many modes to the one substance in the system of Spinoza: the existence of mode 1 (a wave in the ocean) correlates with God's being F (undulating under the attribute of extension), the existence of mode 2 with God's being G, and so on. Such a correlation opens the way for various possible isomorphisms; for example, it might be that God's being F is the immanent cause of his being G iff mode 1 is the transeunt cause of mode 2, and so on. In an analogous way, isomorphism might be possible for Kant.

Let us assume, then, that there is some partitioning of phenomena and noumena that yields numerical one-to-one correspondence.[76] Must the further claim of isomorphism be vacuous? If all Kant could say is that for every relation among phenomena, there is *some* corresponding relation among noumena, the answer would be yes. We could escape vacuity, however, if we could say *what* the noumenal relation is. Various possibilities come to mind. Perhaps whenever two phenomena are close together in space, their noumenal correlates (Leibnizian monads, as they might be) have similar points of view; or perhaps whenever one phenomenon precedes another, their noumenal correlates stand in some atemporal ordering relation;[77] or perhaps whenever two phenomena are related by the schema of causation (regular succession), the corresponding noumena are related by the pure categorial relation of ground and consequent. The question is whether Kant's agnosticism about things in themselves permits him to say things like this. As I showed in the preceding section, one possible reading of his agnosticism equates 'we do not know how things are in themselves' with 'we do not know what their *intrinsic* properties are'; this equation would allow us to have knowledge of their relations. (The matter is complicated by Kant's further view that relations among things in themselves reduce to their intrinsic properties!)

Even if we are not in a position to identify the specific relations under which an isomorphism is to hold but can only say there must be some such relations, we may be able to avoid triviality by imposing further restrictions on the admissible relations. I mention five possible restrictions.

1. An obvious first thought is to require that the relations be genuine relations-in-intension, not just sets of ordered pairs. But this requirement will not do any work if, as some contend, every relation-in-extension has some intensional specification.[78]

2. A relation can admit of intensional specification and still be *unnatural*, like the relation one thing bears to another iff both of them satisfy Goodman's

predicate 'grue'. A further thought, then, is to require that the relations be *natural* relations. The notion of naturalness I am invoking may be resistant to philosophical analysis, but it seems indispensable for a number of philosophical projects.[79] It is by no means clear to me (though I cannot rule it out, either) that any two sets of equal cardinality must be isomorphic with respect to some natural relations.

3. Notice that I obtained the relation R* in the example of the pennies and the subway stops by defining 'xR*y' in effect as 'the stop correlated with x is adjacent to the stop correlated with y'. I am not sure whether to count R* as a natural relation; that may depend on whether the correlation is itself in any sense natural. But in any case, we may note that 'xR*y' as so defined does not express a *self-contained* relation, that is, a relation whose holding depends on the existence of no items but its own relata.[80] We might wish to add the further restriction that the relations under which an isomorphism holds be self-contained.

4. If none of the foregoing requirements does the job, there are others we can try. We can choose relations in the first domain whose holding is a matter of degree, or which admit of comparisons in the following way: a is more R to b than c is to d (e.g., a is closer to b than c is to d). Then we can require that whenever a is more R to b than c is to d, it must be true in the correlated domain that f(a) is more R* to f(b) than f(c) is to f(d). Once again, it is not clear to me that the existence of such an R* to mirror a given R will be trivial. (We must disallow, of course, that which instances of R* are closer to each other than to which others is to be settled simply by drawing up a ranked list of R*-pairs. The present suggestion is meant to be accompanied by the preceding ones.)

5. Finally, we can require that the relations R and R* under which any interesting isomorphism is to hold be subject to the following constraint: whenever R holds between a and b, it does so *because* R* holds between the correlates of a and b. Not only must there be an isomorphism, but also things must be related in the phenomenal order as they are because things are related in the noumenal order as they are. Such explanatory isomorphism (which is what Paton, Broad, and Findlay were all looking for) is not trivially obtainable from set-theoretical manipulations.

The upshot is that a claim of isomorphism need not be a trivial consequence of co-cardinality. Such a claim may well be informative if either (a) specific relations are identified under which the isomorphism holds, or (b) though no specific relations are identified, the admissible candidates must satisfy certain constraints, for example, of naturalness, self-containedness, or explanatory role.

Too Strong?   We must now consider the objection that isomorphism, rather than being empty, has content enough to clash with important Kantian doctrines. In chapter 4 I showed that in the *Prolegomena* Kant cites incongruent counterparts as providing one of the proofs that objects in space are merely phenomena, not things in themselves. Jill Vance Buroker has claimed that Kant can cite incongruent counterparts as showing something further: the properties and relations of objects in space do not even *correspond* in any systematic way with those of noumena.[81] Here is how such an argument might go.

Suppose whenever two phenomena stand in any given spatial relation, it is because the corresponding noumena stand in some corresponding nonspatial relation: p1Rp2 only because n1R*n2. (Paton, Broad, and Findlay are presumably all committed to at least this much.) Now let p1 and p2 be human hands, one left and one right, and let R be the relation of incongruence. As I showed in section C of chapter 4, incongruence among phenomena is not a grounded relation for Kant. That is to say, the incongruence of two hands is not supervenient on their qualities or intrinsic properties, as shown by the fact that two left hands may display all the same qualities as a left and a right, yet without being incongruent. So, we can have p1Rp2 and not-(p1Rp3) despite the qualitative similarity of p1, p2, and p3; under isomorphism, it follows from this that n1R*n2 and not-(n1R*n3).

Consider now the following auxiliary assumption: if a number of phenomena are qualitatively alike, so are the corresponding noumena (which is not to say, of course, that a phenomenon must be qualitatively like its noumenal correlate). It follows that n1–n3 are all qualitatively alike. It further follows that the relation R* must be ungrounded, since it holds between n1 and n2 yet not between n1 and n3, despite the presence in n1 and n3 of all the qualities to be found in n1 and n2. This result contradicts Kant's view, to which I have had occasion to refer several times now, that *all relations among noumena are grounded.* I have apparently shown that Kant's principles are inconsistent with any systematic isomorphism of phenomena with noumena.

But have I really shown this? That depends on whether we were entitled just now to our auxiliary assumption: if two phenomena are qualitatively alike, so are the corresponding noumena. Nothing in isomorphism as so far characterized warrants that assumption.[82] Going back to the example of the score and the melody, notice that qualitatively identical notes in the melody (notes that are the same in pitch, loudness, etc.) could be represented by notes on the page that were printed in different colors of ink. In similar fashion, perhaps noumena could differ among themselves in ways not reflected at the phenomenal level.[83] If so, we could hold that R* is a grounded relation among noumena after all; it would simply have to be grounded in noumenal features that have no phenomenal counterparts. So, Kant's principle that relations among noumena must be grounded, whereas relations among phenomena need not be, does not stand in the way of isomorphism.

As I showed in section D of this chapter, another difference between noumena and phenomena according to Kant is that noumena do and phenomena do not obey Leibniz's principle of the identity of indiscernibles. Does this difference stand in the way of isomorphism? Once again, the answer would be yes if, but only if, we assumed that if phenomena are qualitatively alike, so are the underlying noumena. On that assumption, if two phenomena (e.g., the raindrops of Kant's example) were qualitatively alike but numerically distinct, the underlying noumena would be qualitatively alike but numerically identical, and that would spoil the one-to-one correspondence necessary for isomorphism.

There are still other principles that Kant thinks hold for noumena but not for phenomena. Here is one that I think does stand in the way of a thoroughgoing isomorphism:[84] in the realm of noumena, composite entities must always contain simple parts; in the realm of phenomena, this is not so.[85] To see why this blocks isomorphism, let R be the part-of relation among phenomena and R* the corresponding relation among noumena. I assume that R* will be some relation of the "conditioned" to its "conditions." Now Kant, as I have said, denies that there are phenomenal simples, so in the realm of phenomena we have $-\exists x-\exists y(yRx)$. He insists, however, that among noumena, descent from "conditioneds" to their "conditions" that never reaches an "unconditioned" is forbidden, so in the realm of noumena we have $\exists x-\exists y(yR^*x)$. This gives rise to a breach of isomorphism that may be pictured as follows:

$$p0 \quad R \quad p1 \quad R \quad p2 \quad \text{etc.}$$
$$n1 \quad R^* \quad n2 \quad \text{etc.}$$

The series of ever smaller parts (the R-series) can always be extended to the left, but the series of noumena related by R* must have a leftmost member.[86]

The difficulty I just raised could be avoided if we gave up the assumption that the relation corresponding to R is the one I have proposed as R*. It could also be avoided if we gave up the assumption that *every* noumenon has a cor-related phenomenon. That, of course, would be to give up the idea that there is any isomorphism between phenomena and the *entire* set of noumena, but there could still be isomorphism between phenomena and a *subset* of noumena. If, for example, only composite noumena have phenomenal corre-lates,[87] then the bottom row in the diagram above would not need to have a leftmost member. This is something that Kant could allow, for he does not rule out the idea of endless descent (or leftward retreat) regarding conditioneds and their conditions; the unconditioned element that reason insists on need not be a *member* of the descending series.

I have uncovered so far no obstacle to Kant's holding a doctrine of isomor-phism if it is appropriately limited. The limited doctrine would have to allow for (i) noumenal items with no corresponding phenomenal items (thus ac-commodating Kant's views about composites and simples) and (ii) properties of noumenal items not reflected in the properties of their phenomenal corre-lates (thus accommodating his views about the reducibility of relations and the identity of indiscernibles).

A Final Difficulty.   Kant's Inaugural Dissertation contains the following ar-resting sentence: "Objects do not strike the senses through their form."[88] An echo of this sentence can be heard in section 15 of the *Critique of Pure Reason*: "[T]he combination of a manifold in general can never come to us through the senses" (B129). As I showed in my discussion of synthesis in chapter 7, this means at least that we have no aboriginal awareness of structured arrays. Does it also mean that the form of external things in themselves does nothing to de-termine the form of what we shall experience? If so, it is incompatible with any explanatory doctrine of isomorphism. Findlay, therefore, is at pains to of-fer an alternative reading of the sentence.[89]

There is one strain of Kant's thought, however, that seems to require the anti-isomorphism reading. I am referring to Kant's linkage of what is knowable *a priori* with the features we ourselves impose on our experience, and to the radical version of constructive idealism that occasionally surfaces in sentences such as the following: "[T]he order and regularity in the appearances, which we entitle *nature*, we ourselves introduce" (A125). To the extent that Kant really believes this, he cannot subscribe to anything very extensive by way of noumenal-phenomenal isomorphism. He cannot, in other words, combine the isomorphist thesis 'aRb because the corresponding noumena are related by R*' with the idealist thesis 'aRb because we so arrange things' if it is no part of our doing that the noumena are related as they are. (Of course, we ourselves are noumenal beings, but I am assuming that some of the noumena involved in isomorphism would be alien to us.)

It is possible that the difficulty I am now raising already arises for Kant independent of any doctrine of isomorphism; it may simply be a consequence of his view that the matter of appearances is impressed from without. H.W.B. Joseph once asked how the synthesizing activities of the mind can guarantee that lightning will always be followed by thunder if, as Kant believes, the mind has no control over the qualitative aspects of experience; he compared the task to "that of a man called upon to arrange in sentences that shall express his thought letters which he must take as they are given; the task may be impossible of fulfillment."[90]

G. Affection

On the first page of the introduction to the *Critique of Pure Reason*, Kant speaks of objects that affect the senses to produce representations: "For how should our faculty of knowledge be awakened into action did not objects affecting our senses partly of themselves produce representations . . ." (B1). On the first page of the Transcendental Aesthetic he again tells us that representations arise in us because we are affected by objects, noting that "the capacity (receptivity) for receiving representations through the mode in which we are affected by objects, is entitled *sensibility*" (A19/B33). For any reader of those lines who already knows what lies ahead in the *Critique of Pure Reason*, the following question immediately presents itself: what is the object that is doing the affecting? Is it an appearance—a phenomenal object in space and time? Or is it a thing in itself?

Some passages favor the phenomenal object. At A28 and again at A213/B260, Kant says that our sense of sight is affected by light, which is something phenomenal on his view. In the Anticipations of Perception, he says that the intensity of our sensations is proportional to certain intensive magnitudes of affecting objects in space. And in the Second Analogy, he says that the order of our perceptions is often determined by the order of phenomenal events—for example, by the passage of a ship downstream.

But other passages favor the thing in itself. Here are two:

How things may be in themselves, apart from the representations through which they affect us, is entirely outside our sphere of knowledge. (A190/B235)

[The understanding] does indeed think for itself an object in itself, but only as transcendental object [a term by which Kant sometimes means 'thing in itself'], which is the cause of appearance and therefore not it-self appearance. . . . (A288/B344).[91]

So, once again the question arises, what is it that affects us—appearances or things in themselves?

When confronted with a pair of alternatives A and B, Buddhist philoso-phers traditionally make sure that they cover all the possibilities by consider-ing four alternatives in all: A, B, both, and neither. We may fruitfully do like-wise here, considering the following four answers:

(a) the affecting object is the phenomenal object only;
(b) it is the noumenal object only;
(c) it is both;
(d) it is neither.

All four answers have found advocates among Kant's disciples, interpreters, or critics.[92] Kant's pupil J.S. Beck gave answer (a), holding that the affecting object cannot be a thing in itself, since on Kantian principles the categories have application to phenomena only.[93] Prichard gave answer (b), arguing that the affecting object cannot be an appearance, since appearances are themselves the creatures of representation.[94] Using the arguments of the foregoing parties against each other, the absolute idealists gave answer (d); they dispensed with affecting objects altogether, sweeping away everything but the mind and its states. Finally, not to leave answer (c) without an advocate, Adickes pro-pounded the theory of *double* affection: things in themselves impinge on our transcendental egos, thereby giving rise to the world of appearances in space in time, which then empirically affect our empirical egos and give rise to rep-resentations.[95]

Note that the problems mentioned for answers (a) and (b) are not merely problems for the suppositions that representations are caused by phenomena alone or by noumena alone; they are problems for the suppositions that rep-resentations are caused by phenomena at all or by noumena at all. The double affection theory therefore inherits the problems with both answers; double affection is double trouble. Nonetheless, I find myself strangely partial to it, up to a point. In the remainder of this section, I examine more closely the problems that arise for affection by the two sorts of objects. I am especially concerned with problems (and solutions) that arise on the assumption that Kantian appearances are virtual objects.

I have already mentioned (in section B of this chapter) the chief objections to affection by noumenal objects. First, there is the difficulty that Kant's own ex-plicit teaching demands that the categories, including causation, apply only to phenomena. This is why I have spoken here of "affection" (Strawson uses the even more colorless term "A-relation"), taking this to be something distinct from causation, though somehow analogous to it. As noted above, it could perhaps be the unschematized category of causation, which can be understood as the concept of "something from which we can conclude to the existence of some-thing else" (A243/B301), though not as "the real upon which, whenever posited, something else always follows [in time]" (A144/B183). Second, there is the dif-ficulty of trying to get a grip on a quasi-causal relation that holds between entities that do not exist in space or even in time. I confessed above to the difficulty of understanding such a relation. I repeat what I said before: if in the end we must reject the idea that nonspatial and nontemporal things in themselves affect us, what we should reject in it is not the idea that things in themselves affect us, but rather the idea that things in themselves are outside space and time.

I turn now to difficulties with the idea that phenomenal objects are causes of our representations. The difficulties here fall into three types:

(i) difficulties with the idea that phenomenal objects, as logical constructions, can be causes at all;

(ii) difficulties with the idea that phenomenal objects, as intentional objects, can be causes at all; and

(iii) difficulties with the idea that phenomenal objects, as constructions out of states of perceivers, can be causes of those very states.

Regarding type (i), one of the guiding themes of this book is that phenomena or appearances are virtual objects, and virtual objects are a species of logical construction. How, it might be asked, can mere logical constructions bear any causal efficacy? Are they not too insubstantial for that? Well, a shadow can stunt the growth of a tomato; a wave can wash a bottle ashore; and one nation can destroy another. Yet shadows, waves, and nations are paradigms of logical constructions. So, there must be a sense in which constructions can be causes after all.

Indeed, reflection on any of these examples will reveal what this sense is. Even though there is strictly no such thing as a wave that moves shoreward from yonder (there are only the successive swellings and subsidings of the ocean), it can be true to say that a wave washed a bottle ashore. In what sense is it true? The water heaved up just behind the bottle, nudging it forward a bit, then some neighboring water heaved up, nudging the bottle forward some more, and so on, until the bottle reached the shore. Our causal statement is thereby made true, but as with any statement about a construction, the truth in it has to be implied by truths exclusively about more basic entities—in this case, the ocean or its constituent water particles.

In the example just given, we retained causal language at the level of the more basic entities—we said the water nudged the bottle. This feature is permissible but not obligatory. At any rate, it is not required by the very idea of a construction that causal truths about constructed entities be grounded in causal truths about the more basic entities. This is an instance of the familar point that to say anything about a construction is to say something, though not necessarily the *same* thing, about the more basic entities.

I pass now to the second type of difficulty for phenomenal objects as causes, class (ii). Recall that Kantian appearances are *intentional objects*, objects that exist only as contents of representations. For me, this means that they are constructions out of states of perceivers. This may seem to raise a difficulty over and above any difficulty with constructions as causes. How can an intentional object cause anything? How can it be any more causally efficacious than an object merely dreamt of?

One possible answer is this: intentional objects (or events) of one type can be regularly followed by intentional objects (or events) of another type.[96] In short, intentional objects can satisfy the condition laid down in Kant's schema for causation. So, even if phenomena cannot be causes in the sense of the full category (pure category plus schema), they can stand in the relation of regular succession that serves as the schema for empirical or phenomenal causation. This would bring Kant a step closer to Berkeley, who held that ideas exhibit only lawful succession, causation proper being the prerogative of spirits.

But that is not the only possibility for understanding what it is for phenomena to stand in causal relations. I can simply repeat what I have already said in discussing what it is in general for constructions to be causes: x's being F causes y's being G (where x and y are constructions) if a certain statement is true about the more basic entities out of which x and y are constructed. This point is no less applicable when the constructions are constructions out of conscious states of noumenal beings. The "certain statement," as I pointed out above, may or may not itself be a causal statement. If it is, causal truths about phenomena are grounded in causal truths about noumena; if it is not, causal truths about phenomena are grounded in noncausal truths about noumena.

I do not have any plausible example to offer of the second option (causal truths about phenomena grounded in noncausal truths about noumena), but I mention it as an abstract possibility. For the first option (causal truths about phenomena grounded in causal truths about noumena), a suggestive model can be found in what Jaegwon Kim calls *supervenient causation*.[97] Kim introduces this topic by citing Jonathan Edwards's example of images in a mirror. According to Edwards, "The image that exists at this moment is not at all *derived* from the image which existed at the last preceding moment." Rather, each image is upheld or sustained in its being by rays of light proceeding from the object. Kim observes that successive images in the mirror are not directly causally linked even if all Humean requirements (contiguity and constant conjunction) are met. "The succession of images is only a reflection of the real causal process at the level of the objects reflected." He goes on to suggest that causation between two macro-events, x's having F and y's having G, is epiphenomenal or supervenient causation in the following sense: x's having F supervenes on x's having micro-property m(F), y's having G likewise supervenes on y's having m(G), and x's having m(F) causes y's having m(G). Applied to Kant, the idea would be this: phenomenon p causes phenomenon q iff p supervenes on (or is constructed out of) noumenon Np, q supervenes on noumenon Nq, and Np causes Nq. Of course, if noumena are outside of space and time, the sense in which one noumenon causes another will have to be whatever sense is involved in the pure category of causation.

So, phenomena can be causes, at least of other phenomena. I turn now to the third and most pressing of the difficulties identified above: how is it possible for them to be causes of our representations in particular?

Regarding (iii), constructions can be causes, as now allowed, but how can they be causes of the very items out of which they are constructed? If As are constructions out of Bs (or reducible to Bs or logically supervenient on Bs— the differences among these do not at present matter), how can they be causes of Bs? It is a compelling thought that the cause of an item must have some being and constitution over and above that which it causes. That explains why behaviorists typically do not say that mental states cause behavior: mental states cannot cause pieces of behavior if they reduce to patterns of behavior. It also explains why the general theory of relativity is often regarded as a return to a substantival theory of space (or spacetime): if the curvature of space influences the movements of matter, it is hard to see how space can be a mere construction out of matter. It explains, finally, why Kant himself in some places refuses to allow that bodies cause representations:

> [I]t is not, therefore, the motion of matter that produces representations in us; the motion itself is representation only, as is the matter which makes itself known in this way. (A387)

> [N]o one could dream of holding that what he has once come to recognise as mere representation, is an outer cause [of our representations, as the context makes clear]. (A390)

But are we perhaps being too hasty in rejecting phenomena as causes of representations? One possibility I invoked above to accommodate phenomenal causation was supervenient causation—one supervenient entity causing another by virtue of its base causing the base of the other. Why not invoke a variant of this idea to accommodate the causation of representations by entities that supervene on representations? To be sure, a supervenient entity cannot cause the *very* entities it supervenes on, but perhaps it can be said to cause *other* entities at the base level—whatever entities its own base properly causes. Schematically, the idea would be that if A1 supervenes on B1 and B1 causes B2, then A1, though in no sense a cause of its own base B1, is in some sense a cause of B2.[98]

On further reflection, however, it seems that the variety of "downward" causation I have just tried to accommodate is only causation by courtesy. The supposed relation of causation running from phenomenon to noumenon is simply the logical product of a vertical relation (of a phenomenon to its noumenal base) and a horizontal relation (of the noumenal base to another noumenon). It is not a diagonal relation holding in its own right. Contrast this with the case in which a is three feet north of b and b is four feet west of c: it follows that a is five feet northwest of c, and here the induced relation between a and c is a spatial relation on a par with the inducing relations. But if A1 supervenes on B1 and B1 causes B2, there seems to be no new diagonal relation in addition to the horizontal and vertical relations. That is why I said phenomenal-to-noumenal causation is causation by courtesy.

To summarize the results of this section, phenomena are not debarred from being causes just because they are constructions, or just because they are constructions out of representings. Phenomenal causation (i.e., causation of phenomena by phenomena) can be understood in any of three ways: first, as mere regular succession, in accordance with Hume's definition of causation or Kant's schema for it; second, as supervenient causation in the manner of Kim, causation between phenomena being a reflection of causation between the underlying noumena; third, as derivative causation in the manner appropriate to constructions, where the foundational facts at the base level need not themselves involve causation at all. But none of these ways enables us to make room for the idea of phenomenal-to-noumenal causation.[99] The objects that affect us to produce representations must be things in themselves.

H. Secondary Qualities

I conclude this chapter by discussing Kant's views on the distinction between primary and secondary qualities. I begin with a quick review of Locke and Berkeley on this topic. Here is how Locke defines secondary qualities:

> Such *Qualities*, which in truth are nothing in the Objects themselves, but Powers to produce various Sensations in us by their *primary Qualities, i.e.* by the Bulk, Figure, Texture, and Motion of their insensible parts.[100]

It is clear from this passage that what Locke understands by a secondary quality is something quite definitely in the object, namely, a power. His "subjectivism" about colors, tastes, and the like is expressed not by saying that secondary qualities exist only in the mind, but by saying that our ideas of colors and tastes do not resemble anything in the objects that cause them.[101]

As students of modern philosophy know, Berkeley did not adhere to the definition above in his own discussion of Locke's views. Here is how he has Hylas present the distinction between primary and secondary qualities:

> You must know sensible qualities are by philosophers divided into *primary* and *secondary*. The former are extension, figure, solidity, gravity, motion, and rest. And these they hold exist really in bodies. The latter are those above enumerated [colors, sounds, tastes, etc.]; or briefly, all sensible qualities beside the primary, which they assert are only so many sensations or ideas existing nowhere but in the mind.[102]

As Berkeley uses the term, a secondary quality is a quality that exists only in the mind.[103]

We thus have two senses of 'secondary quality': one deriving from Locke in which a secondary quality is a power to affect us, and another deriving from Berkeley in which a secondary quality is a quality existing only in the mind. The difference between these two usages has been a source of confusion down to the present day.

I showed in section E that Putnam attributes to Kant the thesis that all properties are secondary qualities, evidently having Locke's meaning in mind. In support of this attribution, he cites the following passage from the *Prolegomena*:

> Long before Locke's time, but assuredly since him, it has been generally assumed and granted without detriment to the actual existence of external things that many of their predicates may be said to belong, not to the things in themselves, but to their appearances, *and to have no proper existence outside our representation.* Heat, color, and taste, for instance, are of this kind. Now, if I go farther and, for weighty reasons, rank as mere

appearances the remaining qualities of bodies also, which are called primary—such as extension, place, and, in general, space, with all that which belongs to it (impenetrability or materiality, shape, etc.)—no one in the least can adduce the reason of its being inadmissible. (pp. 36–37, emphasis mine)

Kant is indeed saying here that all the properties of bodies have the status of secondary qualities in one sense of the term—but it is Berkeley's sense, not Locke's. He is not saying (as Putnam would have it) that all properties of bodies are dispositions to affect us; he is saying that the properties of bodies "have no proper existence outside our representation." This, of course, is just what we should expect from one who affirms the ideality of space. The properties traditionally listed as primary—extension, location, and so on—can all be viewed as so many ways of being in space.

It is important to recognize that Kant really did believe that the traditional primaries are mind-dependent. The *Prolegomena* passage seems clear and explicit on this point, but some interpreters would have us set it aside, owing to its ostensible conflict with some things Kant says in the *Critique of Pure Reason*. There Kant gives us two warnings against explaining the ideality of space and its contents by analogy with standard doctrine about secondary qualities. He says that the ideality of space cannot "be illustrated by examples so altogether insufficient as colors, taste, etc." (A29/B45) and also that it "must not . . . be illustrated by false analogies with sensation" (A36/B53).

I do not read these passages as disowning an idealist treatment of the primaries. I believe it is clear from the context in each case that Kant's quarrel with the sensation or secondary quality model is that it is *insufficiently radical*. The problem with the model is not that it makes space too subjective, but quite the reverse: it makes space too objective. The last sentence I quoted reads in full as follows:

This ideality, like that of space, must not, however, be illustrated by false analogies with sensation, because it is then assumed that the appearance, in which the sensible predicates inhere, itself has objective reality.

In other words, we must not think that shapes (like sensed colors, in Locke's view) are effects produced in us by independently existing bodies, for once spatiality is made subjective, bodies are, too. In making spatial properties subjective, we do not merely relocate certain properties to the mind while leaving their bearers behind; we make the bearers themselves mind-dependent. It is because the secondary quality model involves a residual object that Kant thinks it insufficient to illustrate his own view.

So, Kant, like Berkeley, makes the primary qualities depend on minds for their being present in the universe. Yet alongside this similarity, there is a notable difference, to which I now turn.[104] Look again at the passage from B67 discussed in section E:

[E]verything in our knowledge which belongs to intuition . . . contains nothing but mere relations; namely, of locations in an intuition (extension), of change of location (motion), and of laws according to which this change is determined (moving forces). What it is that is present in this or that location, or what it is that is operative in the things themselves apart from change of location, is not given through intuition. Now a thing in itself cannot be known through mere relations; and we may therefore conclude that since outer sense gives us nothing but mere relations, this sense can contain in its representation only the relation of an object to the subject, and not the inner properties of the object in itself. (B67)

Pondering this passage, the reader may be struck by the following thought: there is a sense in which Kant holds that all properties of matter are *primary*. The sense is this: all properties of matter are ways of being in space and time— location, extension, motion, and so on—and are thus contained on the traditional list of primary qualities, extensionally speaking. Kant's inventory of the properties of matter varies somewhat from occasion to occasion but nearly always bears out what I am saying. In the passage just quoted he mentions extension, motion, and forces (which he equates with laws governing motion). At A358, he says that outer sense gives us only "extension, impenetrability, cohesion, and motion," lumping these together under the heading "space and its determinations." In the *Prolegomena* passage, he lists as primary qualities "extension, place, and, in general, space, with all that which belongs to it (impenetrability or materiality, shape, etc.)." The description of external bodies is in each case strikingly similar to what we find in Galileo, Locke, and Descartes.[105]

This is the difference between Berkeley and Kant to which I adverted above. When Berkeley lumped the primary and the secondary qualities together as equally mind-dependent, it was to preserve the place of secondary qualities in the world around us, saving them from the ravages of the scientific worldview. He wanted to keep the scent in the rose and the blue in the sky. These qualities exist only in a mind perceiving them, it is true, but for Berkeley the same goes for "all those bodies which compose the mighty frame of the world." In putting colors in the mind, he was not taking them out of bodies.

Kant, on the other hand, was a defender of the scientific *Weltanschauung* of his day. For him, matter has the primary qualities only; the secondary qualities are definitely second class. This comes out positively in his inventories of the properties of matter, cited two paragraphs above. It also comes out negatively in a number of remarks in which he downgrades the secondary qualities, such as the following:

The taste of a wine does not belong to the objective determinations of the wine, not even if by the wine as an object we mean the wine as appearance, but to the special constitution of sense in the subject that tastes it. Colors are not properties of the bodies to the intuition of which they are attached, but only modifications of the sense of sight. . . . (A28)[106]

The question now to deal with is this: how can we combine these two themes in Kant—the ideality of all the qualities of matter with the privileged place of the primary? This combination, though not outright inconsistent, is nonetheless puzzling.

Kant does not see the two views as inconsistent. Indeed, he sees the first as making the second possible—that, in a way, is what syllogism 2 of section E is all about. The primary properties all distill down to spatial (and presumably also temporal) relations, either of part to part within a whole or of the whole to other wholes outside it. So, if bodies have the primary properties only, they have relational properties only (plus dispositions to have relations). How can anything be like that—all form and no matter, all structure and no stuffing? That is a question Berkeley and Hume raised for "the modern philosophy," and it has been raised again for the scientific realism of our own day by Smart and Armstrong.[107] Kant's response is to hold that although no *thing in itself* can be like that, an *appearance* can be, thus converting the difficulty into one more proof of the ideality of bodies.

We are still left with this question: if both sorts of qualities exist only in our representations, in what way do the secondaries have an inferior and more subjective status? Matter itself exists only in our representations for Kant, so why is it not a fitting locus for colors and tastes?

We can find two distinct but complementary answers to this question in Kant's scattered remarks about the secondary qualities. The first invokes the hoary idea that the secondaries vary with observer and circumstance whereas the primaries are constant:

> Colors, tastes, etc., . . . cannot rightly be regarded as properties of things, but only as changes in the subject, changes which may, indeed, be different for different men. (A29/B45)

> We commonly distinguish in appearances that which is essentially inherent in their intuition and holds for sense in all human beings, from that which belongs to their intuition accidentally only, and is valid not in relation to sensibility in general but only in relation to a particular standpoint or to a peculiarity of structure in this or that sense. (A45–46/B62–63)

The difficulties with this attempt to draw the distinction are well known. As Bayle and Berkeley pointed out, the primaries are in fact just as variable as the secondaries. One can maintain the constancy of the primaries only by taking them at a highly generic or determinable level (e.g., the tower that looks round from a distance and square from up close has *some* shape from every perspective), but then the secondaries are equally invariant when taken at an equally generic level (the mountain that looks blue from a distance and green from up close never appears to have no color at all).

The second answer is that the secondaries "are connected with the appearances only as effects accidentally added by the particular constitution of the sense organs" (A29). What I wish to stress in this remark is not the variability implied by dependence on a sense organ (for variability is what we just considered), but the idea that the secondaries exist as effects in the observer rather than as properties of the external bodies that impinge on observers. Notice what becomes of this idea when we take Kant's larger scheme of things into account. Kant, like Locke, it now appears, wished to maintain that colors, scents, and the like do not reside in bodies, but arise in us as the effects of bodies on our senses. At the same time, it is a tenet of Kant's transcendental idealism that bodies themselves—things in space—are only appearances, arising as the result of the affection of our sensibility by things in themselves. If we are to believe these two tenets together, we evidently have to believe in the theory of *double affection*: things in themselves affect us to produce first-round appearances, which are purely spatial and temporal; these first-round appearances then impinge on us (the same "us," or our phenomenal brains?) to produce second-round appearances, which at last provide a home for the secondary qualities.[108] As discussed in the preceding section, I find the theory of double affection intriguing but in the end untenable. The main problem with it in the present connection is that a *phenomenal cause* (a body in space, existing only as the intentional object of a conscious state) would have a *noumenal effect* (one of those very states, which presumably must belong to a noumenal self).[109] It is hard to make sense of causation that proceeds from phenomena to noumena.

It is regrettable that Kant, having taken one step in Berkeley's direction by making the primary qualities ideal, did not take the further step of giving the primaries and secondaries the same status. As it is, I find much justice in Margaret Wilson's observation that Kant's view offers us "the bitters of idealism without the sweets of Berkeley's commonsense empiricism."[110]

11

Problems of the Self

> '*I think*' is, therefore, the sole text of rational
> psychology, and from it the whole of its
> teaching has to be developed.
> Kant, *Critique of Pure Reason* (A343/B401)

The Paralogisms of Rational Psychology are a series of arguments purporting to demonstrate in *a priori* fashion various important properties of the soul or thinking self, including the following:[1]

that it is a *substance*;

that it is *simple* (i.e., without parts) and therefore immaterial;

that it *endures through time*, and indeed, that it lasts forever.

Kant thinks that these arguments must inevitably fail (as would arguments on the other side). Their conclusions would be synthetic and *a priori*, and he believes that synthetic *a priori* knowledge is to be had only of propositions about objects of possible experience. Yet the self, Kant believes in company with Hume, is *not* an object of possible experience. We may refer to it in our thoughts, but we have no intuition of it and hence no knowledge of its nature. "It is obvious," he says, "that in attaching 'I' to our thoughts we designate the subject of inherence only transcendentally, without noting in it any quality whatsoever—in fact, without knowing anything of it either by direct acquaintance or otherwise [*zu kennen, oder zu wissen*]" (A355). Elsewhere he adds that the representation of the I is "the poorest of all representations" (B408).

The foregoing point, if sound, would show that *something* is wrong with the rational psychologist's arguments, but not *what*. In this chapter, I for the most part ignore Kant's critique of the very idea of rational psychology and try instead to identify (sometimes with Kant's help and sometimes without it) specific places where the Paralogisms go awry. I also suggest an alternative route by which one of the rational psychologist's conclusions might still be reached.

Before I begin, a note on the meaning of the term 'paralogism' is in order. At the beginning of his chapter on this topic, Kant defines a paralogism as "a syllogism that is fallacious in form, be its content what it may" (A341/B399). In his lectures on logic, he says that a formally fallacious syllogism (with the appearance of correctness) "is a *paralogism* in so far as one deceives oneself through it, a *sophism* so far as one intentionally seeks to deceive others through it."[2] In fact, however, all of the so-called paralogisms that Kant presents for discussion are formally valid (or can be made so by minor alterations). They are to be faulted (if at all) only for containing unwarranted premises or equivocal uses of terms. Indeed, in some places, equivocation is Kant's preferred diagnosis of what is wrong with them. He says that the characteristic fallacy of the Paralogisms is *sophisma figurae dictionis* (A402), which he identifies in his logic lectures as the fallacy of ambiguous middle term.[3] But Kant's actual criticisms do not always bear out this general diagnosis.[4]

A. Is the Self a Substance?

Here (with two deletions) is Kant's statement of the First Paralogism ("Of Substantiality") at A348:

1. That which is the *absolute subject* of our judgments and cannot therefore be employed as determination of another thing is *substance*.
2. I, as a thinking being, am the *absolute subject* of all my possible judgments.
3. Therefore, I, as thinking being (soul), am *substance*.[5]

Assuming that "our" in the major premise may be replaced by "my" or "one's," the argument is perfectly valid. So, what does Kant think is wrong with it?

In his critique of the Paralogism in the first edition, Kant appears willing to grant the whole argument, questioning only the usefulness of its conclusion. "The proposition, 'The soul is substance', may quite well be allowed to stand," he says,

> if only it be recognized that [it] does not carry us a single step further, and so cannot yield us any of the usual deductions of the pseudo-rational doctrine of the soul, as, for instance, the everlasting duration of the human soul in all changes and even in death. . . . (A350–51)

In other words, his complaint seems to be that the soul has only been shown to be a substance$_1$ or substance in the unschematized sense—"something which can exist only as subject and never as predicate" (A243/B301). It has not been shown to be a substance$_2$ or substance in the sense of his schematized category—that which is *permanent*, "abiding while all else changes" (A143/B183).

But if this is Kant's criticism, it is inconsistent with other important principles of his. In his proof of the First Analogy of Experience, he argues that all coming-to-be and passing-away is merely alteration of something else. For example, the passing-away of a fist consists merely in the opening up of a hand. This implies that no genuine substance$_1$ can ever pass away, for anything whose passing away is merely an alteration of something else exists merely as a "predicate" of that something else; its mode of being is adjectival rather than substantival. I deal with this point at length in chapter 8.

If Kant wants to deny the "usual deductions" of the rational psychologist, then he had better be able to find something else wrong with the First Paralogism. Fortunately, in the second edition of the *Critique* he does just that, denying (in effect) that the argument can even get as far as showing that the self is a substance$_1$. I identify four possible reasons for its falling short.

First, what is meant by the phrase "subject of all my judgments"? Bennett distinguishes two senses here, *topic* and *maker*: if S judges x to be F, x is the topic and S the maker of the judgment in question.[6] Perhaps the rational psychologist has conflated these two senses, affirming the minor premise because of the obviousness of 'I am the subject (= maker) of all my judgments', but then slipping from here to 'I am the subject (= topic) of all my judgments'. That transition would, of course, be a *non sequitur*; a person can make judgments that are not about himself.

Second, even if we waive the preceding point, the rational psychologist has still not made out his case. What must be pointed out next is that being the subject (= topic) of a judgment [and even, as I show below, being the subject (= topic) of *all* one's judgments] is not yet sufficient for being a substance$_1$.

A subject is anything to which a property is correctly ascribed. The maker of any judgment is a subject in this sense (for the property expressed by 'judges such and such' may correctly be ascribed to it); so is the topic of any true judgment. Now I think one of Kant's points against the rational psychologist may simply be this: being a subject is not all there is to being substance$_1$. There are *two* clauses in the definition of a substance$_1$: a substance$_1$ must be a subject, and it must not be a predicate of anything else. The second clause must be understood as having this implication: the existence of a substance$_1$ must not consist in the having of predicates by something else (as the existence of a fist consists in a hand's being closed). Plainly, the first clause does not imply the second. The rational psychologist may have erroneously concluded from the mere fact that the self is a subject to its being a substance$_1$, ignoring the need to make sure that the second clause is fulfilled.[7] This seems to be just what Kant is saying in the following passage:

> In the second proposition [I think as subject] it has not been determined whether I can exist and be thought as subject only, and not also as a predicate of another being, and accordingly the concept of a subject is here taken in a merely logical sense, and it remains undetermined whether or not we are to understand by it a substance. (B419)

He also notes that the proposition that I am subject "casts no light whatsoever upon the mode of my existence" (B412).

An example of the too-quick inference from subject to substance$_1$ may be found in Bayle's famous objection to Spinoza:

> If it were true then, as Spinoza claims, that men are modalities of God, one would speak falsely when one said, "Peter denies this, he wants that, he affirms such and such a thing"; for actually, according to this theory, it is God who denies, wants, affirms; and consequently all the denominations that result from the thoughts of all men are properly and physically to be ascribed to God. From which it follows that God hates and loves, denies and affirms the same things at the same time. . . .[8]

In assuming that if God is the only substance, he must also be the only subject, Bayle is equating the notions of subject and substance (i.e., substance$_1$). But in declaring Peter to be a mode rather than a substance, Spinoza is not denying that Peter is a subject. He is maintaining that Peter's existence (as well as his having the predicates he does) consists in God's having certain predicates, but these predicates need not include being the real thinker of Peter's thoughts.

I turn now to the third possible mistake of the rational psychologist. The minor premise does not merely say that I am a subject of my judgments; it says that I am the subject of *all* my judgments. Does that make a difference, enabling me now to infer that I am a substance$_1$? The answer is no: that I am topic of all *my* judgments would not imply that I am predicate of *no* judgment. Even if I occur only in subject place in the judgments I make, there might be other judgments (made by others or perhaps not made by anyone, simply obtaining as true propositions) in which I do *not* figure as subject. Such a judgment might be 'God-or-Nature is modified in the Van Clevish manner'. (Compare: even if all the judgments I make about waves employ them as subjects, that leaves quite open the possibility that their mode of being is adjectival.) Once again, it would be correct for Kant to observe that the fact recorded in the minor premise "casts no light whatsoever upon the mode of my existence."

To sum up the first three criticisms: neither from the fact that I am the subject (= maker) of all my judgments, nor from the fact that I am the subject (= topic) of some of them, nor even from the fact that I am the subject (= topic) of all of them, would it follow that I am a substance$_1$.

To set the stage for the fourth criticism, I turn now to a feature of the Paralogism I have so far left out of account. Kant's formulation of it employs the phrase 'absolute subject': what does he mean by the qualifier *absolute*? I think the answer is clear: an absolute subject is something that is a subject in relation to predicates without itself being a predicate (or an adjectival being) in relation to any further subject. This accords with Kant's two-clause definition of substance$_1$; it also accords with his discussion of the term 'absolute' (in the sense in which it is opposed to 'comparative') at A324–26/B380–82, and it makes sense of the interior 'therefore' in the major premise. If we take the phrase 'absolute subject' in this sense, the inference from 'absolute subject' to 'substance$_1$' is valid (and the major premise incontestably true).

Here now is the fourth criticism, which is the one I think Kant would regard as fundamental: none of us knows he is an absolute subject in the required sense. Although there are several senses in which we may know ourselves to figure as subjects of judgments, we cannot know ourselves to be *absolute* subjects. Thus, once we have understood the middle term so as to make the major premise true, the minor premise becomes problematic.[9] So, there is no understanding of the middle term that makes both premises simultaneously acceptable.

B. Is the Self Simple?

Here is Kant's formulation of the Second Paralogism ("Of Simplicity") at A351:

1. That, the action of which can never be regarded as the concurrence of several things acting, is *simple*.

2. Now the soul, or the thinking I, is such a being.
3. Therefore, the soul is simple.

Kant calls this "the Achilles" of all dialectical inferences in the pure doctrine of the soul, one that appears to withstand even the keenest scrutiny (A351). But like the first Achilles, this one has its Achilles heel.

The major premise is perhaps more readily grasped if we restate it in contrapositive form: if something is *non*simple (i.e., composite), its action *can* be regarded as the concurrence of several things acting. Kant himself states it this way a little further on:

> [T]he action of a composite . . . is an aggregate of several actions or accidents, distributed among the plurality of substances . . . (as, for instance, the motion of a body is the combined motion of all its parts). (A351–52)

More generally, we could say that any nonrelational property of a composite whole must follow from the properties of and relations among its parts. Call this the principle of *mereological reducibility*.[10] To illustrate the principle with an example that bears it out, if something is square, its being so follows from its being composed of four straight sides that are equal in length and meet each other at right angles.

The minor premise says that the characteristic activity of the soul—thinking—is *not* thus reducible. If it were thus reducible, Kant has the rational psychologist argue, it would be the concurrence of several things thinking, but that would violate one of Kant's supreme principles—the unity of consciousness:

> For suppose it be the composite that thinks: then every part of it would contain a part of the thought, and only all of them taken together would contain the whole thought. But this cannot consistently be maintained. For representations (for instance, the single words of a verse), distributed among different beings, never make up a whole thought (a verse), and it is therefore impossible that a thought should inhere in what is essentially composite. (A352)[11]

The example of the verse should remind us of James's twelve men each of whom is given one word of a sentence to think of "as intently as he will: nowhere will there be a consciousness of the whole sentence."[12]

As in the case of the First Paralogism, Kant spends most of his time criticizing not the argument itself but the import of its conclusion.[13] The simplicity of the soul is a result of interest to the rational psychologist because it is thought to imply the immateriality of the soul. But Kant contends that for all we know, simplicity is compatible with materiality. He notes that if by 'matter' one means *outer appearances*, then matter is only a species of representations, and the question of whether the soul is the same in kind as matter has so obvious an answer that it should not be a topic for debate: "[F]or it is obvious that a thing in itself is of a different nature from the determinations which constitute only its state" (A360). Properly construed, then, the question must be whether there is any similarity between the soul and matter when matter is taken to be *the thing in itself underlying outer appearances*. When matter is taken in this way, however, we "are in no position to say that the soul is in any inward respect different from it" (A360). For all we know, matter in this noumenal sense may be endowed with thought.

Kant is evidently thinking of a hypothesis like that of Leibniz: the reality underlying the phenomenon of matter may consist of monads, simple beings endowed with consciousness. What puzzles me about this suggestion is why Kant thinks it should dash the hopes of the rational psychologist. Instead of opening the way for a materialist account of the soul, Kant seems to be raising the possibility of a spiritualist account of matter—a theory in which matter is merely a phenomenon generated by the underlying monads.[14]

So, I now return to the Paralogism itself and ask how it fares as an argument for the simplicity of the soul. Since Kant is not very forthcoming about exactly where the argument goes wrong,[15] I invite another critic to join in the discussion. Here is how the merits of the case might be debated by the proponent of the original Paralogism and our new antagonist.

Antagonist: Your reducibility principle as stated in the major premise is reasonable enough: the action of a composite must be the concurrence of several things acting. But why do you suppose that if a composite being thinks, its thinking must be the concurrence of several things *thinking*? Why could it not be the result or concurrence of several things acting in other ways? When a radio emits a sound, we do not suppose that different parts of the radio emit different parts of the sound; rather, the various parts engage in various soundless activities, as a result of which the radio as a whole emits sound. Why may we not similarly suppose that when a composite entity thinks, its parts (brain cells, perhaps) engage in various thoughtless activities (firing or refusing to fire, etc.), as a result of which the whole, but nothing short of the whole, thinks?

Paralogist: Thinking could perhaps be the *nomological* outcome of various purely physical activities of the parts, such as those you describe. What our reduction principle requires, however, is that every property of a whole be the *logical* outcome of properties and interrelations of the parts. And what properties can we cite from which thought or consciousness in the whole would follow logically, save properties already involving thought or consciousness? That is why I say the thinking performed by a composite being would have to be divided among its parts.

Antagonist: Well, if *logical* deducibility is what your reduction principle demands, the principle itself is suspect. The properties of a chemical compound cannot be deduced logically from the properties of the elements and their mode of combination; they flow from these properties with nomological necessity alone. They are *emergent*, in one good sense of that term.[16] You can know all there is to know about hydrogen and oxygen taken separately without being able to deduce in advance the properties of water molecules.

Paralogist: You say that the properties of a chemical compound do not follow logically from the properties and relations of the parts. But how could they not so follow? If a water molecule has the property of being F (whatever that is), must not some of its constituent atoms have the dispositional property of forming an F thing when appropriately united with other atoms?

Antagonist: Yes, of course, so if you allow *such* properties in the reduction base, I make no objection to your principle. In fact, you have made it completely trivial. But I see now where your use of its leads you astray. Perhaps there are no properties of brain cells (or other parts of persons) entailing that the whole person thinks, except for properties already involving thought, but to say that a property *involves* thought in the relevant sense is not yet to say that its *bearer* must think. To take a cue from what you said about the water molecule: the properties of brain cells that entail consciousness in the whole could be properties such as "yielding consciousness when appropriately related to such-and-such other cells." Such properties conceptually involve consciousness, because you cannot specify them without making reference to consciousness. But I see no reason to think that their bearers must *be* conscious, so the kind of reduction you are now holding out for would not in the least require that some of the proper parts of a thinking thing must themselves be things that think. It would not lead to violations of the unity of consciousness.

In my opinion, the antagonist wins this little debate. Now I restate and amplify some of the points that arise within it.

There is only one version of the major premise that will do what the paralogist wants it to do. The needed version implies that every property of a whole that is not possessed by any of its parts (or that is not generically similar to any property of any part) is reducible to properties of the parts in the following sense: it must follow logically from properties of and relations among the parts that are conceptually independent of (or specifiable without reference to) the original property. It is hard to see how consciousness could be thus reducible, so if a composite entity were conscious, some of its parts would have to be conscious, too—thus violating the unity of consciousness.[17] (An 'I' that is a plurality would have to be a plurality of 'I's, as Sellars puts it.[18])

When the major premise is construed in the way just described, however, there is reason to reject it. Properties of chemical compounds are *prima facie* exceptions to it.

We can get a more plausible version of the major premise by weakening it in either of two ways: either (a) by requiring mere nomological following of whole-properties from part-properties, or, if we continue to require logical following, (b) by dropping the requirement that the properties of the parts be specifiable without reference to properties of the whole. In either of these cases, however, we will no longer be able to give the unity-of-consciousness argument for affirming the minor premise (i.e., for holding that consciousness is irreducible). In case (a), consciousness may be the nomological outcome of purely physical doings of the parts. In case (b), consciousness may be the logical outcome of properties the specification of which requires reference to consciousness, but the possession of which does not require the possession of consciousness. In either case, we can accommodate consciousness in the whole without assigning it to any of the parts.

In closing, it may be instructive to compare the rational psychologist's argument to the following argument by Leibniz for the existence of *petites perceptions*:

> A great stupefying roar, as, for example, the murmur of a large assemblage, is composed of all the little murmurs of individual persons which are not noticed at all but of which one must nevertheless have some sensation; otherwise one would not sense the whole.[19]

Leibniz assumed that the parts of what is heard must themselves be things that are heard; the rational psychologist assumes, in effect, that the parts of what hears must themselves be things that hear. The second assumption is no better off than the first.

C. Can a Self Have Emergent Properties?

Can anything be salvaged of the rational psychologist's project from the first two Paralogisms? I believe the answer is yes. Consider the following Mixed Paralogism, which combines features of the First and Second:

1. That the action of which can never be regarded as the logical outcome of other things acting is *substance.*
2. Now the soul, or the thinking I, is such a being.
3. Therefore, the soul is substance.

As before, the major premise is more readily grasped if stated in its contrapositive form: that which is not a substance (but only a mode of other things) must be such that its "action" follows logically from the actions of those other things. This time the major premise can be gained virtually by definition: if x is a mode of y and z (or a logical construction out of them, to use a more recent term), then all of x's properties must follow logically from properties of y and z. Putting the point another way, although there might conceivably be emergent properties of *wholes* (that was the trouble with the major premise of the Second Paralogism), there cannot be emergent properties of *modes.* The properties of a mode must flow logically and not just nomologically from the properties of the underlying substances.

The minor premise now tells us that the characteristic activity of the soul— thinking—is not logically derivable from the "action" or properties of other things, as it would have to be if the soul were a mode. We can appreciate the point by asking: if I am a mode, what am I a mode of? The most plausible answer nowadays is that I am a mode of the cells, atoms, or yet tinier particles of which my body is composed. In accordance with the major premise, then, all my properties (including psychological properties such as having the experiences I am now having and thinking the thoughts I am now thinking) would have to flow logically from properties of my cells or atoms. Yet is that not exactly what we saw to be implausible in discussing the Second Paralogism?

Of course, as before we can find properties of the cells or other parts that entail the possession of various conscious states by the whole if we countenance among the base properties such items as "yielding conscious state C when related thus and so to such-and-such other cells." In similar fashion, we can derive my psychological properties from properties of the planet Pluto if we reckon among Pluto's properties such properties as "being such that JVC is seeing red" and "being such that JVC is contemplating the continuum hypothesis." But that would not be enough to make me a mode of Pluto. If one thing is genuinely a mode of another thing or things, its properties must be logically derivable from *conceptually independent* properties of those other things. The minor premise of the Mixed Paralogism claims that conscious states are not logically derivable from any conceptually independent properties of cells or anything else of which conscious beings might plausibly be thought tc be modes.

The answer to the question posed in the title of this section thus appears to be this: a self can have emergent properties, but only if it is a substance$_1$ and not a mere mode.

D. Does the Self Endure?

Here is how Kant presents the Third Paralogism ("Of Personality") at A361:

1. That which is conscious of the numerical identity of itself at different times is in so far a *person.*
2. Now, the soul is conscious, etc.
3. Therefore, it is a person.

What is at issue in this Paralogism is whether the soul is *veridically* conscious of its identity over time, that is, whether numerically the same soul really does exist at different moments of time. This is clear from the way in which Kant restates the conclusion of the Paralogism elsewhere: "As regards the different times in which it [the soul] exists, it is numerically identical, that is, *unity* (not plurality)" (A344/B402; see also A404). Kant puts the point using the term 'person', probably because Locke had made consciousness of identity a defining feature of persons.[20] But we could just as well state the Paralogism without using the term 'person' at all:[21]

1. That which is conscious of the numerical identity of itself at different times must exist at these different times, i.e., must *endure.*
2. Now, the soul is conscious, etc.
3. Therefore, it endures.

Here 'endurance' is meant to stand for the strict kind of persistence or identity through time that contrasts with what David Lewis has called 'perdurance', that is, persisting by means of having different (but unified) parts or phases at different moments.[22] I say more on this presently.

Like the other Paralogisms, this one is formally valid, and as with the others, Kant thinks that no one knows its conclusion to be true. So, what is wrong this time? I think Kant would agree with the following diagnosis: if by 'consciousness' we mean veridical consciousness, then the major premise is true but the minor open to question, and if by 'consciousness' we mean consciousness that may or may not be veridical, then the minor is true but the major false. This would be in line with his general diagnosis of the Paralogisms as all containing equivocal terms, with no uniform reading that makes both premises acceptable.

The second horn of the dilemma I just stated is developed in the following passage:

> The identity of the consciousness of myself at different times is therefore only a formal condition of my thoughts and their coherence, and in no way proves the numerical identity of my subject. Despite the logical identity of the 'I', such a change may have occurred in it as does not allow of the retention of its identity, and yet we may ascribe to it the same-sounding 'I', which in every different state, even in one involving change of the [thinking] subject, might still retain the thought of the preceding subject and so hand it over to the subsequent subject. (A363)

A footnote attached to this paragraph explains that just as one elastic ball may communicate its entire state of motion to another when they collide, so might one conscious substance transfer all of its representations to a second substance, this second to a third, and so on:

> The last substance would then be conscious of all the states of the previously changed substances, as being its own states, because they would have been transferred to it together with the consciousness of them. And yet it would not have been one and the same person in all these states.

Here it looks very much as though Kant is conceding the minor premise (as long as 'conscious of' does not have "success grammar"), but pointing out that consciousness of identity in this merely phenomenological sense is not sufficient for identity—in which case the major premise is false. I may ostensibly remember doing something that was in fact done by another agent at a time when I did not even exist. If we sought to avoid this objection by making consciousness of identity by definition veridical, Kant could respond by pointing out that doubt is now transferred from the major premise to the minor.

Roderick Chisholm has suggested that Kant is simply indulging here in wholesale skepticism about memory.[23] He need not be doing quite that, since he could still maintain that when I remember my doing or experiencing such-and-such, I am reliably right about the fact that such-and-such was done. My possible error consists only in thinking that it was I (= this subject) who did it. Nonetheless, Kant is certainly challenging something that Thomas Reid took to be a first principle, namely, that our own personal identity and continued existence extend as far back as we remember anything distinctly.[24]

It is worth noting that Kant's standards for what would count as real identity through time are stricter than those of Locke and many contemporary philosophers. Locke held that all that is requisite to personal identity is memory, or continuity of consciousness:[25] if the consciousness of my past deeds should come to be concentrated in my little finger, or transferred to some other substance in just the manner Kant suggests, then my finger (or that substance) would be the same person as the doer of the deeds.[26] In a similar vein, Derek Parfit and many other contemporary philosophers hold that psychical continuity is all that matters to personal identity, so A may be the same person as B who existed twenty years ago even if the stuff of which A is now composed is entirely distinct from the stuff of which B was then composed.[27] Kant is here disagreeing with both Locke and Parfit: where there is not numerical identity of subjects existing at different times, there is not personal identity, either.

But there is also another side of Kant in tension with this one. Kant would certainly want to allow that representations occurring at different times can enjoy unity of apperception. If representations are transferred from subject to subject in the way Kant envisions in his critique of the Third Paralogism, is unity of apperception destroyed? Presumably Kant would say no: it could still obtain, and would moreover still suffice for unity of mind. (See appendix F.) But if so, Kant must relax his standards for real identity through time. He must say that a succession of distinct subjects can add up to one continuing person, provided the representations occurring to these subjects stand in the right unity-conferring relations.

I have noted that Kant seems in some places to be a system theorist and in others to be a center theorist about the unity of mind. Trying to put the two types of theory together causes trouble. If the dictates of the two theories agree, we get a strange kind of overdetermination; if they pull in opposite directions, we get inconsistency.

E. How Many Selves?

Kant speaks of three different selves: the empirical self, the transcendental self, and the noumenal self. The empirical self is the self as encountered in introspection; it is the totality of items disclosed to inner intuition (thoughts, perceptions, emotions, etc.) The transcendental self is the subject of all the states just mentioned: it is the thinker of our thoughts, the haver of our experiences, the willer of our actions, and perhaps also the agent of the various activities of synthesis Kant talks about. Kant calls this self transcendental because, like Hume, he believes that we can never observe it. Recalling Hume's famous remark—"For my part, when I enter most intimately into what I call *myself*, I always stumble on some particular perception or other, of heat or cold, light or shade, love or hatred, pain or pleasure"[28]—we might say that the empirical self is the self on which Hume stumbled, while the transcendental self is that which did the stumbling.[29] Finally, the noumenal self is the "self in itself"— the real self or the self as it really is.

Three selves are surely too many. Can we reduce this number, either by eliminating one of the selves or by collapsing two or more of them together?

I begin by discussing views that eliminate the transcendental self—the I of the 'I think'. Certain passages in Kant and some of his commentators give the idea that the I is some sort of necessary fiction—that 'I think . . . ' is a matrix we must use for reporting psychological facts, but that the symbol 'I' occurring within it does not refer to anything. Here are two passages that may suggest (though I do not believe they imply) such a view:

It follows, therefore, that the first syllogism of transcendental psychology, when it puts forward the constant logical subject of thought as being knowledge of the real subject in which the thought inheres, is palming off upon us what is a mere pretence of new insight. We do not have, and cannot have, any knowledge whatsoever of any such subject. (A350)

[When I think of myself as a subject of thoughts] no object whatsoever is being thought; all that is being represented is simply the relation to self as subject (as the form of thought). (B412n.)

According to this view, our belief in the existence of a self is an illusion engendered by the need to attach 'I think' to reports of our mental lives.

I find this view puzzling and perhaps incoherent. If we *must* use the form of words (or form of thought) 'I think _____' to report certain facts, what better reason could there be for thinking that there *is* an entity to which 'I' refers? It is a well-entrenched point of method in ontology that if there are certain true sentences purportedly referring to an entity of a certain kind, and if there is no known way to restate the content of those sentences without making ostensible reference to that entity, then we are ontologically committed to the entity in question. I illustrate this point with an application that bears precisely on the case at hand.

According to certain versions of the "no-self" or "no-ownership" theory (as held by Buddhists, Humeans, and others), there is no such thing as a thinker of thoughts or haver of experiences, and it should be possible accordingly to state all facts about our mental lives in an 'I'-free idiom. For example, instead of saying 'I am now in pain', one could use the passive construction 'pain is now felt', which refers only to pain and not to any subject who feels it. But there are problems with trying to carry this translation program through. Roderick Chisholm has trenchantly asked: how are we to translate *negative* judgments, such as 'I am *not* now feeling pain', into an idiom free of reference to the I?[30] The passive construction 'pain is not now felt' is obviously too sweeping—perhaps pain is felt by someone, even if not by me. 'Pain is not now felt *here*' similarly oversteps what is known to be the case, for however small *here* may be, perhaps some tiny creature (a microbe coursing through my veins, perhaps?) shares that space with me and feels pain. '*This sensation* is now occurring and is not co-instantiated with pain' is a good try, but still fails to be equivalent with the original; it implies, as 'I am not in pain' does not, that a particular sensation is occurring. It seems that if we are to state only that which we know to be true, we must say '*I* am not now in pain', bringing in just that reference to the I that was supposed to be eliminable.[31] But does that not constitute at least a *prima facie* reason for thinking that there *is* such a thing as the I?[32]

In any event, I do not think that Kant himself subscribed to the view that the I is a fiction. His deprecatory remarks about it generally make an epistemological rather than a metaphysical point. Here are two representative passages:

Through this I or he or it (the thing) which thinks, nothing further is represented than a transcendental subject of the thoughts = X. (A346/B404)

[B]eyond this logical meaning of the 'I', we have no knowledge of the subject in itself, which as substratum underlies this 'I', as it does all thoughts. (A350)

Often enough, he makes it clear that there is a referent for 'I', as in the following passage:

[The indeterminate perception expressed by 'I think'] signifies . . . something which actually exists, and which in the proposition 'I think' is denoted as such. (B422n.)[33]

So, there is such a thing as the transcendental self—a referent for the 'I' of the 'I think'.

If we are going to reduce the number of selves, then, we do better to collapse two or more of them together. In this connection, some have proposed an identification of the transcendental self with the empirical self and others an identification of the noumenal self with the empirical self.[34] I advocate instead an identification of the transcendental self with the noumenal self.

If there is such a thing as the transcendental self at all, it would be astonishing indeed if it were *not* the noumenal self. Recall the phenomenal/noumenal distinction: phenomenal items exist only as contents of representations, whereas noumenal objects exist in their own right. If thinkers or representers were *not* noumenal beings, we would have the absurdity of something that exists only as the content of representations, yet is itself the subject of representations—as in the story by Jorge Luis Borges that ends with the following sentence:

With relief, with humiliation, with terror, he understood that he, too, was all appearance, that someone else was dreaming him.[35]

If we learn anything from Descartes's *cogito*, it is that the predicament described by Borges is impossible. I may be dreaming, but I cannot exist merely as the figment of someone else's dream.

In saying that the transcendental self must exist in its own right, I mean that it must exist independent of being represented—not necessarily that it must be ontologically basic in the manner of a substance. As far as the present argument goes, the self could exist *an sich* yet be ontologically derivative. This, of course, is the possibility Kant himself tries to keep open in his criticism of the First Paralogism.

Whether on the strength of the argument I have just given or not, I think it is clear that Kant regards the transcendental self as a noumenal being. Witness the following:

Indeed, it would be a great stumbling-block, or rather would be the one unanswerable objection, to our whole critique, if there were a possibility of proving *a priori* that all thinking beings are in themselves simple substances. . . . It would then follow that *a priori* synthetic propositions . . . are applicable to things in general and to things in themselves—a result that would make an end of our whole critique, and would constrain us to acquiesce in the old-time procedure. (B409–10)

Clearly, the unstated premise in Kant's enthymeme is that thinking beings are things in themselves.

The same presupposition can be found toward the end of Kant's discussion of the Second Paralogism in the A edition. Kant there introduces a dilemma for the doctrine of the simple soul with the words, "If I understand by soul a thinking being in itself . . ." (A360). It is clear from the rest of the passage that this understanding of things is not simply one horn of the dilemma he propounds, but something taken for granted in both cases.

I call attention finally to a passage in which Kant equates "the transcendental subject" with "the self proper, as it exists in itself":

> Even the inner and sensible intuition of our mind (as object of our consciousness) which is represented as being determined by the succession of different states in time, is not the self proper, as it exists in itself—that is, is not the transcendental subject—but only an appearance that has been given to the sensibility of this, to us unknown, being. (A492/B520)

The transcendental self is none other than the noumenal self.[36]

We are down now to two selves, the transcendental/noumenal self and the empirical self. Which of these is the topic of the Paralogisms? I take it to be the transcendental self. After all, the transcendental self is the I of 'I think', and Kant tells us that 'I think' is "the sole text of rational psychology" (A343/B401). Moreover, the source of the failing of all the Paralogisms is supposed to be that there is no acquaintance with the self, but we *do* have acquaintance with our empirical selves.

It must be conceded, however, that there are passages in the Paralogisms that make sense only if the self Kant is talking about is the empirical or phenomenal self. (i) In the second paragraph of the Third Paralogism, Kant says that judgments of an outside observer have priority over one's own judgments in questions about one's identity through time. Why should this be the case if the identity of the noumenal self were at issue? What is observable by others is only my body and its states, which for Kant are phenomenal. (ii) In the example of the elastic balls, Kant raises the possibility that the subject of our thoughts at one moment may pass on all its thoughts to a different subject at the next moment. How can any of these subjects be noumenal, given that noumenal entities are supposed to be outside time and therefore incapable of doing any "passing on"? Indeed, it would seem that the entire issue of the Third Paralogism—does the self endure through time?—cannot arise for the noumenal self if the noumenal self is not in time.

But to jump back to the other side of the question, we have seen that for Kant the issue of the *Second* Paralogism—is the self of a like nature with matter?—cannot legitimately arise for anything *but* the noumenal self. Surely all the Paralogisms are meant to concern the same self! So, perhaps the Third Paralogism is about the noumenal self, too, and Kant has momentarily forgotten that noumena are not in time. The view that nothing is really in time, not even the noumenal self, is so radically opposed to our ordinary thinking that it would not be surprising if Kant occasionally lost sight of it.

It remains to say something about the ontological status of the empirical self. Kant's official position is that the empirical self is an appearance to no less an extent than any of the empirical objects outside us in space: just as empirical objects exist only as assorted contents of perceptive awareness, so the empirical self exists only as the collective content of apperceptive awareness (see chapter 5). That makes it merely a virtual object, so in one good sense, the noumenal self is the only self there is.[37]

12

Rational Theology

> There are only three possible ways of prov-
> ing the existence of God by means of specu-
> lative reason. All the paths leading to this
> goal begin either from determinate experi-
> ence . . . or they start from experience which
> is purely indeterminate . . . or finally they
> abstract from all experience, and argue com-
> pletely *a priori*, from mere concepts, to the
> existence of a supreme cause.
>
> Kant, *Critique of Pure Reason*, A590/B618

Kant tells us that there are exactly three ways of proving the existence of God by speculative reason. In the first, we begin from "determinate experience and the specific constitution of the world" and ascend from there to a supreme cause. "The world presents to us so immeasurable a stage of variety, order, purposiveness, and beauty" (A622/B650) that we may infer a sublime and wise cause (A625/B654). This is the physico-theological proof or argument from design. In the second, we begin from indeterminate experience or "experience of existence in general" and proceed once again to a cause. Here it does not matter what the world is like, but only that it exists; if the cosmos consisted of nothing but a speck of dust, we would still need to posit a cause for it. This is the cosmological proof. Finally, we may bypass experience altogether and argue "completely *a priori*, from mere concepts." This is the ontological proof, most audacious of all, as it premises nothing about what exists. In this chapter I examine what Kant has to say about the cosmological and ontological proofs. I consider them (as Kant does) as attempts to prove the existence not of the God of Abraham, Isaac, and Jacob, but of a primordial being, whose identity with the God of religion must be a matter of further argument or faith.

A. The Ontological Argument

The version of the ontological argument Kant considers is that of Descartes, not Anselm.[1] It may be set forth as follows:

1. The *ens realissimum* (i.e., God) is, by definition, the being who possesses all perfections.

2. Since (a) existence is a perfection, (b) any being that possesses all perfections must exist.
3. Therefore, the *ens realissimum* exists.

Kant is generally credited with originating what has become the standard criticism of the ontological argument—that existence is not a predicate. His critique contains in addition two other objections that he and his commentators do not always keep separate from the first: in a predicative proposition you may always "reject the subject," and there is something logically defective in the concept of a necessary being. I argue that one of these criticisms is cogent while the other two—including the famous one—are not.

B. Real Predicates

Kant never enunciates the slogan so often attributed to him, that existence is not a predicate. What he says instead is that existence is not a *real* or *determining* predicate, that is, "a predicate which is added to the concept of the subject and enlarges it" (A598/B626). As always, by a 'predicate' he does not mean a linguistic item but a property or a constituent of a concept. His contention may be understood in accordance with the following definitions:

A predicate P *enlarges* a concept C =Df $\Diamond \exists x(Cx \, \& \, -Px)$. (Note that "enlarge" may be a misleading term, insofar as enlarging a predicate typically results in narrowing its extension.)

A predicate P is a *real* predicate =Df P enlarges at least one concept.[2]

It follows from these definitions that a predicate P is *nonreal* iff for any concept C, $\Box(x)(Cx \, \& \, Px \text{ iff } Cx)$. This makes clear the sense in which a nonreal predicate "makes no addition" to any concept: if P is nonreal, then saying that something is both C and P says nothing not already implied by simply saying that it is C.[3]

Is Kant correct in claiming that existence is not, in the sense just defined, a real predicate? Yes, indeed: there is no concept C such that $\Diamond \exists x(Cx \, \& \, -Ex)$. This, at any rate, is a consequence of letting the existential quantifier express existence.[4] To suppose there is something ($\exists x \ldots$) that does not exist ($\ldots$ $-Ex$) is to suppose there is something that there is not.

Relative to widely accepted assumptions, then, Kant's dictum is true. The next question is, how does it show that Descartes's argument is wrong? How does the fact that existence is not a real predicate invalidate the ontological argument or make it unsound?

One common suggestion is that only real predicates may be used in definitions, in which case it would be illegitimate for Descartes to define God as a being who, among other things, exists.[5] But this suggestion is off the mark on two counts. First, Descartes is not guilty as charged. Look at his first premise; it says that God has all perfections but makes no mention of existence. Of course, in the next premise, Descartes says that existence is one of the perfections, so one may wish to say that he is implicitly if not explicitly defining God as a being who exists. But that brings us to the second point: what Descartes is charged with is no crime. There is nothing wrong with using non-real predicates in definitions. Any tautological predicate (e.g., being red or nonred) is as much a nonreal predicate as existence, but there is nothing logically vicious about the definition 'x is square =Df x is an equilateral rectangle & x is red or nonred'. The second conjunct in the definiens is idle but harmless.

Perhaps it will be suggested that the premise that runs afoul of Kant's dictum is not the first but the second, for if existence "makes no difference" to any concept, how can it be a perfection? A perfection might be thought of as a property that contributes to the greatness of a thing, or makes an already good thing better than it would be without it. But if existence "makes no difference" to any concept, how can it be a perfection in this sense? How can an existent thing be better or more perfect than a nonexistent thing?[6]

But this objection is readily sidestepped. As I have formulated the second premise above, it consists of a premise proper (whatever has all perfections exists) and a reason for it (existence is a perfection). Perhaps Kant's dictum undermines or refutes the reason offered for the premise, but it does not refute the premise itself. Quite the contrary: it entails the premise! If existence is implied by any concept whatsoever, then in particular it is implied by the concept *possesses all perfections*, and that makes the second premise true.

Our verdict so far must be that Kant's most famous criticism of the ontological argument leaves it entirely unscathed.

C. Existence and Quantifiers

When the slogan "existence is not a predicate" occurs in contemporary philosophy, it does not generally mean quite what Kant meant by "existence is not a *real* predicate," though it does mean something closely related. It is worth while to inquire into what the contemporary slogan means, how it is related to Kant's views, why we should believe it, and how it affects the ontological argument.

What the slogan usually means is that it is the job of the existential quantifier to make existence statements—that you say that something exists when and only when you say something of the form '∃xFx' (or an equivalent). In short, the existential quantifier deserves its name.[7]

The view that existence is expressed by quantifiers is often accompanied by the Fregean view that quantifiers are second-level predicates—predicates that express properties of concepts rather than properties of objects. For Frege, to say that something exists is always to say that some concept is instantiated.[8] This, of course, is the so-called Kant-Frege view, discussed earlier in chapter 8, section H. It should be noted, however, that the bare linkage of existence with quantifiers need not take this Fregean form. It could instead take a Quinean form, in which '∃x(x is dog)' carries ontological commitment to dogs, but none to doghood or the concept Dog.[9]

Why should we speak of the *Kant*-Frege view? The following passage gives one good reason:

If, now, we take the subject (God) with all its predicates (among which is omnipotence), and say 'God is', or 'There is a God', we attach no new predicate to the concept of God, but only posit the subject in itself with all its predicates, and indeed posit it as being an *object* that stands in relation to my *concept*. (A599/B627)

To say that God exists is to say something not directly about God, but only about the concept of God, namely, that there is an object corresponding to it. That does sound remarkably like Frege's view.[10]

Why should we accept the Kant-Frege view? One reason is that it gives us a neat solution to the ancient problem of nonbeing, or of negative existentials.[11] How can we truly say that unicorns do not exist? Must they not exist in some fashion if we are to say anything meaningful about them? Notoriously, some philosophers solve this problem by distinguishing two modes of being, shadowy subsistence and robust existence: it is because unicorns subsist that we are able truly to deny that they exist. Frege and the post-1903 Russell solve the problem without bringing in a second mode of being: according to them, we say that unicorns do not exist by saying of the *concept* unicorn (which *does* exist) that it has no instances. If we treat positive existentials in parallel fashion, we arrive at precisely the Kant-Frege view: to say that something exists (or that things of a certain sort exist) is to say that some concept is instantiated.[12]

How is the Kant-Frege view related to Kant's doctrine that existence is not a real or determining predicate? The former may be seen as underlying (because entailing) the latter. Recall that a predicate P is *nonreal* iff for any concept C, $\Box(x)(Cx \& Px \leftrightarrow Cx)$. The right-hand side of the entire biconditional is equivalent by elementary logic to 'for any C, $\Box(x)(Cx \rightarrow Px)$'. So, existence will be a nonreal predicate iff it is already entailed by any other predicate or concept. Now, suppose we say, in alliance with Kant and Frege and in opposition to Meinong, that it is the function of the quantifier 'there is' to make existence statements. In that case, we cannot truly say that there are things that do not exist: for any concept C, to say that $(\exists x)(Cx \& -Ex)$ will be to say something contradictory and impossible. Well, if $(\exists x)(Cx \& -Ex)$ is impossible, then $(x)(Cx \rightarrow Ex)$ is necessary, but that is just what is involved in saying that existence is not a real or determining predicate.[13]

We should ask finally how "existence is not a predicate" in its contemporary meaning affects the ontological argument. I showed in the preceding section that Kant's dictum that existence is not a real predicate does nothing to harm the ontological argument. Does the contemporary dictum have any extra punch—any adverse impact on the ontological argument not already delivered by Kant's dictum? As far as I can see, the answer is no: that existence is expressed by quantifiers does nothing to disturb either premise. As for premise 1, there is nothing wrong with defining a being in terms of a clause Px that implies existence. This clause will now have to take the quantified form '$\exists y(y = x)$', but what is wrong with that? As for premise 2, there is nothing wrong with affirming that whatever has all perfections exists; indeed, that is implied by the Kant-Frege view as strongly as it is implied by Kant's dictum.

D. Rejecting the Subject

The doctrine of Kant's (and also, by the way, of Gassendi's)[14] that we have been exploring—that any property implies or presupposes existence—must surely heighten our suspicion that something is wrong with the ontological argument. For, if any property implies existence, do we not have the makings of an ontological argument for the existence of any being we please? Recall Gaunilo's objection to Anselm—by means of the ontological argument, one could prove the existence of a perfect island. In the present context, we could define Fs as items that have the property P, affirm as our next premise that anything with P must exist, and conclude that Fs exist. Surely something has gone wrong, but what?

In the second of his criticisms of the ontological argument, Kant tells us what:

> If, in an identical proposition, I reject the predicate while retaining the subject, contradiction results; and I therefore say that the former belongs necessarily to the latter. But if we reject subject and predicate alike, there is no contradiction; for nothing is then left that can be contradicted. (A594/B623)

As I interpret this passage, Kant is telling us that all that follows from the premises of the ontological argument is a *conditional* proposition, namely, that *if* anything is God (an *ens realissimum*), then it exists. Since this proposition is analytic (following as it does from a definition in the first premise and a logical truth in the second), to deny its consequent while affirming its antecedent would be to contradict oneself. However, one can deny that anything satisfies the antecedent (thus "rejecting the subject") with logical impunity. One can thus deny the existence of God while accepting both premises (and the conclusion, if properly stated) of the ontological argument.[15]

A similar objection was raised against Descartes's version of the ontological argument by Caterus:

> Even if it is granted that a supremely perfect being carries the implication of existence in virtue of its very title, it still does not follow that the existence in question is anything actual in the real world; all that follows is that the concept of existence is inseparably linked to the concept of a supreme being. So you cannot infer that the existence of God is anything actual unless you suppose that the supreme being actually exists; for then it will actually contain all perfections, including the perfection of real existence.[16]

I think this criticism is exactly on target. To appreciate why, it will help to make one other point first. The starting point of the ontological argument is supposed to be a definition, and a definition is not supposed to presuppose the existence of the thing defined. The definition of a K should only say *what* Ks are (or would be if there were any), not *whether* there are any. That is why definitions are typically stated as biconditionals: an item x is a K iff _____.

Now look at the first premise of the ontological argument as I formulated it above: the *ens realissimum* is the being possessing all perfections. That is not a biconditional, but an identity flanked by two definite descriptions. If we understand descriptions *à la* Russell, it unpacks into 'there is exactly one being that possesses all perfections, and that being is the *ens realissimum*'.[17] The resulting proposition asserts the existence of an *ens realissimum*, so it is not neutral on questions of existence as definitions are supposed to be. To get a definition that does not by its very form presuppose the existence of the being it defines, we must move to the conditional or biconditional mode. That is, our proper starting point must be this:

x is an *ens realissimum* iff x possesses all perfections.[18]

Otherwise, we simply beg the question. I think any proponent of the ontological argument would have to accept the stricture on his starting point that I am now urging.

If we accept the stricture, however, we must also accept Kant's criticism. What we are given in the argument are premises of the form 'x is God iff x is F' and 'whatever is F exists'. From these it follows that a being is God only if it exists—but it does not follow that there is anything that is God. We can reject the subject along with its predicates, including the predicate of existence. The point is really just the simple one that from conditional premises we cannot derive a categorical conclusion.[19]

E. The Modal Ontological Argument

There are variants of the ontological argument in which *necessary* existence rather than existence *simpliciter* is claimed to be the relevant perfection of God. Necessary existence (or existence in all possible worlds) is, of course, one of the traditional attributes of God, since a being whose existence was merely contingent would not have the self-sufficiency and explanatory ultimacy that the office of Supreme Being requires. Credit for calling attention to such "modalized" versions of the ontological argument belongs to Hartshorne, Malcolm, and Plantinga;[20] I take my departure here from a version due to Malcolm.

How would it help the ontological argument to enlist necessary existence as a perfection? One suggestion is this:[21] even if simple existence is not a predicate, necessary existence may be one, and that would enable the standard criticism of the ontological argument to be circumvented. It is indeed arguable that necessary existence is a real (or determining) predicate in Kant's sense. I showed above that for no concept C is it possible for there to be instances of C that do not exist, but that seems to leave room for the claim that for some concepts C, it is possible for there to be instances of C that do not *necessarily* exist. If so, necessary existence would be a determining predicate, enlarging or making a difference to the content of a concept.[22]

But how would that save the day for the ontological argument, given the results in sections B, C, and D above? I showed there that the fundamental objection to the ontological argument is *not* that existence is not a determining predicate, or even that it is not a predicate, period. The fundamental objection is rather the one raised by Kant in company with Caterus: all we can derive from the premises of the ontological argument is a conditional proposition, not one affirming the existence of God outright. I have chosen Malcolm's version of the modal ontological argument for consideration precisely because he sees it as offering a way around the objection of Kant and Caterus.

Malcolm's defense of the ontological argument as he actually presents it rests on a confusing misconstrual of Kant. He takes Kant to concede that the statement 'God necessarily exists' follows from the premises of the argument but at the same time takes him to maintain that this statement, when properly analyzed, is equivalent to the conditional statement 'if God exists, then He necessarily exists'. Malcolm further takes Kant to hold that this conditional is compatible with (and indeed, that it entails) 'it is possible that God does not exist'. He then claims that 'God necessarily exists' is in fact *in*compatible with 'it is possible that God does not exist'. So, Malcolm concludes that Kant's rejection of the ontological argument is inconsistent with one of his own admissions. Specifically, Malcolm holds that something Kant allows to follow from the ontological argument does, after all, rule out the possibility of God's nonexistence.

This criticism of Kant mistakes his point. The point is not that 'God necessarily exists' must be analyzed as a conditional; it is rather that *only* a conditional and *not* 'God necessarily exists' follows from the premises of the ontological argument to begin with. Malcolm's rejoinder to Kant's criticism assumes that the conclusion 'God necessarily exists' *can* be extracted from the argument, but that is precisely what Kant denies.

Nonetheless, Malcolm has given us everything we need to make a riposte to the Kant-Caterus "conditionalizing move" (as Bennett calls it). If Kant is willing to concede that the conditional 'if there is a God, then he exists' follows from the premises of the original ontological argument, then he should also be willing to concede that the conditional 'if there is a God, then he necessarily exists' follows from the premises of the modal ontological argument (in which necessary existence replaces existence as the relevant perfection). But the second conditional is not as harmless as the first; when augmented by plausible premises to be identified below, it does imply that God exists.

Here, then, is the Malcolm-inspired version of the modal ontological argument I recommend. To facilitate presentation, the modal operators in what follows are sometimes spelled out and sometimes abbreviated by '□' and '◇'.

1. □(if God exists, then God necessarily exists).

This is the conditional proposition that Kant would concede, asserted now as holding necessarily. Kant would have to concede its necessity, since it follows from premises that are themselves necessary.

2. ◇(God exists).

This is the premise by which Leibniz thought any valid ontological argument would have to be supplemented. Kant acknowledges this premise at A596/B624 and says he will allow it for the sake of argument (even if elsewhere he implicitly challenges it, as I show in sections F and H).

3. $\Diamond$ (God necessarily exists).

This follows from premises 1 and 2 by the modal principle that possibility is transmitted by entailment.

4. $\Box$[if God necessarily exists, then $\Box$(God exists)].

In this premise, we move from necessity *de re* in the antecedent to necessity *de dicto* in the consequent. I comment on the significance of this shortly.

5. $\Diamond \Box$(God exists).

This follows from 3 and 4, again by the principle that possibility is transmitted by entailment.

6. $\Diamond \Box$p only if $\Box$p.

This is a theorem of the modal system S5, provable from that system's axiom that whatever is possible is necessarily possible.

7. $\Box$(God exists).

This follows from 5 and 6 and completes the proof. If the proof is sound, it shows that the conditional proposition Kant concedes implies the necessity of the existential proposition he says we are free to deny.

What is there in the argument that we might reasonably question? Bennett observes that the transition from 'God necessarily exists' to 'it is necessary that God exists' in step 4 is controversial.[23] The difference between these two may appear overly subtle—what does it amount to? Well, suppose that God necessarily exists, that is, that there is a being who is God in our world and who exists in all possible worlds; but suppose also that there are worlds in which this being is no longer God and in which no other being plays the role of God, either. In that case, the antecedent of 4 would be true and its consequent false; that suffices to illustrate the difference between them.

In showing us under what circumstances premise 4 would be false, the scenario just sketched also brings to light a premise we could add to ensure its truth: whatever being is God is *essentially* God. That is to say, the divine attributes cannot be possessed by any being accidentally. It follows that if any world contains a God, that being is God in all possible worlds in which it exists, and if any world contains a necessary being who is God, that being exists in all worlds and is God in all worlds.[24] Thus may premise 4 be vindicated.[25]

Is there anything else in the argument that might be questioned? Perhaps the likeliest target is 2, the premise that the existence of God is possible. Some contemporary opponents of the ontological argument have taken the tough line that the existence of God is, indeed, impossible.[26] Why would anyone say that? The most common answer is that there is something defective or incoherent in the very idea of a necessary being. That, as noted above, is one of Kant's own points, to which I turn next.

F. Could There Be a Necessary Being?

The third of Kant's three criticisms of the ontological argument is that the notion of a necessary being is problematic, if not impossible. It is not immediately clear how this point affects the Cartesian ontological argument that is the target of Kant's criticism, since it is not explicitly part of that argument that God *is* a necessary being.[27] However, it does affect the modal ontological argument we have been considering in an obvious way. If there cannot be a necessary being, and if that is what God would have to be, then the Leibnizian premise affirming the possibility of God's existence is false.

In his debate with Copleston on the existence of God, Russell contended that the term 'necessary' is significantly applicable only to propositions, not to things, and that the notion of a necessary being therefore makes no sense.[28] Kant may be making a similar point in the following passage, which occurs soon after he has raised the question of whether the concept of an absolutely necessary being is legitimate:

> All the alleged examples are, without exception, taken from *judgments*, not from *things* and their existence. But the unconditioned necessity of judgments is not the same as an absolute necessity of things. The absolute necessity of the judgment is only a conditioned necessity of the thing, or of the predicate in the judgment. (A593/B621)

One may think this objection easily overcome. After all, if the notion of a necessary proposition is granted, why not simply define the notion of a necessary being in terms of it as follows?

x is a necessary being =Df the proposition that x exists is necessary.

But this will not do. Since a definition with free variables is tacitly equivalent to its universal closure, we are here quantifying into the context 'the proposition that _____ exists is necessary'. There are familiar reasons for holding that this is illegitimate.[29]

To accommodate the idea of a necessary being, we do better to forget about necessity *de dicto* or the necessity of propositions and appeal straightaway to the idea of necessity *de re*, as in the following definition:[30]

x is a necessary being =Df x is necessarily such that it exists.

Here we attribute necessary existence to a thing, not necessary truth to a proposition.

Notice also that the necessity we attribute is unconditional or absolute necessity—we are not merely saying that x is necessarily such that it exists *if* it has some other feature. In the passage quoted above, Kant seems to deny that there is such a thing as unconditional necessity:

> The absolute necessity of the judgment is only a conditioned necessity of the thing, or of the predicate in the judgment. The above proposition [a triangle has three angles] does not declare that three angles are absolutely necessary, but that, under the condition that there is a triangle ... three angles will necessarily be found in it. (A593–94/B621–22)[31]

Kant is right, of course, about the example, but a defender of the notion of necessary existence (and perhaps also many defenders of the distinction between essential and accidental properties) would dispute Kant's implicit attempt to generalize from it. Not all necessities connect predicates with other predicates; some connect predicates directly with things. On this issue, philosophy in the first half of the twentieth century tended to agree with Kant, but philosophy since then has shown the way to make room for the idea of predicates or properties attaching necessarily and directly to things.[32]

There is another objection to the idea of a necessary being to be found in Kant and in a fair amount of literature inspired by him. This is the objection that no existential proposition can be necessary—that there cannot be necessary propositions of the form '∃xFx'. This objection is distinct from the first, though not always distinguished from it. To say that something has necessary existence, $\exists x \Box Ex$, implies that it is necessary that something exists, $\Box \exists x Ex$,[33] but not conversely. Thus, the objection to the necessity of existential propositions would automatically be an objection to necessary beings, but not conversely. Often the objection takes the form of the following syllogism:

1. No existential proposition is analytic.
2. Only analytic propositions are necessary.
3. Therefore, no existential proposition is necessary.

Kant himself affirms premise 1 at A598/B626: "But if, on the other hand, we admit, as every reasonable person must, that all existential propositions are synthetic. . . ." But since he explicitly challenges premise 2 (that, indeed, is the official occasion for writing the *Critique of Pure Reason*), he is in no position to advance the present objection.

In my view, then, both of the Kantian objections to the notion of necessary being are inconclusive—the first because the notion of absolute necessity *de re* has survived attempts to discredit it, the second because (as Kant himself teaches us) not all necessity is born of analyticity.[34]

So much for defending the idea of a necessary being from objections; I now present a positive argument in its favor. Ironically, it proceeds from a premise that Kant himself accepts—the Kant-Frege view. So, if the argument is correct, one of Kant's criticisms of the ontological argument—that existence is not a predicate—turns out to undermine another—that there cannot be any necessary beings.[35]

In discussing the Kant-Frege view, I have shown that it is a theorem of standard quantification theory that everything exists:

1. (x)Ex.

That is because its negation, $\exists x - Ex$, is contradictory, given that the existential quantifier expresses existence. Now, since what is provable is necessary, we also have

2. $\Box$(x)Ex.

By universal instantiation, '(x)Ex' entails 'Ea':

3. $\Box[(x)Ex \to Ea]$.

From 2 and 3 together with the principle that what is entailed by the necessary is itself necessary, we next obtain

4. $\Box$Ea.

So, not only is it possible for there to be necessary beings; we have just proved that an arbitrary nameable being is one!

There are, to be sure, systems of logic in which the above argument does not go through. In free logic, the rule of universal instantiation is restricted in a way that prevents us from arriving at step 3: we cannot infer from '(x)Fx' to 'Fa' unless we already have the premise that a exists, so all we could get at line 3 is the harmless $\Box$[(x)Ex & Ea → Ea]. It seems to me, however, that if we adopt free logic we depart at least from the spirit of the Kant-Frege view. Free logic places a companion restriction on the rule of existential generalization, requiring 'Ea' as an auxiliary premise before one can get from 'Fa' to '∃xFx', and that requirement has point only on the assumption that a can instantiate the property of being F even if a does not exist. How can that assumption be true if, as on the Kant-Frege view, asserting existence and asserting the instantiation of a property go hand in hand?

Some may think that step 3 is blocked for a different reason. In some of his systems of quantified modal logic, Kripke has imposed a stricture against applying the rule of necessitation (which says you may put a '$\Box$' in front of anything provable) to purported theorems containing free variables, such as '(x)Ex → Ey'. This keeps the Barcan and Converse Barcan formulas from being provable in his systems.[36] It might be thought that the same stricture prevents us from arriving at my step 3, but in fact it does not. The proof I have given uses a name rather than a variable in step 3, so it does not violate Kripke's stricture.

That the Kant-Frege view leads to the necessity of all beings should not be a surprise given the argument of chapter 8. There I argue that the Kant-Frege view leads to the result that there cannot be any absolute existence-changes: if something exists at one time but not at another, what is really going on is that some substance existing at both times is qualified now one way, now another. In the modal case, we are now reaching an analogous conclusion: if something exists in one possible world but not in another, what is really going on is that some substance or substances existing in both worlds are differently qualified or arranged in the two worlds. "This hammer might not have existed," we may say, but that only means that a certain head might not have been attached to a certain handle—or, going deeper, that certain particles might not have been so arranged as to constitute a hammer. Substances themselves exist in all worlds, and the myriad beings of our world that do not exist in other worlds are therefore merely modes. (Modes must here, as in chapter 8, be accorded the status of mere constructions, not to be quantified over in an ontologically perspicuous language.) If Kant and Frege are right, it now appears, so too are Spinoza and the Tractarian Wittgenstein: genuine substances are necessary beings.

But hold! The view we are now flirting with clashes with a conclusion advanced earlier. In chapter 11 I offer the Mixed Paralogism, a blend of the first two Paralogisms of Rational Psychology, as showing that thinking things must be substances. I am arguing here that if the Kant-Frege view is correct, all substances are necessary beings. Yet surely not all thinking things are necessary beings—immortality is not so easily assured. I leave it to the reader to consider which among the following contains a false step that should be rejected: the Mixed Paralogism, the Kant-Frege view, or the contention that the Kant-Frege view requires all substances to be necessary beings.[37]

G. A Meinongian Ontological Argument

In an interesting discussion of Descartes's ontological argument, Anthony Kenny has claimed (a) that Descartes was a proto-Meinongian, and (b) that "if we give Descartes his Meinongian assumptions, there is nothing fallacious in his argument."[38] Others, including Russell, have also thought that within a Meinongian framework the ontological argument would go through. That is the claim I examine in this section.

I begin by identifying the relevant Meinongian assumptions. There are two, the first of which is expressed in the following notorious passage:

(I) Those who like paradoxical modes of expression could very well say: "There are objects of which it is true that there are no such objects."[39]

That is paradoxical indeed, but it is not the contradiction it may appear to be. Meinong's point is that there are objects of which it is true that they do not exist. For this not to be contradictory, 'there are' (*es gibt*) must not mean the same thing as 'there exist'; that is to say, Meinong's quantifier must range over even things that do not exist. As he puts it in another famous passage, "[T]he totality of what exists, including what has existed and will exist, is infinitely small in comparison with the totality of Objects. . . ."[40]

Here is the second relevant assumption, sometimes called the Independence Principle:

(II) [T]he *Sosein* of an Object is not affected by its *Nichtsein*. This fact is sufficiently important to be explicitly formulated as the principle of the independence of *Sosein* from *Sein*.[41]

Thus, an object does not have to be (have existence or *Sein*) in order to be a certain way (have characteristics or *Sosein*). The golden mountain is golden, but it does not exist; it is one of that multitude of things that "there are" but that do not exist.[42]

How do Meinong's views come to the aid of the ontological argument? A natural first thought would be this: with assumption (I), *Meinong breaks the connection between quantifiers and existence.* For him, it is not contradictory to say there are things that do not exist. Hence, we lose the basis offered in section C for saying that existence is not a real predicate. If some winged horses do not exist, existence becomes a real or determining predicate after all; it "enlarges" the concept of a winged horse.

If that were the only relevance of Meinong, he would offer no salvation to the ontological argument. I argued above that the ontological argument is flawed for reasons independent of the slogan "existence is not a predicate," whether taken in its Kantian or in its contemporary meaning. It is flawed for the Kant-Caterus reason that its conclusion can be nothing more than the conditional 'if any being is God, that being exists'.

There is a second way, however, in which Meinong's ideas might be exploited in defense of the ontological argument. For Kenny, the key is assumption (II), the Independence Principle. *Meinong breaks the connection between predication and existence.* According to the Kant-Caterus objection, the starting point of the ontological argument must be conditional if it is not to beg the question, and from a conditional premise no categorical conclusion can be derived. Given Meinong's theory, however, our starting point may be the categorical 'God has all perfections'; since this is noncommittal about existence, it does not beg the question.[43] When we add premise 2 (that whatever has all perfections exists), we may then go on to draw the categorical conclusion that God exists.

Such is Kenny's defense of the ontological argument. He goes on to object to Meinong's theory as bad ontology, but he sticks by the contention that if we grant Meinong's assumptions, the argument is valid.

I disagree. Those who like paradoxical modes of expression could perhaps put my objection to Kenny in this way: yes, we may now draw the conclusion that God exists, but that does not mean that God exists! We are still free, as Kant said, to reject the subject along with its predicate of existence. The Meinongian assumptions about predication that allow the premise 'God has all perfections' to be true regardless of whether God exists also allow the conclusion 'God exists' to be true regardless of whether God exists.[44]

My point is simply that if the predicational form 'Fa' does not require for its truth that a exist, the same remains true when 'exists' itself is the predicate. Some may wish to counter that 'Fa' trivially implies that a is F, so how can 'God exists' fail to imply the existence of God?[45] We seem to have reached a stalemate; how are we to resolve it?

Perhaps the following example will help. Suppose we agree to define a concept of fictional truth according to which a proposition p is true (in novel N) iff it is stated or implied by the author of N within its pages. Let the author now proclaim within his novel: "My characters are real, not imaginary; they have an existence outside these pages." It is then true (in the sense defined) that the characters are real, not merely imaginary. Imagine now a debate in which one party says, "Yes, but it doesn't follow that the characters *are* real outside the novel," and the other replies, "How could it not so follow? What you have conceded is the truth of precisely this, that the characters are real outside the pages of the novel." I hope the reader will agree with the first party. Fictional truth may not be the best model for *Sosein* without *Sein*, but I trust the moral of my little story is clear: no predicates employed within a bracketed form of discourse will ever enable one to transcend the brackets.[46]

Here is another analogy that may be instructive. C.D. Broad once suggested that a lesson to be learned from McTaggart's purported proof of the unreality of time is that we cannot say that an event is present by using a tenseless copula and a temporal predicate: 'e is present' will not do unless the copula is in the present tense, else we would be implying that e is eternally present. So, we need tense as an additional device, and once we have it, temporal predicates are redundant.[47] Similarly, I suggest, we cannot say that something exists by using an existentially neutral form of predication along with a predicate of existence. We need some additional device—an existentially loaded form of predication or an existentially interpreted quantifier—and once we have it, the predicate of existence is redundant.

We are thus led in the end to a further relevant sense of the dictum that existence is not a predicate—a sense in which the dictum is inimical to the ontological argument after all. Existence *is* a predicate (or may be if you like), but it is not by means of any such predicate alone that we ever manage to say that anything exists. To do that, we need some further device—a form of predication that presupposes existence or a non-Meinongian quantifier. If we have the further device, existence as a predicate is redundant. Moreover, the assertion that God exists or that there is a God—in the existentially loaded sense—does not follow from the premises of the ontological argument.

H. Necessary Being and *Ens Realissimum*

I turn now to Kant's treatment of the second way of proving the existence of God: the cosmological argument. The cosmological argument as Kant presents it has two distinct stages. The first stage argues for the existence of a necessary being; the second stage argues that the necessary being can only be God or the *ens realissimum*. ("And this all men call God," as Aquinas says at a similar juncture.) The two-stage structure of the argument is made especially clear at A584–86/B612–14 and A604–6/B632–34.

Kant gives the following compact formulation of the first stage of the cosmological argument:

> If anything exists, an absolutely necessary being must also exist. Now I, at least, exist. Therefore an absolutely necessary being exists. (A604/B632)

I postpone discussion of this argument to the next section. Here I concentrate on the second stage, to which Kant devotes most of his critical attention.

In the second stage of the argument, "reason looks around for a concept that squares with so supreme a mode of existence as that of unconditioned necessity . . ." (A585/B613) and discovers that "[t]he concept of an *ens realissimum* is . . . of all concepts of possible things, that which best squares with the concept of an unconditionally necessary being . . ." (A586/B614). Indeed, the concept of an *ens realissimum* is the *only* concept that is adequate to the concept of a necessary being:

> The necessary being can be determined in one way only, that is, by one out of each possible pair of opposed predicates. It must therefore be completely determined through its own concept. Now there is only one possible concept which determines a thing completely *a priori*, namely, the concept of the *ens realissimum*. The concept of the *ens realissimum* is therefore the only concept through which a necessary being can be thought. In other words, a supreme being necessarily exists. (A605–6/B633–34)[48]

Kant's overall criticism of the cosmological argument is well known: he maintains that it presupposes the ontological argument, which he has already refuted. But how exactly does the one argument presuppose the other?

An obvious first guess would be this: the cosmological argument depends on the ontological argument because it asserts that there is a necessary being, which could be true only if the ontological argument were sound. Thus Russell writes:

> It is clear that Kant is right in saying that this argument depends upon the ontological argument. If the existence of the world can only be accounted for by the existence of a necessary Being, then there must be a Being whose essence involves existence, for that is what is meant by a necessary Being. But if it is possible that there should be a Being whose essence involves existence, then reason alone, without experience, can define such a Being, whose existence will follow from the ontological argument. . . .[49]

Though a good guess, this is a wrong one. Russell's suggestion makes the cosmological proof depend on the ontological proof in its *first* stage. As we read on, however, it becomes clear that Kant thinks the cosmological proof depends on the ontological proof in its *second* stage. Here is a compact statement of his point:

> If I say, the concept of the *ens realissimum* is a concept, and indeed the only concept, which is appropriate and adequate to necessary existence, I must also admit that necessary existence can be inferred from this concept. Thus the so-called cosmological proof really owes any cogency which it may have to the ontological proof from mere concepts. (A607/ B635)

Here Kant is saying that if we can infer from having necessary existence to being an *ens realissimum* (as in stage 2 of the cosmological argument), we can also infer from being an *ens realissimum* to having necessary existence (as allegedly in the ontological argument). But we cannot normally reverse an inference like that; what enables us to do so in this case? Here is Kant's fuller explanation of the point:

> If the proposition, that every absolutely necessary being is likewise the most real of all beings, is correct (and this is the *nervus probandi* of the cosmological proof), it must, like all affirmative judgments, be convertible, at least *per accidens*. It therefore follows that some *entia realissima* are likewise absolutely necessary beings. But one *ens realissimum* is in no respect different from another, and what is true of some under this concept is true also of all. In this case, therefore, I can convert the proposition *simpliciter*, not only *per accidens*, and say that every *ens realissimum* is a necessary being. But since this proposition is determined from its *a priori* concepts alone, the mere concept of the *ens realissimum* must carry with it the absolute necessity of that being; and this is precisely what the ontological proof has asserted. . . . (A608/B636)

The steps in this reasoning may be set out as follows:[50]

1. Every necessary being is an *ens realissimum*. (This is the central claim of stage 2 of the cosmological argument.)
2. Some *ens realissimum* is a necessary being. (From 1 by conversion *per accidens*.)
3. One *ens realissimum* is no different from any other.
4. Every *ens realissimum* is a necessary being. (From 2 and 3.)
5. That is to say, from the mere concept of an *ens realissimum*, the necessary existence of its object may be inferred. (Purportedly from 4.)
6. Line 5 is "precisely what the ontological proof has asserted."
7. Therefore, the cogency of the cosmological proof depends on that of the ontological proof.

One might object straight off to the inference from 1 to 2. The classical inference of conversion *per accidens* (i.e., from 'all F is G' to 'some G is F') is valid only if A-propositions are accorded existential import, but it was implicit in Kant's best criticism of the ontological argument that A-propositions need *not* be given existential import. (You can affirm an A-proposition while "rejecting the subject.") In the present context, however, the inference from 1 to 2 poses no problem. Kant is discussing the position of a cosmological arguer who has *already* proved 'there is a necessary being', and from this result together with 1, 2 *does* follow.[51] So, Kant's inference is all right; we just need to augment the justification he offers for it.

Moving on, step 3 is a consequence of the fact that the concept of an *ens realissimum* is formed by conjoining all the positive predicates from each pair of a predicate with its opposite. So, naturally, all *entia realissima* are just alike.[52] As for step 4, it plainly follows from 2 and 3.

It is steps 5 and 6 that bear close scrutiny. Note that since the premises yielding 4 are necessary truths, we are enabled to reach not just 4 but its necessitation: *necessarily*, every *ens realissimum* is a necessary being. That makes it true in one sense that we may "infer" from being an *ens realissimum* to having necessary existence, as 5 says: we can say that necessarily, if anything is an *ens realissimum*, it is also a necessary being. But this proposition is purely hypothetical; from it alone we could not conclude that there *is* a necessary being. That, indeed, is Kant's own best criticism of the ontological argument. To go on and say as he does in 6 that 5 amounts to the ontological argument is to forget or ignore this criticism.[53]

I am not saying that nothing authorizes us to get past 4 to the existence of a necessary being. If part 1 of the cosmological argument is correct, we already know at this stage that there is a necessary being. The point is rather that the cosmological arguer need not excogitate the existence of the necessary being from step 4 alone, as the ontological arguer tries to do. There is nothing in 4 that allows us to examine the concept of an *ens realissimum* and conclude (on that basis alone) that there must be an object instantiating it. Therefore, the cosmological arguer need not (just in virtue of being committed to proposition 4) be an ontological arguer.

The point of the previous two paragraphs may be encapsulated as follows. In the sense of 5 in which 5 follows from 4, it is not true (as 6 maintains) that 5 amounts to the ontological argument. By the same token, in the sense that 5 must have if it is to amount to the ontological argument, it does not follow from 4.[54] So, Kant's central criticism of the cosmological argument fails.

We should ask at this point whether there is any other criticism Kant would or could make of the cosmological argument. Indeed, it appears that he is committed to finding some flaw in the cosmological argument in addition to the one he highlights. He objects to 5 on the ground that it recapitulates the ontological argument, and he maintains (even if mistakenly) that 5 follows from 4. He is therefore committed to rejecting 4. But 4 follows from 1, 3, and the existence of a necessary being, as I have shown. Kant does not question 3. He must therefore question either 1 (the inference from necessary being to *ens realissimum*) or the existence of a necessary being in the first place. He does, in fact, raise doubts on each score.

On the first point, Kant's attitude appears to be the following. If we had to identify the best candidate for having necessary existence, it would be the *ens realissimum* (A586–87/B614–15). Nonetheless, for all we know, some lesser being might be a necessary being. "[W]e are entirely free to hold that any limited beings whatsoever, notwithstanding their being limited, may also be unconditionally necessary . . ." (A588/B616). This coincides with one of Hume's criticisms of the cosmological argument—that for all we know, the material universe might be the sought-for necessary being.[55]

One who raises this possibility must not, of course, rule the very idea of a necessary being out of court. But in other places Kant does object to the idea of a necessary being (which brings me to the second point).[56] I have already considered two such objections in the context of the ontological argument (section F). Kant raises further objections in a section entitled "Discovery and Explanation of the Dialectical Illusion in All Transcendental Proofs of the Existence of a Necessary Being," which is appended to his discussion of the cosmological argument.

In this section, Kant presents a little paradox together with two ways of resolving it. Here is the paradox:

> If I am constrained to think something necessary as a condition of existing things, but am unable to think any particular thing as in itself necessary, it inevitably follows that necessity and contingency do not concern the things themselves; otherwise there would be a contradiction. (A616/B644)

The paragraph preceding the quoted sentence makes it clear that Kant affirms both conjuncts in the antecedent of his conditional. Thus, we have

(A) I must think $(\exists x)(Nx)$[57]

and

(B) $(x)(I$ must think $-Nx)$.

If to these we add

(C) if I must think p, then p,

we then obtain the contradiction

(D) $(\exists x)(Nx)$ & $(x)(-Nx)$.

What is the way out? Kant says we must view principles (A) and (B) as subjective and regulative, rather than as objective and constitutive. In effect, he denies (C), telling us that what we "must think" about these matters need not be constitutive of reality. Even so, a mild paradox remains, insofar as we are enjoined to think a number of things that cannot all be true.[58]

Kant passes immediately to another way of avoiding the contradiction without remarking that it is different from the first:

> [I]nasmuch as the second rule [i.e., B] commands us always to regard all empirical causes of unity as themselves derived [and contingent] . . . it follows that we must regard the absolutely necessary as being *outside* the world. (A617/B645)

Here we are invited to replace '$(x)(-Nx)$' by '$(x)(Wx \rightarrow -Nx)$', which is compatible with '$(\exists x)(Nx)$' insofar as the being making the latter proposition true may be "outside the world." This is a recapitulation of Kant's strategy for reconciling the Thesis with the Antithesis of the Fourth Antinomy: let everything in nature (the totality of sensible appearances) be contingent, as the Antithesis maintains, but at the same time let there be a necessary being, as the Thesis proclaims, by placing the necessary being outside nature.[59] In the present context, however, this strategy is too conciliatory, for positing a necessary being *anywhere* will still (in the company of 1) bring us to step 4, which Kant is committed to rejecting.

Kant on the whole appears to be agnostic about the existence and even the possibility of a necessary being. If so, he owes us an account of what goes wrong with the *first* part of the cosmological argument, which purports to establish the existence of precisely such a being. He never gives us such a critique. In the next section I undertake an evaluation of part I, which I refer to from now on simply as the cosmological argument.

I. The Cosmological Argument

The central claim of the cosmological argument is that if anything exists, an absolutely necessary being must exist. Kant explains the rationale for this claim as follows:

> This inference is too well known to require detailed statement. It depends on the supposedly transcendental law of natural causality: that everything contingent has a cause, which, if itself contingent, must likewise have a cause, till the series of subordinate causes ends with an absolutely necessary cause, without which it would have no completeness. (A605/B633n.)

That explanation makes the cosmological argument sound too much like its unsophisticated cousin, the first cause argument. In the subtler form in which it was advanced by Leibniz and Clarke, the cosmological argument concedes the possibility of a causal series extending infinitely into the past, but then goes on to insist that the existence of *the whole series* must be explained by the existence of something outside it. As Hume's Demea puts it:

> [T]he whole eternal chain or succession, taken together, is not determined or caused by anything, and yet it is evident that it requires a cause or reason, as much as any particular object which begins to exist in time. The question is still reasonable why this particular succession of causes existed from eternity, and not any other succession or no succession at all.[60]

Since we may assume that all contingent beings are members of the series, the being outside it must be a noncontingent being, which is to say a necessary being.[61] The nerve of the argument is thus better represented when Kant writes: "The whole universe must thus sink into the abyss of nothingness, unless, over and above this infinite chain of contingencies, we assume something to support it . . ." A622/B550).[62]

The cosmological proof in the above form is the target of a famous criticism by Hume, expressed thus by Cleanthes:

> Did I show you the particular causes of each individual in a collection of twenty particles of matter, I should think it very unreasonable, should you afterwards ask me, what was the cause of the whole twenty. This is sufficiently explained in explaining the causes of the parts.[63]

The proponent of the cosmological argument allows that each member of the set of contingent beings is caused by some member of the set that existed earlier. In that case, claims Hume, it is unreasonable to seek any further explanation for the series as a whole.

Although many philosophers profess to be fully satisfied with Hume's reply,[64] I think there is something wrong with it.[65] From the passage quoted above, we may extract the following principle: the existence of a totality is always adequately explained when the existence of each member is explained. A corollary is that if there is an infinite totality of objects or events each of which is explained by the causal efficacy of some other members(s) of the totality, then the existence of the whole totality is thereby adequately explained—no recourse to anything outside the totality is needed. It is this corollary that I wish to challenge.

Consider the following pattern of explanation:

Explanandum: all members of the set {a,b,c,d,e, . . . } of Fs exist.

Explanans: a exists because b and c caused a to exist; b exists because d and e caused b to exist; and so on.

You would be giving an explanation of this type if you tried to explain the existence of zebras by noting, for each zebra, that it is the offspring of two other zebras—Zeb was begotten by Zeke and Zelda, and so on.

I maintain that explanations of this sort are circular. The explanans invokes the existence of Fs, but Fs are the very beings for whose existence an explanation is being sought. To be sure, the circularity is not quite of the 'P because P' variety, since the existence of each zebra is explained by reference to *other* zebras. But if what is to be explained is the existence of zebras *in general* (or why there are zebras *at all*), the explanans provokes the very question it is supposed to answer. This is the sense in which the explanation is circular.

If what is demanded is an explanation of the existence of zebras in general, no amount of appeal to zebras begetting zebras will satisfy it. The demand will be satisfied only when recourse is had to something that is *not* a zebra—as happens equally in the explanations offered by creationists and evolutionists.

In light of the foregoing I wish to propose the following counterprinciple to Hume's, which I call *the anticircularity stricture*:

> The existence of Fs in general (or the fact that Fness is instantiated) can be explained only by appeal to the existence of something that is *not* an F.

The stricture requires qualification, as I show in a moment. But I believe that some principle along these lines must be correct, and that its correctness is acknowledged in other contexts. It is presumably some such principle that leads us to reject explanations of perception in terms of homunculi. "How does vision take place? Well, objects outside us cause patterns on the retina, which are then scanned by a little man seated behind it. . . ." If what is sought is an explanation of vision in general (not just human vision as opposed to homuncular vision), that explanation is worthlessly circular.

Hume's dictum appears plausible only because he illustrates it with a finite case that does *not* violate the anticircularity stricture. We accept his explanation of the twenty particles of matter only because it has recourse at some point to an entity outside the twenty. (Even if the particles are capable of reproducing, we would not accept causal loops.) The entity outside the twenty must be either a particle of matter or not. If it is, we have not explained why there are particles of matter in general; if it is not, we have explained Fs by reference to non-Fs. Either way, we do not run afoul of the anticircularity stricture. But as soon as we try to explain the existence of an *infinite* totality in Hume's fashion, we *do* run afoul of it.

The application of this point to the cosmological argument will by now be obvious. The cosmological arguer demands to know why there are contingent beings at all. The Humean would say that the existence of each contingent being may be explained by the causal efficacy of some other contingent being, and that is explanation enough. If we accept the anticircularity stricture, however, we will insist that the existence of contingent beings in general can be explained, if at all, only by reference to a *non*contingent being. The noncontingent being may or may not be God—that is a matter for further argument. But I suggest that cosmological arguers have always been right to maintain that we can explain everything that needs explaining only if there is a necessary being.

I turn now to the needed qualification in the anticircularity stricture. As presently stated, it is open to the following embarrassing counterexample: the existence of necessary beings can only be explained by the existence of contingent beings! There are also further counterintuitive consequences, such as that the existence of nongreen things can be explained only by reference to the existence of green things. These counterexamples are avoided if we qualify the principle as follows:

If it is contingent that there are Fs, then the existence of Fs can be explained (if at all) only by reference to the existence of things that are not Fs.

This sidesteps the two counterexamples just given, since it is not contingent that there are necessary beings, nor (if one is any sort of Platonist) is it contingent that there are nongreen things, since the number two necessarily exists and is necessarily nongreen. But it *is* presumably contingent that there are contingent things,[66] so the restricted principle retains its intended application to the cosmological argument.

J. The Principle of Sufficient Reason

It is plain that a needed premise in the cosmological argument is the Principle of Sufficient Reason, which Leibniz formulated thus: "[N]o fact can be real or existing and no proposition can be true unless there is a sufficient reason why it should be thus and not otherwise."[67] Were it not for this principle, the existence of one or more of the contingent beings might simply be a brute fact, getting no explanation by reference to a necessary being or anything else.

Why should we accept the Principle of Sufficient Reason? I am enough of a rationalist to find it attractive, but I now argue that it is a principle that can be accepted only at the high cost of banishing contingency from the universe altogether.

Suppose for the moment that there is a necessary being, and suppose further that this necessary being is God. What fact about God is it that explains the existence of all the contingent beings? Is it his sheer existence, or is it some further fact about him—his choosing, say, to bring into being one rather than another of all the possible worlds? In the former case, we are citing as the self-sufficient explanation of the existence of all contingent beings (and presumably also of the holding of all contingent truths) a fact that is itself necessary, namely, that God exists. But on the assumption that one fact adequately explains another only if it entails the other, this implies that the necessity of the explanans will be transferred to the explanandum. Hence, it will be necessary that the totality of mundane beings exists; they will not be contingent after all. So, on the first alternative, the existence of contingent beings is not explained but negated.

It will be instructive to compare the current situation with one I noted in chapter 3, section D. There I showed that the attempt to explain the necessary in terms of the contingent (by citing certain contingent facts as necessary conditions for the necessary) results in doing away with necessity. Here I point out that the attempt to explain the contingent in terms of the necessary (by citing certain necessary facts as sufficient conditions for the contingent) results in doing away with contingency. If the universe is to house both kinds of truths, we must evidently forswear any attempt to explain either of the twain in terms of the other.

I turn, then, to the other alternative: what explains the existence of contingent beings is some fact over and above God's existence, say, his choosing to create one world rather than another. The further fact must be contingent, else we land smack back in the difficulty of the last paragraph. But then what is the explanation of the further fact? It either has none, or we explain it by reference to a prior contingency, thus embarking on the explanatory regress already dismissed above in connection with Hume. It appears, then, that our choices are two: either banish all contingency or admit at least one exception to the Principle of Sufficient Reason.

The point for which I have been arguing is made with admirable compactness in the following passage from Bennett:

> Let P be the great proposition stating the whole contingent truth about the actual world, down to its finest detail, in respect of all times. Then the question 'Why is it the case that P?' cannot be answered in a satisfying way. Any purported answer must have the form 'P is the case because Q is the case' but if Q is only contingently the case then it is a conjunct in P, and the offered explanation doesn't explain; and if Q is necessarily the case then the explanation, if it is cogent, implies that P is necessary also. But if P is necessary then the universe had to be exactly as it is, down to the tiniest detail—i.e., this is the only possible world.
>
> In short, an explanatory rationalist [one who accepts the Principle of Sufficient Reason] is under intense pressure to suppose that there are no contingent truths.[68]

In the next section, I consider a suggestion of Nozick's that is meant to get us out of the dilemma of having to reject all contingency or accept brute facts.

K. The Realization of All Possibilities

The Principle of Fecundity says that *all possibilities are realized*. In a chapter devoted to the above-described dilemma,[69] Robert Nozick commends this principle as one that would drastically reduce the number of unanswerable why-questions. He also explores the idea that the principle itself may be explained by explanatory self-subsumption: it is deducible from itself together with the fact (arguably necessary if it holds at all) that what it states is a possibility. He thus holds out the hope that without eliminating contingency, we might reduce the quotient of brute fact in the universe to nothing.

There are two ways of interpreting the slogan "all possibilities are realized": as shrinking the realm of the possible down to what is actually the case, or as expanding the realm of the realized up to the limits of the possible. The philosophy of Spinoza may provide an example of the former; Nozick plainly intends the latter. Presented with the question, "Why X rather than Y?" Spinoza would say, "Because Y could not have happened"; Nozick would say, "There is no 'rather' about it; X and Y *both* obtain."

Is it not a possibility that *not* all possibilities are realized?[70] If so, the Principle of Fecundity would be undermined by the following syllogism:

1. All possibilities are realized.
2. It is a possibility that not all possibilities are realized.
3. Therefore, not all possibilities are realized.

Nozick identifies several strategies for avoiding this contradiction and others that threaten. I examine three such strategies here.

The first strategy is to restrict the Principle of Fecundity so that it only says that all *first-order* possibilities are realized, where a first-order possibility is one that neither entails nor excludes the existence of other possibilities. We then avoid the syllogism above, since 'not all possibilities are realized' does not state a first-order possibility. Nozick mentions this stategy in a footnote[71] but declines to adopt it, since it would prevent us from explaining the Principle of Fecundity by subsuming it under itself.

Even if we did adopt the first strategy, however, it would not keep the Principle of Fecundity from spawning contradictions. Consider the two possibilities 'there are talking donkeys' and 'there are no talking donkeys'. These are both first-order, so our restricted principle says they both obtain. But if they both obtain, do we not have a contradiction on our hands?

This brings us to the second strategy, which is to relativize the notion of a possibility's obtaining so that mutually incompatible possibilities can all obtain without contradiction. Nozick suggests that we think of the various possibilities as belonging to "noninteracting realms." I take it he means to ban *logical* interaction—no possible world can imply anything about what goes on outside its own boundaries in logical space. If we follow this strategy, we are supposed to be able to say that the possibilities *something exists* and *nothing exists* both obtain! ("Why is there something rather than nothing? There isn't. There's both."[72]) For this to work, it must amount to the following idea: 'nothing exists' really means 'nothing exists *here*, in this region of logical space'. It is thereby rendered consistent with the existence of something in some *other* region of logical space. More generally, the idea seems to be that 'so-and-so happens' is always short for 'so-and-so happens in world w'.

The problem I see for this strategy is the following. Are worlds defined by what happens in them or not? If they are, all contingency is lost. All we can assert are propositions of the form 'so-and-so happens in world w', and these will be necessarily true, by definition of whatever world is in question. On the other hand, if worlds are *not* defined by what happens in them—if they are bare chunks of logical space or arenas in which things happen—then we invite a new host of why-questions: why does so-and-so happen in *this* world rather than *that*? For the entire wheel of possibilities could have been rotated through logical space. Recall Leibniz's objection to Newtonian absolute space: he complained that if space were an arena in which objects were placed, not simply an abstraction defined in terms of the relations among objects, then there would be no sufficient reason why the entire material cosmos is situated here rather than there. Similarly, if worlds are not defined in terms of what goes on in them, there can be no sufficient reason why certain things happen in this world rather than that one. So, the relativization strategy seems to leave us with Bennett's dilemma: either all truths are necessary, or there is at least one brute fact.

I come now to the third strategy, which is the one Nozick favors. He undertakes to restrict the Principle of Fecundity to possibilities of a certain delimited sort in such fashion that the principle will no longer refute itself, yet will still explain itself by way of self-subsumption. Since the restricted principle is to be self-subsuming, he suggests that 'self-subsuming' should help to demarcate the sort itself. In that case, the desired Principle of Limited Fecundity would take the following form:

(LF) All self-subsuming possibilities of sort S are realized.[73]

LF, unlike the original Principle of Fecundity, does not subsume its own negation and therefore does not refute itself.[74] But does it subsume itself? Nozick is content to point out that either answer we give to this question is consistent. I believe the situation is rather more troublesome than this. LF is self-subsuming iff it has the property specified in its antecedent—that is, only if it has the property of being self-subsuming. There seems to be nothing to determine either that it subsumes itself or that it does not. In such a case, I think we should conclude that the matter is simply indeterminate.

Let us set that misgiving aside, however, and assume that LF does subsume itself. I maintain that under that supposition LF would not be true but instead either false or without any truth value at all. It would be false if there were self-subsuming principles of sort S other than LF that were false. Suppose, however, that there were no other self-subsuming principles of sort S that were false. Could we then declare LF to be true? I say no, since our declaration would be groundless: there would be nothing to make LF false, but nothing to make it true, either. An example will illustrate the situation.

Suppose you walk into a classroom and see written on a blackboard the sentence S: 'every sentence now appearing on this board is true'. Elsewhere on the board there appear only true sentences—'2 + 3 = 5' and the like. So far, so good, but is S true? It depends—on whether it is true! The truth of S depends on its own prior truth in much the same way as does that of the so-called "truth-teller" sentence, 'this sentence is true'. Some philosophers are willing to declare the latter sentence true, but my intuition tells me that such sentences are lacking in truth value altogether. The reason is that truth-attributing facts must supervene on (or be determined by) facts that do not involve truth. From this it follows that whenever the truth-free facts do not determine a truth value for a given sentence, we are left with a truth-value gap. To illustrate, the fact that the sentence 'snow is white' is true is determined by its having the meaning it does together with snow's being white—facts that do not themselves involve truth. But whether our sentence S is true is not determined by any truth-free facts, so by the supervenience principle it has no truth value at all.[75]

To return to Nozick, it should be clear that his Principle of Limited Fecundity, if self-subsuming as desired, has the same status as the sentence 'all sentences now appearing on this board are true'. Circumstances could conspire to make it false, but nothing could happen to make it true: in the best-case scenario, it would be without truth value. So, Nozick's favored ultimate explanatory principle, if genuinely self-subsuming, is not true, and if it is not true, it cannot serve as an explanation of itself or anything else.

The prospects for *explaining everything* now look dark indeed. We are left with Bennett's alternatives: either all truths are necessary, or there is at least one brute fact. The "terrible sublimity" of this situation is well brought out in the following passage from Kant:

> We cannot put aside, and yet also cannot endure, the thought that a being that we represent to ourselves as supreme amongst all possible be-

ings should, as it were, say to itself: 'I am from eternity to eternity, and outside me there is nothing save what is through my will; *but whence then am I?*' (A613/B641)

Be it the existence of the primordial being or the disposition of its will, it appears that there is bound to be at least one brute fact.

13

Kant and Contemporary Irrealism

> There is no God's Eye point of view that we can know or usefully imagine. . . . Kant is best read as proposing for the first time what I have called the 'internalist' or 'internal realist' view of truth.
>
> Hilary Putnam,
> *Reason, Truth, and History*

As noted in section E of chapter 1, contemporary irrealism is not typically a variety of idealism. It is more often a theory that insists on a necessary connection between truth and evidence, which need not be the same thing as requiring a necessary connection between reality and minds. Two leading irrealists whose views fit this characterization are Hilary Putnam and Michael Dummett. Roughly, Dummett holds that nothing can be true unless there is adequate evidence for it, while Putnam holds that anything for which there is ideally adequate evidence is true. (Putnam *also* seems to espouse a doctrine of mind-dependence, as I show below.

There are occasional striking similarities between the views of Kant and those of Putnam and Dummett. It is not surprising, therefore, that Putnam has seen in Kant aspects of his own "internal realism" and that others have seen in Kant a version of the view Dummett labels "antirealism." In this chapter I explore some of the parallels, seeking to determine to what extent the appropriation of Kant by contemporary irrealists is well taken.

A. Putnam's Internal Realism

In a series of articles and books spanning more than a decade, Putnam has criticized a position he calls metaphysical realism and advocated in its place a position he calls internal realism. He has also discerned in Kant important anticipations of his own views. In particular, he has suggested that the transcendental realism Kant opposes is equivalent to metaphysical realism, and that the transcendental idealism Kant espouses is similar to his own internal realism. In the following section I assess the parallels, but first I must make clearer what Putnam means by his own pair of "isms."

My task is complicated by the fact that Putnam has offered a variety of accounts of the two "isms" over the years that are by no means obviously equivalent, but that are apparently intended to be formulations of the same doctrines. To simplify matters, I concentrate here on the account given in *Reason, Truth, and History*, where Putnam gives characterizations of metaphysical realism (or "externalism," as he also calls it) and internal realism (or "internalism") in three consecutive sentences each.[1] Here, in Putnam's words, are the tenets of metaphysical realism, with numbers inserted for future reference:

E1. The world consists of some fixed totality of mind-independent objects.

E2. There is exactly one true and complete description of 'the way the world is' [modulo notational variation, as Putnam adds elsewhere].[2]

E3. Truth involves some sort of correspondence relation between words or thought-signs and external things and sets of things.

Elsewhere Putnam characterizes metaphysical realism as a bundle containing four components: Independence, Uniqueness, Correspondence, and Bivalence.[3] The first three of these terms could serve as labels for E1, E2, and E3, respectively; the fourth is a tip of the hat to Michael Dummett, whose views on bivalence as a mark of realism I discuss below in section C.

The corresponding tenets of internal realism are the following:

I1. 'What objects does the world consist of?' is a question that it only makes sense to ask *within* a theory or description.

I2. There is more than one 'true' theory or description of the world [according to "many" internalists].

I3. 'Truth', in an internalist view, is some sort of (idealized) rational acceptability—some sort of ideal coherence of our beliefs with each other and with our experiences *as those experiences are themselves represented in our belief system*—and not correspondence with mind-independent or discourse-independent states of affairs.

Notice that each I-item is evidently meant to be a contrary of the corresponding E-item. Thus, E3 (truth as correspondence) is opposed to I3 (truth as coherence), and E2 (one true theory) is opposed to I2 (more than one true theory). The opposition is less clear in the case of E1 and I1. Is mind-independence really incompatible with theory-relativity? If it is a theory-relative matter what objects there are, does that make objects dependent on minds? The answer would be yes if (i) theory-relativity implied theory-dependence and (ii) there could be no theories without minds to devise them. Otherwise, the matter is not so clear.

Putnam sometimes suggests that a core commitment of metaphysical realism is that even an epistemically ideal theory might be false (a possibility not countenanced by internal realism):

The most important consequence of metaphysical realism is that *truth* is supposed to be *radically nonepistemic*—we might be 'brains in a vat' and so the theory that is 'ideal' from the point view of operational utility, inner beauty and elegance, 'plausibility', simplicity, 'conservatism', etc., *might be false.*[4]

Perhaps that commitment can be seen as a corollary of metaphysical realism as defined by the E3/I3 contrast. If epistemic ideality is explicated in terms of coherence, and if a theory can satisfy the demands of coherence without satisfying those of correspondence, then E3 implies that a theory can be epistemically ideal without being true.

B. Is Kant an Internal Realist?

I now discuss where Kant stands on each of the three issues marking Putnam's divide.

Mind-Independence.   According to the interpretation of transcendental idealism defended in this book, Kant thinks everything in the world of nature—everything in space and time—is mind-dependent. If by 'the world', therefore, one means the world of nature, Kant rejects the realist tenet E1. That is not necessarily to say that he subscribes to I1, however, for he does not connect mind-dependence with theory-relativity as Putnam apparently does.

Nor is it to say that Kant denies the existence of *any* mind-independent objects, for such precisely are his things in themselves. There is *a* world consisting of a fixed totality of mind-independent objects, namely, the noumenal world. Putnam agrees: "[Kant] does not doubt that there is *some* mind-independent reality."[5] On one important score, then, Kant is a metaphysical realist.

One True Theory.   I know of nothing in Kant to suggest that he would not subscribe as well to the second tenet of metaphysical realism. It is even a stock criticism of Kant that he was too wedded to the leading theories of his own day—Aristotelian logic, Euclidean geometry, and Newtonian physics—taking them to be true for all time and without possible alternatives. It is part of the Hegelian reaction to Kant to try to make room for alternative conceptual frameworks (e.g., rival geometries or systems of categories), and Putnam's internal realism is part of this tradition. But Kant himself, for better or worse, gives every indication of having believed in One True Theory.

Truth as Correspondence.   Here is where it may seem likeliest that Kant departed from metaphysical realism. According to Norman Kemp Smith, "Kant is the real founder of the *Coherence* theory of truth."[6] And according to Putnam,

> [Kant] all but says that he is giving up the correspondence theory of truth.
> Kant does not, indeed, *say* he is giving up the correspondence theory of truth. On the contrary, he says that truth is the 'correspondence of a judgment to its object'. But this is what Kant called a 'nominal definition of truth'.[7]

It is true that Kant disparaged the correspondence definition of truth as 'nominal', as Putnam notes. But does this mean he rejected the correspondence theory of truth? I think not. Here is the passage Putnam is referring to:

The question, famed of old, by which logicians were supposed to be driven into a corner, obliged either to have recourse to a pitiful sophism, or to confess their ignorance and consequently the emptiness of their whole art, is the question: What is truth? The nominal definition of truth, that it is the agreement [*Übereinstimmung*, also translatable as "correspondence"] of cognition with its object, is assumed as granted; the question asked is as to what is the general and sure criterion of the truth of any and every cognition. (A57–58/B82, replacing Kemp Smith's "knowledge" by "cognition.")

It is clear that Kant is not rejecting the correspondence definition of truth; on the contrary, he says it is "assumed as granted." Why, then, does he call it *nominal*? The rest of the passage makes that clear, too. The point is that the correspondence definition, though it correctly states the *nature* of truth, does not provide us with an epistemologically helpful *test* of truth. In Kant's terms, it does not give us a *criterion* we can use to tell whether a cognition is true or false.

For further light on this point, compare a parallel passage from Kant's *Lectures on Logic*:

Truth, it is said, consists in the agreement of cognition with its object. In consequence of this mere nominal explanation, my cognition, to count as true, is supposed to agree with its object. Now I can compare the object with my cognition, however, only by *cognizing it*. Hence my cognition is supposed to confirm itself, which is far short of being sufficient for truth. For since the object is outside me, the cognition in me, all I can ever pass judgment on is whether my cognition of the object agrees with my cognition of the object. Such a circle in explanation was called by the ancients *diallelus*.[8]

It should be noted that the phrase in the passage from the *Critique* that Kemp Smith translates as "pitiful sophism" is *elenden Dialele*. The problem to which Kant is adverting in the *Critique* is thus almost certainly none other than the diallelus. What exactly is the problem, and what is Kant's solution?

It is possible to interpret the *Logic* passage along the lines I have suggested for the *Critique* passage. In that case, Kant is accepting correspondence as the definition of truth and questioning only its utility as a test of truth. He is not proposing a coherence definition of truth; on the contrary, he is repudiating it: he says that the agreement of one cognition with (presumably other) cognitions is "far short of being sufficient for truth."

On the other hand, it is also possible to extract from the *Logic* passage an argument against the correspondence theory and in favor of the coherence theory. On this reading, Kant's point would be that all we can ever verify is the agreement of one cognition with another, and that such agreement is "far short of being sufficient for truth" *as truth is defined by the correspondence theory*. Hence, the correspondence theory would have the consequence that truth is unknowable. If we add the premise that truth *is* knowable, we get a transcendental argument for the coherence theory.

Variants of this simple argument (sometimes called "the comparison argument") have exerted a powerful influence down to the present day, having persuaded Neurath, Dewey, Davidson, Rorty, and BonJour among a great many others.[9] However, the argument is not unanswerable. It is no doubt true that I can "compare" a given cognition with its object only by using another cognition, but that is not to say that *what* I am comparing is cognition 1 with cognition 2. The argument confuses the vehicle of knowledge with its content. All one need assume, in order to maintain that it is possible after all to compare a cognition with its object (or as I would prefer to say, to confirm a cognition by checking its object), is that some cognitions do disclose features of the objects they cognize. Putting the point another way, if the diallelus argument is to reach its conclusion, it must be assumed that cognition *never* discloses or gives knowledge of features of the object cognized, but only of its own self. When the needed assumption is thus made explicit, I doubt that many will want to embrace it. (For further discussion of a related argument against the correspondence theory, see appendix N.)

The problem of the diallelus, I would therefore say, arises from a false presupposition. But my main point for now is this: Kant's solution to the diallelus is *not* a coherence theory of truth. Instead, it is a reductive theory of the objects of empirical knowledge—the already familiar phenomenalist theory discussed in chapter 7, section H. For an empirical object to exist (and to have whatever properties it does) is for certain representations to occur and to bear certain relations to other representations that do, will, or would occur. The resulting view *simulates* a coherence theory of truth, insofar as it offers the same truth conditions that a coherence theory might offer for judgments about empirical objects. It says, for example, that the judgment that there is an apple on my desk is true if and only if certain relations hold just among my representations.[10] But as I see things, Kant reaches this result not by way of a coherence theory of truth, but by way of his reductive account of objects.[11]

That Kant does not hold a coherence theory of truth may be reinforced further by the following three considerations.

(i) A proper coherence theory of truth holds that the truth of a judgment consists exclusively in its relations to other *judgments*. The "simulated" coherence theory to which I have just drawn attention holds that the truth of a judgment consists in relations among representations, but not necessarily among judgments or other truth-bearers exclusively.[12]

(ii) At A59–60/B84 Kant says that cognitions that are not in contradiction with themselves may nonetheless be in contradiction with their object. Logical consistency, he concludes, is merely "a *conditio sine qua non*, and is therefore the negative condition of all truth—not a sufficient condition."

(iii) If the general nature of truth for Kant were coherence, we should expect him to say that even the truth of a judgment explicitly about our representations alone, or one about the logical relations among judgments, consists in its coherence with other judgments and representations. But in fact Kant seems to hold no such regressive theory. When we reach judgments about the basic entities of his ontology, truth for him is correspondence with fact.[13]

To summarize, here is where Kant stands on Putnam's three issues. On the first (mind-independence vs. mind-dependence), he is an internal realist regarding the phenomenal world but a metaphysical realist regarding the noumenal world. On the second issue (one true theory vs. more than one), I venture to suggest he is metaphysical realist regarding both worlds. On the third (correspondence vs. coherence), I would say he is again a metaphysical realist concerning both worlds, even though his view coincides with internal realism in what it says about the truth conditions of judgments about objects in the phenomenal world.

In fairness to Putnam, I should note that when he suggests that Kant gives up the correspondence theory of truth, he generally seems to have in mind a version of the theory in which the items corresponding to our judgments are noumenal items outside our minds.[14] In regard to such an understanding of things, I wish to make two points. First, as I show above, it is by no means essential to the correspondence theory as such that it be understood in such a "noumenalized" fashion.[15] Second, even if a "noumenalized" version of the correspondence theory is what is in question, Kant may still subscribe to it. He would not, to be sure, hold a noumenal correspondence theory for judgments about phenomenal objects. But what of judgments that are *about* noumenal items outside our minds? Don't we need a noumenal correspondence theory for them?

To this question, Putnam would reply that there can be no such judgments. He offers an argument for this contention that I set down and comment on briefly.[16] For purposes of the argument, Putnam characterizes metaphysical realism as the view that "we can think and talk about things as they are, independently of our minds, and that we can do this by virtue of a 'correspondence' relation between the terms in our language and some sorts of mind-independent entities."[17] He equates metaphysical realism with the view Kant called transcendental realism.[18] He then goes on to argue against metaphysical realism in this sense as follows, attributing the argument more or less to Kant:[19]

1. We have no direct access to mind-independent things.
2. Without direct access to mind-independent things, we cannot "pick out" a unique correspondence relation between words and the things.
3. Therefore, metaphysical realism (as just defined) is false.

Whatever one thinks of the two stated premises, I think one may fault this argument for its *un*stated premise: the mere *obtaining* of an appropriate correspondence relation (which might be a causal relation, according to Putnam[20]) would not be enough to let us refer to the things on the other end of the relation. Putnam requires in addition that we *single out* (or refer to) the relation as a precondition of referring to its relata. I have given reasons for rejecting this requirement elsewhere.[21] I would also raise the question of how reference to mind-dependent objects is supposed to be any less problematic for internal realism than reference to independent objects is for metaphysical realism, given that the problems Putnam raises for reference seem to have to do with the relation itself and not its relata.

C. Dummett's Antirealism

The phrase 'antirealism' gained currency through the writings of Michael Dummett, who coined it to have a name for a certain kind of opposition to realism that need not take the form of idealism. Here is how Dummett portrays the debate as he sees it between realism and antirealism:

> Realism I characterise as the belief that statements in the disputed class possess an objective truth-value, independently of our means of knowing it: they are true or false in virtue of a reality existing independently of us.
>
> The anti-realist insists, on the contrary, that the meanings of these statements are tied directly to what we count as evidence for them, in such a way that a statement of the disputed class, if true at all, can be true only in virtue of something of which we could know and which we should count as evidence for its truth.[22]

Examples of "disputed classes" of statements are statements about the mental states of others, statements about the past, statements about the theoretical entities of science, and statements of mathematics.

Antirealism according to Dummett's characterization of it is a species of *verificationism*: it is the view that there is no truth (in whatever domain is at issue) without evidence or the possibility of verification. It is not the positivist variety of verificationism, however, which holds that statements on which no evidence could bear are *meaningless*. Dummett's antirealism can accord meaning to such statements, but it denies that they have any truth value. To distinguish it from the older variety of verificationism, I sometimes refer to it here as *evidentialism*.[23]

To spell out Dummettian antirealism a bit further, say that a state of affairs in virtue of which a sentence is true is a *truthmaker* for it, and that a state of affairs is *recognizable* if and only if we would or could know it to obtain if it did obtain. Then we can say that antirealism about a domain D is the view that statements in D are never true except in virtue of the obtaining of recognizable truthmakers. Realism, by contrast, is the view that statements in D may be true in the absence of recognizable truthmakers. Assuming both sides agree that there is never truth without a truthmaker, realism amounts to the view that a statement may be made true by an *un*recognizable truthmaker.

Dummett's model for the realism/antirealism debate is the debate between Platonists and intuitionists in the philosophy of mathematics. Intuitionists say there is no such thing as mathematical truth without proof, proofs being the only kind of recognizable truthmaker in mathematics. Platonists, on the other hand, allow for truth in the absence of proof: a mathematical assertion can be made true simply by the structure of mathematical reality. Generalizing the notion of proof to evidence, Dummett notes that the same form of debate occurs in other areas as well. For example, let the domain be statements about the mental states of others and consider the statement 'Jones was brave', asserted of someone now dead who never faced danger. For the antirealist this will be neither true nor false, since there is no recognizable truthmaker for either it or its negation. For the realist, on the other hand, the statement may well be true or false, because made true or false by a fact about the agent's unobservable inner character.

The foregoing examples lead us naturally to Dummett's well-known test for whether one is a realist or an antirealist in a given domain: does one accept the law of excluded middle as holding in that domain or not?

[A]cceptance of the law of excluded middle for statements of a given class [is] a crucial test for whether or not someone takes a realist view of statements of that class.[24]

The mathematical intuitionists did, of course, reject excluded middle; that is the most famous feature of intuitionist logic.

In later writings, Dummett says that bivalence, rather than excluded middle, should be the touchstone for realism.[25] Excluded middle is the logical law schematized as 'p v –p'; bivalence is the semantic principle that every statement is either true or false. Normally, these go together, but under certain assumptions one may reject bivalence while retaining excluded middle.[26] That combination would count as antirealist under Dummett's revised test.[27]

Why link antirealism with the rejection of bivalence? The connection in one direction is easy to see. Let S be an undecidable statement—a statement such that there is no evidence for asserting it and none for denying it (i.e., asserting its negation) either. Such statements lack recognizable truthmakers, and so do their negations. Examples of such statements are 'Jones was brave' (under the assumptions of a few paragraphs back) and any unsolved conjecture in mathematics (e.g., Goldbach's hypothesis that every even number greater than 2 is the sum of two primes). If S is any such statement, the antirealist will have to say that neither it nor its negation is true, since neither possesses a recognizable truthmaker. Since falsehood is standardly defined as truth of the negation,[28] it follows that S is neither true nor false. The antirealist will thus be led to reject bivalence in any domain in which there are undecidable statements.[29]

The realist, by contrast, will not have this reason for rejecting bivalence. So, Dummett summarizes the matter thus:

The anti-realist cannot allow that the law of excluded middle [bivalence] is generally valid: the realist may, and characteristically will.[30]

Here Dummett says that the realist *may* accept bivalence, not that he *must.* That seems right: a realist might reject bivalence for reasons having nothing to do with the absence of evidence but with something else instead, for example, vague predicates or quantum indeterminacy (which on some accounts is not epistemic in origin).[31]

Is Dummett's antirealism a form of idealism? The answer is no. Perhaps it *would* be a form of idealism if he insisted that nothing is ever true unless there is a truthmaker for it that someone *actually recognizes* (or knows to obtain), for it would presumably take a mind to do the recognizing. But he requires only that truthmakers be recogniz*able*—not that anyone actually take cognizance of them. That suffices to keep his style of antirealism from being a species of idealism.[32]

I do not intend to discuss the merits of Dummett's antirealism here, as I have done so elsewhere.[33] But in the following section I discuss some of the advantages and disadvantages of attributing such a view to Kant.

D. Is Kant an Antirealist?

The most illuminating work interpreting Kant as a Dummettian antirealist is that of Carl Posy.[34] In what follows, I present some of the main features and advantanges of Posy's interpretation; then I say why, despite these advantages, I remain unconvinced that Kant is an antirealist. The showcase for Posy's interpretation is the Mathematical Antinomies, to which I now once more turn.

The Theses and Antitheses of the Mathematical Antinomies may be symbolized as follows:

T: $(\exists x)(y)(-Ryx)$
A: $(x)(\exists y)(Ryx)$

By choosing appropriate ranges of values for the variables and appropriate relations for 'R', we may obtain from these schemata formulas that express all the key propositions of the Mathematical Antinomies. Letting the variables range over events and taking 'Ryx' to express the relation of temporal precedence, we get the Thesis and Antithesis of the temporal version of the First Antinomy (a beginning of the world vs. an infinite sequence of past events). Letting the variables range over bodies and taking 'Ryx' to express the relation 'y is more remote from Earth than x', we get the Thesis and Antithesis of the spatial version of the First Antinomy (an outermost body vs. bodies beyond bodies forever). Finally, letting the variables range over bits of matter and taking 'Ryx' to express the relation of proper parthood, we get the Thesis and Antithesis of the Second Antinomy (ultimate parts vs. parts within parts forever).

Recall that Kant's strategy in the Mathematical Antinomies is to argue that an adherent of transcendental realism (TR) must choose in each Antinomy between Thesis and Antithesis, but that each of these is demonstrably false. Hence, transcendental realism is itself false, giving us an indirect proof that transcendental idealism (TI) is true. In symbols:

1. TR $\to$ (T or A).
2. $-$T & $-$A.
3. Therefore, $-$TR.
4. Therefore, TI.

According to Kant, the transcendental idealist escapes the Antinomy that refutes transcendental realism because he can avoid the choice between T and A. But what entitles him to avoid this choice? In my discussion of the Second Antinomy in chapter 6, I could offer no satisfactory answer to this question. Indeed, if T and A are symbolized as above, it will appear impossible for the transcendental idealist to avoid the choice, since in standard logic T and A are logical contradictories, each being equivalent to the negation of the other. How can one avoid the choice between a proposition and its negation?

It is here that antirealism comes to the rescue. We must choose between a proposition and its negation only if bivalence holds, and I just showed in section C that antirealists reject bivalence and sometimes excluded middle. If Kant's transcendental idealism is a species of antirealism, he can escape the Antinomy.

Posy interprets Kant along these general lines, attributing to him a semantic theory that ties truth to evidence after the fashion of Dummett. It is not exactly the view canvassed in the preceding section, however; a difference or two will emerge presently.

Among the clauses in the semantic theory Posy makes integral to transcendental idealism are the following:[35]

1. An atomic formula holds at a time if and only if there is confirming evidence for it at that time.
2. A negation '−P' holds at a time if and only if P does not hold at that time or at any subsequent time. (Thus, if P is atomic, its negation holds at a time only if there is no evidence for P at t or any later time.) A variation on this clause that Posy favors would have it that −P holds at t only if there is evidence at t that P will remain unevidenced at later times.
3. A universal generalization '(x)(Fx)' holds at a time if and only if 'Fx' holds of every object at that time and all later times.

The clause for negation makes for one of the differences between Posy and the antirealist described in the preceding section. As I show below, Posy's clauses work jointly to open up the possibility that unevidenced P and −P are both false, rather than (as for the antirealist) both without truth value.

If we apply these clauses to Thesis and Antithesis of the spatial version of the First Antinomy, we get the following results: T holds at t only if there is some body that is an outermost discovered body (i.e., a body than which none is known to be farther out) at t and subsequently; A holds at t only if for every body discovered at t, a body known to be farther out has also been discovered at t. It is easy to see that under these stipulations, T and A might both be false. Suppose we discover new planets at the rate of one per year, each the remotest known when discovered, and that the years run on endlessly. Then T will be false because no body is the outermost ever discovered, and A will be false because at no time will there be, for every discovered body, a more remote body that is already discovered. So, Thesis and Antithesis are both false, just as Kant claims.

This is the first promised advantage of Posy's interpretation: it vindicates Kant's contention that T and A do not exhaust the possibilities. It does this by associating with transcendental idealism a semantic theory under which T and A, though contradictories in standard logic, can both be false.

A second advantage of Posy's interpretation is that it makes sense of a stretch of Kant's reasoning that has struck many readers as a bald *petitio*. Here is the crux of Kant's argument against the spatial half of the First Antinomy's Antithesis—the proposition that the world is infinite in space:

> In order, therefore, to think, as a whole, the world which fills all spaces, the successive synthesis of the parts of an infinite world must be viewed as completed, that is, an infinite time must be viewed as having elapsed in the enumeration of all coexisting things. This, however, is impossible [as the refutation of the temporal half of the Antithesis has shown]. (A428/B456)

The Antinomies are supposed to constitute an indirect proof of transcendental idealism. But in the passage just quoted, it looks as though Kant is simply *assuming* a key element of transcendental idealism, namely, that the various parts of the cosmos depend for their existence on the cognitive activity of synthesis. Why should a transcendental realist agree with that? It looks as though Kant has simply begged the question.

Posy defends Kant against the charge of question begging by making two suggestions. First, synthesis should be understood not as the activity of *generating empirical objects*, but as the activity of *confirming empirical judgments*. Second, the transcendental realist no less than the transcendental idealist abides by the requirement that an empirical judgment holds true at a time *only if there is confirming evidence for it* at that time. So, in assuming that the parts of the cosmos depend on synthesis, Kant is not making any sort of *esse est percipi* assumption that the transcendental realist would reject; he is only making the more innocent assumption of evidentialism, which on Posy's view the transcendental realist accepts, too. So, the argument above does not beg the question.

On Posy's interpretation, then, transcendental idealism is not a form of ontological idealism but of epistemic antirealism or evidentialism, and transcendental realism is evidentialist, too. But that gives rise to a pressing question. I showed above that linking truth to evidence may lead to breaches of bivalence. If transcendental realism shares with transcendental idealism the evidentialist principles that give rise to nonbivalent logic, why must the transcendental realist accept the disjunction of T and A? Why may she not escape the Antinomy by the same route as the transcendental idealist?

Posy's answer is that making truth depend on evidence does not automatically issue in failures of bivalence.[36] Whether an evidential theory of truth leads to nonbivalent logic depends on at least two other issues. First, do we say that something's being true now depends on there being evidence for it *now* (the "short view"), or only on there being evidence for it *eventually* (the "long view")? Second, what assumptions do we make about the future course of inquiry? Do we say (as Hilbert optimistically did in the case of mathematics) that eventually all questions *will be settled*—that for any proposition, there will sooner or later be proof on one side or the other? Or do we take the more pessimistic view that some questions will remain *forever undecided*? An evidential theory of truth that embraces either the short view or pessimism will indeed imply that the principle of bivalence sometimes fails. But an evidential theory of truth that combines the long view with optimism will uphold bivalence: if all it takes to make a proposition true now is evidence for it eventually, and if there will eventually be either evidence for p or evidence for −p, then one of them is true now.[37]

We are now in a position to say why the transcendental realist, though as much an evidentialist in Posy's view as the transcendental idealist, is barred from escaping the Antinomy by the idealist's route. *The realist is a long-view optimist.* She is thus committed to bivalence, and in particular to the truth of either Thesis or Antithesis. Hence, she is refuted when both of them prove untenable.[38]

An interesting sidelight that emerges from Posy's view is this: though he was claimed as a forerunner by the intuitionist Brouwer, Kant is not himself constrained to adopt an intuitionist logic for mathematics. That is because in mathematics (and perhaps in the sphere of the *a priori* generally) Kant is an optimist:

> [T]here are sciences [Kant later cites mathematics and ethics as cases in point] the very nature of which requires that every question arising within their domain should be completely answerable in terms of what is known, inasmuch as the answer must issue from the same sources from which the question proceeds. (A476/B504)[39]

It is rather in the empirical sphere that Kant countenances failures of bivalence, according to Posy, for it is here that our questions may outrun our ability to answer them. Compare: "[N]o one can say how far [our knowledge of nature] may in time extend" (A278/B334).

I now consider the overall plausibility of Posy's interpretation. Its key points are that epistemic antirealism or evidentialism is an essential ingredient not only of Kant's transcendental idealism but also of his opponent's transcendental realism. Here I raise some doubts concerning each point.

Is Kant's transcendental realist really an epistemic antirealist? I find this difficult to believe for two reasons. First, Kant thinks that by refuting transcendental realism, he thereby achieves an indirect proof of transcendental idealism. But if transcendental realism and idealism are both committed to evidentialism, they are no longer exhaustive alternatives, and refuting one would *not* suffice to establish the other. There would be occupiable ground outside the area of their common presupposition, and a *thoroughgoing* realist—one who rejects evidentialism along with ontological idealism—could safely occupy this ground. Using Kant's own terminology, he might say that both isms "presuppose an inadmissible condition" (viz., that truth depends on evidence), and that his own position is therefore untouched. The upshot is that if Posy is right about the commitments of transcendental realism, refuting it would not establish transcendental idealism, as Kant thinks it does; it would only establish that the truth lies either with transcendental idealism or with a more thoroughgoing realism.[40]

Second, if Kant had taken for granted that some form of evidentialism is assumed even by transcendental realism, his arguments against the antinomial alternatives could have taken a much simpler and directly epistemic form. He could simply have pointed out that there could never be evidence sufficient to verify either Thesis or Antithesis, which on evidentialist principles would make both of them untrue. What we find instead is that Kant deploys a number of distinctively *metaphysical* arguments against the various alternatives: (a) A beginningless series of events is ruled out because it would involve a completed infinite—something Kant opposes for reasons not having anything to do with transcendence of the evidence. Evidential concerns about an infinite cosmos could be allayed if an infinite quantity of evidence could be "all in," but a completed infinite totality of evidence would boggle Kant's mind for the same reason as an infinite cosmos. (b) A first event is ruled out because it would violate the Principle of Sufficient Reason—there could be no explanation for the world's beginning at this rather than that moment of time.[41] (c) The infinite complexity of matter (parts within parts forever) is ruled out because it would mean there could be total annihilation through mere scattering (see chapter 6, section A). Finally, (d) ultimate simple parts of matter are ruled out for the Baylean reason that everything in space must be extended and therefore composite (see chapter 6, section B).[42]

These arguments may be good or they may be bad; my point just now is that they are metaphysical, not epistemological. They would be effective (if at all) even against an adversary who was not an evidentialist; they would be needlessly baroque against one who was.

What now of Kant's own transcendental idealism—should it be construed as a species of evidentialism? Of this, too, I am unconvinced, this time for three reasons.

It is common in philosophy to try to ground the truth of assertions about facts at one level in facts belonging to another level: mental facts in behavioral facts, past facts in present or future facts, facts about micro-objects in facts about macro-objects (or sometimes vice versa), facts about potentialities in facts about actualities, facts about wholes in facts about parts, general facts in singular facts, and so on. The reasons for doing this are sometimes epistemological: one wants truth to be grounded in evidence, and one believes that the lower stratum facts provide the evidence for the higher stratum facts. But the reasons are not always epistemological: in the whole-part and potentiality-actuality cases (to mention only two), they are more likely to be ontological, and they *may* be ontological in nearly any of the cases. Moreover, to the extent that a philosopher's concerns *are* epistemological, one would expect him to apply evidentialist principles across the board, admitting truth in *no* area of discourse that is not grounded in epistemically privileged fact. For example, an evidentialist about the past ought to extend his evidentialism to the future, too, allowing future fact only to the extent that it is determined by presently knowable fact.

To come to the point I have obviously been leading up to, Kant sometimes grounds facts at one level in facts at another but gives no sign of being an across-the-board evidentialist. For example, in giving the truth conditions for some present facts about material things, he has recourse to future and even subjunctive facts about experience (if I may apply a grammatical term to the facts themselves). That there are creatures on the moon, he says, means that under an appropriate "advance of experience" we would encounter them. (For more on this, see appendix D.) Again, to say that such-and-such has happened in the remote past is to say something about what future inquiry would disclose concerning the causal antecedents of present experience (A495/B523).[43] But Kant gives no hint that the future and subjunctive facts need themselves be anchored in anything knowable. I think he would allow that 'a city will never be built on this spot', one of Dummett's paradigms of an unverifiable statement,[44] might be made true by the future course of human sense experience, even though at no point will anyone ever have evidence that establishes it. This strongly suggests that his motives are not at bottom evidentialist.

For a second reason to doubt that Kant is an evidentialist, note that he affirms the following principle:

[E]very *thing*, as regards its possibility, is likewise subject to the principle of *complete* determination, according to which if *all the possible* predicates of things be taken together with their contradictory opposites, then one of each pair of contradictory opposites must belong to it. (A571–72/B599–600)[45]

As Posy has pointed out, this is not full-strength excluded middle but only a restricted version of it, insofar as it applies only to singular judgments.[46] Nonetheless, it covers enough ground to run afoul of evidentialism, since some pairs of predicates and their opposites will generate pairs of singular judgments such that there might well never be evidence conclusively establishing either member. Did Caesar dream of three pink elephants on the eve of his assassination or not? The Principle of Complete Determination implies that he did or he did not, even if there will never be evidence settling which.

For my last reason, I note that even if evidentialism makes sense of much of what Kant says in the Antinomies, it does little as far as I can see to account for the force Kant attributes to his other main arguments for transcendental idealism—the argument from geometry and the argument from incongruent counterparts. How would an evidentialist construal of transcendental idealism explain Kant's contention that our synthetic *a priori* knowledge in geometry can be accounted for only if transcendental idealism is true? And how would it help us to see why the paradox of incongruent counterparts is resolvable only if transcendental idealism is true? These are questions I hope Posy addresses as he develops his interpretation further. In the meantime, I continue to regard Kant as an old-fashioned idealist.

Appendices

Appendix A. Reds, Greens, and the Synthetic *A Priori*

As I noted in chapter 2, 'nothing is both red and green all over at the same time' has been a contested example of a proposition that is both synthetic and *a priori*. The example goes back to Wittgenstein's *Tractatus* and further back to Leibniz, who called such propositions 'disparates'.[1] Opponents of the synthetic *a priori* have generally conceded that the proposition is *a priori* and have devoted their ingenuity to showing that it is analytic. The best attempts along these lines I know of grow out of an essay by Hilary Putnam in the 1950s. Putnam's proposals were emended and criticized by Arthur Pap, then further emended and defended by Lambert and van Fraassen.[2] Interest in the question has died down, owing no doubt to growing disenchantment with the analytic-synthetic distinction, but it merits a brief reprise.

Putnam's strategy has two parts. The first is to show that the following theorem is analytic in the strict sense that has figured in this book, that is, demonstrable using only definitions and logic:

A. $(F)(G)[Col(F) \& Col(G) \& F \neq G \rightarrow -\exists x(Fx \& Gx)]$

That is, if F and G are distinct colors, nothing has them both. Would the analyticity of A imply that it is analytic that nothing is both red and green? Yes, provided we add the assumption that red and green are distinct colors, and provided that the added assumption is itself analytic. So, the second half of Putnam's strategy is to show that the following statement, an instance of the antecedent of A, is also analytic:

B. $Col(red) \& Col(green) \& red \neq green$

To prove A, Putnam employs two definitions. First, he defines what it is for two objects to be the same in color, xSy, in terms of the relation I of phenomenal indistinguishability:

D1. $xSy =_{Df} (z)(zIx \leftrightarrow zIy)$

Although the relation I is intransitive (and thus not itself sufficient for identity in color), the relation S (as defined by D1) is demonstrably an equivalence relation: transitive, reflexive, and symmetric.

Next, Putnam defines the property of being a color in terms of the relation S:

D2.   Col(F) =Df $\exists y(x)(Fx \leftrightarrow xSy)$

That is, F is a color iff there is an object such that something is F iff it is the same in color as that object. This definition is a natural companion to the idea (though Putnam does not endorse it) that particular colors are defined ostensively by reference to paradigm objects, for example, $(x)(red(x) \leftrightarrow xSa)$—to be red is to be the same in color as *this*. From this definition it would follow by existential generalization that red is a color in the sense defined by D2. (Thus, part of the task of showing B to be analytic would have been accomplished— it would have been shown to follow logically from a definition that red is a color. The remaining part would be to show that it is analytic that red $\neq$ green.)

I do not reproduce here Putnam's derivation of proposition A from the above two definitions.[3] I simply note that at a crucial stage, Putnam needs to use a purely extensional criterion of property identity: $F = G$ iff $(x)(Fx \leftrightarrow Gx)$. That, of course, is highly implausible, as shown by such well-worn examples as the coextensive but distinct properties of having a heart and having a kidney.

Noting the inadequacy of the extensional criterion of property identity, Pap suggests that a stronger modal criterion be used instead: $F = G$ iff $(x)\Box(Fx \leftrightarrow Gx)$. (Many who countenance properties would say we need a criterion that is stronger yet, but I shall let that point pass.) He also notes that Putnam's D2 has the consequence that if all and only blue things were round, roundness would be a color, and he therefore proposes that D2 also be replaced by a modal definition:

D2'.   Col(F) =Df $\exists y(x)\Box(Fx \leftrightarrow xSy)$

While we are at it, perhaps we should also replace D1 by a modal definition: xSy =Df $\Box(z)(zIx \leftrightarrow zIy)$.[4] However, this change is not required for Putnam's proofs to go through.

Pap contends that under his proposed emendations, A and B can still be derived from definitions and logic. He goes on to raise further difficulties to which I return below. But first I pause to note that in fact A does *not* follow from Pap's definitions and identity criterion, as the following countermodel devised by Lambert and van Fraassen shows:

World 1	World 2
a,b,c all red	a,c red (and not green)
a,b,c all green	b green (and not red)
all possible pairs of a,b,c related by S	aa, bb, cc, ac, ca related by S

In this model, red and green count as colors by Pap's D2' and as distinct colors by his modal criterion (since they are not coextensive in world 2), so the antecedent of A is true. Yet the consequent of A is false, as a glance at world 1 shows.

Lambert and van Fraassen propose to salvage the situation by replacing modal operators with quantification over possible individuals. In place of Pap's criterion, they propose F = G ↔ (/x)(Fx ↔ Gx), where '(/x)' is a quantifier ranging over possibilia. Thus, properties are distinct iff some possible object has one but not the other. With this understanding of the quantifiers, a proof formally analogous to Putnam's original (and valid) proof goes through, but since the range of the quantifiers is now expanded to include all possible objects, there is no longer any objection to Putnam's overly extensional assumptions. The trouble with this saving move is that quantification over possibilia is highly suspicious: despite impressive lobbying on their behalf by David Lewis, there are no merely possible individuals. Even if there were, their existence could scarcely be analytic.

I come now to the difficulty Pap himself raises against his emended approach. Both definitions of 'Col(F)' make colors dependent on particulars in an unacceptable way. Putnam's D2 has the consequence that red is not a color unless ∃y(red y)—that is, there are no uninstantiated colors. Pap's D2' has the same consequence and another more implausible yet, namely, that red is a color only if ∃y□(red y). Take one of the paradigms that is used to define redness: to be red is to be the same in color as it, whence it follows that the paradigm itself, being necessarily the same in color as itself, will be necessarily red. That is absurd.

Readers familiar with Kripke's discussion of the standard meter stick will know how to avoid this absurdity.[5] When we say 'x is one meter long iff x is the same in length as stick S', we are only fixing the reference, not giving the sense, of 'x is one meter long'. We are not giving a definition that implies that the standard meter stick (i.e., stick S) has the same length in all possible worlds just because it is self-congruent in all possible worlds. Rather, we are saying that the length possessed by S in the actual world is such that to be one meter long is to have that length. Similarly, when we define red in terms of a paradigm object, we are not making it necessary that the paradigm is red. In effect, we are saying that the color possessed by the paradigm in the actual world is such that to be red is to have that color.

We can thus avoid Pap's absurdity, but at what cost for present purposes? Recall his emended definition of color: Col(F) =Df ∃y(x)□(Fx ↔ xSy). If we are to avoid the inference from the definiens to □(Fa ↔ aSa) and its consequence □(Fa), we must rewrite the definition thus: Col(F) =Df ∃y∃G(G is the color of y & (x)□[Fx ↔ Gx]). In other words, a color is a property that is necessarily coextensive with the color of something—which is a circular definition. In giving it, we abandon the definition of colors in terms of the relation S, on which the analyticity of both A and B depended.

To sum up: the Putnam-inspired attempts to demonstrate the analyticity of 'nothing is red and green' by demonstrating the analyticity of A and B all fail. As for A, Putnam's proof of it uses an inadequate principle of individuation for properties, Pap's turns out to be invalid, and Lambert and van Fraassen's makes dubious commitment to possibilia. As for B, the proof of its analyticity depends on defining colors in a way that implausibly implies that certain objects have their colors necessarily. We can avoid this implausible implication by using Kripke-style definitions instead, but they are no longer of use in demonstrating the analyticity of either A or B.

Appendix B. Five Questions about Causation and Necessity

I showed in chapter 2, section D, that Hume and Kant both distinguish the following two questions: is the general causal maxim necessary? and are particular causal laws necessary? The latter question should be distinguished in turn from a closely related question: is causation to be *analyzed* in terms of necessity? That question itself splits into two, depending on whether the necessity in question is physical or logical. We may thus distinguish four questions so far:

1. Is causation to be analyzed in terms of physical necessity?
2. Is causation to be analyzed in terms of logical necessity?
3. Are particular causal laws logically necessary?
4. Is the general causal maxim logically necessary?

Hume says no to all four questions. Kant says no (at least implicitly) to 2 and 3 but yes to 1 and 4. Below I indicate the textual bases for these answers, but first it is useful to say something about the logical relations among the questions. In brief, an affirmative answer to 2 requires an affirmative answer to 3, but in every other case the questions are independent.

Here is why yes to 2 implies yes to 3. Suppose we accept the following analysis (call it A), in conformity with a yes answer to 2:

C causes E iff it is logically necessary that whenever an event of C's type occurs, an event of E's type follows.

I abbreviate the analysans as '$\Box(C > E)$'. The argument that we must now say yes to 3 runs as follows:

1. C causes E—assumption for conditional proof.
2. $\Box(C > E)$—from 1 and analysis A.
3. $\Box\Box(C > E)$—from 2 and the modal principle that what is necessary is nessarily necessary.
4. $\Box$(C causes E)—from 3 and analysis A.
5. If C causes E, then $\Box$(C causes E)—from 1–4.

As for the converse relationship, I cannot see that yes to 3 implies yes to 2, even though I know of no philosopher who has answered yes to 3 without basing this on a yes to 2.

Questions 3 and 4 are independent of one another, at least formally. To see that yes to 3 does not imply yes to 4, consider the following analog: if a natural number has a certain predecessor, it is (logically) necessary that it have that predecessor, but it is not necessary (because not even true) that a natural number have some predecessor or other (zero does not). To see that yes to 4 does not imply yes to 3, consider this analog: it is necessary that a colored thing have some shape or other, but contingent that any colored thing has the particular shape that it does. In just the same way, it could be necessary that an event have some cause or other, but contingent that it has the particular type of cause that it does.

I assume that it will be sufficiently clear without comment in the remaining combinations of cases that the questions are independent. I now briefly indicate why I attribute the answers I do to Hume and Kant.

That Hume says no to 3: The argument from conceivability and the argument from Adam in section IV of the *Inquiry Concerning Human Understanding* both show that causal laws are not *a priori*; for Hume this means they are not necessary, either.[6]

That Kant says no to 3: He believes, just as Hume did, that specific causal laws are empirical (see, e.g., A766/B794) and that the empirical coincides with the contingent (see, e.g., B4).

That Hume and Kant must both say no to 2: This is required by their no to 3, since as I showed above, yes to 2 would imply yes to 3.

That Hume says no to 1: This is implied by his denial that we have any idea of necessary connection in the sense of power, force, energy, and so on—any idea of efficacy that goes beyond constant conjunction with an effect.

That Kant says yes to 1: He does believe that the concept of causation involves the concept of a connection that is in *some* sense necessary (see, e.g., B5 and p. 5 of the *Prolegomena*). But the necessity cannot be logical necessity, as I have already shown. So, a natural move is to attribute to him the view that causation is to be analyzed in terms of physical necessity.

That Hume says no to 4: This is the argument of *Treatise* I.3.iii, discussed in chapter 2.

That Kant says yes to 4: See, for example, B5, B19–20, and A766/B794. The general causal maxim is of course none other than the Second Analogy of Experience, one of Kant's "principles of pure understanding," all of which are supposed to be *a priori* and therefore necessary. It was Hume's opining to the contrary that aroused Kant from his dogmatic slumber.

Kant's combination of yes to 4 with no to 3 is formally consistent, as I point out above; nonetheless, it is a combination that can seem puzzling. I discuss the puzzling aspects in appendix I.

Here is a fifth question about causation and necessity:

5. Is the principle *same cause, same effect* necessary?

Beck and Dodge have discussed whether Kant was committed to the italicized principle and whether he has any argument in its favor.[7] I believe this issue may be resolved quickly. If we take the principle as stated—same *cause*, same effect—it is analytic. A cause of event E is by definition (for both Hume and Kant) an event C such that whenever an event of C's type recurs, so does an event of E's type. So of course Kant is committed to it, and he need not do anything special by way of proving it. On the other hand, we can construe the principle this way: same total antecedent event, same total ensuing event. Taken this way, the principle is not analytic. If we let events be as wide as entire momentary states of the universe, the principle is tantamount to LaPlacean determinism—which is in turn equivalent to Kant's Second Analogy or Kantian determinism.[8] So, once again, Kant is committed to the principle, but he need not do anything extra by way of proving it once he has proved the Second Analogy.[9] If the Second Analogy is a necessary truth, so is "same cause, same effect" under its second meaning.

Appendix C. Incongruent Counterparts and Absolute Space

In this appendix I briefly summarize some of the issues surrounding Kant's argument of 1768 from incongruent counterparts to the existence of absolute space. This is a compressed presentation of issues I have dealt with more thoroughly elsewhere.[10]

Here is how I reconstruct Kant's argument of 1768:

1. A hand is left or right (as the case may be) either (a) solely in virtue of the *internal* relations among the parts of the hand or (b) at least partly in virtue of the *external* relations of the hand to something outside it—if not other material objects, then absolute space.
2. But a hand is not left or right solely in virtue of its internal relations, since these are the *same* for right and left. ("The right hand is similar and equal to the left hand. And if one looks at one of them on its own, examining the proportion and the position of its parts to each other, and scrutinising the magnitude of the whole, then a complete description of the one must apply in all respects to the other, as well."[11])
3. Nor is a hand right or left even partly in virtue of its relations to other material objects, since a hand that was all alone in the universe would still be right or left. ("Imagine that the first created thing was a human hand. That hand would have to be either a right hand or a left hand."[12])
4. Therefore, a hand is left or right (as the case may be) at least partly in virtue of its relation to absolute space. ("Our considerations, therefore, make it clear that differences, and true differences at that, can be found in the constitution of bodies . . . [that] relate exclusively to *absolute* and *original* space. . . ."[13])

Since the argument is plainly valid, there are four possible responses to it. (i) One may reject the first premise, maintaining that left and right do not consist in relations at all, but are irreducible monadic properties. This view is not very plausible, and I do not know of anyone who has embraced it. (ii) One may reject the second premise, maintaining that right and left consist in relations only among a hand's own parts. Call this view *internalism*. (iii) One may reject the third premise, maintaining that right and left consist in relations to material objects outside the hand. Call this view *externalism*. (iv) One may accept the conclusion, and with it the existence of absolute space. Call this view *absolutism*. In recent critical commentary on Kant's argument, internalism has been advocated by Earman, externalism by Gardner, and absolutism by Nerlich.[14]

Two phenomena relevant to the evaluation of Kant's argument are *the fourth dimension* and *the fall of parity*.

The Fourth Dimension. For Kant, that space has three dimensions is a paradigm of a synthetic but necessary proposition. But for many thinkers since

Kant, propositions about the topological structure of space, including this one, are contingent, and dimensions beyond the familiar three are perfectly possible. How would the possibility of a fourth spatial dimension bear on Kant's argument?

In 1827, the mathematician Möbius observed that in a space of four dimensions, an object like a hand could be flipped over so as to become its own incongruent counterpart. The point is readily grasped with the help of lower dimensional analogs. If tokens of the letters 'p' and 'q' are confined to a two-dimensional sheet of newsprint, neither can be twisted or turned so as to make it occupy the space of the other, but if we are permitted to lift one of the letters out of the plane of the page and turn it over, the feat can be accomplished. Just so in a four-dimensional space: a left hand could be turned around so as to fit in the space now occupied by a right. Glovemakers would no longer have to manufacture separate left and right gloves, since the same model would fit all hands.

These facts are relevant to Kant's argument in two ways. First, they reinforce the case against internalism. Kant rejected internalism because he thought the relevant internal relations were exhausted by distances between points and angles between lines, and those relations are indeed the same for a right hand as for a left. Defenders of internalism have protested that Kant overlooked two other possibilities: according to some, the *direction* in which some points lie from others is different for corresponding points in left and right hands; according to others, there are *sui generis* relations of standing in a right-making configuration or a left-making configuration. Either way, the rightness of a hand would be a property of it intrinsic to the hand as a whole. But if rightness (or leftness) is an intrinsic property, how can it be altered by mere motion in the way I have just noted?

Second, the possibility of a fourth dimension undercuts the thought-experiment of the solitary hand by which Kant sought to refute externalism. Kant contends that a hand entirely alone in the universe would still be left or right. Weyl, Gardner, and others have denied this, maintaining that the first created hand would be neither right nor left until God created a second. Their position gains enormously in plausibility if we accept the possibility of a fourth dimension. If four-dimensional spaces are possible (even if not actual), then the difference between a right and a left hand comes to no more than the difference between a 'p' and a 'q'. That is to say, it is a matter of orientation (alterable by mere motion in a wide enough space) rather than shape. Now, can a solitary object have an orientation? It is hard to see how: two hands can be the same or different in orientation, but one hand alone can have no orientation at all. Externalism appears vindicated.

So matters stood until 1973, when Graham Nerlich gave a new twist to Kant's argument and defended its absolutist conclusion. In effect, Nerlich conceded the externalist criticism of Kant's argument regarding right and left, but he ran the argument all over again for a new pair of properties: being enantiomorphic and being homomorphic. Roughly, an object is enantiomorphic if it *could* have an incongruent counterpart (whether it actually does so or not) and homomorphic otherwise. A symmetrical object like a basketball is homomorphic in any possible space, for in no possible space does it have an incongruent counterpart. But an asymmetrical object like a hand may be either enantiomorphic or homomorphic, depending on the topological structure of the surrounding space. In a three-dimensional space it will be enantiomorphic (since it could have an incongruent counterpart in that space); in a four-dimensional space it will be homomorphic (since any counterpart of it will be superposable with it and thus congruent with it). Thus, Nerlich defends Kant's argument at a more abstract level: a solitary hand must be enantiomorphic or homomorphic; which of these it is will depend on the nature of the containing space, so there must be such an entity as space.

Not everyone has been convinced. Earman, though now an externalist rather than an internalist about right and left, has offered in opposition to Nerlich an internalist account of homomorphism and enantiomorphism. The debate among our "isms" continues at the more abstract level.

The Fall of Parity.   This refers to the finding, first made in the 1950s, that some laws of nature are sensitive to the distinction between right and left. For example, some particles more often decay in a left-handed configuration than a right, and the outcome of some physical processes can depend on whether the initial conditions assume a right- or a left-handed form. It would not be more suprising in principle if we were to discover that a left glove, when tossed into the air, generally lands palm up, whereas a right lands palm down.

The fall of parity has been adduced as showing that Kant was wrong to maintain (as he did in 1770) that the difference between right and left was intuitive or ostensive, and thus presumably not communicable to a distant galaxy. We *could* communicate the difference (according to Kant's critics) simply by sending the directions for one of the parity-violating experiments: "Let a bunch of X-particles decay; the decay configuration you will get most often is what we call left." However that may be, it seems to me that the fall of parity shows that Kant was correct about something else, namely, that externalism is mistaken. If being right or left is only a matter of being the same or different in orientation as some other object, how can it be a law of nature that certain processes always or usually have left-handed outcomes? That would be like a law of nature that instructs a seed to grow, not into a watermelon vine or something of such-and-such an intrinsic description, but into the same type of plant that a neighboring seed will grow into.[15]

If the points briefly developed in this appendix are correct, a significant conclusion follows. I have suggested (1) that in response to Kant's argument we must be either internalists, externalists, or absolutists; (2) that externalism is refuted by the fall of parity; and (3) that internalism would be refuted if four-dimensional spaces were possible. It follows that either absolutism is correct (as Kant maintained) or that four-dimensional spaces are impossible (as he also maintained). So, Kant was right about at least one thing.[16]

Appendix D. Unperceived Phenomena

Kant does not always maintain a strict *esse est percipi* view regarding appearances or phenomena.[17] He sometimes grants existence to items that are not actually perceived, provided they stand in some other suitable relation to perception. Just how far he wishes to liberalize the *esse est percipi* requirement is my topic here.

Kant's most extensive discussion of this issue occurs in his exposition of the Postulates of Empirical Thought, which are the synthetic *a priori* principles embodying the categories of modality. There he tells us this:

> The postulate bearing on the knowledge of things as *actual* does not, indeed, demand immediate *perception* (and, therefore, sensation of which we are conscious) of the object whose existence is to be known. What we do, however, require is the connection of the object with some actual perception in accordance with the analogies of experience. . . . (A225/B272)

The relevant Analogies here are presumably the second and the third, those dealing with causation. Kant is telling us that to be actual is to be either given in perception or causally connected with perception. He elaborates in the following passage, whose sentences I have numbered:

> [1] Thus from the perception of the attracted iron filings we know of the existence of a magnetic matter pervading all bodies, although the constitution of our organs cuts us off from all immediate perception of this medium. [2] For in accordance with the laws of sensibility and the context of our perceptions, we should, were our senses more refined, come also in an experience upon the immediate empirical intuition of it. [3] The grossness of our senses does not in any way decide the form of possible experience in general. [4] Our knowledge of the existence of things reaches, then, only so far as perception and its advance according to empirical laws can extend. (A226/B273)

Three distinct proposals are suggested by these remarks. According to the first, for something not presently perceived to be actual is for it to be a cause of something that is perceived. This proposal is suggested by the example of magnetic fields in sentence 1. According to the second, for something not presently perceived to be actual is for it to be the object of some perception that will occur in the future. (In light of Kant's determinism, we could replace "some perception that will occur in the future" by "some perception whose occurrence is now causally determined to happen.") This proposal is suggested by the phrase "perception and its advance according to empirical laws" in sentence 4.[18] According to the third, Kant is giving us a subjunctive account of unperceived existents of the sort favored by many latter-day phenomenalists: to say that something not perceived is actual means that under certain possible circumstances we *would* perceive it, regardless of whether we actually will. This proposal is suggested by the phrase "were our senses more refined" in sentence 2.

In brief, the alternatives are that unperceived phenomena are (i) causes of actual perceptions, (ii) objects of actual (present or future) perceptions, or (iii) objects of possible perceptions. (i) and (ii) have in common that unperceived items are actual by virtue of some relation to actual perceptions rather than merely possible ones, while (ii) and (iii) have in common that unperceived items are actual by virtue of being the objects of perceptions (actual or possible) rather than their causes.

I think alternative (i) can probably be ruled out as Kant's considered view for two reasons. First, Kant holds that inferences from effect to cause are always somewhat conjectural, owing to the multiplicity of possible causes (see A227/ B279 and A368). We could only verify the magnetic hypothesis if we came one day to observe magnetic fields, but in that case one of the other two accounts of unperceived actuality would be brought into play. Second, alternative (i) will not secure the existence of the back side of a house or of a tree in the darkened quad, since these need not function as causes of any actual perceptions.

It is hard to decide between the remaining two alternatives, but I am inclined to favor the second. The following remark seems to count against the third:

> What is possible only under conditions which themselves are merely possible is not *in all respects* possible. (A232/B284)

If the conditions under which we would perceive magnetic fields will never in fact come to pass, the fields are not (according to this remark) in all respects possible. It may—though I am not sure of this—be Kant's view that what is not in all respects possible is not actual, either.[19]

Kant says more about unperceived existents in his discussion of the Mathematical Antinomies, which includes the following remark:

> That there may be inhabitants in the moon, although no one has ever perceived them, must certainly be admitted. This, however, only means that in the possible advance of experience we may encounter them. (A493/ B521)

Here Kant equates the claim that lunar creatures may exist (*geben konne*) with the claim that we may encounter them (*auf sie treffen konnten*). From this it is hard to know whether he thinks their actual existence would require that we actually encounter them, or only that we would encounter them under appropriate circumstances.

A few sentences later, however, Kant is more definite:

> To call an appearance a real thing prior to our perceiving it, either means that in the advance of experience we must meet with such a perception, or it means nothing at all. (A493/B521)

Now the 'may' has given way to a 'must'. On the whole, then, it appears that Kant ties actual existence to actual perception (present, future, and perhaps also past), not merely to possible or hypothetically available perception.

Appendix E. Singularity and Immediacy

At A320/B377 Kant cites two marks of intuitions that distinguish them from concepts, singularity and immediacy:

> The former [intuition] relates immediately to the object and is single; the latter [concept] refers to it mediately by means of a feature which several things may have in common. (A320/B377)

For a full understanding of Kant's distinction between intuitions and concepts, we must know how these marks are themselves to be understood and how they are related to each other.

Immediacy.   An immediate (*unmittelbar*) relation between a representation x and an object y is one that is not mediated. A mediated relation is one that decomposes into two subrelations and a mediating item z, such that xRy iff xR'z & zR*y. When the relation between a representation and its object is mediated, what is the mediating item z?

Some passages suggest that it is *another representation*:

> Since no representation, except an intuition, is in immediate relation to an object, no concept is ever related to an object immediately, but to some other representation of it, be that other representation an intuition, or itself a concept. (A68/B93)

Kant's position here seems to imply that I cannot make a singular judgment (a judgment in which I apply a concept to a particular object) unless I have an intuition of that object. This may prompt an objection: can I not make judgments about my dog Fido even at times when I am not seeing him? Perhaps Kant would reply that a singular judgment about Fido must incorporate some intuition, though not necessarily an intuition of Fido, as in 'the dog who eats from *this dish* is friendly'. Or perhaps there are memory-representations that count as intuitions; Hintikka quotes Kant's contemporary Eberhard as saying "[sense] presents the particular that is present, [imagination] presents the particular that is absent."[20]

Other passages suggest that the mediating item is a *property* or *feature*, as in the quotation with which we began: a concept refers to an object "mediately by means of a feature which several things may have in common." In that case, the following question arises: is the clause 'which several things may have in common' (*was mehreren Dingen gemein sein kann*) restrictive or nonrestrictive? The grammar of Kant's sentence seems not to settle the issue. If the clause is restrictive, concepts and intuitions may *both* be mediated in their reference by properties, but concepts by properties that several things may have in common and intuitions by properties that are possessed by one thing uniquely. If it is nonrestrictive, the reference of concepts is mediated by properties (which *as such* are potentially common to many things) and the reference of intuitions is *not* mediated by properties. Hintikka has opted for the former alternative,[21] but I find the latter more likely: the reference of concepts is mediated by properties; that of intuitions is not.

Perhaps Kant's view is that the relation of concepts to objects is *doubly* mediated, by properties *and* by intuitions, as suggested by Parsons.[22] There is support for this suggestion at A19/B34: "But all thought must, directly or indirectly, by way of certain characters, relate ultimately to intuitions. . . ."

Singularity.   According to Manley Thompson, Kant holds that intuitions are not only single (i.e., nonrepeatable, such that there cannot be two intuitions of the same object) but also *singular.* He notes that although Kemp Smith's translation of the *Critique*'s *einzeln* as "single" is plausible, Kant uses the Latin term *singularis* when he characterizes intuitions in his lectures on logic.[23] "An intuition thus differs from a concept," Thompson says, "both in being *single* (a single occurrence) and in being a *singular* representation (a representation of but one object)."[24]

What does it mean to say that an intuition has only one object? Here are three successively stronger possibilities:

(a) it has only one object as a matter of contingent fact;
(b) it has only one object by virtue of its own nature;
(c) it has only one object by virtue of its own nature, and has moreover the *same* object in every possible world.

The concept 'kangaroo that is exactly six feet tall' is for all I know singular in sense (a), but if so, that would not turn it into an intuition. Whether a representation is singular (and hence whether it counts as an intuition or a concept) should depend on intrinsic features of the representation, not on extraneous facts about how many kangaroos of a certain height there happen to be.

The concept 'tallest kangaroo' is singular in sense (b), but for all that it is still a concept, not an intuition. So, singularity in sense (b) is not by itself sufficient for intuitionhood, either.

To be singular in sense (c), a representation must not only have just one object; it must also have the *same* object in every possible world. 'Tallest kangaroo' never has more than one object in any world, but it may have different objects in different worlds, so it is not singular in sense (c). I propose below that (c) is better than (a) or (b) as an explication of singularity.

How Are the Marks Related?   There are two main views about how the marks of singularity and immediacy are related. According to Parsons, immediacy implies singularity, but not conversely; according to Hintikka and Thompson, the two conditions are equivalent.[25] They thus differ as to whether singularity implies immediacy. If it does, singularity is sufficient for something being an intuition; if it does not, immediacy is a separately necessary condition. I believe Hintikka and Thompson are right on this issue, though for reasons neither of them states.

Here are some bits of textual evidence suggesting that for Kant singularity and immediacy go together. (i) In his Inaugural Dissertation, Kant speaks of apprehending something "immediately, that is, as singular."[26] (ii) In the third of the arguments of the Metaphysical Exposition of Space in the B edition, Kant infers from the uniqueness of space the intuitional status of our representation of it (B39). (iii) At A32/B47, he says, "[T]he representation that can be given only through a single object is intuition." (iv) At B41, Kant speaks of "*immediate representation*, that is, *intuition*." Point (i) strongly suggests that immediacy and singularity are equivalent. Points (ii) and (iii) suggest that singularity suffices for intuitionhood, and (iv) suggests that immediacy suffices for intuitionhood. Given that both marks are necessary for intuitionhood, neither would suffice by itself for intuitionhood unless it also sufficed for the other. Thus, (ii), (iii), and (iv) taken together strongly suggest as (i) does that the two marks are equivalent.

If the marks are equivalent, then singularity is sufficient for intuitionhood. But I showed above that singularity in senses (a) and (b) is *not* sufficient for intuitionhood.[27] So, we need to understand singularity in some stronger fashion; I suggest two possibilities here.

First, we could understand singularity in sense (c) above: a singular representation is one that has the same object in every possible world.[28] Along with this, we would need to assume that there are no individual essences in the sense discussed in chapter 8—properties that are exemplifiable only by one given individual. Then we could argue as follows: if representation R refers mediately via property P, it can refer to different individuals in different worlds and is thus not singular in sense (c).[29] By contraposition, singularity would imply immediacy and thus be sufficient for intuitionhood.

Second, we could understand singularity to involve not only uniqueness in sense (b), but also existence. That is, a singular representation would guarantee not only the uniqueness of its object, but also the existence of its object. According to Kant, no concept can do this. Only one concept even purports to do so (viz., the concept of the *ens realissimum* or God), but the ontological argument fails. Thus, singularity by itself would again be a guarantee of intuitionhood.

Two Difficulties.   The views sketched above about the singularity and immediacy of intuitions give rise to two difficulties when juxtaposed with Kant's other views.

First, as Thompson notes, "Whether or not a given intuition is a veridical perception is contingent on the occurrence of other intuitions."[30] How are we to square this with the guaranteed existence of the object I proposed as the second way of understanding singularity? Perhaps the distinction between objects$_1$ and objects$_2$ drawn in chapter 7 can resolve this difficulty: every intuition has by its own nature an object$_1$, but it has an object$_2$ only if it is suitably related to other intuitions.

Second, it seems to be Kant's eventual view in the *Critique* that intuitions have objects only through the offices of conceptual thought. "Intuitions without concepts are blind," he tells us (A51/B75), and "thought is the act which relates given intuition to object" (A247/B304).[31] Does this not conflict with the immediacy of intuitions? A satisfactory resolution would require more space than I can give it here. I simply note two points. (i) Even if the relation of intuitions to their objects is effected only by conceptual thought, it might still be immediate in the sense that it does not decompose into two subrelations and an intervening item. (ii) The distinction between objects$_1$ and objects$_2$ may again be of service. Perhaps intuitions have objects$_1$ on their own but objects$_2$ only through the offices of thought.

Appendix F. Two Concepts of Unity

Although many writers use the terms interchangeably, unity of mind and unity of apperception are not the same thing: unity of apperception implies unity of mind, but not conversely. It might nonetheless be possible to construct unity of mind as a more complex relation involving unity of apperception as one component; that is the possibility I explore here.

As noted in chapter 7, theories of the unity of mind may be divided into two types: center theories, according to which unity consists in the relation of representations to an item outside the system of representations (typically, either a substantial self or a material body), and system theories, according to which unity consists in relations strictly among the representations. Descartes is perhaps the best-known center theorist; Hume, the best-known system theorist. Kant's footprints may be found in each camp.

As I showed in chapter 11, Kant certainly believed in a transcendental or noumenal self, and that, one might think, is precisely to believe in a center of consciousness. At any rate, if there is such an entity in one's philosophy, why not say that representations all belong to the same mind just in case they are all states of the same noumenal self?

Nonetheless, there are also passages in Kant that suggest a system theory. Like Hume, Kant believed that there is no awareness of the self, as distinct from the various representations that occur in it:

> The 'I' is indeed in all thoughts, but there is not in this representation the least trace of intuition. . . . (A350)

> The consciousness of myself in the representation 'I' is not an intuition, but a merely *intellectual* representation of the spontaneity of a thinking subject. (B278)[32]

> It is obvious that in attaching 'I' to our thoughts we designate the subject of inherence only transcendentally, without noting in it any quality whatsoever—in fact, without knowing anything of it either by direct acquaintance or otherwise. (A355)

This gave him a motive for adopting a system theory. The supposed center is never observed, but only inferred, so the occasion is ripe for applying Russell's maxim that logical constructions are always to be preferred to inferred entities. As I showed in chapter 7, that is what Kant does when it comes to accounting for the relation of representations to an object. In places it seems also to be what he does in accounting for the relation of representations to a self.

If Kant is indeed a system theorist, what are the relations among representations that constitute unity of mind? What ties the bundle of representations together? My suggestion is that unity of apperception figures centrally in Kant's answer. That would help to explain why Kant thinks the principle of unity of apperception is analytic. It is not, to be sure, analytic that all representations belonging to the same mind have unity of apperception (or are U-related)—that is not even true. But some qualifed version of this thesis may, perhaps, turn out to be analytic—for example, that all representations belonging to the same mind are U-related with some other representations belonging to that mind.

To implement this suggestion, we need an understanding of unity of apperception that differs in an important way from all accounts of the U-relation canvassed in chapter 7. Each of those accounts has the U-relation *presuppose* a subject of consciousness: all are defined with the existential quantifier 'for some subject S'. If our project is to analyze unity of mind (or ownership by a single subject) in terms of the unity of apperception, we need an understanding of the latter that does not already presuppose such a subject.

Is there an understanding of unity of apperception that does not presuppose a self or subject of awareness? I see two main possibilities. First, unity of apperception among n representations might be a primitive n-ary relation holding only among those representations.[33] On this alternative, 'being apprehended together by the same subject' would be a phrase like 'occurring at the same time': just as the latter can be understood as denoting a two-term relation of simultaneity, not involving a moment of time as a *tertium quid*, so the former might be understood as denoting a two-term relation of "compresence" (as Russell once called it), not involving a subject as a *tertium quid*. In Russell's view, compresence is an introspectible relation among items in a sense field and does not involve any onlooking self.[34]

The second possibility is that unity of apperception among n representations holds in virtue of an $(n + 1)$-ary relation among the representations and a further item, but an item that is not a self or a subject. Instead, the further item could be an apperceptive act—assuming, of course, that there can be acts without agents. Such a view is espoused by some Buddhist philosophers as part of their "no self" theory; it is also espoused by William James, who speaks of some thoughts and perceptions in the stream of experience as "appropriating" others.[35] James's "appropriators" are not subjects or agents outside the stream of experience, but are fellow floaters in the stream. A similar view is perhaps suggested by Kant's occasional remarks that the 'I think' that accompanies other representations is itself a representation (see, e.g., B132).

If a "subjectless" relation of unity of apperception of either of the foregoing sorts were available to us, we could proceed to analyze unity of mind in two steps. First, we could analyze *synchronic* unity of mind (or membership of representations in the same "total temporary state") directly in terms of unity of apperception. Next, we could analyze *diachronic* unity of mind (or membership of total temporary states in the history of a single mind) in terms of memory and other relations linking elements in different total temporary states. A contemporary version of an analysis along these lines (and one with definite Kantian overtones) has been provided by H.P. Grice.[36] Grice analyzes 'experiences E1 and E2 belong to the same total temporary state' as 'E1 and E2 would, given certain conditions, be known, by memory or introspection, to be simultaneous'. This comes close to analyzing synchronic unity of mind in terms of potential unity of apperception. He then goes on to analyze diachronic unity in terms of various direct and indirect linkages in memory.

I now mention a problem with such accounts. Note that I spoke just now of analyzing unity of mind in terms of *potential* unity of apperception. It would be a stretch to say that all my representations at a given moment *actually* have unity of apperception; it is more plausible to say that they *could* have unity of apperception, or that they *would* have it under certain conditions. Recognition of this fact is reflected in Grice's using the formulation "would, given certain conditions" and in Kant's saying that it must be *possible* for the 'I think' to accompany all my representations. In the present context of analysis, this resort to possibility raises the following question: can actualities be analyzed in terms of possibilities, or must possibilities themselves be grounded in actualities? The same question arises concerning reductive strategies in other areas, for example, the phenomenalist's attempt to define actual but unperceived matter in terms of the possibility of perceptions. Those who think actualities come first will find such strategies wanting.[37]

The problem I am raising here also affects a somewhat different account of mental unity ascribed to Kant by Kitcher. Kitcher has Kant analyze unity of mind directly in terms of synthesis (rather than, as on my account, analyzing it in terms of unity of apperception and then holding that unity of apperception is produced by synthesis). According to her account, "[C]ognitive states belong to one consciousness just in case they are connectible by synthesis with a set of states already connected by synthesis, and all such states are connectible with each other."[38] Compare this with the following: two plots of land belong to the same landmass iff they are connectible by road building to plots already connected by road building, and all such plots are connectible with each other. Again we have the question of which side of the biconditional comes first.[39]

Appendix G. Split Brains and Unity of Apperception

One version of the principle of the unity of apperception may be put as follows: if a subject S is in conscious mental states F and G, then S will know (or be capable of knowing on reflection) that he is in *both* F and G.[40] This is not quite the same as any version attributed to Kant in chapter 7, partly because I was there trying to tailor the principle for its role in the Transcendental Deduction. It is nonetheless recognizably Kantian in spirit, and something very like it was espoused by Brentano.[41] My concern in this appendix is with the apparent challenge to this principle provided by the truly puzzling experiments with split-brain patients that have been conducted from the 1960s on.

The essential facts needed for understanding these experiments are the following. First, the neural "wiring" between eye and brain is such that information from the two right halves of each retina (and thus from the left side of the visual field) is transmitted to the right hemisphere of the brain, while information from the two left halves of each retina (and thus from the right side of the visual field) is transmitted to the left hemisphere of the brain. Second, in most people the left hemisphere controls the right side of the body and produces speech; the right hemisphere controls the left side of the body and understands speech but does not produce it. Third, patients suffering from uncontrollable epilepsy are sometimes treated by commissurotomy, or severing of the corpus callosum, a channel through which information is transmitted from one hemisphere of the brain to the other. A number of such patients have been the subjects of the experiments I describe below.

In a useful monograph on this topic, Charles E. Marks provides the following epitome of the relevant experimental findings:

The abnormal behavior of split-brain patients in such controlled conditions is illustrated by the following. A subject, S, is told to fixate a point on a screen before him. "Key ring" is flashed on the screen for a tenth of a second, with "key" appearing to the left of the fixation point and "ring" to the right. Since the time is too brief for eye movement, information from the right visual field ("ring") is projected exclusively to the left hemisphere and information from the left visual field ("key") is projected exclusively to the right hemisphere. If S is asked to say what he saw, he responds that he saw "ring". . . . S's verbal responses show no awareness of "key." On the other hand, if S is instead asked to retrieve, with his left hand, what he saw from an array of items (concealed from sight), he will retrieve a key while rejecting all varieties of rings. . . . S's response with his left hand indicates an awareness of "key," but none of "ring". . . . Someone seems to have seen "key" and someone seems to have seen "ring" and they seem unaware of each other. No one is aware of seeing "key ring".[42]

On the strength of the foregoing, we may construct the following argument:

1. Someone (call him S1) saw "ring" and was aware of seeing "ring" (as shown by the subject's verbal responses).
2. Someone (call him S2) saw "key" and was aware of seeing "key" (as shown by the subject's manual responses).
3. No one saw "key ring," nor was anyone aware that he saw both "key" and "ring" (as shown by the fact that no one said he saw "key ring" or selected a key ring with his fingers).
4. There are not *two* subjects in the experiment, but only one: S1 = S2.
5. Therefore, (a) someone saw "key" and "ring" but not "key ring," and (b) someone was aware of seeing "key" and aware of seeing "ring" but not aware that he saw *both* "key" and "ring".[43]

Premise 5 follows from 1–4 and appears to run counter to the unity of consciousness as formulated above (at least assuming the experimenters give the subjects opportunity for reflection). As Marks puts it, "[T]he split-brain patient has one mind and is one person, although he has on occasion a disunified consciousness. The experimental results . . . do falsify the common belief that a single mind can always jointly introspect its simultaneous conscious contents."[44]

Notice that if the experiment is to demonstrate a disunified consciousness (as Marks suggests it does), premise 4 is crucial. Without that premise, the experiment might be taken instead to demonstrate the phenomenon of two persons inhabiting the same body, which is not at all the same thing as one person with a disunified consciousness.[45]

Some thinkers have responded to the argument by denying one or more of the inferences drawn from the patient's behavior to his mental states that underlie the first three premises. One such is the neurophysiologist J.J. Eccles, who is reported by Marks as denying that right-hemisphere processes are conscious,[46] and who would therefore apparently deny premise 2's claim that someone was aware of seeing "key." In that case, there would be no failure of unity of apperception. If we allow that the subject did nonetheless see "key", what there would be instead is a failure of apperception to begin with—seeing without awareness of seeing.

I would note myself that anyone who insists on premise 4 must certainly temper the inferences leading to premises 1–3. If 4 is true, deciding what inferences to draw from the patient's behavior is a very delicate business. If the evidence warrants our saying (as we do in 3) that no one saw "key ring," it equally warrants our saying that no one saw "key": no one says he saw "key ring," but equally, no one says he saw "key." But if we say as we do in premise 2 that S2 saw "key," and if we insist as we do in premise 4 that there is only one subject, then we must say that S1 saw "key", too—contrary to what I just said is warranted by the evidence if 3 is.

Using the terms distinguished in chapter 7 and appendix F, what appears to be uncontroversial about the split-brain experiments is just this much: *if* we accept the normally acceptable behavioral evidence for ascribing or withholding ascription of states of consciousness (thus accepting 1–3), then *either* the experiences associated with split-brain patients lack unity of *mind* (we have two subjects) *or* they lack unity of *apperception* (we have one subject with a disunified consciousness).

Appendix H. Synthesis and the Binding Problem

Kant's views about the need for synthesis in generating representations may be interestingly compared with the "binding problem" in contemporary cognitive science. The problem may be put thus: how is it possible to achieve representations of *what goes with what*, that is, representations indicating which features are combined in the same object?[47] To illustrate the problem, imagine that a visual system has receptors that fire whenever an object is present at any given x-coordinate of its visual field and other receptors that fire whenever an object is present at any given y-coordinate. Suppose receptors fire for $x = 3$ and $y = 5$. Does the system thereby "know" that an object is present at the location $<3, 5>$? Not at all, for one receptor might have been triggered by an object at $<3, 3>$ and the other by an object at $<5, 5>$. So, how is the system to register that a given x-coordinate "goes together" (in the same object) with a given y-coordinate? More generally, given that it can represent the information $\exists x Fx$ and $\exists x Gx$, how is it to represent the information $\exists x (Fx \ \& \ Gx)$?

Experimental work bearing on this topic by Ann Treisman and others has led Treisman to theorize that there are at least two levels in visual processing: an earlier level at which single features (e.g., colors and shapes) are extracted preattentively and a later level at which objects with conjunctions of features (e.g., objects that are both red and X-shaped) are identified.[48] Treisman proposes that conjunctions of features are apprehended by serial acts of focused attention—metaphorically speaking, by a searchlight directed now at one, now at another area in the field of view. Setting aside questions about the brain mechanisms of the searchlight,[49] it seems clear that apprehension of conjunctions of features involves a further layer of processing beyond whatever is required for the extraction of single features. This is suggested by the following experimental finding among others: boundaries marked out by objects with conjunctions of features (e.g., the boundary between a field of red Vs and blue Os on one side and red Os and blue Vs on the other) are not as salient—they do not "pop out" as much—as boundaries marked out by single features (e.g., the boundary between a field of red Vs and red Os on one side and blue Vs and blue Os on the other).

Patricia Kitcher cites Treisman's work as dramatic confirmation of Kant's views on the need for synthesis.[50] That it may well be. At the same time, however, it needs to be pointed out that the work of Treisman and other cognitive scientists *fails* to confirm the more extreme aspects of Kant's views. Kant maintains that the awareness of *any* manifold is achieved only through synthesis—that "combination" (i.e., the state of being combined) is never given through the senses. Here are some representative passages:

> All appearances are, in their intuition, extensive magnitudes. . . . I entitle a magnitude extensive when the representation of the parts makes possible, and therefore necessarily precedes, the representation of the whole. I cannot represent to myself a line, however small, without drawing it in thought, that is, generating from a point all its parts one after another. Only in this way can the intuition be obtained. (A162)

> [T]he combination (*conjunctio*) of a manifold in general can never come to us through the senses. . . . To this act the general title 'synthesis' may be assigned, as indicating that we cannot represent to ourselves anything as combined in the object which we have not ourselves previously combined, and that of all representations *combination* is the only one which cannot be given through objects. (B129–30)

As far as I know, cognitive scientists do not commit themselves to any such view of things. The features extracted in early visual processing according to Treisman include simple properties of lines such as tilt, curvature, and topological closure. A curved or tilted line is already what Kant would call a manifold; it consists of a plurality of elements related in certain ways. (Insofar as we can't see a line without seeing a line of some color, it is even arguable that the representation of a line already involves some "conjunctive encoding.") If synthesis *starts* with the awareness of such rudimentary manifolds as lines and curves, then it is not the case that *all* awareness of things together is produced by synthesis.

Appendix I. Determinism, Projection, and Imposition

As I have shown, Kant holds the following combination of views: the principle of universal causation (or determinism) is necessarily true, but particular causal laws are only contingently true. This combination, though logically consistent as I argue in appendix B, raises two puzzles that I discuss here.

Projecting Determinism. Simon Blackburn has propounded an interesting two-part argument against moral realism.[51] First premise: it is necessary that if two items (agents, acts, or things) are alike in their natural properties, they are also alike in their moral properties, but it is *not* necessary that an item with a certain set of natural properties must have any particular set of moral properties. Blackburn puts this premise by saying that moral properties supervene on natural properties but are not necessitated by them.[52] Second premise: the combination of supervenience without necessitation would be highly puzzling on a realist view of moral properties but is easily explicable if moral properties are only projections of our moral sentiments.

If Blackburn is right, the combination of supervenience without necessitation should be equally puzzling wherever it occurs, inviting a projectivist account of whatever features exhibit the combination. It is therefore of interest to note that the Kantian combination stated in the first paragraph is also an instance of the Blackburn combination. Since this may not be obvious, let me explain.

A world is deterministic iff given any two total temporary states S and S' belonging to its history, if S is exactly like S' (qualitatively speaking), then the sequence of states following S is exactly like the sequence of states following S'. In other words, a world is deterministic iff the repetition of any state carries in its train repetitions of all states that followed it before.[53] This is the doctrine sometimes misleadingly expressed by the slogan "same total cause, same total effect."

To assert that determinism is a necessary truth is to assert that every possible world is deterministic in the foregoing sense. That is, in the history of any world, the same state again means the same sequel again. This amounts precisely to the (weak) supervenience of subsequent states on prior states.

In holding that particular causal laws are contingent, Kant is holding that a given state of the world does not logically necessitate the succeeding state. That is to say, it could be that S1 is followed by S2 in the actual world and that a state S1' exactly like S1 occurs in some other world but is not followed in that world by a state S2' exactly like S2. In short, while holding that subsequent states supervene on prior states, Kant denies that subsequent states are necessitated by prior states. This is exactly the Blackburn combination, so if Blackburn is right, Kant must hold a projectivist theory.

But must the Blackburn combination always betoken projectivism? Here is a counterexample adapted from James Dreier.[54] McTaggart's A-characteristics (being past, present, or future) supervene on position in the B-series (the series of events as ordered by before, after, and simultaneous with), since it is necessary that if two events have the same position in the B-series (the same date, in effect), they are either both present, both past, or both future. But an event's position in the B-series does not necessitate its A-status, as shown by the fact that its A-status may change while its B-location remains the same. So, here we have the Blackburn combination again, but I think we should hesitate to conclude from this that the A-characteristics are mere projections. (Of course, McTaggart himself did regard the A-characteristics as illusory, as have others; my point just now is that we need some further argument for so regarding them.)

Moreover, in the case at hand, if Kant's view is projectivist, what is it that we would be projecting? It seems scarcely credible that we could project the patterns of sequence and similarity among states themselves. (Hume is sometimes interpreted as holding that when confronted with constant conjunctions, we project causality. But how could we project the very conjunctions?) Perhaps the most plausible suggestion would be that we do not project similarity forward but difference backward. Whenever we find that two apparently similar sets of initial conditions are followed by dissimilar sequels, we suppose there must have been some difference in the initial states after all, even if no such difference disclosed itself.

But that proposal does not take us as far as Kant wants to go. It suggests that determinism is merely a regulative principle for Kant—a principle enjoining us to posit differences in what precedes to account for differences in what follows, but with no guarantee that there actually are any such differences. Kant instead regards the Second Analogy as constitutive: though we may not discover a cause for every event (or a prior difference for every subsequent difference), such causes are guaranteed to exist.

Imposing Determinism.   Perhaps Kant embraces after all the view I just called "scarcely credible"—or even something stronger. As I noted in section F of chapter 10, Kant sometimes holds that there is guaranteed to be a cause for any event because *we see to it* that this will be the case—we synthesize the manifold in such a way that the Second Analogy is true. If this is Kant's view, what he holds is not merely a projection theory but an imposition theory. The difference is that a projected feature need not actually characterize the reality on which it is projected, whereas an imposed feature must do so—just as surely as the imprint of the seal characterizes the wax.

This brings us to the second puzzle. If the general causal maxim is necessary, but particular causal laws are not, and if the necessity in question is the product of imposition, we have two consequences. First, since regarding any event E it is necessary that it have a cause,[55]

we see to it that for some event C, C causes E.

Second, since particular laws or causal relationships are contingent,

there is no event C such that we see to it that C causes E.

But how can that be? How can we impose orderliness in general without imposing any particular order? It is as though one were given the following task: "Clean up this mess—but be careful not to put the socks in any particular place!"

The second puzzle does not arise for the "determinism is necessary and particular laws are contingent" combination as such, but it does arise as soon as we add Kant's imposition theory to the mix.

Appendix J. Relational Predicates and Relativized Predicates

Only in time can two contradictorily opposed predicates meet in one and the same object, namely, *one after the other.*
    Kant, *Critique of Pure Reason* (A32/48)

In chapter 10 I raise the following question for the double-aspect theory: how is it possible for something to be F as we know it, yet *not* F as it is in itself? How do the modifiers "as we know it" and "as it is in itself" serve to remove what would otherwise be a contradiction? I proceed to invoke David Lewis's inventory of three ways in which modifiers remove contradictions, and I claim that none is satisfactory for purposes of the double-aspect theory. In this appendix, I consider the possibility that Lewis's inventory is incomplete.

Lewis introduces his three ways in the course of discussing "the problem of temporary intrinsics": how is it possible to report without contradiction simple facts of change—for example, the fact that a leaf is green on Monday and no longer green on Tuesday? None of us senses a contradiction there, of course, thanks to the modifiers "on Monday" and "on Tuesday." But how do the modifiers do their work? Lewis offers us three models:[56]

1. By analogy with 'the building is round on the third floor, square on the fourth'. Here we are dividing the original subject, finding within it two different subjects of predication to bear the contrary predicates.
2. By analogy with 'the mayor is crooked according to the *Times*, honest according to the *News*'. Here we are adding operators in front of the original incompatible statements: the *Times* says p, the *News* says not-p. The contradiction goes away because we presume that at least one of the papers gets things wrong; we need not assert both of the embedded contents.
3. By analogy with 'Ted is tall compared to Ed, short compared to Fred'. Here we make the predicate relational: Ted bears R (in this case, the taller-than relation) to Ed and does not bear R to Fred. Because it is not the same thing to which R is borne and not borne, the contradiction again goes away.

In the case of temporary intrinsics, Lewis thinks that the second and third ways are both unsatisfactory. He rejects the third way because he thinks it converts what are intrinsic properties *par excellence*—for example, colors and shapes—into relations. Following the third way, we can't say that x is red, period, but only that it bears the 'red at' relation to a time; yet "[i]f we know what shape is, we know that it is a property, not a relation."[57]

Lewis rejects the second way because according to it, "[o]ther times are like false stories." The leaf is green at or "according to" t1, red "according to" t2, and at least one of the times "gets things wrong." Lewis assimilates this approach to philosophies of time that make the past and the future unreal, and is understandably unenthusiastic.

That leaves us only with the first way, which in the temporal case means dividing continuants into temporal parts. Lewis thinks there is no contradiction in what we say about the leaf because it is the Monday segment of the leaf that that is green and the Tuesday segment of it that is red. Such is his brief for an ontology of temporal parts.

I am on record as opposing the doctrine of temporal parts.[58] So, how would I respond to Lewis's argument?

One possible thought is that we should treat *relativized* predication as a primitive device, not reducible to *relational* predication or any of the other ways above. In its syntax, relativized predication might take the form '$(Fa)_{t1}$ and $(-Fa)_{t2}$', as opposed to '$F(a,t1)$ and $-F(a,t2)$'. The parameter of relativization would occur as a subscript to an entire formula rather than as a term in relational predication. In formal semantics, the difference between relational predication and relativized predication would show up as the difference between a one-place function assigning a set of ordered pairs to a two-place predicate and a two-place function assigning a set of individuals to a one-place predicate and the added parameter. But is there any philosophical significance to this distinction?

If the fourth way is to be distinct from the third, the relativized content must be a syntactically well-formed component of the larger expression; it must stand on its own as something intelligibly entertainable (unlike, e.g., 'x is to the left of'). At the same time, if relativization is to block contradictions, the relativized content must not be detachable from the larger expression in which it is embedded. "Parameter-dropping" inferences must be forbidden.

It is just this combination—understandability apart from the embedding context and assertability only within it—that seems to me to constitute the main objection to relativized predication. If 'Fa' can stand alone as the expression of an intelligible content, why can't it also be true or false *simpliciter*? If 'Fa' expresses a genuinely monadic property—an accident with its legs in just one substance, as Leibniz might have put it—why should it be incapable of standing if the support of some other substance is taken away? So, I am inclined to agree with Lewis: "relativized predication" is really just relational predication in a misleading guise.

How, then, are we to avoid the introduction of temporal parts? My answer is that there is an obvious device for reporting changes that Lewis has overlooked, namely, *tense*. If I say 'x *was* green & x *is* red', I imply that a change has occurred without contradicting myself. At the same time, I neither divide the subject, make the past unreal, nor turn colors into relations.

Is tense a *sui generis* device that should take its place as a way alongside Lewis's three? Not necessarily. On A.N. Prior's treatment of tense, past and future tense statements are analyzed in terms of operators attaching to present-tense statements.[59] To say 'John ran' is to say that 'it was the case that John runs'. If this is a correct reconstruction of tense, then rather than being a *sui generis* device in addition to Lewis's three, tense is an instance of the second way. What, then, of Lewis's complaint that the second way makes the past and future unreal? It is true, in a sense, that other times "get things wrong": from 'it was the case yesterday that it is snowing', one cannot infer 'it is (now) snowing'. Yet the reality of the past is secured well enough if we simply admit the truth of the past-tense statements as wholes. As Prior notes, "[A]lthough Whitrow's lecture isn't now present and so isn't real, isn't a fact, nevertheless its pastness, its *having* taken place, *is* a present fact, *is* a reality, and will be one as long as time shall last."[60]

I do not believe that there is any analog of tense that will save the double-aspect theory from the objections raised in chapter 10.

Appendix K. Can You Eat Your Cake Empirically and Still Have It Transcendentally?

Philosophers who are in one way or another antirealists (e.g., reductive phenomenalists, Kantian transcendental idealists, and Putnamian internal realists) often wish to make room within their systems for such commonsense claims as the following: the physical world could exist even if there were no minds, there was a time when it actually did exist in the absence of any minds, and the physical world's being as it is explains the course of our sense experience. But how can philosophers of the antirealist persuasion say such things? Is there not a plain incompatibility between any of them and the proposition that the physical world is constituted by the organization of human experience, or by any other facts involving human minds?

Not so, say some antirealists. The truths cited above about the independence of the physical can be acknowledged within their view after all, they maintain, as long as one makes an appropriate distinction between two levels, two points of view, or two assertive frameworks. In this vein, some interpreters or defenders of Kant tell us that although from the transcendental point of view, physical objects (objects in space) are dependent on minds, from the empirical point of view they are not. This is supposed to be one possible gloss on Kant's combination of transcendental idealism with empirical realism. But what does the distinction between the two points of view really amount to? How can you eat your cake empirically and still have it transcendentally? I have always wondered how this can be anything but doublethink.

It was therefore with great interest that I read John Foster's discussion of "The Two Frameworks" in his book *The Case for Idealism*.[61] Addressing the problem for antirealists raised in the first paragraph of this appendix, Foster tries to resolve it with a distinction between two assertive frameworks: the mundane framework within which we make ordinary first-order claims about physical reality and the philosophical framework within which we try to assign to physical reality its correct metaphysical status. He goes on to offer a novel elucidation of this distinction in terms of a distinction between the relative scopes of two operators.

The problem Foster sets himself is this: on the one hand, it is a conceptual truth (or so Foster believes) that if there is a physical world, it is something whose existence is independent of the existence of human minds; on the other hand, it is a consequence of reductive phenomenalism (which Foster defends in detail) that "the physical world is the logical creation of the constraints on human experience."[62] Foster understands this to imply that the physical world could not exist in the absence of human minds. Thus, his phenomenalism appears to conflict with the commonsense belief in mind-dependence or externality. Foster seeks to reconcile the apparent conflict by distinguishing between claims made *within* the framework of physical theory and claims made *about* this framework—physical and meta-physical claims, as he later calls them. He further explicates this distinction as one between the relative scopes of two operators, logical possibility and physical truth:

(a)   It is physically true that $\exists w(Fw$ & $\Diamond[Fw$ & $-h])$

(b) $-\Diamond$ (it is physically true that $\exists wFw$ & $-h$)

Here '$\Diamond$' stands for logical possibility, '$\exists wFw$' asserts the existence of a physical world of a certain sort (consisting of a space with a certain geometrical structure, a set of space-occupying objects, and a set of laws governing them), and h is the proposition that there are minds. A proposition is physically true "iff, as a proposition of physical theory, its truth is logically sustained by the experiential constraints."[63] Foster observes that (a) asserts the physical truth of a certain possibility while (b) denies the possibility of a certain (conjectured) physical truth. He claims that (a) does justice to the belief in mind-independence that is characteristic of first-order physical theory, and that (b) captures the sense in which the physical world is mind-dependent according to phenomenalism. And he claims that (a) and (b) are compatible.

Here for once is a way of making sense of the distinction between the two frameworks (or the empirical and the transcendental viewpoints, etc.) that is perspicuous and plausible. Alas, however, I find that on further scrutiny the distinction proposed by Foster collapses.

Foster is correct in maintaining that there is no *formal* incompatibility between (a) and (b).[64] I argue, however, that (a) and (b) become incompatible as soon as phenomenalism is assumed to be true. The root of the problem is that for phenomenalists, physical truth coincides with truth simpliciter (at least in the case of propositions about physical reality), making the operator "it is physically true that" redundant as it occurs in (a) and (b). But once that operator is dropped, (a) and (b) are easily seen to conflict.

Let us use 'Pp' to say that a proposition belongs to physical theory (or has physical reality for its subject matter), 'Tp' to say that a proposition is true, 'PTp' to say that it is physically true, and 'Ep' to say that its truth is sustained by the obtaining experiential constraints. Foster's phenomenalism holds that if Pp, then Tp $\Leftrightarrow$ Ep, and in view of this he defines PTp as Pp & Ep. From phenomenalism and its attendant definition of physical truth, it is easy to derive the following lemmas: (i) PTp $\Rightarrow$ Tp and (ii) if Pp, then Tp $\Rightarrow$ PTp.[65] Putting (i) and (ii) together, we have Pp $\rightarrow$ (PTp $\Leftrightarrow$ Tp), or equivalently (in view of the redundancy property of the truth operator), Pp $\rightarrow$ (PTp $\Leftrightarrow$ p).

Now for the derivation of a contradiction from (a) and (b). Since physical truth suffices for truth simpliciter [by lemma (i) above], we may deduce our way from (a) to

(a1) $\exists w(Fw$ & $\Diamond[Fw$ & $-h])$.

From (a1) by existential instantiation we may infer

(a2) Fw' & $\Diamond[Fw'$ & $-h]$,

which by simplification implies

(a3) $\Diamond[Fw'$ & $-h]$.

The following entailment (from the bracketed portion of (a3) to the result of replacing one conjunct of it by its existential generalization) is obvious:

(a4) $[Fw' \ \& \ -h] \Rightarrow [\exists wFw \ \& \ -h]$

From (a3), (a4), and the law that what is entailed by the possible is itself possible, we may now derive

(a5) $\Diamond [\exists wFw \ \& \ -h]$.

Turning now to (b), we may write it in our notation as

(b1) $- \Diamond (PT[\exists wFw] \ \& \ -h)$.

Since $\exists wFw$ is a proposition of physical theory, we have by lemmas (i) and (ii) above the following logical equivalence:

(b2) $PT(\exists wFw) \Leftrightarrow \exists wFw$

Interchanging in (b1) in accordance with (b2), we obtain

(b3) $- \Diamond [\exists wFw \ \& \ -h]$.

And there we have it: (b3), which follows from (b), is the direct contradictory of (a5), which follows from (a). So, (a) and (b) conflict after all, at least relative to assumptions to which phenomenalism is essentially committed.

Perhaps Foster should not have defined physical truth in terms of experiential sustainment. He wants (a) to be acceptable to phenomenalists and realists alike, yet as he defines physical truth, (a) implies that $\exists wFw$ is true only because of experiential constraints—something that realists presumably would not accept.[66] For purposes of (a), then, perhaps Foster should have defined PTp simply as Pp & Tp, letting it be collateral phenomenalist doctrine that Pp & Tp iff Pp & Ep. Would this change have blocked our derivation of a contradiction from (a) and (b)? The answer is no. Since what is physically true is true simpliciter (whether you are a phenomenalist or not), we could still have derived $\Diamond [\exists wFw \ \& \ -h]$ from (a). (In case it is objected that the modal portion of (a) is not properly a physical proposition, we can point out that our physical theory of the world does not merely tell us that it is *possible* that Fw and $-h$; it tells us that for millions of years it was *actually the case* that Fw and $-h$. From this and the principle 'ab esse ad posse' we again get $\Diamond [\exists wFw \ \& \ -h]$.) As for the other side of the contradiction, $- \Diamond [\exists wFw \ \& \ -h]$, that still follows from (b) via the phenomenalism that underwrites the assertion of (b) to begin with. So, Foster's scope distinctions do not remove the contradiction with which we began.

Nonetheless, the feeling may linger that there is something to the distinction between assertions made within a framework and assertions made about it after all, even if Foster's proposed way of defining it fails. "It could be the case, and in fact once was the case, that stars and planets existed in a universe devoid of minds"—that, one may want to say, is a plain fact of physical theory, and one that phenomenalists can admit as well as anyone else, as long as the experiential constraints make it true. But inconsistency arises as soon as one adds that minds are necessary for the obtaining of the experiential constraints.[67] A proposition that excludes the existence of minds cannot be made true by a state of affairs that essentially includes them.

The alleged contrast between claims of mind-independence made *within* a framework and claims of mind-dependence made *about* it is initially suggestive, but here as elsewhere, I think the distinction evaporates when one tries to think it through.[68]

Appendix L. Under a Description

The idea is abroad that events cause other events only "under descriptions," for example, that drinking the contents of a certain vessel may cause one's death under the description 'drinking such-and-such a quantity of hemlock', but not under the description 'drinking the drink offered by the guard'. The popularity of this idea has encouraged some forms of the double-aspect theory in interpreting Kant, especially in connection with the problem of affection and the Antinomy of causation and freedom. There has been a temptation to say things like this: objects or events under their phenomenal descriptions (as spatial and temporal) affect us in certain ways, but these same objects under their noumenal descriptions do not. In another application of the idea, it may be suggested that an action can be causally determined (by earlier events) under some of its descriptions, yet undetermined under others. It is my contention here that the "under a description" idea, when properly understood, gives no aid or comfort to the double-aspect theory.

The truth in the "under a description" idea (as brought out by Davidson, perhaps its leading advocate[69]) is this: one event causes another if and only if the two events have descriptions that enter into a strict law. Somewhat more precisely, e1 causes e2 iff there are descriptions (or properties—we need not be so relentlessly linguistic about it) F and G such that e1 has F, e2 has G, and there is a strict law to the effect that every F-event is followed by a G-event. This is really no more than the Humean requirement "no causation without law," together with a conception of events as particulars simultaneously instantiating a multitude of properties (or satisfying a multitude of descriptions).[70]

It is important to note that this account of what it is for events to be causally related does not imply either of two doctrines that are sometimes associated with it: (i) that the context '——————— causes . . . ' is nonextensional, or (ii) that causation is "relative" in a sense implying that whether it holds can vary depending on how the relata are described (or perhaps in the sense that it is a relation of more than two terms, bringing in descriptions as relata in addition to the events themselves).

To scotch point (i), note that if Socrates' drinking of the hemlock caused his death and if the former event was identical with his drinking of the potion offered by the guard, *it follows* that his drinking of the potion offered by the guard caused his death. Describing the drinking in the latter way gives no clue as to the law in virtue of which it caused the death, but yields a causal statement that is true if the original statement was.[71]

To scotch point (ii), note that if two events e1 and e2 satisfy descriptions that enter into a strict law, then it is true of e1 and e2 by themselves that one caused the other. We need not say that causation is really a triadic or tetradic relation, relating not just events but also descriptions under which they fall. Still less need we say that causation holds between events described in some ways but not between the same events described in other ways.[72] If causation were relative in *that* way, an appropriate response to "Look out for that lethal load of falling bricks!" would be "Quick! Describe it some other way!"

I believe we are now in a position to see that there is nothing in the "under a description" idea that is of much use to the double-aspect theory. Consider first the problem of affection (as set out in chapter 10, section G): what are the things that affect us to produce representations, phenomenal objects or noumenal objects? A one-worlder may recast this as the question of whether it is objects under their phenomenal descriptions (as events in space and time) that affect us, or objects under their noumenal descriptions (as objects independent of our forms of sensibility).[73] But if an object affects us under *any* description, it affects us *simpliciter*;[74] and if a phenomenal event causes a representation in a perceiver, so does any noumenal event with which that phenomenal event is identical. If there are problems with noumenal causation, they are not avoided by saying that events are causes only under their phenomenal descriptions.

Turning now to the Third Antinomy, Ralf Meerbote[75] has suggested that Kant's resolution of the Antinomy should be seen as involving Davidson's "anomalous monism." Meerbote's discussion might be taken to suggest that the same action may be determined under some of its descriptions and anomalous under others. There is one good sense in which this is true, but I think it is not a sense that helps us to square freedom with determinism. To see why, note two things. First, as we have seen above, 'determined under some description' implies determined, period. That an action is anomalous under other descriptions does nothing to undo such determination.[76] Second, any event whatever is anomalous under many of its descriptions; that is to say, it has many descriptions that do not enter into laws. An eclipse of the moon, predictable for centuries, is in this sense anomalous under the description 'third lunar event witnessed by Smith since New Year's Day.' How do we make room for freedom simply by pointing out that an event or action has some descriptions that would not have enabled us to predict it?

Appendix M. Concepts of Isomorphism

It may be useful to present in summary fashion the main definitions and results of chapter 10, section F.

D1. Sets A and B are isomorphic *with respect to* function f and relations R and R* (exemplified in A and B) =Df (i) f is a function setting up a one-to-one correlation between members of A and members of B, and (ii) whenever the relation R holds between two members x and y of A, the relation R* holds between their correlates in B, and conversely; that is to say, xRy iff f(x)R*f(y).

D2. A and B are *in some way* isomorphic =Df for some f, R, and R*, A and B are isomorphic with respect to f, R, and R*.

D3. A and B are in *thoroughgoing* isomorphism =Df (i) there is a function f setting up a one-to-one correlation between members of A and members of B; (ii) for every relation R in A, there is a relation R* in B such that A and B are isomorphic with respect to f, R, and R*; and (iii) for every relation S* in B, there is a relation S in A such that A and B are also isomorphic with respect to f, S, and S*. [Note that in this definition, the quantifier (∃f) precedes the quantifier (R)—i.e., the same correlation of entities underlies all isomorphisms.]

D3 defines the notion of thoroughgoing isomorphism that was briefly discussed (though not officially defined) in the main text. If we allow "unary" relations (i.e., monadic properties) to count as degenerate relations, then D3 implies that the distributions of qualities in two isomorphic sets must mirror each other just as their patterns of relation do.

The main results of the section may now be summarized as follows:

1. The notion defined by D2 is a trivial consequence of equinumerosity.
2. The notion defined by D1 need not (in the foregoing sense) be trivial at all; everything turns on what relations are chosen as R and R*.
3. The notion defined by D3 threatens to be trivial if no restrictions are placed on R* and S, but we can avoid triviality by imposing further requirements—for example, that the relations be self-contained. (Roughly, this means that they are intensionally specifiable without reference to members of the correlated domain.)
4. Thoroughgoing isomorphism of phenomena and noumena is ruled out by Kant's view that certain principles valid for noumena are not valid for phenomena (e.g., the reducibility of relations and the grounding of the composite in the simple). However, Kant would be free to maintain that various particular isomorphisms (in the D1 sense) hold between phenomena and noumena, or at least between phenomena and a subset of noumena.
5. He cannot believe in very many particular isomorphisms, however, if the Copernican Revolution takes the extreme form that Kant sometimes hints at: we ourselves are responsible for the order that is to be found in the phenomenal world. Kant's philosophy seems at times to require a delicate balancing act. On the one hand, we must posit things in themselves to account for the brute givens of experience; on the other hand, we must not allow what we posit to thwart our ability to construct a well-arranged world.

Appendix N. A Kantian Argument Against the Correspondence Theory?

Even if Kant himself did not reject the correspondence theory of truth (as I argue in section B of chapter 13), we need to consider the possibility that his philosophy furnishes a decisive objection to it. In particular, we need to consider the view that Kant's teachings about the impossibility of nonjudgmental awareness stand in the way of the correspondence theory. A good example of the mobilization of Kantian considerations for this purpose is found in a brief but pungent discussion by Simon Blackburn entitled "Fact and Judgment: Kant."[77]

According to Blackburn, all experience is infused with interpretation, conceptualization, or judgment in such a way that there is no mode of access to the facts that is not judgmental: "[E]xperience can no more be a judgment-independent source of acquaintance with facts than dough can be a flour-independent source of bread."[77] He credits Kant with making this point, citing the dictum "intuitions without concepts are blind." Let us grant (despite my misgivings about the portions of the Transcendental Deduction relevant to this issue) that there is a good Kantian case to be made against nonconceptual or nonjudgmental access to facts. What now is supposed to follow regarding truth as correspondence? Blackburn writes:

Is it even possible to think of our beliefs as *responding* to facts, let alone corresponding to them? . . . It is this problem that leads to the coherence theory of truth.[79]

I assume that the intended argument may be spelled out as follows:

1. We have no access to any facts except by way of concept-infused beliefs or judgments.
2. If premise 1 is correct, we can never know that any of our beliefs corresponds with the facts.
3. If truth were correspondence with the facts, then we could know that a belief is true only by knowing that it enjoys such correspondence.
4. Therefore, if truth were correspondence with the facts, we could never know that any of our beliefs is true.[80]
5. But we *do* sometimes know that certain of our beliefs are true.
6. Therefore, truth is not correspondence with the facts.

When the argument is thus made explicit, we see that it is a classic transcendental argument, an argument from the actuality of knowledge to its necessary conditions. It is similar to the argument of the diallelus I discuss in chapter 13, section B, bolstered this time by Kantian doctrine on the impossibility of nonconceptual cognition.

The argument does not stop with the negative result 6. The next step is to affirm positively that truth is coherence:

7. Therefore, truth is coherence of belief with belief.

It is worth asking how the coherence theory is supposed to avoid the epistemological difficulties that allegedly beset the correspondence theory. In my opinion, coherentists should be chary of setting anything like the present argument in motion, for the diallelus (literally, the *wheel*) is a juggernaut that will crush nearly every theory in its path. It spares only skepticism, which, however, the present argument thinks itself entitled to reject in premise 5. To highlight the difficulty, how is the coherence theory supposed to escape the problem of gaining access to the facts? The answer must be that although I cannot know whether my beliefs correspond with the facts, I *can* know whether they cohere with one another. But why is the latter knowledge supposed to be any easier to come by than the former? The considerations adduced against the correspondence theory were apparently quite general: the only form of access to anything is judgment, and no judgment has "a pure footing in the way things are, uncontaminated by our powers of thought and imagination."[81] In that case, knowledge of what our own beliefs are (a species of introspective knowledge) and knowledge of how the contents of our various beliefs are logically related to one another (a species of *a priori* knowledge) are just as problematic as any purported knowledge of external fact. Or does our coherentist suppose that there is something special about our own states of mind, some privilege attaching to our knowledge of them that does not attach to knowledge of anything else? And does she likewise suppose that there is something special about our knowledge of logical relations? If so, she joins company with Descartes, who held that the contents of the mind are better known than anything in the external world and that the logical relations among such contents are securely within the province of clear and distinct perception. Cartesians and coherentists—strange bedfellows! In any event, our coherentist has now parted company with Kant, whom she was glad to cite on the interweaving of conceptualization and experience, but whose views on knowledge of the inner sphere, as in principle no different from or superior to our knowledge of the outer sphere (see chapter 5, section C), she must now implicitly renounce.

If a completely generalizable case for skepticism is to be avoided, we must reject one of the first three premises in the argument above. Though not completely sold on any of the premises,[82] I recommend in any case that we reject premise 2. Why should we assume that if a belief is laden with concepts, it is thereby prevented from being the ascertainment of fact?[83]

Appendix O. Williams Contra Lichtenberg

Es denkt, sollte man sagen, so wie man sagt:
es blitzt.

Georg Licshtenberg, *Sudelbücher*

According to Lichtenberg's famous dictum, instead of saying "I think," one should merely say "it is thinking," just as one says "it is raining" or "it is lightening." The remark is often taken to be a pithy expression of the "no subject" or "no ownership" view of the self.[84] Bernard Williams has offered an interesting argument against this view, of which I would like to present a modified version here.[85]

Consider the following two thought-episodes (I begin *in medias res* with Williams's numbering):

(T4) It is thought: it is not doubted whether Q.
(T5) It is doubted: Q?

We would like to say that the occurrence of thought-episode T5 need not automatically falsify the content of thought-episode T4, since the two episodes might occur in different "thought worlds" (as Williams puts it) or (as he also puts it) be "separate" from each other. Yet as the content of T4 is presently formulated, it would be falsified even by a "separate" occurrence of T5. To protect the content of T4 from irrelevant falsification, we must make it refer only to its *own* thought world, perhaps thus: it is not doubted *here* whether Q. The word "here" is a metaphor, not to be taken spatially; the important point is that it indicate a concrete "point of relativization."

So, here is the argument:

1. The occurrence of T5 does not automatically falsify the content of T4.
2. It *would* do so unless the content of T4 were relativized thus: it is not doubted *here* whether Q.
3. Therefore, the content of T4 must be thus relativized.

It is then to be argued further that the "here" that occurs as content of thought in the relativized T4 must refer to a figurative "place" outside thought, yielding

(T10) It is thought at place A: it is not doubted here whether Q,

and further yet, that the "place" is really an I.

Notes

Chapter 1

1. Sometimes Kant distinguishes the meanings of the terms 'thing in itself' and 'noumenon'; see chapter 10, section A. For the most part, however, I use the terms interchangeably, as Kant himself and many of his commentators often do.

2. Page references in this style refer to Norman Kemp Smith's translation of Kant's *Critique of Pure Reason* (New York: St. Martin's Press, 1965), "A" indicating the first and "B" the second edition, and to Lewis White Beck's translation of Kant's *Prolegomena to Any Future Metaphysics* (Indianapolis, Ind.: Bobbs-Merrill, 1950).

3. H.E. Matthews, "Strawson on Transcendental Idealism," *Philosophical Quarterly*, 19 (1969), 204–20; reprinted in *Kant on Pure Reason*, edited by Ralph C.S. Walker (Oxford: Oxford University Press, 1982), pp. 132–49.

4. Ralph C.S. Walker, *Kant* (London: Routledge & Kegan Paul, 1978), pp. 125 and 135.

5. Henry E. Allison, "The Non-spatiality of Things in Themselves for Kant," *Journal of the History of Philosophy*, 14 (1976), 313–21, and *Kant's Transcendental Idealism: An Interpretation and Defense* (New Haven, Conn.: Yale University Press, 1983).

6. Allison, "Non-spatiality of Things in Themselves," p. 319. To make his case that it is analytic that things in themselves are not in space and time, Allison would also have to show that it is analytic that space and time are forms of human sensibility. I do not think Kant so regards the matter.

7. Allison, *Kant's Transcendental Idealism*, p. 30.

8. "The undetermined object of an empirical intuition is entitled *appearance*" (A20/B34); "an object of sensible intuition, that is, an appearance" (Bxxvi).

9. G.E. Moore, *Some Main Problems of Philosophy* (New York: Collier Books, 1962; reprint of 1953 edition), ch. 9.

10. See W.V. Quine, *Set Theory and Its Logic* (Cambridge, Mass.: Harvard

University Press, 1969; revised edition), p. 16. Peter van Inwagen also uses the term 'virtual object' in the sense in which I am using it here on p. 112 of *Material Beings* (Ithaca, N.Y.: Cornell University Press, 1990).

11. The *locus classicus* for Russell's views on logical constructions is his 1918 series of lectures on logical atomism, published as "The Philosophy of Logical Atomism" in *Logic and Knowledge*, edited by Robert C. Marsh (London: Allen & Unwin, 1956), pp. 175–281.

12. Roderick M. Chisholm, *Perceiving: A Philosophical Study* (Ithaca, N.Y.: Cornell University Press, 1957), chs. 8–10, and C.J. Ducasse, *Nature, Mind, and Death* (La Salle, Ill.: Open Court, 1951), especially pp. 259–60 and 284.

13. There are hints of an adverbial theory in Kant's frequent references to appearances as "modifications," as in the following: "For since a mere modification of our sensibility can never be met with outside us, the objects, as appearances, constitute an object which is merely in us" (A129).

14. David Hume, *A Treatise of Human Nature*, I.i.7. As I have stated it, Hume's principle is open to the objection that a whole and any of its parts are distinct yet not capable of separate existence. I would therefore restate the principle thus: if two concrete things are not only distinct but discrete (having no part in common), then it is possible for either to exist in the absence of the other.

15. Indeed, in his "Refutation of Idealism" of 1903 (*Mind*, 12, 433–53), G.E. Moore insists on the act-object distinction precisely in order to secure the possibility of objects of awareness whose *esse* is not *percipi*.

16. R.M. Chisholm, "Intentionality," in *The Encyclopedia of Philosophy*, edited by Paul Edwards (New York: Macmillan, 1967), vol. 4, pp. 201–4.

17. Alexius Meinong, "The Theory of Objects," in *Realism and the Background of Phenomenology*, edited by R.M. Chisholm (New York: Free Press, 1960), pp. 76–117, esp. sec. 4.

18. As Meinong observes: "[I]t is no more necessary to an object that it be presented (to the mind) in order not to exist than it is in order for it to exist" (*Theory of Objects*, p. 83).

19. Franz Brentano, *The True and the Evident*, edited and translated by Roderick M. Chisholm et al. (New York: Humanities Press, 1966), p. 68.

20. Ibid., p. 78.

21. For Russell, to say that entities of a certain sort are logical constructions is to say that terms purportedly referring to them are incomplete symbols, and one mark of an incomplete symbol is that sentences containing it can be translated into other sentences in which it no longer occurs. See Russell, *Logic and Knowledge*, p. 262. For Ayer's views on logical constructions and translation, see *Language, Truth, and Logic* (New York: Dover, 1952; reprint of 1946 edition), ch. 3.

22. This is so for two reasons. First, we need not insist on *two-way* implication or mutual entailment between each A-statement and some B-statement, as would be involved in reducibility. It is enough that each A-statement is implied by some B-statement. Second, we need not insist that the implication in question hold solely in virtue of meanings, as the term "translation" suggests. It is enough that the implication hold necessarily, whether by dint of meanings or no.

23. Ernest Sosa, "Subjects among Other Things," in *Philosophical Perspectives*, edited by James Tomberlin (Atascadero, Calif.: Ridgeview, 1987), vol.1, pp. 155–87.

24. I pause, though, to note an advantage of the supervenient entity construal: it more literally accommodates the talk of appearances as entities dependent on being perceived. If appearances are virtual objects, then strictly speaking we cannot say that an appearance is an entity that would not exist

unless it were perceived, since strictly speaking there is no *it*. But we can say this: there being an appearance entails the occurrence of certain perceptions.

25. Wilfrid Sellars interprets Kant's distinction between things in themselves and appearances as the distinction between things having "formal reality" and things having "objective reality" (in the medieval and Cartesian senses of these terms). Thus, things in themselves exist *simpliciter* while appearances exist only as contents of thought and awareness. See his *Science and Metaphysics: Variations on Kantian Themes* (London: Routledge & Kegan Paul, 1968), ch. 2, and "Kant's Transcendental Idealism," in *Proceedings of the Ottawa Congress on Kant*, edited by P. Laberge, F. Duchesneau, and B.E. Morrisey (Ottawa: University of Ottawa Press, 1976), pp. 165–81. Similar interpretations are advanced and illuminatingly discussed by Phillip Cummins in "Kant on Outer and Inner Intuition," *Nous*, 2 (1968), 271–92, and Richard Aquila, *Representational Mind: A Study of Kant's Theory of Knowledge* (Bloomington, Ind.: Indiana University Press, 1983), especially ch. 4. For Aquila's views, see also his "Things in Themselves: Intentionality and Reality in Kant," *Archiv für Geschichte der Philosophie*, 61 (1979), 293–307.

26. R.J. Hirst, "Realism," in *The Encyclopedia of Philosophy*, edited by Paul Edwards (New York: Macmillan, 1967), vol. 7, p. 77.

27. This is R.B. Perry's "cardinal principle of idealism" as quoted in Curtis Brown, "Internal Realism: Transcendental Idealism," in *Midwest Studies in Philosophy*, vol. 12, edited by Peter A. French, Theodore E. Uehling, Jr., and Howard K. Wettstein (Minneapolis: University of Minnesota Press, 1988), pp. 145–55.

28. Definitions get tricky at this point. I said above (n. 24) that virtual objects are mind-dependent in the sense that their existence entails the occurrence of cognitive acts. On a Cartesian view of the mind, according to which a mind must be thinking at every moment at which it exists, minds would be mind-dependent in just this sense. If we said 'x is mind-dependent iff x would not exist unless there were a cognitive act *apprehending x*,' then perhaps even Cartesian minds would no longer be mind-dependent. But then, strictly speaking, virtual objects would not be mind-dependent either, since they are not in the range of our quantifiable variables.

29. Michael Dummett cites this as a possible view in *Truth and Other Enigmas* (Cambridge, Mass.: Harvard University Press, 1978), p. 231.

30. Another important contemporary form of antirealism does away with *facts* altogether, holding that there is nothing in the world to make sentences in the target area evaluable as either true or false. Expressivist or noncognitivist theories about ethical discourse are one paradigm here. For a canvassing of possibilities, see Simon Blackburn, *Spreading the Word* (Oxford: Clarendon Press, 1984), ch. 5, and Crispin Wright, *Truth and Objectivity* (Cambridge, Mass.: Harvard University Press, 1992), pp. 1–7.

31. For Dummett's views, see *Truth and Other Enigmas*, especially the preface and essay 10, and *The Logical Basis of Metaphysics* (Cambridge, Mass.: Harvard University Press, 1991). For Putnam's views, see "Realism and Reason," in *Meaning and the Moral Sciences* (London: Routledge & Kegan Paul, 1978), pp. 123–40, and *Reason, Truth, and History* (Cambridge: Cambridge University Press, 1981). It is a seldom-noted point of commonality that both philosophers employ a "BIV" test for realism: do you accept BIValence, and do you allow that we might all be Brains In Vats?

Chapter 2

1. Gottlob Frege, *The Foundations of Arithmetic*, translated by J.L. Austin (Evanston, Ill.: Northwestern University Press, 1980), p. 3.

2. Alvin Plantinga, *The Nature of Necessity* (Oxford: Oxford University Press, 1974), pp. 1–2.

3. I do not discuss here Saul Kripke's suggestions that there are *a priori* truths that are not necessary and necessary truths that are not *a priori*. See his *Naming and Necessity* (Cambridge, Mass.: Harvard University Press, 1980), pp. 53–56 and 97–105.

4. For anticipations of the synthetic *a priori* in Kant's predecessors, however, see Lewis White Beck, "Analytic and Synthetic Judgments Before Kant," in *Essays on Kant and Hume* (New Haven, Conn.: Yale University Press, 1978), pp. 80–100.

5. In the *Prolegomena* Kant puts the point this way: "Analytical judgments express nothing in the predicate but what has been already actually thought in the concept of the subject, though not so distinctly or with the same (full) consciousness" (p. 14).

6. See Lewis White Beck, "Kant's Theory of Definition," in *Studies in the Philosophy of Kant* (Indianapolis, Ind.: Bobbs-Merrill, 1965); reprinted in *Kant: Disputed Questions*, edited by Moltke S. Gram (Chicago: Quadrangle Books, 1967), pp. 215–27.

7. For discussion of this, see Henry E. Allison, *The Kant-Eberhard Controversy* (Baltimore: Johns Hopkins University Press, 1973), pp. 42–43.

8. Quoted in Allison, *The Kant-Eberhard Controversy*, pp. 174–75.

9. To avoid this objection, one might try to unpack Kant's notion of "covert" containment in terms of latency or dispositionality: we say that property P is contained in concept S if anyone who thinks of something as S *and considers whether it is also P* must think that it is P. But this proposal will classify as analytic some propositions that Kant wants to count as synthetic—for example, a straight line is the shortest distance between two points.

10. In chapter 1 of *Kant's Analytic* (Cambridge: Cambridge University Press, 1966), Jonathan Bennett notes the narrowness of Kant's definition and complains that it makes the existence of synthetic *a priori* judgments too easy to establish. He therefore suggests a broader notion according to which a proposition should count as analytic if it may be verified by purely conceptual considerations. I think this threatens to make the *non*existence of synthetic *a priori* judgments too easy to establish: if 'purely conceptual' equals *a priori*, it is trivially true that everything *a priori* is analytic. On the other hand, if conceptual considerations are limited (as I propose below) to those mobilizing definitions or analyses and logic, there is still room for the synthetic *a priori*.

11. Ironically, those who criticize Kant's definition for being subjective or psychologistic often rely on a loose notion of contradiction that is at least as subjective as anything Kant offers. They call a statement contradictory not because it has the logical form of a contradiction, but because it has a contradictory ring to their ears.

12. Accurately speaking, this is a definition of what it is to be *analytically true*. We need also to recognize the category of the *analytically false*: A is analytically false iff from A itself, a formal contradiction may be derived, and so on. Synthetic statements then comprise all those that are neither analytically true nor analytically false.

13. Gottlob Frege, *The Foundations of Arithmetic*, sec. 3.

14. Rudolf Carnap, *The Logical Structure of the World*, translated by Rolf A. George (Berkeley: University of California Press, 1967), p. 176.

15. C.I. Lewis, *An Analysis of Knowledge and Valuation* (La Salle, Ill.: Open Court, 1946), p. 96.

16. W.V. Quine, "Two Dogmas of Empiricism," in *From a Logical Point of View* (New York: Harper Torchbooks, 1963), pp. 20–46, in sec. 1.

17. Question: why is there no analytic *a posteriori*? Answer: the definition

of '*a posteriori* proposition' that complements our definition of '*a priori* proposition' is that p is such that no one *could* know it save through experience. Although there may be analytic propositions that a given person actually comes to know on the basis of experience (someone looks out the window, sees that it is raining, and deduces 'it is raining or it is not raining' by the law of addition), there are arguably no analytic propositions that could be known *only* through experience.

18. Note, however, that classifying logical principles as analytic does nothing to explain how we know them to be true. As we have defined 'analytic', logical principles are included within the sphere of the analytic simply by courtesy; it is analytic that they are analytic.

19. Compare Kant's letter to Schulz of November 25, 1788, in which he points out that one may form different concepts of the same number by many different additions and subtractions. If equations of arithmetic were analytic, he argues, then in thinking 3 + 4, one would also be thinking 2 + 5, which "does not jibe with my own awareness." See Arnulf Zweig, ed., *Kant: Philosophical Correspondence, 1759–99* (Chicago: University of Chicago Press, 1967), pp. 128–30.

20. For a brief discussion of these two points and related matters, see Karel Lambert and Gordon Brittan, *An Introduction to the Philosophy of Science* (Englewood Cliffs, N.J.: Prentice-Hall, 1970), ch. 2.

21. Kant claims synthetic *a priori* status for geometry at large, making exception only for propositions such as 'a = a' that serve as "links in the chain of method" (B16–17). Other examples of synthetic *a priori* propositions in geometry he cites are the following: space has three dimensions (B41); two straight lines cannot enclose a space (A47/B65); the sum of the angles of a triangle is equal to two right angles (A716/B744).

22. David Hume, *A Treatise of Human Nature*, I.ii.4 (pp. 49–50 in Selby-Bigge's edition). This passage also gives the following reason for regarding the common maxim as synthetic: "A right line can be comprehended alone; but this definition [of a right line as the shortest] is unintelligible without a comparison with other lines. . . ."

23. Accurately speaking, what it makes analytic is 'any straight line between two points is shorter than any nonstraight line between the points'. The additional implication of the Hume-Kant proposition that there is only one such straight line is not a matter of definition, and is indeed not even true in Riemannian geometry.

24. Ludwig Wittgenstein, *Tractatus Logico-Philosophicus*, translated by D.F. Pears and B.F. McGuinness (London: Routledge & Kegan Paul, 1961), proposition 6.36111. In my copy of the *Tractatus*, Wittgenstein's figure b unfortunately contains an erroneous extra hyphen, destroying the congruence of a and b.

25. For more on this point, see section XI of my "Right, Left, and the Fourth Dimension," *The Philosophical Review*, 96 (1987), 33–68, and also in *The Philosophy of Right and Left*, edited by James Van Cleve and Robert E. Frederick (Dordrecht: Kluwer, 1991), pp. 203–34.

26. Compare the following passage from II.xiii.3 of the *New Essays on Human Understanding* in which Leibniz distinguishes between an absolute and a relative sense of distance:

> To put it more clearly, the distance between two fixed things— whether points or extended objects—is the size of the shortest possible line that can be drawn from one to the other. This distance can be taken either absolutely or relative to some figure which contains the two distant things. For instance, a straight line is abolutely the dis-

tance between two points; but if these two points both lie on the same spherical surface, the distance between them *on that surface* will be the length of the smaller arc of the great circle that can be drawn from one to the other. [*New Essays on Human Understanding*, translated by Peter Remnant and Jonathan Bennett (Cambridge: Cambridge University Press, 1981), p. 146; emphasis mine]

27. It must be confessed that this way of defending Kant affords no guarantee that absolutely straight lines are actually exemplified: they would not be if a curved space were the whole of space. But that is all right, since the synthetic *a priori* status of principles about lines or figures does not depend on whether the lines or figures are actually exemplified. For more on this point, see Gary Rosenkrantz, "The Nature of Geometry," *American Philosophical Quarterly*, 18 (1981), 101–10.

28. This is not one of Kant's own examples. What he says at B44 implies that there are no synthetic *a priori* truths about colors, but I think he was surely wrong about that.

29. Why not simply say 'for each color distinct from redness'? Because determinates of redness (e.g., scarlet) are distinct from it, as are its determinables (e.g., being red-or-orange), yet we do not want our definition to imply that red things cannot be scarlet or red-or-orange.

30. The physical definitions could be more sophisticated than this, perhaps making reference as well to effects on the human nervous system.

31. F.P. Ramsey, "Critical Notice of L. Wittgenstein's *Tractatus Logico-Philosophicus*," *Mind*, 32 (1923), 465–78, at p. 473. In "Some Remarks on Logical Form" [*Proceedings of the Aristotelian Society*, 9 Suppl. (1929), 162–71], Wittgenstein in effect concedes Ramsey's point, allowing that atomic propositions may exclude one another even though they do not contradict one another.

32. It is also the chief supporting example used by C.H. Langford in "A Proof That Synthetic *A Priori* Propositions Exist," *The Journal of Philosophy*, 46 (1949), 20–24. Langford at first appears to make his task too easy by defining an analytic proposition as "one that can be certified solely by reference to logical principles" (p. 22). It emerges, however, that recourse to definitions is also permitted. It will become clear below that I agree with Langford on this point: "[I]t is sufficient for our purposes that there should be at least one adequate definition from which this consequence [having twelve edges] does not follow" (p. 22).

33. This paragraph gives my answer to the title question of Lewis White Beck's "Can Kant's Synthetic Judgments Be Made Analytic?" *Kant-Studien*, 46 (1955), 168–81; reprinted in *Kant: Disputed Questions*, edited by Moltke S. Gram (Chicago: Quadrangle Books, 1967), pp. 228–46. A synthetic sentence 'S is P' can always be made analytic by enriching the meanings of the subject term, but the sentence 'every S in the old sense is an S in the new sense' will be synthetic and *a priori* if the original sentence was. There is no banishing the synthetic *a priori* by this method.

34. Thanks to my former student Jeremy Bernstein.

35. D. Hilbert and S. Cohn-Vossen, *Geometry and the Imagination*, translated by P. Nemenyi from the 1932 German edition (New York: Chelsea, 1956). According to Imre Lakatos, *Proofs and Refutations* (Cambridge: Cambridge University Press, 1976), p. 15, this definition comes originally from Möbius, who used it to prevent two polyhedra with an edge or a vertex in common from counting as a single polyhedron.

36. I do not know what the formulation of this clause generalized to cover all polyhedrons should be.

37. Here is another strategy: if it is analytic that cubes have six faces and twelve edges, we may use Euler's formula ($V - E + F = 2$) to deduce that they have eight vertices. But now we must determine whether Euler's formula is analytic or synthetic. I invite the reader to consult Lakatos's discussion of the proof of this formula in *Proofs and Refutations*, asking himself whether the various lemmas that are needed are true by definition or simply seen to be true on the strength of their intuitive (*anschauliche*) evidence.

38. As pointed out by A.C. Ewing in *The Fundamental Questions of Philosophy* (London: Routledge and Kegan Paul, 1951), ch. 2.

39. A notable exception is Anthony Quinton, "The *A Priori* and the Analytic," *Proceedings of the Aristotelian Society*, 64 (1963–64), pp. 31–54; reprinted in *Philosophical Logic*, edited by P.F. Strawson (Oxford: Oxford University Press, 1967), pp. 107–28. Quinton's purported proof consists in the following chain of claimed implications: a priori ⇒ necessary ⇒ not contingent ⇒ not contingent on anything outside ⇒ true in virtue of factors internal to itself ⇒ true in virtue of its meaning. I question the equation of 'contingent' with 'contingent on something'—'contingent' just means 'possibly false'. I also question the significance of the conclusion that necessary truths are true in virtue of meanings. It is by virtue of its meaning that a sentence expressing a necessary truth expresses the truth that it does; it is not by virtue of the meaning of the sentence expressing it that a given truth is necessary.

40. I find that some take him to deny (v). But merely to deny (v) is to leave open the possibility that some statements are clearly analytic and others clearly synthetic, which Quine would surely dispute. I find that others take him to deny (vi), holding that there is never a fact of the matter whether a given statement is analytic or synthetic.

41. W.V. Quine, "Two Dogmas of Empiricism," in *From a Logical Point of View*, pp. 20–46.

42. For more on this side of Kant's views, see the selections in Van Cleve and Frederick, *The Philosophy of Right and Left*. Especially relevant are the selections from Kant's Inaugural Dissertation of 1770 and the pieces by Jonathan Bennett and Martin Gardner.

43. H.P. Grice and P.F. Strawson, "In Defense of a Dogma," *Philosophical Review*, 65 (1956), 141–58. One can make this claim without hypostasizing meanings, contrary to what Quine has urged in reply in *Word and Object* (Cambridge, Mass.: MIT Press, 1960), p. 206. Compare: if there is such a thing as an object's having a shape, then there is such a thing as two objects' having the same shape; this is so even if the logical form of 'x has a shape' is 'Fx' and not the hypostasizing 'xRy'.

44. Grice and Strawson, "In Defense of a Dogma."

45. P.F. Strawson, "Propositions, Concepts, and Logical Truths," *Philosophical Quarterly*, 7 (1957), 15–25. In *Word and Object*, Quine says that this is an objection he "cannot claim to have answered anywhere" (p. 65, n. 3).

46. See, for example, Quine, *Word and Object*, ch. 2.

47. The full quote is, "Conversely, by the same token, no statement is immune from revision," coming just one sentence after, "Any statement can be held true come what may, if we make drastic enough adjustments elsewhere in the system." I have always wondered by *what* token Quine deems both of these doctrines true. The Duhemian possibility of holding onto any statement in the face of recalcitrant experience is sufficiently secured if there is always *something* else we can deny to save a given hypothesis; from this it does not follow that to save a given hypothesis we may deny *anything* else we please. That is, it does not follow that *everything* is revisable.

48. Instead of construing statements as propositions, we could to the same end construe them as sentences with their meanings held constant.

49. Here is a way to put this without invoking an ontology of propositions: if a sentence is analytic (as used by us now), then no one could reject it while meaning the same by it as we do now.

50. See Donald Davidson, *Inquiries into Truth and Interpretation* (Oxford: Clarendon Press, 1984), esp. essays 9–11, 13, and 14. Quine himself would also deny that anything whatever can be rejected, thanks to the dictum "deny the doctrine and change the subject," which he thinks governs the standard laws of logic among other things. For further discussion of this dictum, see my "Analyticity, Undeniability, and Truth," *Canadian Journal of Philosophy*, 18 Suppl. (1992), 89–111.

51. Roderick M. Chisholm, *Theory of Knowledge* (Englewood Cliffs, N.J.: Prentice-Hall, 1977; 2nd edition), pp. 42–43. Chisholm makes all *a priori* knowledge depend on axioms, which are defined as propositions that are necessarily certain for any subject who understands them; this implies that they could never be reasonably rejected. So, if *anything* could be reasonably rejected, there are no axioms and hence no items of *a priori* knowledge.

52. John L. Pollock, *Knowledge and Justification* (Princeton, N.J.: Princeton University Press, 1974), ch. 10. The essential idea is that a proposition is *a priori* if having an intuition that it is true gives one a *prima facie* reason for believing it—a reason that normally confers knowledge but that can on occasion be defeated.

53. Hilary Putnam, "Analyticity and Apriority: Beyond Wittgenstein and Quine," *Midwest Studies in Philosophy*, vol. 4, edited by Peter French, Theodore E. Uehling, Jr., and Howard K. Wettstein (Minneapolis: University of Minnesota Press, 1979), pp. 423–41.

54. Hume, *A Treatise of Human Nature*, I.iii.3 (p. 78 of the Selby-Bigge edition).

55. On page 82 of the *Treatise*, Hume says he is going to "sink" the first of these questions into the second. This does not mean that he no longer distinguishes them, but only that he thinks an answer to the second will furnish us with an answer to the first. The connection comes out most clearly on page 172: if we analyze particular causal relationships in the way Hume recommends, we will readily see that the causal maxim is not a necessary truth.

I am ignoring here the view of some scholars that for Hume causal laws are necessary after all. For discussion, see Kenneth Winkler, "The New Hume," *The Philosophical Review*, 100 (1991), 541–79.

56. Norman Kemp Smith, *A Commentary to Kant's 'Critique of Pure Reason'* (New York: Humanities Press, 1962; reprint of 1923 edition), pp. xxv–xxix and 61–64. One way Kant misleads the reader is by discussing only the first of Hume's questions in the introduction to the *Prolegomena*.

57. Here, but not always; he conflates the questions at B5.

58. Kemp Smith, *Commentary*, p. 30.

59. Hume, *Treatise*, I.3.iii (pp. 79–80 in Selby-Bigge). I have also taken a hint or two from section IV of Hume's *Inquiry Concerning Human Understanding*. The argument in the *Treatise* is followed by critiques of four arguments in favor of the maxim.

60. As Kemp Smith points out (*Commentary*, pp. xxviii–xxix), Kant probably had not read the *Treatise*, which was not available in German, but could have learned of its teachings on causation through Beattie.

61. An enlightening interpretation of Hume along these lines has been offered by Georges Dicker in "Hume's Fork Revisited," *History of Philosophy Quarterly*, 8 (1991), 327–42. Dicker goes on to suggest that Hume can admit synthetic *a priori* propositions as long as they concern only "relations of ideas" and not "matters of fact," that is, as long as they are not propositions asserting the existence of nonabstract entities or permitting the inference to some such

propositions from others. The resulting view would let arithmetic and geometry count as synthetic *a priori* but would exclude the causal maxim.

62. According to Arthur Pap, *Semantics and Necessary Truth* (New Haven, Conn.: Yale University Press, 1958), ch. 4, all Hume *means* in saying that a proposition implies a contradiction is that it is inconceivable. If this is correct, premise 1 is already equivalent to the telescoped premise.

63. In other words, the premise Hume needs is not 'for any c, it is conceivable that e occurs without being caused by c', but rather 'it is conceivable that for any c, e occurs without being caused by c'. Could the latter be what is intended by his saying that we can separate the idea of an event e from the idea of "a cause" of it?

64. Immanuel Kant, "On the Form and Principles of the Sensible and Intelligible World," in *Theoretical Philosophy, 1755–1770*, translated and edited by David Walford in collaboration with Ralf Meerbote. The Cambridge Edition of the Works of Immanuel Kant, vol. 1 (Cambridge: Cambridge University Press, 1992), pp. 373–416.

65. The letter may be found in Zweig, *Kant: Philosophical Correspondence, 1759–99*, pp. 70–76.

66. It is sometimes unclear whether in raising questions about "relation to an object" Kant is asking how representations have intentionality or what makes them veridical. I say more about this in chapter 7.

67. Hilary Putnam, *Reason, Truth, and History* (Cambridge: Cambridge University Press, 1981), ch. 1; Jerry Fodor, *A Theory of Content* (Cambridge, Mass.: MIT Press, 1990), esp. ch. 4. Fodor says that the "foundational intuition" of his theory is that "a symbol means *cat* in virtue of some sort of reliable causal connection that its tokens bear to cats" (p. 127).

68. The typical concept empiricist will question whether we even *possess* concepts not derived from experience, not merely whether such concepts have denotation.

Chapter 3

1. For a discussion of this objection, see Henry Allison, *The Kant-Eberhard Controversy* (Baltimore: Johns Hopkins University Press, 1973), pp. 34–35, and *Kant's Transcendental Idealism: An Interpretation and Defense* (New Haven, Conn.: Yale University Press, 1983), pp. 111–14. The "neglected alternative" may be made vivid by the much maligned but highly suggestive "red spectacles" analogy: granted that we see everything as red owing to the red spectacles permanently affixed to our noses, why could it not be the case that the things on the other side of the spectacles happen to be red?

2. See B168, where Kant may be making a similar point.

3. I ignore here the following problem, which is created by the so-called paradox of strict implication: if B is true, it is necessarily true, in which case it follows from any premise whatsoever.

4. If the 1–2 inference is to be valid as it stands (and not just as an enthymeme), the missing premise must itself be a necessary truth. This presents no problem; surely 'cubes exist only in being constructed' is the sort of thing that would be true necessarily if true at all.

5. "Empirical intuition is possible only by means of the pure intuition of space and of time. What geometry asserts of pure intuition is therefore undeniably valid of empirical intuition" (A165/B206). "The formative synthesis through which we construct a triangle in imagination is precisely the same as that which we exercise in the apprehension of an appearance" (A224/B272).

6. For example, at A226/B274 Kant says that the existence of anything too subtle for our senses to perceive consists in the following fact: "[W]e should,

were our senses more refined, come also in an experience upon the immediate empirical intuition of it." In other places, he lays down stricter requirements for unperceived existence, replacing the subjunctive "should" by a future-oriented "must": "[T]o call an appearance a real thing prior to our perceiving it, either means that in the advance of experience we must meet with such a perception, or it means nothing at all" (A493/B521). I discuss this side of Kant's views in greater detail in appendix D.

7. This is reminiscent of ideas sometimes put forth in connection with intuitionistic mathematics—for example, that all numbers have a certain property if in constructing any number you would have to give it that property.

8. Here I am in agreement with Paul Guyer, one of the few recent commentators who does not downplay the role of the argument from geometry in Kant's philosophy. See his *Kant and the Claims of Knowledge* (Cambridge: Cambridge University Press, 1987), pp. 354–69, esp. p. 363.

9. This explains why "the conditions of the *possibility of experience* in general are likewise conditions of the *possibility of the objects of experience*" (A158/B197).

10. Up to a point, I find an ally on this issue in Michael Dummett, who seems to say as I do that *Sein*-dependence and *Sosein*-dependence should go together:

> Any thesis concerning the ontological status of objects of a given kind must be, at the same time, a thesis about what makes a statement involving reference to such objects true. . . . To say that something is an object of sense—that for it *esse est percipi*—is to say that it has only those properties it is perceived as having. . . . [*Truth and Other Enigmas* (Cambridge, Mass.: Harvard University Press, 1978), p. 230]

Unlike Dummett, however, I do not regard ontological theses as metaphors whose nonmetaphorical content can be provided only by a theory of meaning.

11. Bertrand Russell, *The Problems of Philosophy* (London: Oxford University Press, 1912), pp. 86–87. Contrary to what Russell suggests, Kant does not (as far as I know) say that our forms of intuition have anything to do with the truths of logic.

12. G.E. Moore, *Some Main Problems of Philosophy* (New York: Collier Books, 1962; first published by Macmillan in 1953), p. 171. This book is based on lectures Moore gave in 1910 and 1911.

13. Compare Nicholas Rescher, "Kant and the 'Special Constitution' of Man's Mind: The Ultimately Factual Basis of the Necessity and Universality of *A Priori* Synthetic Truths in Kant's Critical Philosophy," in *Studies in Modality*, American Philosophical Quarterly Monograph Series, 8 (Oxford: Oxford University Press, 1974), pp. 71–83. Rescher does not explicitly make the suggestion, about to be aired in the text, that Kant would reject the axiom of S4. He does, however, defend the idea of principles that are "relatively necessary for rational creatures equipped with a mind of a type akin to our own" (p. 71).

14. This theorem is an immediate corollary of 'if P entails Q and P is possible, so is Q'.

15. I have developed the point of the next several paragraphs at greater length in "Descartes and the Destruction of the Eternal Truths," *Ratio*, 7 (1994), 58–62.

16. Letter to Mersenne, April 15, 1630, in René Descartes, *Philosophical Letters*, edited and translated by Anthony Kenny (Minneapolis: University of Minnesota Press, 1981), p. 11.

17. Harry Frankfurt, "Descartes on the Creation of the Eternal Truths," *The Philosophical Review*, 86 (1977), 36–57.

18. P.T. Geach, "Omnipotence," *Philosophy*, 48 (1973), 7–20, and E.M. Curley, "Descartes on the Creation of the Eternal Truths," *The Philosophical Review*, 93 (1984), 569–97.

19. The passages imply the contingency of our forms of intuition given one of the following as a further premise: (i) if a proposition is necessary, it is not inexplicable to us; (ii) if a proposition is necessary, there are no alternatives to it that are epistemically possible for us.

20. More accurately, any contingency the proposition has will be owing to the contingency of my existence; it will be necessary that my powers are thus and so *if* I exist.

21. Moore, *Some Main Problems of Philosophy*, p. 171.

22. I have entertained the idea of trying to save Kant from Moore's objection by calling into play a distinction I have developed elsewhere between *sources* of knowledge and *grounds* for knowledge. In Descartes's philosophy, clear and distinct perception is a source of knowledge, but not (except in special cases) a ground for it. That is to say, attaining a state of clearly and distinctly perceiving a proposition p puts you in a state of directly (i.e., noninferentially) knowing p. There is no need to infer the truth of p from the higher order proposition that you do clearly and distinctly perceive it, or any need to have knowledge of that higher order proposition. [For further details, see my "Foundationalism, Epistemic Principles, and the Cartesian Circle," *The Philosophical Review*, 88 (1979), 55–91, esp. secs. 5 and 8.] Were we to mobilize this idea in defense of Kant, we would say that there is no need to have any knowledge about the operations of one's own faculties in order to acquire geometrical knowledge. Rather, the state of "purely intuiting" some geometrical proposition, like the state of clearly and distinctly perceiving a proposition for Descartes, would give one noninferential knowledge of the proposition. The trouble with taking this line on Kant's behalf, however, is that the case for transcendental idealism would be circumvented. If the direct deliverance of one's intuition is that cubes must have eight corners, then what one thereby comes to know is that *all* cubes—even cubes *an sich*—have eight corners.

23. Of course, one could avoid this difficulty by saying that the role of convention is only to map sentences onto propositions—to make sentence S express proposition p. In that case, however, one is only explaining why certain sentences express necessary truths, not why the truths expressed are necessary. Most conventionalists have pursued the latter and larger game, thereby committing the same mistake as Kant.

24. W.V. Quine, *Philosophy of Logic* (Englewood Cliffs, N.J.: Prentice-Hall, 1970), p. 96.

25. Proof: (1) Assume $\Box$p. (2) $\Box\Box$p (from 1 and the S4 axiom). (3) $\Box\Box$p → (q ⇒ $\Box$p) (instance of the theorem $\Box$p → (q ⇒ p) obtained by putting $\Box$p for p). (4) (q ⇒ $\Box$p) (from 2 and 3). (5) $\Box$p → (q ⇒ $\Box$p) (from 1–4 by conditional proof).

26. Simon Blackburn, "Morals and Modals," in *Truth, Fact, and Value*, edited by Graham MacDonald and Crispin Wright (Oxford: Oxford University Press, 1986), pp. 119–41. See esp. pp. 120–21.

27. Here is another possible problem presented by the second horn, however, that arises even if our explanans merely possesses necessity without invoking it: how can there be an asymmetrical order of explanation among necessary truths? How can one necessary truth lie deeper than another, in such fashion as to let us say that one holds *because* the other does? In a way, this is the problem raised by Quine: how can a necessary truth owe its necessity more to one thing than to another?

Chapter 4

1. The qualification "spatial" is important: two objects that differed in color (e.g., a red left glove and a green right one) could still qualify as counterparts in Kant's sense. Writers who cite incongruent counterparts as a counterexample to Leibniz's principle of the identity of indiscernibles are therefore jumping the gun.

2. Immanuel Kant, "Concerning the Ultimate Ground of the Differentiation of Directions in Space," in *Theoretical Philosophy, 1755–1770*, translated and edited by David Walford in collaboration with Ralf Meerbote. The Cambridge Edition of the Works of Immanuel Kant, Vol. 1 (Cambridge: Cambridge University Press, 1992), pp. 365–72. In some earlier translations, the German word *Gegenden* is misleadingly rendered as "regions" rather than "directions." On the reasons for preferring "directions" to "regions," see ibid., pp. 456–57.

3. Immanuel Kant, *On the Form and Principles of the Sensible and the Intelligible World*, in *Theoretical Philosophy*, pp. 373–405.

4. Kant, *Prolegomena to Any Future Metaphysics*, translated by Lewis White Beck (Indianapolis, Ind.: Bobbs-Merrill, 1950), sec. 13. The *Prolegomena* argument is briefly repeated in *Metaphysical Foundations of Natural Science*, translated by James Ellington (Indianapolis, Ind.: Bobbs-Merrill, 1970), pp. 23–24.

5. James Van Cleve, "Right, Left, and the Fourth Dimension," *The Philosophical Review*, 96 (1987), 33–68, and "Introduction to the Arguments of 1770 and 1783," in *The Philosophy of Right and Left*, edited by James Van Cleve and Robert E. Frederick (Dordrecht: Kluwer, 1991), pp. 15–26 (this volume also includes "Right, Left, and the Fourth Dimension").

6. Norman Kemp Smith, *A Commentary to Kant's 'Critique of Pure Reason'* (New York: Humanities Press, 1962; reprint of 1923 edition), pp. 161–66.

7. Or would anyone suggest that perhaps *symmetrical* objects, which lack incongruent counterparts, might for all the argument shows be things in themselves? To take this suggestion seriously would be to countenance the possibility that while my fingers are things in themselves, my hand as a whole is appearance!

8. See B307–9 for the distinction between the positive and negative senses of 'noumenon'.

9. I discuss the two points that follow in more detail in "Right, Left, and the Fourth Dimension."

10. Some would deny this, maintaining that 'b lies in direction D from a' can only mean something like 'b lies along the line from a to c', where c is the North Pole or some other reference point.

11. Spherical triangles, though themselves objects of two dimensions, can exist only in a space of three dimensions and would require for their interchange a space of four dimensions. Hands, Kant's favorite examples of incongruent counterparts, are three-dimensional objects that cannot be interchanged in a space of three dimensions but could be interchanged in a space of four.

12. Jill Vance Buroker, *Space and Incongruence* (Dordrecht: Reidel, 1981), p. 85.

13. All that strictly follows is that *either* space *or* one of the triangles is not a thing in itself—a conclusion that leaves room for someone to maintain that the triangles are things in themselves although space is not. But this position is ruled out in comment (e) below.

14. The assumption that relations among things in themselves must be reducible may also underlie premise 1 in the argument from interchangeability. For further discussion of the role of the reducibility principle in Kant's think-

ing, see my "Inner States and Outer Relations: Kant and the Case for Monadism," in *Doing Philosophy Historically*, edited by Peter H. Hare (Buffalo, N.Y.: Prometheus Books, 1988), pp. 231–47.

15. Buroker, *Space and Incongruence*, pp. 4 and 69.

16. Ibid., p. 87.

17. See esp. ibid., p. 83.

18. See Paul Benaceraff, "What Numbers Could Not Be," *The Philosophical Review*, 74 (1965), 47–73.

19. See D.P. Dryer, *Kant's Solution for Verification in Metaphysics* (London: Allen & Unwin, 1966), ch. 11, sec. 6, esp. pp. 513–14.

20. See Gerold Prauss, *Kant und das Problem der Dinge an Sich* (Bonn: Grundmann, 1974), for the view that *an sich* functions canonically for Kant as an adverb modifying *betrachtet* (considered). For a brief discussion of Prauss's views, see Richard Aquila, "Things in Themselves: Intentionality and Reality in Kant," *Archiv für Geschichte der Philosophie*, 61 (1979), 293–307.

21. See, for example, Wilfrid Sellars, *Science and Metaphysics: Variations on Kantian Themes* (London: Routledge and Kegan Paul, 1968), ch. 2.

22. At any rate, it seems self-evident to me that every genuine existent must be fully determinate; perhaps it may be questioned whether the law of the excluded middle is a sufficient test for such determinacy.

23. Of course, I still find it perplexing why Kant was so convinced of the reducibility principle. For me it has nothing like the evidence of the determinacy principle—certainly not enough evidence to make me give up the reality of things in space.

24. For example:

> If we enquire what new character *relation to an object* confers upon our representations, what dignity they thereby acquire, we find that it results *only* in subjecting the representations to a rule, and so in necessitating us to connect them in some one specific manner. (A197/B242, second emphasis mine)

25. Compare Kant's observation in the *Metaphysical Foundations of Natural Science*: "For with regard to what is actual only by its being given in representation, there is not more given than is met with in the representation" (p. 54).

26. More accurately, the experiences constituting the real beast have relations to one another and to other experiences that are not possessed by the experiences constituting the dragon. As Kant puts it:

> [T]he difference between truth and dreaming is not ascertained by the nature of the representations which are referred to objects (for they are the same in the two cases) but by their connection according to those rules which determine the coherence of the representations in the concept of an object, and by ascertaining whether they can subsist together in experience or not. (*Prolegomena*, sec. 13, remark 3, p. 38 in Beck's translation)

Chapter 5

1. At A31/B47, Kant cites two examples of *a priori* principles about time, our knowledge of which is presumably to be explained by the same idealist explanation he has already given for propositions of geometry: time has only one dimension, and different times are not simultaneous but successive. Other putatively necessary topological features of time he might have mentioned here are its unity or connectedness, its continuity, its unboundedness, and its being neither looping nor branching.

2. Lorne Falkenstein, "Kant, Mendelssohn, Lambert, and the Subjectivity of Time," *Journal of the History of Philosophy*, 29 (1991), 227–51.

3. Letter of October 13, 1770, in *Kant: Philosophical Correspondence, 1759–99*, edited and translated by Arnulf Zweig (Chicago: University of Chicago Press, 1967), p. 63.

4. Letter of December 25, 1770, ibid., p. 69.

5. For these claims, see Falkenstein, "Kant, Mendelssohn, Lambert," n. 9 on p. 234. Though I focus here just on an incidental remark, I recommend Falkenstein's essay for an interesting alternative interpretation to mine of Kant on the ideality of time.

6. I am assuming here, as I think Lambert and Falkenstein both do, that a representation is a slice of psychic actuality—a state of a perceiver or a Humean selfless idea. What if a representation were instead a piece of represented content—an intentionalium rather than a representing? I consider this possibility below.

7. Lambert's version can hardly be worse off, since Mendelssohn's premises imply Lambert's.

8. Letter of February 21, 1772, in Zweig, *Kant: Philosophical Correspondence*, p. 75.

9. David Park, as quoted in Rudolf Rucker, *Geometry, Relativity, and the Fourth Dimension* (New York: Dover, 1977), p. 123.

10. One may also be reminded here of McTaggart, who pointed out that his own views on the unreality of time imply that there is *false perception*, that is, the appearance to perceivers of traits and relations that characterize nothing whatever in the universe—not even states of consciousness [J.M.E. McTaggart, *The Nature of Existence* (Cambridge: Cambridge University Press, 1927), vol. 2, ch. 44]. It is thus that McTaggart would sidestep the objection by Dummett in the epigraph to this chapter.

11. In the notation I am using here, 'e' is an operator that may be attached either to a formula or to a term, in either case yielding a term. The experiences symbolized thereby may have either propositional or nonpropositional contents (depending on whether 'e' has been attached to a formula or a term).

12. D.H. Mellor, *Real Time* (Cambridge: Cambridge University Press, 1981), p. 8.

13. This argument was inspired by one Mellor gives for a different purpose (ibid., p. 8). In his argument, 'e(aPb) occurs → eaPeb' is apparently a premise; in mine it is a conclusion. Mellor's conclusion is that temporal order is fixed by causal order.

14. My conjecture is that it would be the first. On the other hand, when Kant sets forth his account of the threefold synthesis in the Transcendental Deduction, he endorses something very like the first implication. This probably reflects the fact (to be documented before we are done) that Kant did not consistently adhere to the radical line.

15. Daniel Dennett, *Consciousness Explained* (Boston: Little, Brown, 1991), p. 148ff.

16. John Foster, *The Case for Idealism* (London: Routledge & Kegan Paul, 1982), ch. 16.

17. There is a way of construing Foster's project that does not put it at odds with Kant's. Perhaps he means only to offer us an ordering relation for experiential states that has the same formal properties as temporal order without *being* temporal order—somewhat along the lines of McTaggart's C-series. Under this construal, Foster would be telling us how to specify the order of experiences in terms of the contents of the experiences, but the order would be ersatz rather than real temporal order. I note in passing that Foster does not tell us what *noncontentual* features of an experience underlie its being of abc

rather than bcd (and thus serve as the ultimate basis of mental time order). It is an interesting question whether there must be such features; it is in effect the question of whether intentionality is supervenient on the nonintentional features of mental acts.

18. Foster's ordering relation for experiences is nontemporal in the relevant sense, but will not serve in the present connection, since it uses the notion we are trying to analyze.

19. Compare William James:

> [B]etween the mind's own changes *being* successive, and *knowing their own succession*, lies as broad a chasm as between the object and subject of any case of cognition in the world. *A succession of feelings, in and of itself, is not a feeling of succession. And since, to our successive feelings, a feeling of their own succession is added, that must be treated as an additional fact requiring its own special elucidation.* . . . [*The Principles of Psychology* (New York: Dover, 1950; reprint of 1890 edition), vol. 1, pp. 628–29; emphasis original]

20. Of course, such infallibility does not extend even for Descartes to *all* features of our mental lives. But it does presumably cover features wholly exemplifiable within a specious present, and thus covers some instances of the relation of precedence.

21. "How could a mental state—or a *state* of anything—exist *an sich* or in itself?" some readers may ask. It is of course true that a state is not something that exists "in itself" in Spinoza's sense; it is not substantival. But substances and nonsubstances alike can qualify as existing in themselves in Kant's sense, as long as they do not depend for their existence on being cognized.

22. Compare B152–53: inner sense "represents to consciousness even our own selves only as we appear to ourselves, not as we are in ourselves."

23. "It is a proposition which must indeed sound strange, that a thing can exist only in the representation of it, but in this case the objection falls, inasmuch as the things with which we are here concerned are not things in themselves, but appearances only, that is, representations" (A374n.).

24. If the difficulty to be raised for the denial of (i) by itself proves fatal, it will not be necessary to consider the response to the Cartesian tradition that denies *both* (i) and (ii).

25. This is the possibility I promised to consider in n. 6.

26. The hopelessness of the view we fall into here is well noted by Phillip Cummins in "Kant on Outer and Inner Intuition," *Nous*, 2 (1968), 271–92. I observe that the regress may be vicious not because it has no end, but because there is already an absurdity in the first step, that is, in the idea that one item can be an object of awareness to another that is itself merely an intentionalium. That would be like saying the figments of my dreams have dreams of their own.

27. To judge by his words, Norman Kemp Smith also finds the radical view in section 7; see his *A Commentary to Kant's 'Critique of Pure Reason'* (New York: Humanities Press, 1962; reprint of 1923 edition), pp. 138–40. However, he finds the view so unremarkable that I am unsure whether to claim him as an interpretive ally on this point.

28. G.E. Moore, *Some Main Problems of Philosophy* (New York: Collier Books, 1962; first published by Macmillan in 1953), ch. 9.

29. Compare P.F. Strawson, *The Bounds of Sense* (London: Methuen, 1966), p. 193, on the "mixed solution" to the Antinomies, which involves the assumption that "one type of essentially temporal series is accorded a real existence which belongs to no other temporal or spatial series whatever," this being the series of representations or experiences.

Chapter 6

1. Leibniz believed that there are simple substances (the monads), but in his view matter is not *composed* of them; it is a *phenomenon bene fundatum.* So, despite believing in simples, Leibniz did not accept 2a or 2b.

2. I am ignoring the second clause of both Thesis and Antithesis.

3. Russell once suggested that someone might complete an infinite series of tasks by doing each task in half the time taken by its predecessor. For discussion of this idea, see James Thomson, "Tasks and Super-Tasks," *Analysis,* 15 (1954–55), 1–13, and Paul Benacerraf, "Tasks, Super-Tasks, and the Modern Eleatics," *The Journal of Philosophy,* 59 (1962), 765–84.

4. This distinction is drawn by C.D. Broad in "Kant's Mathematical Antinomies," *Proceedings of the Aristotelian Society,* 55 (1954–55), 1–22. Kant's own terminology is somewhat different: to occupy a space is to be present at every point of it, and to fill a space is not only to occupy it but also to resist the entry of other things [see Immanuel Kant, *Metaphysical Foundations of Natural Science,* translated by James Ellington (Indianapolis, Ind.: Bobbs-Merrill, 1970), p. 40ff.]. The additional Kantian implication of 'filling' will not matter for present purposes.

5. He does say, however, that simples can never be given in experience and are therefore absent from "nature" or the world of sense (A437/B465).

6. Pierre Bayle, *Historical and Critical Dictionary,* translated by Richard Popkin (Indianapolis, Ind.: Bobbs-Merrill, 1965), p. 359.

7. Ibid., p. 360.

8. I owe this suggestion to R.M. Chisholm.

9. Roger Boscovich, *A Theory of Natural Philosophy* (Cambridge, Mass.: MIT Press, 1966; English translation of the 1763 edition); Immanuel Kant, "The Use in Natural Philosophy of Metaphysics Combined with Geometry" (generally known as the *Physical Monadology*), in *Kant's Latin Writings,* edited by Lewis White Beck (New York: Peter Lang, 1986), pp. 111–34. Beck notes that Boscovich's ideas were published as early as 1745 and that Kant may have known of them.

10. As noted above, Kant himself subscribed to the Boscovichian hypothesis in the *Physical Monadology* of 1756, but he repudiated it in the *Metaphysical Foundations of Natural Science* of 1786. For his reasons for giving it up, see *Metaphysical Foundations,* pp. 49–50.

11. Adolf Grünbaum, *Modern Science and Zeno's Paradoxes* (Middletown, Conn.: Wesleyan University Press, 1967), pp. 115–35.

12. For another argument against the set-theoretic approach to physical continuity, see Chris Mortensen and Graham Nerlich, "Physical Topology," *Journal of Philosophical Logic,* 7 (1978), 209–23.

13. These conditions are taken from Broad, "Kant's Mathematical Antinomies." For an alternative construction of continuous intervals out of points, see Mortensen and Nerlich, "Physical Topology."

14. I suspect, however, that his own rationale may have involved the mistaken belief that *any* part series beginning with an object composed of simples must eventually terminate. This is not true. An object composed of extensionless points could have as one of its part series an infinite series of concentric spherical shells.

15. P.F. Strawson, *The Bounds of Sense* (London: Methuen, 1966), pp. 194–95.

16. Ibid., pp. 190–97.

17. Strawson says (ibid., p. 195) that transcendental idealism provides support ("metaphysical stiffening") for verificationism, but I fail to see how this

is so. On this point, recall what was said about the distinction between mind-dependence and evidence-dependence in chapter 1, section E.

18. This point is made by Carl Posy in "Dancing to the Antinomy: A Proposal for Transcendental Idealism," *American Philosophical Quarterly*, 20 (1983), 81–94. Posy offers an interpretation of Kant's solution to the Antinomies that is itself broadly verificationist but that does not incur any of the three objections I have leveled against Strawson. Posy's verificationism makes truth (rather than meaningfulness) depend on verifiability, thereby avoiding the second two objections, and it explicitly embraces the consequence that transcendental idealism as *I* am construing it is unnecessary for Kant. I discuss Posy's interpretation in chapter 13, section D.

19. I thus agree with Bennett that a major element in Kant's solution to the Antinomy is what he calls "the futurizing move." [See his "The Age and Size of the World," *Synthese*, 23 (1971), 127–46; reprinted in *Kant on Pure Reason*, edited by Ralph C.S. Walker (Oxford: Oxford University Press, 1982), pp. 176–94.] As I see things, however, Kant's objective in throwing a series into the future is not (as Bennett suggests) to make it a harmless actual infinite; it is to make it a series that is neither finite nor infinite (as in what Bennett calls "the weakening move").

20. Kant, *Metaphysical Foundations*, pp. 53–54.

21. This has been denied by Russell; for discussion of the issue, see Thomson, "Tasks and Super-Tasks," and Benacerraf, "Tasks, Super-Tasks, and the Modern Eleatics."

22. For more on this point, see Fred Dretske, "Counting to Infinity," *Analysis*, 25 (1965), 99–101.

23. I have had second thoughts about this point. It is hard for me to see how 'there will be infinitely many Fs' can be true unless either (i) it will be the case at some time that infinitely many Fs exist then (which is not true when the Fs are someone's perceptions) or (ii) we quantify at *t* over things that are not actual at *t* (which offends against the doctrine sometimes called "presentism"). But to the extent to which these second thoughts are well taken, they enforce the finite alternative rather than Kant's purported "neither finite nor infinite" alternative.

24. The contrast between these two forms of phenomenalism will be important for us at a number of places, especially in connection with the Second Analogy—see chapter 9, section A.

25. Of course, by definition of a logical construction, every *true* sentence about As must have a sufficient truth condition statable in sentences about Bs.

Chapter 7

1. Writers in this tradition include (among many others) P.F. Strawson, *The Bounds of Sense* (London: Methuen, 1966), and Edwin McCann, "Skepticism and Kant's B Deduction," *History of Philosophy Quarterly*, 2 (1985), 71–89. See, however, Karl Ameriks, "Kant's Transcendental Deduction as a Regressive Argument," *Kant-Studien*, 69 (1978), 273–87, for a downplaying of Kant's antiskeptical intent.

2. C.I. Lewis, *Mind and the World Order* (New York: Dover, 1956; reprint of 1929 edition by Scribner's), p. 30.

3. Ibid. p. 54.

4. Norman Kemp Smith's *A Commentary to Kant's 'Critique of Pure Reason'* (New York: Humanities Press, 1962; reprint of the 1923 edition) cites three such remarks on pp. xlix–l, including one in a letter to Marcus Herz of

May 26, 1789. For the remark to Herz, see Arnulf Zweig, ed., *Kant: Philosophical Correspondence, 1759-99* (Chicago: University of Chicago Press, 1967), pp. 150-56, esp. p. 154.

5. The first entry in Kant's table under "representation with consciousness" is *sensation*, suggesting that sensations are by definition conscious. I am not sure that this is Kant's settled view, for what, if not sensations, would be examples of representations *without* consciousness? However, if sensations are by definition conscious for Kant, one may replace my (e1) with "having *representations*" and (e2) with "having *sensations*, that is, representations with consciousness."

By a "representation with consciousness" does Kant mean a representation *of* which we are conscious or a representation *by* which we are conscious? I assume the former. The latter would imply that sensations have objects, in which case they would no longer be sensations but intuitions, as I am about to show.

6. It is an interesting question whether the two marks of intuitionhood just mentioned must go together. If the only sense in which a mental state could have spatial extent is by having an object with spatial extent, the second mark of intuitionhood (having extensive magnitude, or at any rate spatial magnitude) would presuppose the first (having an object).

Kant apparently holds (along with Condillac, Burke, and Reid) that there are no sensations of shape. [For an excellent discussion of these matters, see Rolf George, "Kant's Sensationism," *Synthese*, 47 (1981), 229-55, esp. p. 236.] But these philosophers also hold that there are no sensations "of" anything at all, so I wonder what the nonspatiality of sensation amounts to for them beyond the nonintentionality of sensation. Relatedly, if there is some nonintentional sense in which they would allow that a sensation can be "of" color, why cannot it also be "of" shape?

7. For a defense of this point of view, see Wilfrid Sellars, "Empiricism and the Philosophy of Mind," in *Science, Perception, and Reality* (London: Routledge & Kegan Paul, 1963), pp. 127-96. On the other side, see H.H. Price, *Perception* (London: Methuen, 1973; reprint of the 1932 edition), ch. 1. Two versions of the doctrine that all consciousness is conceptual should be distinguished. According to the stronger, being conscious of something *is* conceptualizing it; according to the weaker, conceptualizing something is *necessary for*, but not *identical with*, being conscious of it. If the stronger version is true, there is *no such thing* as mere thin experience; if the weaker version is true, there is such a thing, but it occurs only as a constituent within thicker conceptual episodes.

8. See Kemp Smith, *Commentary*, pp. xlii and 168.

9. W.V. Quine, *Word and Object* (Cambridge, Mass.: MIT Press, 1960), sec. 1.

10. There is a weaker sense, discussed below, in which awareness of experiences *as* experiences would count as self-conscious experience even if there is no accompanying awareness of a self.

11. For the last view, see Richard Rorty, "Strawson's Objectivity Argument," *The Review of Metaphysics*, 24 (1970), 207-44.

12. Some may resist this assimilation of the conceptual to the judgmental. A possible counterexample is the phenomenon of *seeing as*: if I see x *as* F, my experience is conceptual but not yet judgmental. But I think this appearance of an intermediate form of experience is illusory. When subjected to analytical pressure, the notion of seeing x as F tends to topple in either of two directions: toward seeing x to be F, which is judgmental (in a broad sense that includes belief *de re* as well as belief *de dicto*), or toward x's looking F, which is purely sensory or intuitional, not conceptual. In neither case do we get a kind of experience that is both conceptual and nonjudgmental.

For a defense of the view that "lookings" are nonconceptual, see G.N.A. Vesey, "Seeing and Seeing As," reprinted in *Perceiving, Sensing, and Knowing*, edited by Robert J. Swartz (Berkeley: University of California Press, 1976), pp. 68–83. Sellars, in "Empiricism" (pp. 140–49), argues for the contrary view that 'x looks F to S' expresses a conceptual episode, but his arguments, if sound, would also show that it expresses a propositional attitude. His views, therefore, are compatible with my contention that there is no mean between the nonconceptual and the judgmental.

13. Kemp Smith, *Commentary*, pp. 168 and 222–23. Kemp Smith attributes to Kant the view that "save in and through *a priori* concepts no representations can exist for consciousness" (p.223). For Wolff's views, see Robert Paul Wolff, *Kant's Theory of Mental Activity* (Cambridge, Mass.: Harvard University Press, 1963), pp. 147 and 159. Wolff says that the Transcendental Deduction "will not work unless the categories are viewed as necessary conditions of any consciousness whatsoever" (p.159).

14. Lewis, *Mind and the World Order*, pp. 320–21; D.P. Dryer, *Kant's Solution for Verification in Metaphysics* (London: Allen & Unwin, 1966), p. 290; Paul Guyer, *Kant and the Claims of Knowledge* (Cambridge: Cambridge University Press, 1987), pp. 73–87. Guyer classifies starting premises for the Transcendental Deduction in accordance with two intersecting distinctions: does the premise assume (I) knowledge of objects distinct from the self or only (II) knowledge of the self, and does the knowledge in question include (A) knowledge of synthetic necessary truths or only (B) knowledge of empirical truths? In each of the four cases (IA, IB, IIA, and IIB), it appears that some form of propositional knowledge is involved (though Guyer sometimes leaves one unsure of this by using "judgment" instead of "knowledge").

15. George, "Kant's Sensationism."

16. Strawson, *Bounds of Sense*.

17. H.J. Paton, *Kant's Metaphysic of Experience* (London: Allen & Unwin, 1970; first published in 1936), vol. 1, pp. 329–44, esp. pp. 332 and 337, n. 2; S. Körner, *Kant* (Baltimore: Penguin Books, 1955), pp. 56–59.

18. Jonathan Bennett, *Kant's Analytic* (Cambridge: Cambridge University Press, 1966), pp. 105 and 124. Paton (*Kant's Metaphysic of Experience*, vol. 1, p. 333) also holds the categories to be necessary for self-knowledge.

19. Here are some other instances in which Kant equates 'experience' with 'knowledge of an object' or at least with 'knowledge': "*Empirical knowledge* . . . is what we entitle experience" (B147). "Experience is knowledge by means of connected perceptions" (B161). "Experience is an empirical knowledge, a knowledge which determines an object through perceptions" (B218). (Translating *Erkenntnis* by "cognition" rather than "knowledge" would better accommodate the indefinite article.)

20. For a definition of perceptual taking, see Roderick M. Chisholm, "'Appear,' 'Take,' and 'Evident,'" *The Journal of Philosophy*, 53 (1956); reprinted in *Perceiving, Sensing, and Knowing*, edited by Robert J. Swartz (Berkeley: University of California Press, 1976), pp. 473–85.

21. Wolff, *Kant's Theory of Mental Activity*, p. 125.

22. Ibid., pp. 157–59.

23. Ibid., p. 158.

24. G.W. Leibniz, "Principles of Nature and Grace, Founded on Reason," in *Philosophical Writings*, edited by G.H.R. Parkinson (London: Everyman's Library, 1973), pp. 195–204, at p. 197.

25. "The term 'transcendental' . . . signifies such knowledge as concerns the *a priori* possibility of knowledge, or its *a priori* employment."

26. The other point made here, that unity of apperception comes about only through synthesis, is discussed below.

27. A note of clarification: my concern at the moment is only with expli-cating candidates for the *property* (or relation) of unity of apperception, that is, with saying what it is for several representations to have unity of apper-ception. That is why each of (u1)–(u8) begins with an existential quantifier. I undertake below to formulate candidates for the *principle* of unity of apper-ception, and it would be natural to take such formulations as beginning with a universal quantifier: for any subject S, if r1 and r2 are representations be-longing to S, then ⸻. What fills the blank might then be any of (u1)–(u8) or, better yet, any of the open sentences that result when the '(∃S)' quan-tifiers in (u1)–(u8) are deleted, allowing the 'S' variable to be bound by the initial universal quantifier.

A further wrinkle: I show below that there may be reason to formulate the property of unity of apperception without quantifying over subjects at all, but that is getting ahead of the story.

28. William James, *The Principles of Psychology* (New York: Dover, 1950; reprint of the 1890 edition), vol. 1, p. 160.

29. Wolff, *Kant's Theory of Mental Activity*, p. 106.

30. Note that (u3) is not necessarily meant to imply that only representa-tions occurring at the same time can be U-related, for 'A' may be allowed to cover acts of memory as well as acts of acquaintance. It is the acts, not neces-sarily their objects, that are required to be co-temporaneous.

31. R.M. Chisholm has asked whether my " + " might not be taken to denote the sum-forming operation of mereology, in which case two representations would have unity of apperception in the (u4) sense iff someone were aware of their mereological sum. This is an intriguing suggestion, but it would proba-bly require us to construe representations as existent particulars in the man-ner of classical sense-datum theories—a construal I have not adopted here. A further possible difficulty with the suggestion is the following: let w be a whole of which I am aware, let x be a miniscule part of it that I have never noticed, and let y be the remainder. In classical mereology, a whole is identical with any sum of parts of which it is composed, so in being aware of w, I would ipso facto be aware of the sum (x + y). Under the current suggestion, that would mean that x and y enjoy unity of apperception, which presumably implies that I am aware of each individually. Yet I just stipulated that x is a part I have never noticed. Perhaps Kant (or a sense-datum theorist) would respond by denying that a perceived whole can have unperceived parts; that, at any rate, is sug-gested by Kant's solution to the Second Antinomy.

32. This point stands even if awareness of an item requires judgment about it, for I might attribute a monadic property (e.g., a color) to each of the spots without judging them to be related.

33. Hector-Neri Castañeda, "'He': A Study in the Logic of Self-Cons-ciousness," *Ratio*, 8 (1966), 130–57; Roderick M. Chisholm, *The First Person* (Minneapolis: University of Minnesota Press, 1981), ch. 3.

34. "Through this I or he or it (the thing) which thinks, nothing further is represented than a transcendental subject of the thoughts = X" (A346/B404).

35. A view along these lines was briefly advocated by Roderick M. Chisholm; see his "The Self and the World," in *Wittgenstein and His Impact on Contemporary Thought: Proceedings of the Second International Wittgenstein Symposium* (Vienna: Hölder Pichler Tempsky, 1978), pp. 407–10.

36. C.D. Broad, *Mind and Its Place in Nature* (London: Routledge & Kegan Paul, 1925), pp. 558–72.

37. Ibid.

38. "Only in so far as I can grasp the manifold of representations in one consciousness do I call them one and all *mine*" (B134).

39. "The thought that the representations given in intuition one and all be-

long to me is therefore equivalent to the thought that I unite them in one self-consciousness, or *can* at least so unite them" (B134, emphasis mine). One way of understanding 'r1 and r2 are possibly U-related' would be this: under certain conditions, they *would* be U-related.

40. For further confirmation of this point, see A99. I should add that I sometimes sense an inconsistency between the Transcendental Deduction and the Axioms of Intuition on the one hand and Kant's solution to the Second Antinomy on the other. In the former, the sequence of awareness seems to be bottom-up (from part to whole); in the latter, it seems to be top-down (from whole to part).

41. For another example to reinforce the point, imagine a page full of circles. Which circles did you fill in first, those in the top half or the bottom half? If you are like me, you set the whole array down at once. Even if you filled in one half of the page first, I bet you put the individual circles down whole, rather than generating them point by point.

42. Compare George's alternative account: "Rather, to have an image is to have gone through a certain sequence of sensory affections and to have judged that they constitute one object" ("Kant's Sensationism," p. 236).

43. There is another regress that may be thought to threaten Kant's account, this one on the input side rather than the output side. As mentioned above, Kant's views imply that any representation of an extent or a duration must be brought about by synthesis. If the inputs to synthesis were always themselves representations of extents or durations, there would be a regressive process with no beginning. However, Kant can avoid this regress as long as there are bottom-level inputs that are not themselves representations of items with extent or duration. Kantian sensations probably fill the bill, either because they are punctiform or because they are not representations "of" anything at all. (I sometimes wonder whether the theory of punctiform sensations drives the doctrine of synthesis or vice versa.)

44. James, *Principles of Psychology*, vol. 1, p. 278.

45. Kant defines 'function' as follows, having just contrasted functions with affections: "By 'function' I mean the unity of the act of bringing various representations under one common representation" (A68/B93). This passage would make more sense to me if we replaced "unity of the act" by "unifying act."

46. H.A. Prichard, *Kant's Theory of Knowledge* (Oxford: Clarendon Press, 1909), p. 141.

47. Paton, *Kant's Metaphysic of Experience*, vol. 1, p. 240.

48. Dryer, *Kant's Solution,* pp. 108–13.

49. A categorical judgment will exemplify exactly four of the twelve forms; for example, it might be an Apodeictic Categorical Universal Affirmative. But a compound judgment (e.g., an if-then judgment) will involve more than four forms, since it is itself built out of two judgments.

50. See, for example, Arthur Lovejoy, "Kant's Classification of the Forms of Judgment," *The Philosophical Review*, 16 (1907), 588–603; reprinted in Moltke S. Gram, *Kant: Disputed Questions* (Chicago: Quadrangle Books, 1967), pp. 269–83. Lovejoy maintains that Kant gerrymandered the logic of his day to get a table of judgment forms yielding precisely his twelve categories.

51. This is explicit in the *Prolegomena*, pp. 45–52; it is also a consequence of the definition of 'function' as an act of bringing various representations under a common representation.

52. Some commentators take a line that would circumvent the criticism I have just raised: they say that the (unschematized) categories *are* the forms of judgment (see, e.g., Paton, *Kant's Metaphysic of Experience*, vol. 1, p. 260). Now, that may sound like a mistake—indeed, a category mistake!—for how

can a concept be a form of judgment? But there is a better way to make this point. Instead of saying that categories "are" forms of judgment, we could say that each category is to be defined contextually in terms of its corresponding form of judgment: category C is instantiated iff a judgment of correlated form F is true. This line is not open to the criticism I have just raised. However, Kant's enterprise will still be open (and now more obviously so) to the fundamental criticism I am about to raise.

53. Moreover, as Bennett has pointed out (*Kant's Analytic*, pp. 81–82), even if we could not make any judgments without making judgments of *some* of Kant's favored types, it would not follow that we must eventually make judgments of *each* of the types.

54. See A84–85/B116–17 on the aim of a transcendental deduction. See also the various places in which Kant characterizes "objective validity" or "objective reality," for example, A35/B52, A93/B126, B150–51, and A155–56/B194–95. Although he does not do so in the passages I have cited, some commentators [e.g., Henry E. Allison, *Kant's Transcendental Idealism: An Interpretation and Defense* (New Haven, Conn.: Yale University Press, 1983), pp. 133–36] think Kant distinguishes between 'objective validity' and 'objective reality'. If there is such a distinction, it is objective reality and not merely objective validity that must be established in the Transcendental Deduction.

55. Here are the sources for the various numbered transitions. 1 (consciousness/mine to unity): in A, 113, 116, and 122; in B, section 16. 2 (unity to synthesis): in A, 108 and 122; in B, section 16. 3 (synthesis to categories): in A, 119 and 125 (with help from 79–80); in B, section 20. 4 (synthesis to unity): in A, 106–7; in B, section 17. 5 and 6 (object-relatedness to synthesis and conversely): in A, 105 and 109; in B, section 17. 7 and 8 (object-relatedness to unity and conversely): in A, 129; in B, section 17. 9 (object-relatedness to categories): a consequence of 5 and 3.

56. René Descartes, *The Philosophical Works of Descartes*, translated by Elizabeth S. Haldane and G.R.T. Ross (Cambridge: Cambridge University Press, 1931), vol. 2, p. 10.

57. Here is another passage in which Kant calls attention to the twofold sense of 'object':

> All representations have, as representations, their object. . . . Appearances are the sole objects which can be given to us immediately, and that [in a representation, *sich darin*] which relates immediately to the object is called intuition. But these appearances are not things in themselves; they are only representations, which in turn have their object—an object which cannot itself be intuited by us. (A108–9)

There may appear to be a difference between this passage and the one I quoted in the text. The first says that representations *are* objects and may also relate to objects in a further sense. The second says that representations *have* objects (called appearances—see Bxxvi and A20/B34), which may also relate to objects in a further sense. But given the ing-ed ambiguity of "representation" (which also characterizes *ung*-words like *Vorstellung* in German), I think it is quite possible that the two passages are making exactly the same point. The first says that representeds *are* objects, the second puts this another way by saying that representings *have* objects, and both passages go on to say that there is a further question to be raised about what it is for objects in the thinner sense to be "related to an object" in the thicker sense.

58. Some commentators take Kant to be concerned with elucidating the first sense as well (or instead). I examine the views of Rolf George in this connection below.

59. 'Transcendent object' misleadingly suggests Kant's "transcendental ob-

ject = x", which is not what Kant's objects$_2$ turn out to be. 'Internal' and 'external' misleadingly suggest Kant's distinction between objects of inner sense and objects of outer sense—a distinction that cuts across the distinction between objects$_1$ and objects$_2$.

60. It might be asked whether my construal of objects$_1$ (the objects of intuitings) as virtual objects, subject to adverbial reduction, does not actually *deprive* intuitions of their objects, making them nonintentional states like sensations. This is a good question. Its aptness is reinforced by considering the views of Thomas Reid, who is generally credited with holding both (i) a precursor of the adverbial theory of sensation and (ii) the view that sensation is nonintentional, having no object distinct from itself. It is natural to think that (i) and (ii) go together. If Kant holds an adverbial theory of the objects of intuition, then, in what sense are intuitions intentional and mere sensations not? I do not have a good answer. I can only point out that Kant himself seems to see no incompatibility between the statuses of being an object and existing only in being apprehended. The next sentence after the two I have quoted earlier in this section from A189/B235 is this: "The appearances, in so far as they are objects of consciousness simply in virtue of being representations, are not in any way distinct from their apprehension, that is, from their reception in the synthesis of imagination. . . ."

61. Perhaps it would be useful to remind the reader of what was said in note 57—that which bears "relation to an object" may be taken to be either a representing or its indwelling object$_1$.

62. Kant does sometimes use the phrase "transcendental object" in reference to things in themselves. See, for example, A358, A366, A379–80, and (arguably) A494/B523. At A492/B520 he uses "transcendental subject" for "the self proper, as it exists in itself".

63. Lewis, *Mind and the World Order*, p. 140; see also pp. 135–39. Lewis's phenomenalist views are more explicitly and elaborately worked out in *An Analysis of Knowledge and Valuation* (La Salle, Ill.: Open Court, 1946).

64. The passage continues as follows: "Now all unification of representations demands unity of consciousness in the synthesis of them. Consequently it is the unity of consciousness that alone constitutes the relation of representations to an object. . . ."

65. Note that in the clause following "conversely" (*umgekehrt*), Kant is saying that interrepresentational relations of a certain sort are *necessary* for objective meaning. If the preceding clause is (as Kant says) the converse of this, it must be saying that such relations are *sufficient* for (or that they *exhaust*) objective meaning. That confirms my reductive reading of the passage.

66. Lest anyone think that my reading is gainsaid by the omitted sentence marked by my ellipsis—"Objective meaning cannot consist in the relation to another representation (of that which we entitle object)"—let me point out that the parenthetical phrase *restricts* the meaning of what precedes it. Kant is making the obvious point that 'r is related to an object' cannot be analyzed as 'r is related to some other representation r* that is related to an object' without taking for granted the notion we are trying to analyze.

67. Bertrand Russell, "Logical Atomism," in *Logic and Knowledge*, edited by Robert C. Marsh (London: Allen & Unwin, 1956), p. 326.

68. The condition here is the unity of consciousness, whose connection to "relation to an object" is the topic of the next section.

69. A more cautious statement of this claim would be the following: the members of a group of representations stand in relations whereby each of them is related to an object iff they also stand in relations whereby they have unity of apperception. This formulation does not require the relations referred to by the two sides of the biconditional to be the same relations.

70. For an ingenious defense of a limited version of Kant's idea, however, see Jay Rosenberg, "'I Think': Some Reflections on Kant's Paralogisms," in *Midwest Studies in Philosophy*, vol. 10, edited by Peter A. French, Theodore E. Uehling, Jr., and Howard K. Wettstein (Minneapolis: University of Minnesota Press, 1986), pp. 503–31, esp. pp. 505–10. I call Rosenberg's version limited because (as far as I can see) the "objects" it brings into play could be synthesized complexes of representations in a dream.

71. See the first paragraph of Lewis White Beck, "Did the Sage of Königsberg Have No Dreams?" in *Essays on Kant and Hume* (New Haven, Conn.: Yale University Press, 1978), pp. 38–60; Bennett, *Kant's Analytic*, pp. 61–62 and 156–58; and Strawson, *The Bounds of Sense*, pp. 32, 88–89, and 97.

72. This is not to say that no epistemological challenges remain. We still have whatever epistemological problems attend induction from past and present realities to future and counterfactual realities.

73. T.H. Green, *Prolegomena to Ethics* (Oxford: Clarendon Press, 1883), secs. 38–54. For a summary of Green's views, see Peter Hylton, *Russell, Idealism, and the Emergence of Analytical Philosophy* (Oxford: Clarendon Press, 1990), pp. 36–39.

74. George, "Kant's Sensationism."

75. Ibid., p. 243.

76. Even if a representation could be its own object, that would be presupposing a self-reflexive kind of intentionality.

77. George makes it clear in "Kant's Sensationism" (p. 233) that the problem he sees Kant concerned with is intentionality as such, and thus even with "internal" intentionality or having an idea before one's mind. He constrasts Kant on this score with the British Empiricists, whose "consuming problem" is said to be external intentionality.

78. Lewis, *Mind and the World Order*, p. 221; Beck, *Essays on Kant and Hume*, pp. 38–60.

79. Beck, *Essays on Kant and Hume*, p. 47. The first of our three alternatives is also to be found in Beck: "The categories do not differentiate veridical from non-veridical experience; they make the difference between dumbly facing chaos without even knowing it—'less even than a dream'—and telling a connected story, even if it is false" (p. 54).

80. The argument occupies chapter 2 of part II of Strawson's *Bounds of Sense*, especially pp. 97–112. See page 102 for the claim that UC entails OT and page 97 for the claim that CE is the fundamental premise, underlying and entailing UC.

81. That is to say, if we formulate unity principles as I suggested in note 27, letting the open sentences following the initial '(∃S)' serve as consequents, the results will approximate the unity theses with Strawson's endings (a) and (b), respectively.

82. Strictly speaking, virtual objects are not identical with anything!

83. To establish that UC implies OT as defined by all four conditions, Strawson would have to show that any experience that violated any of conditions (i)–(iv) would also violate UC. What he actually argues is that a pure sense-datum experience, defined as I am about to show by its violation of condition (i), would violate UC. Hence, what follows by contraposition is just that any experience satisfying UC must also satisfy the first condition of objectivity; we get the other conditions of objectivity only to the extent that they are already bound up with the first.

84. Strawson's characterization of a sense-datum experience misrepresents the position of many classical sense-datum theorists, such as Price, who *did* distinguish object from act—see his *Perception*, p. 3. As I argue in section D

of chapter 1, however, it is hard to see how such sense-datum theorists could have any rationale for holding, as they typically did, that the datum cannot exist apart from the act of sensing it.

85. Objection: Strawson does not insist on a center theory of unity of mind; he seems to ascribe to Kant nothing more than a system theory. Why, then, could there not be present in the second figure the relations among sense data needed to make them belong to a single consciousness? Reply: UC, for Strawson, requires more than unity of mind: it requires that unity of mind, in whatever it consists, be capable of being known to obtain, and it is such knowability that is threatened by the "absorption."

86. If Strawson is right about this, the premise connecting CE and UC is apparently unnecessary, since experience violating OT would directly violate CE.

87. My understanding of Strawson's argument here has been much aided by Rorty, "Strawson's Objectivity Argument," esp. p. 217.

88. Ibid., p. 217.

89. To see that the argument is valid, note that –OT, the denial of the conclusion, combines with (2) to yield –UC, which combines with (1') to yield the disjunction –CE or OT, which combines with (3) to yield OT. Denying the conclusion in the company of the premises thus yields contradiction.

90. This question has been asked by a number of Strawson's critics, including J.L. Mackie, *The Cement of the Universe* (Oxford: Clarendon Press, 1974), pp. 99–102, and Leslie Stevenson, "Wittgenstein's Transcendental Deduction and Kant's Private Language Argument," *Kant-Studien*, 73 (1982), 321–37, at p. 325.

91. A judgment regarding two experiences that one bears a certain relation (e.g., resemblance or simultaneity) to the other would confer on them unity in my sense (u5), but not unity in any of the stronger senses that Strawson's argument requires.

92. Strawson presents this argument not as an answer to my third objection, but to an objection of his own, namely, how can objectivity make self-ascription possible when Kant has told us so little about the criteria for reidentifying subjects of experience? Strawson's reply is that objectivity does not indeed provide the *full* conditions of self-ascription but does deliver the "fundamental basis" or "core" of self-ascription. This core Strawson dubs the "self-reflexiveness" of experience and explains thus: "[E]xperience must be such as to provide room for the thought of experience itself" (*Bounds of Sense*, p. 107).

93. The second way of putting the matter goes beyond the first insofar as it implies *believing* in objective items (not just having the concept of them), but in either case we have something far weaker than the actual existence of objective items. The weaker language had already crept into Strawson's formulations earlier in the argument, for example, "experience of objects conceived as distinct from" awareness of them (ibid., pp. 90 and 98).

94. Barry Stroud, "Transcendental Arguments," *The Journal of Philosophy*, 65 (1968), 241–56; reprinted in *Kant on Pure Reason*, edited by Ralph C.S. Walker (Oxford: Oxford University Press, 1982), pp. 117–31.

95. Kant draws the distinction between problematic and dogmatic idealism at A377 and again at B274.

Chapter 8

1. Jonathan Bennett, *Kant's Analytic* (Cambridge: Cambridge University Press, 1966), p. 181.

2. See *Aristotle's Categories and De Interpretatione*, edited with notes by J. L. Ackrill (Oxford: Clarendon Press, 1963), 2a11, p. 5; René Descartes, *Reply to the Second Set of Objections to the Meditations*, Cottingham, vol. 2, p. 114;

Leibniz, *Discourse on Metaphysics*, sec. VIII Parkinson, p. 18; J.M.E. McTaggart, *The Nature of Existence* (Cambridge: Cambridge University Press, 1927), vol. 1, secs. 65 and 72; Bertrand Russell, "On the Relations of Universals and Particulars," in *Logic and Knowledge*, edited by Robert C. Marsh (London: Allen & Unwin, 1956), pp. 103–24, at p. 109.

3. McTaggart (ibid.) stuck resolutely to the letter of the "not a property" definition of substance (that which "has qualities and is related, without being a quality or a relation"); this led him to count sneezes as substances. Kant clearly would *not* want to count sneezes as substances, hence the need to construe his "always subject, never predicate" formula in the stricter way that I suggest. Nor would Aristotle, Descartes, or Leibniz count sneezes as substances; perhaps that is why they make it an additional mark of substances that they be independent beings. Kant, too, sometimes sounds the independence theme; see A435/B463 and A440/B468.

4. Here I agree with H.J. Paton, *Kant's Metaphysic of Experience* (London: Allen & Unwin, 1970; first published in 1936), vol. 2, pp. 69–70. Textual evidence for this answer occurs at A147/B186, A181/B224, and A242–43/B300. I air a second thought about this point in section K.

5. Bennett, *Kant's Analytic*, p. 182.

6. Kant acknowledges this at A184/B227: "Certainly the proposition, that substance is permanent, is tautological." As he makes clear in the next two sentences, however, there is a synthetic proposition in the neighborhood: "[I]n all appearances there is something permanent, and . . . the transitory is nothing but determination of its existence."

7. See Immanuel Kant, *Metaphysical Foundations of Natural Science*, translated by James Ellington (Indianapolis, Ind.: Bobbs-Merrill, 1970), p. 102. The key to the argument Kant gives here is the definition of "quantity of matter" as *number of parts*, together with the lemma that every part of matter is a substance. Add that no substance ever arises or perishes and it follows that the total quantity of matter in the universe is constant. The chief difficulty with this argument is that there is no guarantee that "quantity of matter" as Kant defines it is proportional to *mass*, as it is supposed to be in the eighteenth-century conservation principle he is trying to prove. For further discussion of this point, see section VII of my "Substance, Matter, and the First Analogy," *Kant-Studien*, 70 (1979), 149–61.

8. "Alteration" and "change" are the words by which Kemp Smith translates *Veränderung*, and *Wechsel*, respectively. As an alternative to the translation of *Wechsel*, Bennett (*Kant's Analytic*, p. 187) has proposed "existence-change" and Henry E. Allison [*Kant's Transcendental Idealism: An Interpretation and Defense* (New Haven, Conn.: Yale University Press, 1983), p. 204], "replacement change." I shall stick with "change," trusting the reader to keep its technical meaning in mind.

9. It will emerge that a hand is not a true substance for Kant, since it may itself cease to be if there is a certain derangement of flesh and bone. So, my example does not illustrate (1A). It is *compatible* with (1A), however, provided the ceasing to be of the fist is an alteration not only in the hand but also in substances composing the hand.

10. I so call it because Allison (*Kant's Trancendental Idealism*, p. 201) refers to the central contention of the argument as the Backdrop Thesis.

11. The phrase is Allison's (ibid., p. 208). Allison cites W.H. Walsh, *Kant's Criticism of Metaphysics* (Chicago: University of Chicago Press, 1975), pp. 129–35, for a similar argument.

12. Bennett also follows this strategy in section 47 of *Kant's Analytic*, but with different results.

13. Bennett (ibid., p. 199) denies that from the thesis that all happenings

are alterations (which is tantamount to 1A′ given other things Bennett says) it follows that there are any substances$_2$. But this conclusion *does* follow with the help of three additional premises: that all alterations are alterations of substances$_1$ (which Bennett calls a truism on p. 187), that all substances$_1$ are substances$_2$ (which Bennett grants for the sake of argument on p. 199 and which I demonstrate below), and that there are happenings (which Bennett would not deny).

14. D.P. Dryer, *Kant's Solution for Verification in Metaphysics* (London: Allen & Unwin, 1966). Dryer concedes to Kant the principle that all change is alteration (pp. 351, 354–55) and regards as analytic the principle that only substances$_1$ alter (p. 348). (Dryer uses "change" where Kemp Smith has "alteration" and "thing" where I have "substance$_1$." In his terminology, therefore, the two principles just mentioned are expressed by "every event is a change" and "only things change".) These principles entail that all change is alteration of something permanent, as I show in the text. But Dryer claims that Kant can establish only that all change is alteration of something relatively lasting, not that all change is alteration of something absolutely permanent (pp. 367–68).

15. I often encounter the suggestion that Kant's demand for permanent substances is the result of an illicit quantifier shift: from 'every change is an alteration of some underlying substance$_1$,' to 'there is a substance$_1$ that underlies all changes'. (See, e.g., Walsh, *Kant's Criticism of Metaphysics*, pp. 129–30.) But this move is both too weak and too strong for the purpose of securing what Kant wants. It is too weak because it does not imply that there is a permanent substance unless we add that changes are happening at all times; it is too strong because it implies a kind of monism—for example, that the same substance underlies the melting of a snowflake in Königsberg and the opening of a rosebud in Paris.

16. Note that properties are evidently being conceived of here as so-called "particularized properties" or tropes.

17. I offered a similar argument for the same conclusion in "Substance, Matter, and the First Analogy." However, that argument took the division of substance$_1$ and property to be exhaustive; the argument I now offer allows for the additional category of modes.

The argument is easily seen to imply that every substance$_1$ is a substance$_2$. Jim O'Shea has objected in conversation that Kant would surely classify a stone as a substance$_1$ (see *Metaphysical Foundations*, pp. 49–50), yet a stone can be shattered and so is presumably not a substance$_2$. I think Kant may simply have fallen into inconsistency here. To be consistent, he should maintain either (i) that compound objects are modes, not substances$_1$, or (ii) that compound objects survive fragmentation as scattered objects. See "Substance, Matter, and the First Analogy" for more on these alternatives.

18. We do not want to make 1A″ trivially true by saying that when one thing x (e.g., an ice cube in London) goes out of existence, any other thing y (e.g., a pyramid in Egypt) alters by becoming such that x no longer exists. We could rule out this cheap way of getting 1A″ by stipulating that the alteration not be a mere "Cambridge" alteration, but rather that it consist in the gain or loss of an intrinsic property (or of a relation that is intrinsic to its relata). But actually there is no need of this stipulation. When I say that x's change *is* an alteration in y, I imply that *necessarily*, x changes only if y alters. This will not be true if x and y are "distinct existences" such as the ice cube and the pyramid. Bennett makes a similar point in *Kant's Dialectic* (p. 57).

19. For another example of this structure, consider the classical cosmological argument for the existence of God (discussed in chapter 12), which admits the possibility of a beginningless causal series but insists that the entire series be grounded in a being outside it. Note that groundedness excludes circles.

20. For the contrast between logical fictions and supervenient entities, see chapter 1, section D. For the suggestion that the difference makes a difference to the possibility of ungroundedness, see my "Inner States and Outer Relations: Kant and the Case for Monadism," in *Doing Philosophy Historically*, edited by Peter H. Hare (Buffalo, N.Y.: Prometheus Books, 1988), pp. 231–47.

21. I am indebted here to conversations with Carl Posy.

22. The reader may recall that these are the same questions I pressed above as revealing a hole in the Backdrop Argument.

23. Dryer, *Kant's Solution,* p. 353ff.

24. Bertrand Russell, *An Inquiry into Meaning and Truth* (Baltimore: Penguin Books, 1962; first published by Allen & Unwin in 1940), pp. 153–55.

25. Arthur Melnick, *Kant's Analogies of Experience* (Chicago: University of Chicago Press, 1973), p. 75. I have recast Melnick's argument somewhat.

26. Bennett, *Kant's Analytic*, p. 189ff.

27. In conversation. For relevant discussion, see Felicia Ackerman, "How Does Ontology Supervene on What There Is?" in *Supervenience: New Essays*, edited by Elias E. Savellos and Umit D. Yalçin, (Cambridge: Cambridge University Press, 1995), pp. 264–72.

28. Still, mightn't we raise questions about how we learned the meaning of all the predicates figuring in such truths? Mustn't it be piecemeal and by ostension, rather than systematically through composition principles? In that case, how can we understand infinitely many such predicates, as we apparently do? Such questions are pressed by Donald Davidson in "Theories of Meaning and Learnable Languages," in *Inquiries into Truth and Interpretation* (Oxford: Clarendon Press, 1984), pp. 3–15.

29. Or does the principle only let us make a change in any portion of the universe an alteration of the rest, thus affording no protection against the annihilation of the whole shebang?

30. Compare the definition of substance Kant uses in the First Paralogism: "[T]hat the representation of which is the *absolute subject* of our judgments and cannot therefore be employed as determination of another thing" (A348).

31. Jonathan Bennett, *Kant's Dialectic* (Cambridge: Cambridge University Press, 1974), pp. 62–65, and *Kant's Analytic*, pp. 198–99.

32. Bennett, *Kant's Dialectic*, p. 63.

33. Ibid., p. 64.

34. A.N. Prior offers '∃F(Fx)' as a definition of 'x exists' in *Time and Modality* (Oxford: Clarendon Press, 1957), p. 31.

35. In sections F and G of chapter 12, I provide two additional ways of avoiding the contradiction—one by restricting existential generalization, the other by letting quantifiers range over the nonexistent—but both of them involve "going Meinongian" in ways that are at odds with the Kant-Frege view. They do not challenge the argument of this section that *if* the Kant-Frege view is correct, there can be no absolute existence-changes.

36. Bennett locates the problem rather in the fact that (D) contains the locution "it exists."

37. In symbols, S is an individual essence of x iff (i) □[∃y(y = x) only if Sx] and (ii) □[(y)(Sy only if y = x)].

38. For more about singularity, see appendix E. The one exception Kant admits to the rule that concepts are never singular is the concept of the *ens realissimum*—the most real of all beings, or God. This is a harmless exception in the present connection, since the *ens realissimum* is not susceptible of existence-changes. If existence-changes are only reportable using (%) and if nothing but the *ens realissimum* is a possible satisfier of (%), then there are no existence-changes.

39. I describe such an ontology in "Three Versions of the Bundle Theory,"

Philosophical Studies, 47 (1985), 95–107; it is the third of the three versions.

40. The definition occurs in section 193 of Baumgarten's *Metaphysica*; it is cited in Ermanno Bencivenga, *Kant's Copernican Revolution* (Oxford: Oxford University Press, 1987), p. 33.

41. Karl Ameriks, *Kant's Theory of Mind* (Oxford: Clarendon Press, 1987), p. 299, n. 79.

42. René Descartes, *The Principles of Philosophy*, I.51 Cottingham, vol. 1, p. 210.

Chapter 9

1. I survey and criticize four such attempts in "Four Recent Interpretations of Kant's Second Analogy," *Kant-Studien*, 64 (1973), 71–87.

2. Lewis White Beck, *Essays on Kant and Hume* (New Haven, Conn.: Yale University Press, 1978), pp. 130–64.

3. For further discussion of the differences between the two doctrines, see Jonathan Bennett, *Kant's Analytic* (Cambridge: Cambridge University Press, 1966), pp. 126–27.

4. I propose this as an alternative to the gloss Beck offers in *Essays on Kant and Hume*, p. 146.

5. In Beck's gloss of the paragraph (ibid., pp. 141–46), the ontological phenomenalism is suppressed. I do not think the result expresses what Kant had in mind when he wrote the paragraph, but I agree that it provides a better introduction to the arguments that follow.

6. "This [a succession is to be met with in appearance itself] *is only another way of saying* that I cannot arrange the apprehension otherwise than in this very succession" (A193/B238, emphasis mine).

7. Here I temporarily drop the stipulation that A and B be opposites.

8. For more on the difficulties, see my "Four Recent Interpretations."

9. See Beck, *Essays on Kant and Hume*, pp. 128 and 151–52.

10. Ibid., pp. 148–49.

11. Beck defines this as "the condition that there be no relevant difference in the modes of causal dependence of A_r on A and of B_r on B."

12. I use the all-purpose variables 'X' and 'Y' in this definition because I shall want to speak later of items other than perceptions as being irreversible$_1$. Notice that even the sequence of perceptions I obtain when I scan an unchanging object like a house is irreversible$_1$, since presumably my perceptions are caused to occur in the order they do by my own movements. If we wanted to define a sense in which the ship-perceptions but not the house-perceptions are irreversible, we could say this: a sequence $[A_r B_r]$ is irreversible$_1$, if and only if A_r and B_r are caused to occur in the order they do by A's preceding B. Irreversibility$_1$, would thus be a special case of irreversibility$_1$.

There is a tendency on the part of some commentators to think that what I am calling irreversibility$_1$, is a kind of *logical* necessity, but as far as I can see this is a confusion stemming from the modal fallacy of inferring a *necessitas consequentis* from a *necessitas consequentiae*. For examples of what I am talking about, see Graham Bird, *Kant's Theory of Knowledge* (London: Routledge & Kegan Paul, 1962), p. 155, and P.F. Strawson, *The Bounds of Sense* (London: Methuen, 1966), p. 138.

13. Thus I leave unstated the further requirement that tokens of X's type and tokens of Y's type are never simultaneous.

14. Beck, *Essays on Kant and Hume*, pp. 137–38. It is to be understood here that the definition concerns only those perceptions R' and R" that are perceptions of the same object by the same subject on the same occasion. Thus, the sequence [glimpse of egg unbroken, glimpse of egg scrambled] may count as

irreversible$_2$, even though I see a scrambled egg today and an unbroken egg tomorrow, or a scrambled egg in the pan and an unbroken egg in the carton, and so on. The definition may be extended to cover items other than perceptions, in which case it should be understood to concern only those states R′ and R″ that are states of the same object on the same occasion.

15. Arthur Lovejoy, "On Kant's Reply to Hume," *Archiv für Geschichte der Philosophie* (1906); reprinted in *Kant: Disputed Questions*, edited by Moltke S. Gram (Chicago: Quadrangle Books, 1967), pp. 284–308, at p. 303. This is not the same, incidentally, as what Strawson calls "a *non sequitur* of numbing grossness" (*Bounds of Sense*, p. 137). To put it in a nutshell, the fallacy discerned by Strawson is "$[A_rB_r]$ is irreversible$_{1'}$; therefore, $[AB]$ is irreversible$_1$," whereas that discerned by Lovejoy is "$[A_rB_r]$ is irreversible$_{1'}$; therefore, $[A_rB_r]$ is irreversible$_3$."

In the case of each critic, however, matters are actually a bit more complicated than this. Strawson says Kant's fallacy involves not only a shift in the *application* of 'irreversible' (Strawson's term is 'necessary'), but also a shift in its *sense* (from conceptual to causal necessity). But if there is a shift in sense, it is only the shift from irreversibility$_{1'}$ to irreversibility$_1$, which is *not* a shift from conceptual to causal necessity, since irreversibility$_{1'}$ and irreversibility$_1$ are *both* species of causal necessity. (On this point, see my "Four Recent Interpretations," p. 82.)

To come to Lovejoy, it is not clear that what he means by 'irreversible' involves causation in the way irreversibility$_{1'}$ does, but it *is* clear that the fallacy he blames on Kant consists in supposing that what holds of perceptions on one occasion holds of them on all, rather than in supposing (as in Strawson's fallacy) that what holds of perceptions holds of their objects.

16. Beck, *Essays on Kant and Hume*, p. 138.

17. Ibid., p. 148, n. 3.

18. Premises 2 and 4 support 3, 5 shows how the conclusion is applicable against Hume, and 6 follows from earlier steps.

19. Arthur Schopenhauer, *On the Fourfold Root of the Principle of Sufficient Reason*, translated by E.F.J. Payne (La Salle, Ill.: Open Court, 1974), pp. 126–29.

20. More accurately, in every sequence of opposites that is known to occur, the first member causes (and thus is always followed by) the second.

21. Note, however, that the qualification is not authorized by Beck's premises as now formulated. Premises 3(ii) and 7 entail that if [AB] is an event known to have occurred, then A is (and does not merely contain) a cause of B. To authorize the qualification in the conclusion, 3(ii) would have to carry a similar qualification, requiring irreversibility not of [AB], but of [XB] for some X contained in A.

22. Kant's point in this paragraph [contra H.J. Paton, *Kant's Metaphysic of Experience* (London: Allen & Unwin, 1936), vol. 2, p. 284] is not merely that there is never a temporal gap between cause and effect; it is that cause and effect are often fully simultaneous. This calls for a revision in the schema of causation, which should now run as follows: whenever a token of X's type occurs, a token of Y's type occurs at the same time or immediately afterward.

23. Beck addresses this point in a footnote (*Essays on Kant and Hume*, p. 149, n. 4). He says that until it is extended in the Third Analogy, Kant's model of causation is Leibnizian (immanent?), not Humean (transeunt?). However, it seems to me that the examples of the ball and the stove contradict this.

24. On this point, see Arthur Melnick, *Kant's Analogies of Experience* (Chicago: University of Chicago Press, 1973), pp. 98–100.

25. More accurately, I must know something that, together with premise 7, implies this.

26. Lovejoy, "On Kant's Reply to Hume," p. 297.

27. Ibid.

28. Beck, *Essays on Kant and Hume*, p. 148.

29. Ibid., p. 139.

30. This proposal is suggested by what Beck says (ibid., pp. 139–40), though he is there discussing point (ii) rather than point (i). Note that we are not yet saying that something caused the apple to fall, as 3(ii)' would require.

31. This much Kant accepts, too:

> The accepted view is that only through the perception and comparison of events repeatedly following in a uniform manner upon preceding appearances are we enabled to discover a rule according to which certain events always follow upon certain appearances. (A195/B240)

What he rejects is the idea that the concept of causation and the principle of the Second Analogy are derived empirically.

32. What threatens here is a regress and not, as in the apple example, a circle, since the causal connections on which knowledge of a given event E depends may be connections between events of types other than E.

33. Kant occasionally seems to say that not even the order of two *representations* can be known without appeal to causation (e.g., at A201/B246). I suspect that such passages simply reflect his confusing tendency (for which his ontological phenomenalism is responsible) to use the terms "appearance" and "representation" interchangeably. See Bennett (*Kant's Analytic*, pp. 224–28), however, for an interesting argument that takes the passages at face value.

34. The point is significant, for Kant evidently thought that mental events were subject to the Second Analogy no less than physical events. For evidence bearing on this, see A.C. Ewing, *Kant's Treatment of Causality* (London: Kegan Paul, 1924), pp. 131–42.

35. This is not to say that effects never outlast their causes, but only that they cannot gain or lose the status of having been caused.

36. "That there may be inhabitants in the moon, although no one has ever perceived them, must certainly be admitted. This, however, only means that in the possible advance of experience we may encounter them" (A493/B521). On the next page Kant goes further, saying that in the advance of experience we *must* encounter them, but this does not affect the point I am about to make.

37. Recall in this connection what was said in chapter 1, section E, about mind-dependence versus knowledge-dependence.

Chapter 10

1. See P.F. Strawson, *The Bounds of Sense* (London: Methuen, 1966), p. 16, where a "Principle of Significance" is articulated and attributed to Kant, and part 4, section 7 (esp. p. 264), where Kant's own metaphysics of transcendental idealism is charged with running afoul of this principle. And Jonathan Bennett says this: "[A]part from those licensed by its definition, every sentence containing 'noumenon' is unintelligible" [*Kant's Analytic* (Cambridge: Cambridge University Press, 1966), p. 24].

2. J.N. Findlay, *Kant and the Transcendental Object* (Oxford: Clarendon Press, 1981), p. 34.

3. See Wilfrid Sellars, *Science and Metaphysics: Variations on Kantian Themes* (London: Routledge & Kegan Paul, 1968), p. 41, for the suggestion that "there cannot be representeds without representings" is an improvement on Kant's "[there cannot be] appearance without anything that appears" (Bxxvi–xxvii).

4. I have taken this translation of Jacobi's remark from Hoke Robinson's "Two Perspectives on Kant's Appearances and Things in Themselves," *Journal of the History of Philosophy*, 32 (1994), 411–441, at p. 415.

5. Compare A181/B224: "The category expresses a function which is restricted by no sensible condition. . . ." The schema would be a restricting condition.

6. H.E. Matthews, "Strawson on Transcendental Idealism," *Philosophical Quarterly*, 19 (1969), 204–20; reprinted in *Kant on Pure Reason*, edited by Ralph C.S. Walker (Oxford: Oxford University Press, 1982), pp. 132–49. The quoted passage occurs on page 137 in Walker.

7. For this diagnosis of the "bare particular" fallacy, see P.T. Geach, *Truth, Love, and Immortality: An Introduction to McTaggart's Philosophy* (Berkeley: University of California Press, 1979), pp. 45–47.

8. Nelson Goodman, *Ways of Worldmaking* (Indianapolis, Ind.: Bobbs-Merrill, 1978), p. 3.

9. Ibid., p. 6.

10. George Berkeley, *Principles of Human Knowledge*, edited by Kenneth Winkler (Indianapolis, Ind.: Hackett, 1982), sec. 23.

11. George Berkeley, *Three Dialogues Between Hylas and Philonous*, edited by Robert M. Adams (Indianapolis, Ind.: Hackett, 1979), dialogue I.

12. A.N. Prior, "Berkeley in Logical Form," *Theoria*, 21 (1955), 117–22.

13. Read 'Cx' (with 'C' prefixed to a term or variable) as 'one conceives of x'; read 'Cp' (with 'C' prefixed to an entire formula) as 'one conceives it to be the case that p'. For a uniform reading of 'C', we could define 'Cx' as '∃F[C(Fx)]'; that is, one conceives some fact to hold of x.

14. Hilary Putnam, *Realism and Reason* (Cambridge: Cambridge University Press, 1983), p. 45; see also his *Meaning and the Moral Sciences* (London: Routledge & Kegan Paul, 1978), pp. 131–33.

15. Alternatively, one could give a one-world rendition of the argument with the first premise stated as follows: a thing has, in itself, the property P only if P is not theory-relative. For present purposes it does not matter whether we give the argument a one-world or a two-worlds reading.

16. C.I. Lewis, *Mind and the World Order* (New York: Dover, 1956; reprint of 1929 edition by Scribner's), p. 168.

17. Max Born, "Physical Reality," *Philosophical Quarterly*, 3 (1953), 139–49.

18. Putnam, *Meaning and the Moral Sciences*, p. 132.

19. See Jaegwon Kim, "Concepts of Supervenience," *Philosophy and Phenomenological Research*, 45 (1984), 153–76.

20. I have made the case for the self-refuting character of the "no-difference" principle in greater detail in "Does Truth Supervene on Evidence?" in *Supervenience: New Essays*, edited by Elias E. Savellos and Umit D. Yalçin (Cambridge: Cambridge University Press, 1995), pp. 306–15.

21. Michael Devitt, *Realism and Truth* (Princeton, N.J.: Princeton University Press, 1984), p. 59.

22. Graham Bird, *Kant's Theory of Knowledge* (London: Routledge & Kegan Paul, 1962), p. 37; most of Bird's chapter 3 is relevant to this theme.

23. D.P. Dryer, *Kant's Solution for Verification in Metaphysics* (London: Allen & Unwin, 1966), ch. 11, sec. vi; the quoted sentences are from p. 513.

24. Matthews, "Strawson on Transcendental Idealism," p. 137.

25. H.J. Paton, *Kant's Metaphysic of Experience* (London: Allen & Unwin, 1970; reprint of 1936 edition), vol. 1, p. 61 and elsewhere; L.W. Beck, *A Commentary on Kant's Critique of Practical Reason* (Chicago: The University of Chicago Press, 1960); Gerold Prauss, *Kant und das Problem der Dinge an Sich* (Bonn: Grundmann, 1974), ch. 2; Henry E. Allison, *Kant's Transcendental Idealism: An Interpretation and Defense* (New Haven, Conn.: Yale University Press, 1983), which I discuss further below. For a discussion and critique of Prauss's contention that the phrase *Ding an sich selbst* in Kant should be regarded as a contraction of *Ding an sich selbst betrachtet*—'thing *considered* in

itself'—see Richard Aquila, "Things in Themselves: Intentionality and Reality in Kant," *Archiv für Geschichte der Philosophie*, 61 (1979), 293–307. For a survey of some of some of the rest of the debate on one world versus two, see Karl Ameriks, "Recent Work on Kant's Theoretical Philosophy," *American Philosophical Quarterly*, 19 (1982), 1–24.

26. John Locke, *Essay Concerning Human Understanding*, edited by Peter H. Nidditch (Oxford: Oxford University Press, 1975), II.8.viii.

27. Berkeley, *Three Dialogues Between Hylas and Philonous*, dialogue I.

28. "This predicate [spatiality] can be ascribed to things only in so far as they appear to us, that is, only to objects of sensibility" (A27/B43).

29. I should mention that according to Allison, the distinction between things in themselves and appearances may be drawn at two levels. At the empirical level, what we have is the distinction between physical items and mental items. At the transcendental level, which is what concerns us here,

> the distinction between appearances and things in themselves refers primarily to two distinct ways in which things (empirical objects) can be 'considered': either in relation to the subjective conditions of human sensibility (space and time), and thus as they 'appear,' or independently of these conditions, and thus as they are 'in themselves'.
> (Allison, *Kant's Transcendental Idealism*, p. 8)

30. 'These same things': see ibid., pp. 25 and 60, for confirmation.

31. Devitt, *Realism and Truth*, pp. 59–60. He explains objectivity in terms of independence of human cognition on page 13.

32. David Lewis, *On the Plurality of Worlds* (Oxford: Blackwell, 1986), pp. 200–4. Lewis is especially concerned with modifiers such as 'at time t' and 'in world w'.

33. Lewis thinks temporal modifiers—as in 'x is red on Monday and green on Tuesday'—can remove contradictions only in this first way. In other words, he thinks the statement just given must be taken as equivalent to 'the Monday segment of x is red and the Tuesday segment of x is green'. He argues analogously that transworld variation in properties must be understood in terms of counterpart theory.

34. For an account of objective relativism, see Arthur Murphy's essays on this topic in *Reason and the Common Good: Selected Essays of Arthur E. Murphy*, edited by W.H. Hay and M.G. Singer (Englewood Cliffs, N.J.: Prentice-Hall, 1963). For discussion of a view similar to objective relativism, see C.D. Broad's discussion of the "Theory of Multiple Inherence" in *Mind and Its Place in Nature* (London: Routledge & Kegan Paul, 1925), p. 160ff. Incidentally, the three views Broad discusses there—the Sensum Theory, the Multiple Relation Theory of Appearing, and the Theory of Multiple Inherence—may be regarded as instances (though not the only possible ones) of Lewis's three models as applied to perceptual situations.

35. See Lewis, *On the Plurality of Worlds*, p. 53, for the contention that "relativized properties" are really relations.

36. Ibid., p. 204.

37. As Allison has suggested to me in correspondence.

38. Allison, *Kant's Transcendental Idealism*, p. 5.

39. Allison (ibid., p. 5) faults Prichard and Strawson for foisting such an "illusion thesis" on Kant—or rather, for attributing to Kant a view that incurs the illusion thesis as one of two dilemmatic horns.

40. Suggestive in this connection are Thomas Reid's views on the difference between primary and secondary qualities as set forth in *Essays on the Intellectual Powers of Man*, edited by Baruch Brody (Cambridge, Mass.: MIT Press, 1969; originally published in 1785), essay II, ch. 17. Reid writes:

[O]ur senses give us a direct and a distinct notion of the primary qualities [including extension and figure], and inform us what they are in
themselves: but of the secondary qualities, our senses give us only a
relative and obscure notion. They inform us only, that they are qualities that affect us in a certain manner. . . .

A relative notion of a thing, is, strictly speaking, no notion of the
thing at all, but only of some relation which it bears to something
else. . . .

Our notion of primary qualities is not of this kind; we know what
they are, and not barely what relation they bear to something else.
(pp. 252–54)

41. For further discussion of the Amphiboly section, see my "Inner States
and Outer Relations: Kant and the Case for Monadism," in *Doing Philosophy
Historically*, edited by Peter H. Hare (Buffalo, N.Y.: Prometheus Books, 1988),
pp. 231–47. I raise the question there of whether it is Kant's view that Leibniz's
principles do definitely hold for things in themselves (as he sometimes says),
or only that they *would* hold for noumena in the positive sense, it being problematic whether things in themselves are noumena in that sense. (They are not
noumena in the positive sense for us, but may be so for other beings.) If the
Leibnizian principles do not definitely hold for things in themselves, my argument in the text would have to be recast somewhat. The difficulty presented
for the one-world view would be this: principles that definitely fail for phenomena (e.g., the identity of indiscernibles) may, for all we know, hold of
things in themselves.

42. Elsewhere Kant lists additional principles that hold for things in
themselves but not for appearances. In his solution to the Mathematical
Antinomies, he says that the principle 'if the conditioned is given, the entire
series of its conditions is likewise given [i.e., *geben* and not just *aufgegeben*,
set as a task]' is true when we are dealing with things in themselves, but not
when we are dealing with appearances. See A497–99/B525–27. In section
13 of the *Prolegomena* he says, "That is to say, the part is possible only
through the whole, which is never the case with things in themselves, as objects of the mere understanding, but which may well be the case with mere
appearances."

43. To be sure, the doctrine of "relative identity" (x and y are the same F,
but not the same G) has found favor in some quarters recently, but there is really nothing to recommend it. For criticisms, see John Perry, "The Same F,"
The Philosophical Review, 79 (1970), 181–200, and David Wiggins, *Sameness
and Substance* (Cambridge, Mass.: Harvard University Press, 1980), ch. 1.

44. The following sentence from A379 might be cited as showing that Kant
approved of relative identity: "Though the 'I', as represented through inner
sense in time, and objects in space outside me, are specifically quite distinct
appearances, they are not for that reason thought as being different things."
Kant's use of the pronoun "they" to refer back to the 'I' of inner sense and to
spatial objects admittedly suggests relative identity. As the very next sentence
makes clear, however, his point can also be expressed by saying that diverse
phenomena can have the same noumenal ground—not that they *are* the same
as noumena.

45. For the moment I equate 'nonrelational' with 'intrinsic', but I show below that there are senses of these terms in which a property that is nonrelational may still fail to be intrinsic.

46. More accurately, knowledge of things as they appear would be knowledge of a subclass of relational facts about objects—facts about how they are

related *to us*. More needs to be said about how knowledge of the relations of objects to objects other than us would fit into this scheme.

47. Lewis, *Mind and the World Order*, pp. 154–94.

48. John Stuart Mill, *An Examination of Sir William Hamilton's Philosophy* (Boston: Spencer, 1865), vol. 1, p. 16ff.; Dryer, *Kant's Solution*, ch. 11, sec. vi, esp. pp. 513–14; Hilary Putnam, *Reason, Truth, and History* (Cambridge: Cambridge University Press, 1981), p. 59ff. A conception of the in itself as the intrinsic was also discussed by Daniel Warren in "Things in Themselves and in Relation to Others," a paper presented at Brown University in 1992. Allison's one-world interpretation, which was criticized in the last section, might also be developed in this direction, but as elaborated by Allison it seems to me to lie within a different camp. To cite one difference, Allison's view implies that indiscernible items may be numerically distinct considered in relation to us but numerically identical considered in themselves, while the view I discuss in this section has no such implication.

49. Mill, *An Examination of Sir William Hamilton's Philosophy*, vol. 1, p. 16.

50. Ibid., p. 18.

51. Putnam, *Reason, Truth, and History*, p. 59.

52. Ibid., p. 61. On page 63 he equates 'all properties are secondary' with 'all properties are Powers' and adds that for Kant the powers are ascribed to the noumenal world *as a whole*. That is why 'all properties are secondary' is only a first approximation to Kant's view.

53. Here is how Locke defines secondary qualities in the *Essay Concerning Human Understanding*, II.viii.10: they are "[s]uch *Qualities*, which in truth are nothing in the Objects themselves, but Powers to produce various Sensations in us by their *primary Qualities, i.e.* by the Bulk, Figure, Texture, and Motion of their insensible parts."

54. Hilary Putnam, *The Many Faces of Realism* (La Salle, Ill.: Open Court, 1987), p. 9; see also p. 24.

55. This is actually Moore's account of when a kind of *value* is intrinsic, but it is readily extendible to properties in general. See G.E. Moore, "The Conception of Intrinsic Value," in *Philosophical Studies* (Totowa, N.J.: Littlefield, Adams, 1968; first published in London by Routledge & Kegan Paul in 1922), pp. 253–75, at p. 265. David Lewis has more recently offered a similar test for intrinsic properties: an intrinsic property is one that can never differ between two duplicates. See his *On the Plurality of Worlds*, pp. 59–63.

56. Such, at any rate, is the import of Putnam's slogan "*all* properties are secondary." On the other hand, if the view he wishes to attribute to Kant is only that "everything we say" about an object is dispositional in form, it is closer to Mill's "Relativity of Knowledge" and to the view discussed by some contemporary philosophers under the label "Global Response-Dependence." See Philip Pettit, "Realism and Response-Dependence," *Mind*, 100 (1991), 587–626, or Michael Smith and Daniel Stoljar, "Global Response-Dependence and Noumenal Realism," manuscript in preparation.

57. I myself advocate a limited version of this thesis, namely, that things never differ in their dispositions without differing in their categorical properties. For my reasons, along with an application of the limited thesis to Putnam's Kant, see my "Putnam, Kant, and Secondary Qualities," *Philosophical Papers*, 24 (1995), 83–109, esp. 90–92 and 102–3.

58. Locke, *Essay Concerning Human Understanding*, II.viii.10.

59. In both of the passages, Kant uses 'thing in general' as a synonym for 'thing in itself'. For other instances of this practice, see Bxxvii and A34–35/B51.

60. The quoted sentence occurs as part of Kant's reconstruction of a Leibnizian argument for monadism. In the further development of the argument, it is premised that representations (e.g., sensations) are examples *par excellence* of "inner determinations." For a good discussion of the senses in which sensations are and are not purely "inner" for Kant, see Ralf Meerbote, "Kant's Functionalism," in *Historical Foundations of Cognitive Science*, edited by J.C. Smith (Dordrecht: Kluwer Academic Publishers, 1990), pp. 161–87.

61. See Reid's *Essays on the Intellectual Powers of Man*, essay II, ch. 17.

62. Does the alternative first premise thereby return us to the thesis of Putnam's Kant, that all properties of external things are dispositions to affect us? No, for two reasons. In the first place, Kant's premise allows thing-thing relations, whereas Putnam's thesis allows only thing-us relations. In the second place, Putnam's thesis is about external things in the sense of *noumena*, whereas Kant's premise is about *objects of outer sense*. As I show below, it is the very point of the argument to distinguish objects of outer sense from noumena.

63. Here is a reminder that Kant does indeed hold the doctrine about appearances I just attributed to him:

> It is a proposition which must indeed sound strange, that a thing can exist only in the representation of it, but in this case, the objection falls, inasmuch as the things with which we are here concerned are not things in themselves, but appearances only, that is, representations. (A375n.)

See also A490/B518.

64. Immanuel Kant, *Metaphysical Foundations of Natural Science*, translated by James Ellington (Indianapolis, Ind.: Bobbs-Merrill, 1970), p. 105.

65. Letter to Hellwag, January 3, 1791, in Arnulf Zweig, ed., *Kant: Philosophical Correspondence, 1759–99* (Chicago: University of Chicago Press, 1967), p. 170.

66. Findlay, *Kant and the Transcendental Object*, p. 34.

67. Paton, *Kant's Metaphysic of Experience*, vol. 2, p. 417.

68. C.D. Broad, *Kant: An Introduction* (Cambridge: Cambridge University Press, 1978), pp. 23–27. There is an intermediate alternative that Broad does not consider: the difference between the perceptual objects is due to a difference in the underlying sensory states, but this difference in turn is not due to any difference in foreign things in themselves. I suspect, however, that Broad would find this just as incredible as the first alternative.

69. Findlay, *Kant and the Transcendental Object*, pp. 92–93.

70. Ludwig Wittgenstein, *Tractatus Logico-Philosophicus*, translated by D.F. Pears and B.F. McGuinness (London: Routledge & Kegan Paul, 1961), prop. 4.014.

71. Isomorphism may even be an aspect of Kant's philosophy that requires two orders in a stronger sense than I allowed at the end of section D. That is to say, it may be a doctrine that goes better with a conception of appearances as supervenient entities than with a conception of them as virtual objects.

72. Bertrand Russell, *The Analysis of Matter* (London: Kegan Paul, Trench, Trubner, 1927).

73. M.H.A. Newman raised his difficulty in "Mr. Russell's 'Causal Theory of Perception'," *Mind*, 37 (1928), 138–48. The difficulty was rediscovered in an apparently independent article in *Mind* almost thirty years later: Hiram J. McLendon, "Uses of Similarity of Structure in Contemporary Philosophy," *Mind*, 64 (1955), 79–95. Newman's criticism is summarized and endorsed in William Demopoulos and Michael Friedman, "The Concept of Structure in

The Analysis of Matter," in *Minnesota Studies in the Philosophy of Science*, vol. 12, edited by C. Wade Savage and C. Anthony Anderson (Minneapolis: University of Minnesota Press, 1989), pp. 183–89. Demopoulos and Friedman connect the Newman problem with the "model-theoretic argument against metaphysical realism" advanced by Hilary Putnam.

74. To this McLendon added that since any material plenum is divisible into arbitrarily many parts, there is guaranteed to be, for any such plenum, a set of parts to match the cardinality of any given set.

75. Later on, Russell held that "compresence" is a relation among our percepts that is also instantiated in the physical world. See his *Human Knowledge: Its Scope and Limits* (New York: Simon and Schuster, 1948), pp. 294ff.

76. Failing this, we could no longer claim isomorphism, but we could still claim that how things are with the noumenal world as a whole determines how things are with the phenomenal world as a whole. This could be understood as a case of what Jaegwon Kim calls "uncoordinated multiple domain supervenience." See his "Supervenience for Multiple Domains," in *Supervenience and Mind* (Cambridge: Cambridge University Press, 1993), pp. 109–30, esp. pp. 113 and 121–22.

77. Like McTaggart's C-series, perhaps; see J.M.E. McTaggart, *The Nature of Existence* (Cambridge: Cambridge University Press, 1927), vol. 2, ch. 33, secs. 347–51.

78. Demopoulos and Friedman ("The Concept of Structure") claim that for every "fictitious relation" (Newman's term for a relation specified only by giving its extension), there is a "real relation" co-extensive with it.

79. For more on the distinction between natural and unnatural properties and relations, see Lewis, *On the Plurality of Worlds*, pp. 59–69, and Eli Hirsch, *Dividing Reality* (Oxford: Oxford University Press, 1993).

80. We could also define a self-contained relation as a relation that is either internal or external in the senses of these terms defined by Lewis on page 62 of *On the Plurality of Worlds*: such a relation supervenes either on the intrinsic natures of the relata taken separately (as does similarity in color) or on the intrinsic nature of the composite of the relata taken together (as does distance).

81. Jill Vance Buroker, *Space and Incongruence* (Dordrecht: Reidel, 1981), pp. 82–83.

82. In fairness to Buroker, I should note that she formulates the Leibnizian "Correspondence Principle" that she thinks is falsified by incongruent counterparts as follows: "The properties and relations of phenomena correspond in an exact way with the properties and relations of noumena" (ibid., p. 82). It sounds as though this principle, with its mention of properties as well as relations, has our auxiliary assumption built into it. In that case, it is stronger than isomorphism and is indeed incompatible with Kantian principles.

83. What about the converse of our lemma, that if phenomena *differ* qualitatively, so must the underlying noumena? That much is a consequence of the idea, required by the theory of virtual objects and the theory of supervenient objects alike, that every feature of a phenomenon derives from features of an underlying noumenon.

84. The notion of "thoroughgoing" isomorphism goes beyond what was defined above. Roughly, it requires that for every relation in either domain there be a relation in the other such that the domains are isomorphic with respect to the two relations. For a more exact definition, see appendix M.

85. See the Amphiboly section of the *Critique* and my discussion in chapter 6 of the Second Antinomy. That there are no phenomenal simples is reaffirmed in the *Metaphysical Foundations of Natural Science*, ch. 2, prop. 4

(p. 49 in Ellington): "Matter is divisible to infinity, and indeed into parts each of which is again matter."

86. Findlay (*Kant and the Transcendental Object*, p. 38) says that Kant's chief reason for regarding things in space and time as phenomenal is that they do not obey the same ontological laws as noumena—for example, they violate the principle that composites require simples. Ironically, this turns out to be a reason for denying, or at least limiting, the isomorphism Findlay attributes to Kant.

87. This would be reminiscent of the Leibnizian idea that no single monad well-founds any phenomenon; only infinite aggregates of monads do that.

88. *Dissertation on the Form and Principles of the Sensible and Intelligible Worlds*, sec. 2, paragraph 4; the translation of the sentence is from Immanuel Kant, *Kant's Inaugural Dissertation and Early Writings on Space*, translated by John Handyside (Chicago: Open Court, 1929).

89. Findlay, *Kant and the Transcendental Object*, pp. 84–85.

90. H.W.B. Joseph, "A Comparison of Kant's Idealism with that of Berkeley," *Proceedings of the British Academy* (1929), 213–34; reprinted in *The Real in the Ideal*, edited by R.C.S. Walker (New York: Garland, 1989), pp. 47–68. The quotation is taken from page 63 in Walker.

91. The passage continues as follows: ". . . and which can be thought neither as quantity nor as reality nor as substance, etc. (because these concepts always require sensible forms in which they determine an object)." Since the "etc." must presumably cover the category of causation, the second half of the passage may seem to take back the first. That constitutes part of the problem I discuss in this section.

92. See Robinson, "Two Perspectives," for discussion and further references. Robinson also mentions the double-aspect theory as providing a fifth answer—the very same objects are causes qua phenomena but not qua noumena. For critical discussion of one possible development of this fifth answer, see appendix L.

93. Letter of June 20, 1797, pp. 227–31 in Zweig, *Philosophical Correspondence*.

94. H.A. Prichard, *Kant's Theory of Knowledge* (Oxford: Clarendon Press, 1909), pp. 30–32. Prichard's reasoning here is not entirely clear, but he evidently holds that the cause of our sensations must, on Kantian principles, be a metaphysical thing in itself rather than a physical body.

95. Erich Adickes, *Kants Lehre von der doppelten Affektion unseres Ich* (Tübingen: Mohr, 1929). There is a brief English summary of Adickes's view in T.D. Weldon, *Kant's Critique of Pure Reason* (Oxford: Clarendon Press, 1958; 2nd ed.), pp. 252–53, and a version of the double affection theory along Adickes's lines is advocated by Findlay in *Kant and the Transcendental Object*, ch. 8. Also suggestive in this connection is Moltke S. Gram, *The Transcendental Turn* (Gainesville: University of Florida Press, 1984), ch. 1.

96. This option works better if the ideality of time does not take the radical form discussed in chapter 5.

97. Jaegwon Kim, "Epiphenomenal and Supervenient Causation," *Midwest Studies in Philosophy*, vol. 9, edited by Peter A. French, Theodore E. Uehling, Jr., and Howard K. Wettstein (Minneapolis: University of Minnesota Press, 1984), pp. 257–70; reprinted in his *Supervenience and Mind*, pp. 92–108.

98. We are dealing now with a version of the old question of whether emergents must be epiphenomenal. The twist is that the emergents are ontological emergents, not just nomological emergents.

99. Actually, I sometimes wonder whether phenomenal-to-phenomenal causation, if understood in the second or third of the ways, is not just as much a matter of causation by courtesy as is phenomenal-to-noumenal causation.

100. Locke, *Essay Concerning Human Understanding*, II.viii.10.

101. See ibid., II.viii.15.

102. Berkeley, *Three Dialogues Between Hylas and Philonous*, p. 22 (First Dialogue).

103. I think it likely that in the passage I have just quoted, Berkeley is defining secondary qualities simply by enumerating them, letting it then be a further doctrine about them that they exist only in the mind. I nonetheless speak in what follows of existence in the mind as the Berkeleyan "meaning" of 'secondary'. That is the meaning of 'secondary' generally associated with Berkeley and, since Berkeley's writings, perhaps the most common meaning of the term. On the latter point, see Reginald Jackson, "Locke's Distinction Between Primary and Secondary Qualities," *Mind*, 38 (1929); reprinted in *Locke and Berkeley*, edited by C.B. Martin and D.M. Armstrong (Notre Dame, Ind.: University of Notre Dame Press, 1968), pp. 53–77. Writing in 1929, Jackson noted that the term 'secondary quality' was by then generally used to refer to mind-dependent sensations, not to Lockean powers. [The difference in terminology between Locke and Berkeley should not be allowed to obscure substantive points of agreement between them—e.g., that color as sensed ("color as idea," Locke would say) exists only in the mind.]

104. The difference between Kant and Berkeley that I am about to discuss is well brought out by Margaret Wilson, "The Phenomenalisms of Berkeley and Kant," in *Self and Nature in Kant's Philosophy*, edited by Allen W. Wood (Ithaca, N.Y.: Cornell University Press, 1984), pp. 157–73, and Findlay, *Kant and the Transcendental Object*, ch. 8.

105. Having said this, I must point out that there are also passages in Kant seemingly at odds with a conception of matter wholly in terms of extension and its modes. In the Anticipations of Perception (A166–76/B207–18), he ascribes *intensive magnitude* both to sensations and to whatever it is in external objects that causes sensations. He defines intensive magnitudes simply as magnitudes whose possible values form a continuum; he does not define them as nonextensive. However, it seems to be a further doctrine of Kant's that intensive magnitudes are in no way reducible to extensive magnitudes. If this is so, the properties of matter cannot be limited to extension and its modes. If they are still in some sense primary, it will not be in a narrow Cartesian sense.

106. I should note that in the footnote to B69–70, Kant says things that depart from his normal line. Here he seems to be saying that redness and extension can both be ascribed to the rose, as long as we remember to ascribe them to the rose only in relation to us. Is this perhaps an anticipation of the twentieth-century doctrine of "objective relativism?"

107. J.J.C. Smart, *Philosophy and Scientific Realism* (New York: Humanities Press, 1963), pp. 72–75, and D.M. Armstrong, *Perception and the Physical World* (London: Routledge & Kegan Paul, 1961), ch. 15.

108. A version of the double affection theory along these lines is advocated in Findlay, *Kant and the Transcendental Object*, ch. 8. For further references, see note 94 above.

109. Suppose that, to avoid this difficulty, one makes the second relatum of the second round of affection an event in a phenomenal brain, rather than a noumenal event. The problem now is that brains, as phenomena, cannot be subjects of states of consciousness.

110. Wilson, "The Phenomenalisms of Berkeley and Kant," in Wood, *Self and Nature*, p. 170.

Chapter 11

1. I do not discuss here the fourth of the four Paralogisms, since it is concerned not with the nature of the self but with whether we must be skeptics

about the existence of material things. Kant's answer is that we do not have to be skeptics, provided we recognize that material things are "only a species of representations" (A370) and are therefore immediately perceived rather than problematically inferred. This section of the *Critique* provides us with one of the most explicit statements of Kant's idealism.

2. Immanuel Kant, *Lectures on Logic*, translated by J. Michael Young (Cambridge: Cambridge University Press, 1992), p. 628 (sec. 90 of the Jäsche logic).

3. Ibid.

4. For example, at A402–3 Kant says that in the First Paralogism the term 'substance' is used equivocally, but in that argument 'substance' is the major term, not the minor. And as I show below, Kant sometimes criticizes not the Paralogism itself but the usefulness of its conclusion.

5. I have eliminated one phrase from the major premise and one clause from the minor. From the major I have eliminated the phrase "That the representation of which" in favor simply of "That which." The longer phrase is unnecessary and causes nothing but confusion. The major is supposed to be true by definition, and Kant's definition of substance is simply "that which is always subject, never predicate" (A243/B301)—it is not 'that the representation of which is always subject . . . .' From the minor I have deleted the clause "and this representation of myself cannot be employed as predicate of any other thing," since this clause would be redundant if the major were true.

6. Jonathan Bennett, *Kant's Dialectic* (Cambridge: Cambridge University Press, 1974), p. 75.

7. I thus disagree with Patricia Kitcher, who dismisses the second clause in Kant's definition of substance as playing no essential role in his discussion [*Kant's Transcendental Psychology* (Oxford: Oxford University Press, 1990), p. 188]. As I see things, it is precisely through failing to demonstrate that the second clause is satisfied that the First Paralogism fails to demonstrate the substantiality of the soul.

8. Pierre Bayle, *Historical and Critical Dictionary*, translated by Richard Popkin (Indianapolis, Ind.: Bobbs-Merrill, 1965), p. 311. (The passage is from note N of article "Spinoza.")

9. Here is a possible twist on this verdict. Suppose I am absolute subject of the judgments *I* make, but not of all judgments whatever, and suppose that 'our judgments' in the major means 'one's judgments' rather than 'all judgments'. Then the minor would be true, but the major false.

10. As with other reducibility principles stated in this book (e.g., the reducibility of relations), supervenience rather than reducibility is all that is strictly required.

11. Kemp Smith's translation has "every part of it would *be* a part of the thought," but Roderick Chisholm has pointed out to me that this is a mistake. The German verb is *enthalten*.

12. William James, *The Principles of Psychology* (New York: Dover, 1950; reprint of 1890 edition), vol. 1, p. 160.

13. The critique of the usefulness of the conclusion occupies paragraphs 10–16 of the eighteen paragraphs constituting Kant's discussion of the paralogism in the A edition.

14. In the course of making this point, Kant makes the following remark:

Accordingly, the thesis that only souls . . . think would have to be given up; and we should have to fall back on the common expression that men think, that is, that the very same being which, as outer appearance, is extended, is (in itself) internally a subject, and is not composite, but is simple and thinks. (A360)

This passage may remind one of Strawson's well-known view that persons are the proper logical subjects of both P-predicates (predicates ascribing states of consciousness) and M-predicates (predicates ascribing corporeal characteristics). However, a closer look at the passage reveals that Kant is not suggesting that the same being has both sorts of predicate: he says that what thinks is noncomposite, whereas the extended is composite. Thinking things are not themselves extended, but appear as extended, just as colorless raindrops give rise to an appearance of the rainbow.

15. Some of Kant's criticism is leveled at an argument that is *not* the argument of the Paralogism as he has stated it. I have in mind the argument discussed and criticized in paragraphs 7–9 of his critique of the Paralogism in the A edition. A premise of the argument is that our representation of the I is simple in the sense that it "never contains a synthesis of the manifold" (A356). But that, Kant goes on to say, is only because this representation is so impoverished to begin with. "Nothing, indeed, can be represented that is simpler than that which is represented through the concept of a mere something" (A355). Our representation of the I is not the representation of anything composite, but from that it does not follow that it is the representation of something simple. On this issue, our representation of the I is simply indeterminate. For a good discussion of this aspect of Kant's critique, see Wilfrid Sellars, "Metaphysics and the Concept of a Person," in *Essays in Philosophy and Its History* (Dordrecht: Reidel, 1974), pp. 214–43, at pp. 236–38. I wonder myself what, if anything, Kant thought would follow if our representation of the I *were* a representation of something simple.

16. For more on the relevant sense of 'emergence,' see my "Mind-Dust or Magic? Panpsychism Versus Emergence," in *Philosophical Perspectives*, edited by James Tomberlin (Atascadero, Calif.: Ridgeview, 1990), vol. 4, pp. 215–16. Other discussions of emergence may be found in A. Beckermann, H. Flohr, and J. Kim, eds., *Emergence or Reduction?* (Berlin: De Gruyter, 1992).

17. Suppose we tried to avoid violating the unity of consciousness by saying that a composite entity thinks a thought in virtue of just *one* of its proper parts thinking it. We would have to ask in that case whether the proper part is itself simple or composite. If simple, the ultimate thinker of the thought is simple, as the paralogist maintains; if composite, there must be another thinker within it, giving rise to a plurality of thinkers within the original after all.

18. Sellars, "Metaphysics and the Concept of a Person."

19. Gottfried Wilhelm Leibniz, *Philosophical Papers and Letters*, edited and translated by Leroy E. Loemker (2nd ed.; Dordrecht: Reidel, 1969), p. 557.

20. In II.xxvii.9 of the *Essay Concerning Human Understanding*, John Locke defines a person as "a thinking intelligent being, that has reason and reflection, and can consider itself as itself, the same thinking thing in different times and places; which it does only by that consciousness, which is inseparable from thinking. . . ."

21. For discussion of possible "practical" or "forensic" dimensions of the concept of a person that I am leaving out of this account, see C. Thomas Powell, *Kant's Theory of Self-Consciousness* (Oxford: Oxford University Press, 1990), pp. 165–73.

22. David Lewis, *On the Plurality of Worlds* (Oxford: Blackwell, 1986), p. 202.

23. Roderick M. Chisholm, *Person and Object* (LaSalle, Ill.: Open Court, 1976), pp. 105–6.

24. Thomas Reid, *Essays on the Intellectual Powers of Man*, essay 6, ch. 5. Reid's statement of this principle occurs on page 625 of the edition edited by Baruch Brody (Cambridge, Mass.: MIT Press, 1969).

25. Some of Locke's remarks suggest that I am the same person as the per-

son who did A only if I have the "same consciousness" of A that that person did when doing it; other remarks suggest that I need only have consciousness of A in the sense of remembering doing it.

26. This must be stated carefully if Locke's view is not to imply (as it is indeed sometimes taken to do) the doctrine of relative identity—the doctrine, for example, that a substance s1 can be the same person as a substance s2 without being the same substance as s2. To avoid this result, instead of saying that s1 and s2 are the same person, we could say that s1 constitutes at t1 the same person that s2 constitutes at t2 (constitution being a relation that falls short of identity).

27. See, for example, Derek Parfit, *Reasons and Persons* (Oxford: Clarendon Press, 1984), esp. pp. 216–17.

28. David Hume, *A Treatise Concerning Human Nature*, I.iv.6 (p. 252 in the Selby-Bigge edition).

29. I owe this way of putting the matter to Arnold Cusmariu.

30. Roderick M. Chisholm, "On the Observability of the Self," *Philosophy and Phenomenological Research*, 30 (1969), 7–21.

31. A related problem for the 'I'-free idiom has been raised by Bernard Williams in *Descartes: The Project of Pure Inquiry* (New York: Humanities Press, 1978), pp. 95–101. See appendix O.

32. In chapter 7 I criticize Kant's Transcendental Deduction for showing only that we must use certain concepts, not that they must actually apply to anything. Here I am saying that if we must use the concept of the I, it applies to something. Exam question: Am I operating with a double standard?

33. With ellipsis filled in, the sentence reads as follows: "[The indeterminate perception expressed by 'I think'] signifies only something real that is given, given indeed to thought in general, and so not as appearance, nor as thing in itself (*noumenon*), but as something which actually exists, and which in the proposition 'I think' is denoted as such" (B422n.).

34. The identification of the transcendental self with the empirical self is advocated by Patricia Kitcher in *Kant's Transcendental Psychology*. Kitcher wants to see Kant as a contributor to cognitive science, so it is not surprising that she favors a view that makes the agent of cognitive operations empirically accessible. The identification of the noumenal self with the empirical self is the natural view for upholders of the double-aspect theory.

35. Jorge Luis Borges, "The Circular Ruins," in *A Personal Anthology*, edited by Anthony Kerrigan (New York: Grove Press, 1967), pp. 68–74.

36. Quanhua Liu has asked me whether the following passage does not show that the transcendental self is distinct from the noumenal self (as well as from the empirical self): "[I]n the synthetic original unity of apperception, I am conscious of myself, not as I appear to myself, nor as I am in myself, but only that I am" (B157). There are similar passages at B422n. and B429. I take them all simply to imply that the transcendental self knows nothing about its own intrinsic nature (= how it is in itself); it knows only that it exists and is the subject of thoughts.

37. Moreover, even if Kant were a direct realist about awareness of one's mental states, there would still be only one self. In being aware of the states of one's noumenal self, one is not being aware of a second self any more than in being aware of the qualities of an apple one is being aware of a second piece of fruit.

Chapter 12

1. "The attempt to establish the existence of a supreme being by means of the famous ontological argument of Descartes is therefore merely so much

labour and effort lost . . . " (A602/B630). The argument as Kant formulates it in the seventh paragraph of his discussion is actually Descartes's argument as supplemented with the Leibnizian premise that a supreme being is *possible*, but for the time being this addition may be ignored.

2. I find that this explication of 'real predicate' is equivalent to one also proposed by Alvin Plantinga in *God, Freedom, and Evil* (New York: Harper Torchbooks, 1974), p. 97.

3. This interpretation of 'real predicate' is confirmed by Kant's remark that a real predicate "must not be already contained in the concept" (A598/B626). According to D1 and D2, a nonreal predicate is contained in any concept whatsoever (or at least entailed by it, if not "contained" in it in the strict sense Kant uses when explicating analyticity). There is further confirmation at A600/B628: "By whatever and by however many predicates we may think a thing . . . we do not make the least addition to the thing when we further declare that this thing *is*."

4. More explicitly, the assumption here is Ex iff $\exists y(y = x)$.

5. Jerome Shaffer attributes this idea to Kant (without endorsing it himself) in "Existence, Predication, and the Ontological Argument," *Mind*, 71 (1962), 307–25. Jonathan Bennett both attributes the idea to Kant and endorses it himself in *Kant's Dialectic* (Cambridge: Cambridge University Press, 1974), pp. 228–32 (and again on p. 248, where the inclusion of 'existent' in a defininiens is said to be a "logical defect").

6. "Existence is a perfection" might be interpreted to mean that of two otherwise similar objects, one existent and the other not, the existent one is better or more perfect. This turns out to be true rather than false if existence is not a real predicate—true vacuously because of an impossible antecedent: (x)(y)(if x exists & y does not exist, then . . .).

7. Writers for whom "existence is not a predicate" has this meaning include Jonathan Bennett, *Kant's Analytic* (Cambridge: Cambridge University Press, 1966), p. 198, and *Kant's Dialectic*, pp. 62 and 231; and Georges Dicker, *Descartes: An Analytical and Historical Introduction* (Oxford: Oxford University Press, 1993), p. 163.

8. Gottlob Frege, *The Foundations of Arithmetic*, translated by J.L. Austin (Evanston, Ill.: Northwestern University Press, 1980), esp. sec. 53. Frege puts this misleadingly by saying that "existence is a property of concepts." To affirm the existence of dogs is to affirm something about the concept Dog, but not *its* existence, since you would do that even in denying that there are dogs.

9. W.V. Quine, "On What There Is," in *From a Logical Point of View* (New York: Harper Torchbooks, 1963), pp. 1–19. There are actually three ways in which formulas of existential quantification may be understood. For Frege, '∃xFx' carries commitment both to the existence of a concept and to the existence of one or more objects falling under it. For Quine, it carries commitment to the objects only; for the pure Platonists discussed in chapter 8, section J, it carries commitment to the concepts only.

10. In an earlier publication (1762), Kant gives us another clear statement of the Kant-Frege view: he tells us that instead of saying, "Regular hexagons exist in nature" we should say, "The predicates that are thought together in a hexagon belong to certain things in nature, such as honeycombs and rock crystals." This is from Immanuel Kant, *The One Possible Basis for a Demonstration of the Existence of God*, translated by Gordon Treash (Lincoln: University of Nebraska Press, 1994; reprint of the 1979 Abaris Books edition), p. 59; see also pp. 57 and 61 for similar remarks.

11. For an especially clear exposition, see Dicker, *Descartes: An Analytical and Historical Introduction*, pp. 165–67. See also Richard Cartwright, "Negative Existentials," *The Journal of Philosophy*, 57 (1960), 629–39.

12. What if instead we hold the Quinean form of the Kant-Frege view, according to which '∃xFx' carries no ontological commitment to properties or concepts? I suppose that the thing to say then is that 'there are no unicorns' is not about unicorns and not about the concept Unicorn, either: it is not *about* anything at all.

13. Here is another route from the Kant-Frege view to Kant's dictum. In standard logic, the rule of existential generalization holds without restriction: from 'Fa' we may always infer '∃xFx'. If the existential quantifier expresses existence, endorsing that inference amounts to saying that the possession of a property by anything entails its existence. The latter is another way of putting Kant's dictum that existence is not a real predicate.

14. Here is Gassendi objecting to Descartes: "In fact, however, existence is not a perfection either in God or in anything else; it is that without which no perfections can be present" [René Descartes, *The Philosophical Writings of Descartes*, translated by John Cottingham, Robert Stoothoff, and Dugald Murdoch (Cambridge: Cambridge University Press, 1984), vol. 2, p. 224].

15. Kant makes this point in the middle paragraph of three paragraphs that question the concept of an absolutely necessary being. It is not always noticed that it stands on its own as a separate criticism of the ontological argument.

16. Descartes, *Philosophical Writings*, vol. 2, p. 72.

17. I have only unpacked the description that occurs in the definiens, which is enough to make my point. Unpacking the description in the definiendum as well would yield 'there is exactly one *ens realissimum*, there is exactly one being possessing all perfections, and these beings are one and the same'.

18. Or, to build in uniqueness, 'x is the *ens realissimum* iff x possesses all perfections and nothing else does'.

19. The present point is pithily made by Russell near the end of "On Denoting" [*Logic and Knowledge*, edited by Robert C. Marsh (London: Allen & Unwin, 1956), pp. 41–56, at p. 54]. He notes that the ontological argument fails "for want of a proof of the premise 'there is one and only one entity x which is most perfect'." With a proper conditional starting point, the argument can be made to prove that "all members of the class of most perfect beings exist," but not that this class has members.

20. Charles Hartshorne, "The Logic of the Ontological Argument," in *Philosophy of Religion*, edited by William L. Rowe and William J. Wainwright (New York: Harcourt Brace Jovanovich, 1973), pp. 108–10, and "The Necessarily Existent," in *The Ontological Argument*, edited by Alvin Plantinga (Garden City, N.Y.: Anchor Books, 1965), pp. 123–35; Norman Malcolm, "Anselm's Ontological Arguments," *Philosophical Review*, 69 (1960); reprinted in Plantinga, *The Ontological Argument*, pp. 136–59; Alvin Plantinga, *The Nature of Necessity* (Oxford: Oxford University Press, 1974), ch. 10.

21. Cf. Malcolm, "Anselm's Ontological Arguments," pp. 148–56 in Plantinga, *The Ontological Argument*, and Bennett, *Kant's Dialectic*, pp. 232–33.

22. I give reason to question this further below. Assuming for the moment that it is true, however, note that it would indicate a further difference between what Kant means by "existence is not a real predicate" and what Frege means by "existence is not a predicate." Part of what Frege means by his dictum is that existence is a second-level predicate, something predicated of concepts. If existence is a second-level predicate, so presumably is necessary existence. So, for Frege, existence and necessary existence must be in the same boat.

23. Bennett, *Kant's Dialectic*, p. 234. Bennett does not quarrel with the move if the necessity is taken to be logical (as in fact it is in the version of the modal ontological argument I am presenting), but there is reason to question it in this case, too.

24. The resulting argument is similar to one presented by Peter van Inwagen in *Metaphysics* (Boulder, Co.: Westview Press, 1993), ch. 5, esp. pp. 85–91. In his version, the work done here by premises 1 and 4 is done by defining God as a being that possesses necessary existence and all other perfections essentially.

25. A parallel version of the modal ontological argument may be constructed using 'is God' as a predicate rather than 'God' as a name. The parallel version more clearly exhibits the *de re* to *de dicto* move in premise 4:

1. $\Box(x)(Gx \to \Box Ex)$
2. $\Diamond(\exists x)Gx$
3. $\Diamond(\exists x)(Gx \ \& \ \Box Ex)$ (1,2)
4. $\Box[(\exists x)(Gx \ \& \ \Box Ex) \to \Box(\exists x)(Gx \ \& \ Ex)]$
5. $\Diamond\Box(\exists x)(Gx \ \& \ Ex)$ (3,4)
6. $\Diamond\Box p \to \Box p$
7. $\Box[(\exists x)(Gx \ \& \ Ex)]$ (5,6)

Premise 4 may be derived from the auxiliary premise identified in the text—that whatever is God is essentially God, that is, $(x)[Gx \to \Box(Ex \to Gx)]$—provided the underlying modal logic permits one to infer from '$(\exists x)\Box Ex$' to '$\Box(\exists x)Ex$'. Although the inference from '$(\exists x)\Box Fx$' to '$\Box(\exists x)Fx$' is questionable in general, there seems nothing wrong with it in the special case where 'F' stands for existence.

26. See J.N. Findlay, "Can God's Existence Be Disproved?" reprinted in Plantinga, *The Ontological Argument*, pp. 111–22.

27. The notion of a necessary being does not figure in the premises of Descartes's argument. The conclusion is simply that God exists, or that there is a God. If the conclusion followed, it would be necessary, since the premises are necessary. But to say 'necessarily, there is a God' is not yet to say that there is a necessary being: $\Box\exists x Fx$ does not imply $\exists x\Box Fx$.

28. The debate is reprinted in Paul Edwards and Arthur Pap, *A Modern Introduction to Philosophy* (New York: Free Press, 1965), pp. 473–90.

29. For example, if the terms 'the number two' and 'John's favorite number' designate the same number, we may instantiate the definition twice to get the result that the same object both is and is not a necessary being.

30. If it is possible to analyze necessity *de re* in terms of the necessity *de dicto* of a special type of proposition (as proposed by Plantinga in *The Nature of Necessity*, ch. 3), we may appeal to the necessity of propositions after all. But our definition of a necessary being will have to be more subtle than the one rejected in the text.

31. Bennett cites this passage as making a similar point, connecting it with Locke's doctrine that there are no essences of individuals (*Kant's Dialectic*, pp. 234–35).

32. The *locus classicus* is Plantinga, *The Nature of Necessity*.

33. The formula '$\exists x\Box Fx \to \Box\exists x Fx$' (a version of what Plantinga calls the Buridan formula) is questionable and fails to hold in many systems of quantified modal logic. [For discussion, see Kenneth Konyndyk, *Introductory Modal Logic* (Notre Dame, Ind.: University of Notre Dame Press, 1986), ch. 4.] However, the special case of the Buridan formula in which F is existence seems to be acceptable.

34. For further defense of the possibility of necessary existence against some of the standard objections, see Robert M. Adams, *The Virtue of Faith* (Oxford: Oxford University Press, 1987), essays 13 and 14.

35. There may be a similar inconsistency in Hume. Hume is sometimes said to have anticipated the "existence is not a predicate" doctrine with his view that the idea of existence "is the very same with the idea of what we conceive

to be existent" (David Hume, *A Treatise of Human Nature*, I.ii.7, p. 66 in Selby-Bigge's edition). Yet he also criticizes the idea of necessary being by saying "whatever we conceive as existent, we can also conceive as non-existent" [*Dialogues Concerning Natural Religion*, edited by Nelson Pike (Indianapolis, Ind.: Bobbs-Merrill, 1970), dialogue IX, p. 58].

36. See Saul Kripke, "Semantical Considerations on Modal Logic," *Acta Philosophica Fennica*, fasc. XVI, 83–94; reprinted in *Reference and Modality*, edited by Leonard Linsky (Oxford: Oxford University Press, 1971), pp. 63–72. Kripke's stricture is discussed and endorsed in Konyndyk, *Introductory Modal Logic*, ch. 4.

37. Since writing this section I have learned that some of it is a rediscovery of the wheel. Avoiding the result that all substances are necessary beings was the objective of A.N. Prior's search for a "logic for contingent beings." For a good survey of the problem (including solutions not canvassed here), see Harry Deutsch, "Logic for Contingent Beings," *Journal of Philosophical Research*, 19 (1994), 273–329.

38. Anthony Kenny, *Descartes: A Study of His Philosophy* (New York: Random House, 1968), ch. 7, at p. 164.

39. Alexius Meinong, "The Theory of Objects," in *Realism and the Background of Phenomenology*, edited by R.M. Chisholm (New York: The Free Press, 1960), pp. 76–117, at p. 83.

40. Ibid., p. 79. The concluding phrase of Meinong's sentence is "Objects of knowledge"; I have deleted "of knowledge" so that readers unfamiliar with Meinong will not be misled into thinking that Meinongian Objects depend in any way on being known.

41. Ibid., p. 82.

42. Kant himself observes that the judgment 'God is omnipotent' is true even if God does not exist (A595/B623). Does he thereby accept Meinong's Independence Principle? Not necessarily, for his observation can be accommodated by construing the predication as a conditional: if any being is God, that being is omnipotent. That in turn can be construed as asserting a link between two concepts rather than a link between a Meinongian object and a predicate.

43. See Anthony Kenny, *Descartes: A Study of His Philosophy* (New York: Random House, 1968), pp. 157–58.

44. Meinong's assumptions also seem to undermine the case I made earlier for accepting premise (2) of the ontological argument—in which case any help he offers the ontological argument at one point is offset at another.

45. Compare Descartes's defense of the ontological argument in paragraphs 9 and 10 of the fifth of his *Meditations*. He allows that from the inseparability of A from B (e.g., right triangularity from the Pythagorean property) it does not in general follow that As exist, but only that they are Bs. But he then goes on to insist that in the special case where B is existence, it *does* follow that As exist.

46. The point I am now urging may throw light on one aspect of the debate between Meinong and Russell in the first decade of the twentieth century. [For an account of the debate, see Peter Simons, "On What There Isn't: The Meinong-Russell Dispute," in *Philosophy and Logic in Central Europe from Bolzano to Tarski* (Dordrecht: Kluwer, 1992), pp. 159–91.] In "On Denoting" (*Logic and Knowledge*, pp. 41–56), Russell accused Meinong of flouting the law of noncontradiction by admitting into his realm of objects such items as the round square. Meinong replied that the law of noncontradiction holds only for existing things, so there is no problem. Russell rejoined that on Meinong's principles, one must admit that the *existent* round square exists, so one has a contradictory object among existing things after all. (This is why Russell thought Meinong committed to the validity of ontological arguments.)

Meinong replied that it is indeed true that the existent round square is existent, but that any round square exists does not follow.

Meinong's final reply may leave one flabbergasted. What distinction can there possibly be between being existent and existing? But I think there is a way to interpret his reply that makes it perfectly correct and consonant with his own principles. We should take him to be distinguishing *not* between the predicate 'exists' and the predicate 'is existent' (as was perhaps his intent), but between a predicative tie to existence and existence as we would express it by a (Quinean, not Meinongian) quantifier. To say that existent round squares are (in the predicative way) existent is not to say that there exist any round squares. Similarly, to say that God is in the predicative way existent is not to say that God exists (i.e., that there exists such a being). On Meinongian assumptions, God can be predicatively existent without existing just as he can be predicatively perfect without existing.

47. C.D. Broad, *An Examination of McTaggart's Philosophy* (New York: Octagon Books, 1976; reprint of the 1938 Cambridge edition), vol. 2, part I, pp. 264–323, especially pp. 314–15. I discuss this further in "If Meinong Is Wrong, Is McTaggart Right?" *Philosophical Topics*, 24 (1996), 231–54.

48. A page later, Kant writes:

> Reason therefore abandons experience altogether, and endeavours to discover from mere concepts what properties an absolutely necessary being must have, that is, which among all possible things contains in itself the conditions (*requisita*) essential to absolute necessity. Now these, it is supposed, are nowhere to be found save in the concept of an *ens realissimum*; and the conclusion is therefore drawn, that the *ens realissimum* is the absolutely necessary being. (A606–7/B634–35)

49. Bertrand Russell, *A History of Western Philosophy* (New York: Simon & Schuster, 1945), pp. 587–88. Bennett (*Kant's Dialectic*, sec. 80) offers the same criticism as what Kant could and should have said, though not as what he did say.

50. Here I follow J. William Forgie, "Kant on the Relation Between the Cosmological and Ontological Arguments," *International Journal for Philosophy of Religion*, 34 (1993), 1–12. Forgie's exposition of the matter is the clearest I have seen.

51. This point is well made by Forgie, who also cites Peter Remnant, "Kant and the Cosmological Argument," *The Australasian Journal of Philosophy*, 37 (1959), 152–55, and Allen W. Wood, *Kant's Rational Theology* (Ithaca, N.Y.: Cornell University Press, 1978).

52. Contrary to what Wood suggests, Kant does not need to assume the identity of indiscernibles. His argument only requires that all *entia realissima* be qualitatively alike, in a sense implying that none is a necessary being unless all are.

53. As Bennett puts it, "Kant has insisted that the conditionalizing move is correct, so how can he refuse to allow the cosmological arguer to make it?" (*Kant's Dialectic*, p. 252). This is not the only place in which Kant is oblivious to his own best criticism of the ontological argument. In *The One Possible Basis* (p. 57 in Treash), he gives the following argument for "Existence is not a predicate or determination of any thing": in deciding whether to create Caesar, God consults the complete concept of Caesar, which includes all his predicates. If existence were among these predicates, it would not be left up to God whether Caesar exists or not. But it *is* up to God whether Caesar exists or not; therefore, existence is not a predicate. To argue in this way is not to expose the error in the ontological argument, but to commit it.

54. Here again I am in essential agreement with Forgie. Incidentally, I am not saying that 4 does not imply the existence of a necessary being. As Forgie notes, if there is a necessary being, than anything implies that there is a necessary being. (I think he is assuming that '∃x☐Ex' implies '☐∃x☐Ex' and that anything implies any necessary truth.) What I am saying is that on the basis of 4 alone we cannot *know* that there is a necessary being.

55. The objection occurs in the mouth of Cleanthes in part IX of Hume's *Dialogues Concerning Natural Religion*.

56. It is all right for Kant (and Hume) to raise two objections that are inconsistent with each other. Although they cannot both be correct, one can be a backup in case the other fails.

57. Perhaps (A) should really be 'I must think (∃x)(–Nx) → (∃x)(Nx)'; that will still lead to the contradiction below.

58. We are enjoined to think ∃xNx, which is true only if (for some item *a*) N*a*, but we are also enjoined to think –N*a*. I offer Kant the following alternative way out of the contradiction: allow that what we "must think" is true, but say that our inability to think any particular being as necessary is a matter of 'cannot think Nx' rather than 'must think not-Nx'. This would parallel what he seems to say in the Second Paralogism: from our inability to think of the self as composite, it does not follow that we must think of it as simple.

59. Matters are a little more complicated than this. The Thesis of the Fourth Antinomy is as follows: "There belongs to the world, either as its part or as its cause, a being that is absolutely necessary." The Antithesis: "An absolutely necessary being nowhere exists in the world, nor does it exist outside the world as its cause." Kant's reconciling proposition: "All things in the world of sense may be contingent, and so have only an empirically conditioned existence, while yet there may be a non-empirical condition of the whole series; that is, there may exist an unconditionally necessary being" (A560/B588). Bennett makes the following complaint (*Kant's Dialectic*, p. 243): "With this supposedly reconciling suggestion, Kant manages to contradict both the Thesis and the Antithesis!" Things are not quite that bad. The Antithesis is not contradicted by the reconciling proposition unless the necessary being outside the world is said to be its *cause*; Kant characterizes it instead as a ground. (If appearances are virtual objects, as I maintain, they certainly do require grounds that are not themselves appearances. It could be left open to speculation—which is all Kant's purposes in the Fourth Antinomy require—that the ground is a necessary being.) As for the Thesis, there is justice in the complaint that Kant's reconciling proposition does not give the Thesis proponent what he explicitly asks for—a necessary being within the sensible world.

60. Hume, *Dialogues Concerning Natural Religion*, sec. IX.

61. For Leibniz's version of this argument, see "On the Ultimate Origination of Things" and "A Resumé of Metaphysics" in *Philosophical Writings*, edited by G.H.R. Parkinson (London: Everyman's Library, 1973), pp. 136–44 and 145–47. (At A604/B632, Kant identifies the cosmological proof with Leibniz's proof *a contingentia mundi*.) For an account of Clarke's version, see William L. Rowe, *The Cosmological Argument* (Princeton, N.J.: Princeton University Press, 1975), pp. 58–59 and 168–69.

62. Does supporting the infinite chain mean causing it to exist? If so, since each member is also caused by its predecessor, is the existence of each member causally overdetermined? Or is the relation of support to chain rather like that of God to the modes in Spinoza? If the argument of section F that every substance is a necessary being is correct, that would be further reason for adopting the Spinozist model: contingent beings would dissolve into contingent truths about necessary substances; that is to say, they would be modes.

63. Hume, *Dialogues Concerning Natural Religion*, sec. IX.

64. For a good contemporary example, see Paul Edwards, "The Cosmological Argument," *The Rationalist Annual*, 1959; reprinted in Rowe and Wainwright, *Philosophy of Religion*, pp. 136–48.

65. As does Rowe in *Cosmological Argument*, pp. 151–58. Rowe suggests that once you have explained the existence of each member of a set, you still have to answer the question of why the set has the members it does rather than none at all. Since I take it to be essential to any set that it have just the members it does, I do not think the question Rowe formulates needs an answer. But as will become clear in what follows, I think Rowe is right to insist that there *is* an important question that Hume leaves unanswered; it just needs to be formulated in terms of properties rather than sets.

66. Might it be suggested to the contrary that it is necessary that some contingent beings or other exist, though of course not necessary (on pain of contradiction) regarding any particular contingent being that *it* exist? This is a *formal* possibility, as shown by a possible worlds model in which each world contains some individual that fails to exist in some other world. But I would cite David Lewis's "principle of recombination" against it. [See his *On the Plurality of Worlds* (Oxford: Blackwell, 1986), pp. 87–88.] If a world is possible in which Socrates does not exist and a world is possible in which Plato does not exist (and so on), then why not a world in which none of them exists?

67. Leibniz, *Monadology*, paragraph 32; p. 184 in *Philosophical Writings*.

68. Jonathan Bennett, *A Study of Spinoza's Ethics* (Indianapolis, Ind.: Hackett, 1984), p. 115.

69. Robert Nozick, *Philosophical Explanations* (Cambridge, Mass.: Harvard University Press, 1981), pp. 115–64, esp. pp. 128–37.

70. If we say no, we wind up making every truth a necessary truth. Here's how: (a) $-\Diamond-$(all possibilities are realized) (assumption); (b) $\Box$(all possibilities are realized) (rewrite of b); (c) $\Box$(w)(w is possible $\to$ w is realized) (rewrite of c); (d) $\Box$(w)(w is possible $\leftrightarrow \Box$[w is possible]) (from the modal principle that what is possible is necessarily possible); (e) (w)(w is possible $\to \Box$[w is realized]) (from c and d). Our last step, (e), in effect tells us that whatever is possible is necessarily the case.

71. Nozick, *Philosophical Explanations*, p. 131.

72. Ibid., p. 130.

73. Ibid., p. 134.

74. If we tried to construct an analog of the undermining syllogism it would be as follows:

1. All self-subsuming possibilities of sort S are realized.
2. It is a self-subsuming possibility of sort S that not all self-subsuming possibilities of sort S are realized.
3. Therefore, not all self-subsuming possibilities of sort S are realized.

Here the second premise is false. The words following "that" do not express a self-subsuming possibility because they do not state a generalization (but rather the negation of one), and only generalizations subsume themselves.

75. The idea that truth-attributing facts supervene on truth-free facts is made precise and defended by Matthew McGrath in his doctoral dissertation, *Between Deflationism and the Correspondence Theory: An Account of Truth* (Ph.D. dissertation, Brown University, 1998). McGrath shows that this idea underwrites a truth-value gap solution to the Liar Paradox and provides a rationale for the semantic apparatus developed by Saul Kripke in his "Outline of a Theory of Truth," *The Journal of Philosophy*, 72 (1975), 690–716.

Chapter 13

1. Hilary Putnam, *Reason, Truth, and History* (Cambridge: Cambridge University Press, 1981), pp. 49–50.

2. Hilary Putnam, "Why There Isn't a Ready-Made World," in *Realism and Reason* (Cambridge: Cambridge University Press, 1983), pp. 205–28, at p. 211.

3. Hilary Putnam, *Representation and Reality* (Cambridge, Mass.: MIT Press, 1988), p. 107.

4. Hilary Putnam, "Realism and Reason," in *Meaning and the Moral Sciences* (London: Routledge & Kegan Paul, 1978), pp. 123–40, at p. 125. See also his *Reason, Truth, and History*, p. 50.

5. Putnam, *Reason, Truth, and History*, p. 61.

6. Norman Kemp Smith, *A Commentary to Kant's 'Critique of Pure Reason'* (New York: Humanities Press, 1962; reprint of the 1923 edition), p. 36.

7. Putnam, *Reason, Truth, and History*, p. 63. For other places where Putnam says Kant repudiates the correspondence theory of truth, see *Realism and Reason* (Cambridge: Cambridge University Press, 1983), pp. 177, 209–210, 225–26, and 272.

8. Kant, *Lectures on Logic*, translated by J. Michael Young (Cambridge: Cambridge University Press, 1992), p. 557. This passage is from the *Jaesche Logic*; similar definitions of truth occur in the Blomberg Logic (p. 61), the Vienna Logic (pp. 280 and 289), and the Dohna-Wundlacken Logic (p. 455).

9. Carl Hempel, "On the Logical Positivists' Theory of Truth," *Analysis*, 2 (1935), 49–59; John Dewey, "Propositions, Warranted Assertibility, and Truth," in *Problems of Men* (New York: Philosophical Library, 1946), pp. 331–53; Donald Davidson, "A Coherence Theory of Truth and Knowledge," in *Truth and Interpretation: Perspectives on the Philosophy of Donald Davidson*, edited by Ernest LePore (Oxford: Blackwell, 1986), pp. 307–19; Richard Rorty, *Consequences of Pragmatism* (Minneapolis: University of Minnesota Press, 1982), pp. 154 and 180; Laurence BonJour, "Can Empirical Knowledge Have a Foundation?" *American Philosophical Quarterly*, 15 (1978), 1–13. For a critical survey of versions of the argument since Kant, see Douglas McDermid, *Is Pragmatism Coherent?* (Ph.D. dissertation, Brown University, 1997), ch. 3.

10. Somewhat more formally, my point is as follows. By what Crispin Wright calls the Correspondence Platitude, a judgment is true iff things are as the judgment says they are [*Truth and Objectivity* (Cambridge, Mass.: Harvard University Press, 1992), p. 25]. By the reductive theory of objects, what the judgment that o is F says is equivalent to a fact of the form $R(r_1 \ldots r_n)$. Therefore, the judgment that o is F is true iff $R(r_1 \ldots r_n)$.

11. See the important paragraph running from A189/B234 to A191/B236 for an argument that employs the formula, "truth consists in the agreement of knowledge with the object," in the midst of a discussion that plainly takes it for granted that the object in question is in some fashion reducible to representations.

12. I owe this point to McDermid, "Is Pragmatism Coherent?," ch. 3.

13. Let me mention, however, two suggestive points that might be exploited in defense of the interpretation of Kant I am opposing. (1) On pages 128–29 of *Meaning and the Moral Sciences*, Putnam notes that a thoroughgoing internal realist should use verificationist semantics "all the way down," never arriving at a bedrock of hard facts (e.g., sense-datum reports) in connection with which one uses truth-conditional semantics. (2) On page 62 of *Reason, Truth, and History*, Putnam says that Kant regards "all of these points" as applying to sensations as well as to external objects. He does not make as clear as one would like exactly *which* points he has in mind, but one of them may be Kant's supposed repudiation of correspondence as the theory of truth.

If we put (1) and (2) together, we can perhaps glimpse the possibility of a Kant for whom not even judgments strictly about representations possess correspondence truth.

14. See Putnam, *Reason, Truth, and History*, p. 63, and "Why There Isn't a Ready-Made World," in *Realism and Reason*, pp. 205–28 and p. 272.

15. See Michael Devitt, *Realism and Truth* (2nd edition; Princeton: Princeton University Press, 1997), p. 42, for the point that a correspondence theory of truth need not have realist assumptions built into it. See also A191/B236 as already noted.

16. Putnam's argument occurs in "Why There Isn't a Ready-Made World."

17. Ibid., p. 205.

18. Ibid., p. 206.

19. "How can we pick out any *one* correspondence between our words (or thoughts) and the supposed mind-independent things *if we have no direct access to the mind-independent things?* (German philosophy almost always began with a particular answer to this question—the answer 'we can't'—after Kant.)" (ibid., p. 207; p. 225 makes it clear that Putnam also takes Kant to have affirmed the italicized antecedent.)

20. Ibid., p. 205.

21. James Van Cleve, "Semantic Supervenience and Referential Indeterminacy," *The Journal of Philosophy*, 89 (1992), 344–61.

22. Michael Dummett, "Realism," in *Truth and Other Enigmas* (Cambridge, Mass.: Harvard University Press, 1978), pp. 145–65, at p. 146.

23. With apologies to Richard Feldman and Earl Conee, who use the term for the view that epistemic justification (not truth) depends on evidence in "Evidentialism," *Philosophical Studies*, 48 (1985), 15–34.

24. Dummett, *Truth and Other Enigmas*, p. 155.

25. See, for example, the preface to Dummett's *Truth and Other Enigmas*, p. xxx.

26. Bas C. van Fraassen's supervaluation semantics provides one scheme for accommodating this combination; see his "Presuppositions, Supervaluations, and Free Logic," in *The Logical Way of Doing Things*, edited by Karel Lambert (New Haven, Conn.: Yale University Press, 1969), pp. 67–91. To make the combination possible, one must reject the Tarski schema that permits one to infer from 'snow is white' to '"snow is white" is true.'

27. In still later writings, Dummett distinguishes three grades of antirealism. The mildest rejects referential semantics while retaining bivalence. The next rejects bivalence but keeps the idea of truth conditions. The strongest rejects the idea of truth conditions altogether in favor of assertibility conditions. See his "Realism" in *Synthese*, 52 (1982), 55–112. These refinements are not necessary for the present purposes.

28. Michael Dummett, *The Logical Basis of Metaphysics* (Cambridge, Mass.: Harvard University Press, 1991), p. 49.

29. In the next section, I note the possibility of a more liberal antirealism that requires, for the truth of S at t, not evidence at t, but evidence at t or later.

30. Dummett, *Truth and Other Enigmas*, p. 155.

31. In some places, however, Dummett seems to have lost sight of this possibility, insisting that realists *must* accept bivalence. In the later article "Realism," Dummett says that bivalence is necessary, but not sufficient, for realism. In the introduction to *Logical Basis of Metaphysics*, he again affirms that bivalence is an essential ingredient in all varieties of realism.

32. There may be pressure toward idealism in some cases, however. Intuitionists say there is no truth in mathematics without proof. Well, what does it take for a proof to exist? Must it be written down somewhere? Then mathematical truth would depend on how much paper there is in the universe.

May it exist as an abstract structure, not needing any concrete realization? Then we are a step closer to the Platonism that intuitionists abjure. Must the proof be apprehended by some mind? Now we are idealists after all—as indeed some of the intuitionists were.

33. James Van Cleve, "Minimal Truth Is Realist Truth," *Philosophy and Phenomenological Research*, 56 (1996), 869–75, and "The Manifestation Argument Against Realism," forthcoming in *Realism: Responses and Reactions (Essays in Honour of Pranab Kumar Sen)*, edited by D.P. Chattopadhyaya et al.

34. I rely here mainly on the following two papers by Posy: "Dancing to the Antinomy: A Proposal for Transcendental Idealism," *American Philosophical Quarterly*, 20 (1983), 81–94, and "Kant's Mathematical Realism," *The Monist*, 67 (1984), 115–34. Also instructive is the symposium by Leslie Stevenson and Ralph Walker, "Empirical Realism and Transcendental Anti-Realism," *Proceedings of the Aristotelian Society* (1983), 131–77.

35. Posy, "Dancing to the Antinomy," pp. 84–85.

36. Here I am drawing on Posy's "Kant's Mathematical Realism."

37. I am oversimplifying Posy's account somewhat; for example, I am ignoring his distinction between strict and mild constructivisms, which combines with the long/short and optimist/pessimist distinctions to yield eight possible scenarios.

38. This is what Posy suggests in "Kant's Mathematical Realism." In "Dancing to the Antinomy," he gives a somewhat different explanation of why the transcendental realist must accept the disjunction of Thesis and Antithesis: the realist operates with an intellectualized notion of evidence, "a notion of omniscience to which the idea of evidential growth does not apply" (p. 85). But on either account we get a bivalent semantics.

39. The quotation comes from section 4 of the Antinomy chapter. It is clear that in this section Kant wishes to hold that in certain domains of inquiry, there are no questions with unknowable answers. However, the *reason* he gives—that in these domains, "the object is not to be met with outside the concept" (A477/B505)—seems to me to support only something weaker. The weaker contention is that every question in the domain either (i) has a knowable answer or (ii) has no answer at all. The objective indeterminacy countenanced in alternative (ii) would arise if there were cases in which a concept dictated no answer to a particular question.

40. I note here that Dummett ventures to suggest that *everyone*, realists included, agrees that there is no truth that is not at least in principle knowable, at least by a superhuman being (*The Logical Basis of Metaphysics*, p. 345). But I am not sure that I agree with that! Such is the hold of one's deepest presuppositions—that one takes it for granted that everyone else shares them.

41. A relationist about time could dismiss the question, "Why did the first event occur *when* it did?" but would still be left with the question, "Why did that event occur at all?"

42. Kant makes it a further argument against simples that their existence could never be established by any possible perception. This is admittedly a point that is relevant only on idealist or evidentialist assumptions.

43. I am actually uncertain as to whether Kant is saying here that the events of past time consist in past, future, or possible experiences.

44. Dummett, *Truth and Other Enigmas*, p. 16.

45. Kant further explains: "The proposition, *everything which exists is completely determined*, does not mean only that one of every pair of *given* contradictory predicates, but that one of every [pair of] of *possible* predicates, must always belong to it" (A573/B601).

46. Carl Posy, "Kant and Conceptual Semantics," *Topoi*, 10 (1991), 67–78, at p. 72.

Appendices

1. G.W. Leibniz, *New Essays on Human Understanding*, IV.ii.1.

2. Hilary Putnam, "Reds, Greens, and Logical Analysis," *The Philosophical Review*, 65 (1956), 206–17; Arthur Pap, "Once More: Colors and the Synthetic A Priori," *The Philosophical Review*, 66 (1957), 94–99; Hilary Putnam, "Red and Green All Over Again: A Rejoinder to Arthur Pap," *The Philosophical Review*, 66, (1957), 100–3; Karel Lambert and Bas van Fraassen, "Meaning Relations, Possible Objects, and Possible Worlds," in *Philosophical Problems in Logic*, Karel Lambert, ed. (Dordrecht: Reidel, 1970), pp. 1–19. The Putnam-Pap exchange is reprinted in L.W. Sumner and John Woods, eds., *Necessary Truth* (New York: Random House, 1969), pp. 71–93.

3. Here, however, is an informal version of it. Assume that red and green are colors and that some object *o* has them both. By the right side of D2, that means there are an object *a* (one of the paradigm red objects) such that *o* is the same in color as *a* and an object *b* (one of the paradigm green objects) such that *o* is the same in color as *b*. Since 'same in color as' is an equivalence relation (a consequence of D1), it further follows that *a* is the same in color as *b*. But now it follows that everything red is green and vice versa, since whatever matches our paradigm for red will also match our paradigm for green and vice versa. Invoking the identity criterion 'F = G iff (x)(Fx ↔ Gx)', Putnam draws the further conclusion that red is the same property as green. Finally, by conditionalizing and contraposing, we reach the intended result that if red is a distinct property from green, no object can have them both.

4. That is, we should say that objects are the same in color only if it is *impossible* for there to be anything indistinguishable from one but not the other. We do not want mere *de facto* gaps in the spectrum of exemplified colors to make certain objects count as the same in color.

5. Saul Kripke, *Naming and Necessity* (Cambridge, Mass.: Harvard University Press, 1980), p. 53ff.

6. This nonnecessitarian reading of Hume, fairly standard for two centuries, is now challenged by proponents of "the new Hume." For discussion, see Kenneth Winkler, "The New Hume," *The Philosophical Review*, 100 (1991), 541–79.

7. Lewis White Beck, "A Prussian Hume and a Scottish Kant," in *Essays on Kant and Hume* (New Haven, Conn.: Yale University Press, 1978), pp. 111–29; Jeffery Dodge, "Uniformity in Empirical Cause-Effect Relations in the Second Analogy," *Kant-Studien*, 73 (1982), 47–54.

8. For a discussion of LaPlacean determinism, see John Earman, *A Primer of Determinism* (Dordrecht: Reidel, 1986), ch. 2.

9. To get from 'every event has a cause' to LaPlacean determinism, we need the further assumption (denied by theorists of agent causation such as Thomas Reid) that the cause of any event is always itself an event. However, this further assumption is already implicit in Kant's statement of the Second Analogy, which does not merely say that every event has a cause, but that for every event there is "something upon which it follows according to a rule." His discussion makes plain that this something is another event or state.

10. James Van Cleve, "Right, Left, and the Fourth Dimension," *The Philosophical Review*, 96 (1987), 33–68; reprinted in *The Philosophy of Right and Left*, edited by James Van Cleve and Robert E. Frederick (Dordrecht: Kluwer, 1991), pp. 203–34. Also relevant is my "Introduction to the Arguments of 1770 and 1783," in the same volume, pp. 15–26.

11. Immanuel Kant, "Concerning the Ultimate Ground of the Differentiation of Directions in Space," in *Theoretical Philosophy, 1755–1770*, edited and translated by David Walford in collaboration with Ralf Meerbote.

The Cambridge Edition of the Works of Immanuel Kant, vol. 1 (Cambridge: Cambridge University Press, 1992), pp. 365–72.

12. Ibid., p. 371.

13. Ibid.

14. John Earman, "Kant, Incongruous Counterparts, and the Nature of Space and Space-Time," *Ratio*, 13 (1971), 1–18; Martin Gardner, *The Ambidextrous Universe* (3rd ed.; San Francisco: Freeman, 1989), ch. 17; Graham Nerlich, "Hands, Knees, and Absolute Space," in *The Shape of Space* (Cambridge: Cambridge University Press, 1976), ch. 2. Relevant work by these authors and others is reprinted in Van Cleve and Frederick, *The Philosophy of Right and Left*.

15. For further development of this point, see my "Introduction to the Arguments of 1770 and 1783," esp. pp. 20–22.

16. One sometimes encounters the claim that the assignment of weird or intuition-challenging topological features to space makes sense only if a relational account of space is assumed (e.g., that 'space is finite' asserts something possible only if it just means that the greatest distance between any two bodies populating space is finite). [For a suggestion along these lines, see D.P. Dryer, *Kant's Solution for Verification in Metaphysics* (London: Allen & Unwin, 1966), pp. 165–66.] If the fourth dimension were a feature for which this claim is true, we could extend the argument just given as follows: (4) either absolutism is correct or four-dimensional spaces are impossible; (5) four-dimensional spaces are possible only if a relational theory of space is correct; (6) if a relational theory is correct, absolutism is not correct; therefore, (7) four-dimensional spaces are impossible.

17. Nor does Berkeley. In paragraph 3 of the *Principles of Human Knowledge*, he tells us that if he were out of his study, he would still say that his writing table exists, "meaning thereby that if I was in my study I might perceive it, or that some other spirit actually does perceive it."

18. I should note, however, that Kemp Smith has read the *Anhang* (connection) of Kant's text as *Fortgang* (advance).

19. Could it be Kant's view in the Postulates section that the categories of possibility, actuality, and necessity all coincide? Incredible though it seems, there are hints of such a view in his discussion.

20. Jaakko Hintikka, "On Kant's Notion of Intuition (*Anschauung*)," in *The First Critique: Reflections on Kant's Critique of Pure Reason*, edited by T. Penelhum and J. McIntosh (Belmont, Calif.: Wadsworth, 1969), pp. 38–53, at p. 44, n. 19.

21. This is according to Manley Thompson, "Singular Terms and Intuitions in Kant's Epistemology," *The Review of Metaphysics*, 26 (1972), 314–43, at p. 315. Thompson criticizes Hintikka for making intuitions a special kind of concept.

22. Charles Parsons, "Kant's Philosophy of Arithmetic," in *Kant on Pure Reason*, edited by Ralph C.S. Walker (Oxford: Oxford University Press, 1982), pp. 13–40.

23. Thompson, "Singular Terms and Intuitions," p. 328n.

24. Ibid.

25. Ibid., p. 314; Parsons, "Kant's Philosophy of Arithmetic," pp. 15–16.

26. Paragraph 10 of the *Dissertation on the Form and Principles of the Sensible and Intelligible World*, in Immanuel Kant, *Kant's Inaugural Dissertation and Early Writings on Space*, translated by John Handyside (Chicago: Open Court, 1929), p. 50.

27. I think Parsons understands singularity in sense (b); he thus naturally denies that singularity is sufficient for intuitionhood and enlists immediacy as a separate requirement.

28. It would thus be the mental counterpart of a rigid designator in Kripke's sense. For a closely related suggestion—that empirical intuitions are the mental analogs of pure demonstrative singular terms—see Robert Howell, "Intuition, Synthesis, and Individuation in the *Critique of Pure Reason*," *Nous*, 7 (1973), 207–32.

29. Two further assumptions are actually needed in this argument: (i) if representation R refers to an object through the mediation of property P, it does so in every possible world in which R exists; and (ii) if there are possible worlds in which P is instantiated by y rather than x, there are also possible worlds in which this happens *and* R still exists and refers to an object. In such worlds, R would have y rather than x for its object, and thus would not be singular in sense (c).

30. Thompson, "Singular Terms and Intuitions," p. 33.

31. On the significance of the second quoted sentence, see Beck, "Did the Sage of Königsberg Have No Dreams?" in *Essays on Kant and Hume*, pp. 38–60, at p. 43.

32. This sentence occurs in the Refutation of Idealism. A paragraph earlier is this: "Certainly, the representation 'I am', which expresses the consciousness that can accompany all thought, immediately includes in itself the existence of a subject; but it does not so include any *knowledge* of that subject . . ." [for which we would require intuition in addition to thought].

33. In strictness we need to add: and not holding among the representations only in virtue of an $(n + 1)$-ary relation among the representations and something else. We should probably also allow that unity of apperception is a multigrade relation, capable of holding among any number of representations.

34. Bertrand Russell, *Human Knowledge: Its Scope and Limits* (New York: Simon & Schuster, 1948), pp. 294–97 and 302–7. See also C.D. Broad, *An Examination of McTaggart's Philosophy* (New York: Octagon Books, 1976; reprint of 1938 Cambridge edition), p. 178. Broad says that if we had a term 'sympsychic' standing to 'belonging to the same self' as 'collinear' stands to 'lying on the same straight line', we might not regard the unity relation as involving a self.

35. For a discussion of James's views and references, see A.J. Ayer, *The Origins of Pragmatism* (San Francisco: Freeman, Cooper, 1968), pp. 247–60.

36. H.P. Grice, "Personal Identity," *Mind*, 50 (1941); reprinted in *Personal Identity*, edited by John Perry (Berkeley: University of California Press, 1975), pp. 73–95.

37. For this general point, see Lawrence Sklar, *Space, Time, and Spacetime* (Berkeley: University of California Press, 1974), pp. 171–73. For discussion of further difficulties facing theories like Grice's, see John Perry, "Personal Identity, Memory, and the Problem of Circularity" in Perry, *Personal Identity.*

38. Patricia Kitcher, *Kant's Transcendental Psychology* (Oxford: Oxford University Press, 1990), p. 119.

39. I note also the following feature of Kitcher's analysis (and perhaps of any system theory): it gives us a way of analyzing '∃x(the rs belong to x)' but not 'the rs belong to x' where x is a free variable, replaceable by a constant. In other words, it gives us a way of analyzing 'the rs all belong to one self' but not 'the rs all belong to *me*' (or to you or Jones). So, it answers an analog of van Inwagen's "Special Composition Question" but not the analog of the more difficult "General Composition Question." For this distinction, see Peter van Inwagen, *Material Beings* (Ithaca, N.Y.: Cornell University Press, 1990), ch. 4.

40. Spelling this out further, for any subject S and conscious states F and G, if S is in F & S is in G & S considers whether he is in F & S considers whether he is in G, then S will know that he is in the conjunction of states F and G. Note that the consequent does not merely say 'S knows that he is in F & S

knows that he is in G', for that would not yet express the unity of apperception. However, the clause about consideration in the antecedent *does* merely
say 'S considers whether he is in F & S considers whether he is in G' (as opposed to the stronger 'S considers whether he is in the conjunction of states F
and G'); this is because the stronger antecedent clause would result in a principle that is simply a special case of the self-presenting character of conscious
states. I am trying to formulate a version of the unity of apperception that goes
beyond self-presentation. That said, I should point out that if the experimental findings about to be described constitute an exception to unity of apperception, they probably also constitute an exception to self-presentation.

41. Franz Brentano, *Psychology from an Empirical Standpoint*, edited and
translated by Linda L. McAlister et al. (New York: Humanities Press, 1973; first
published in 1874), pp. 155–76.

42. Charles E. Marks, *Commissurotomy, Consciousness, and Unity of Mind*
(Montgomery, Vt.: Bradford Books, 1980), pp. 4–5.

43. See ibid., p. 13.

44. Ibid., p. 2.

45. If the experiment is interpreted as confronting us with two persons in
one body, other puzzling questions arise. Were two subjects there even before
the commissurotomy, or only one? If only one, how is that one related to the
two that emerge later?

46. Marks, *Commissurotomy, Consciousness*, p. 10.

47. This formulation and the illustration that follows are taken from G.E.
Hinton, J.L. McClelland, and D.E. Rumelhart, "Distributed Representations,"
in *Parallel Distributed Processing: Explorations in the Microstructure of
Cognition*, edited by David E. Rumelhart and James L. McClelland (Cambridge,
Mass.: MIT Press, 1986), pp. 77–109, p. 88ff.

48. Ann Treisman, "Features and Objects in Visual Processing," *Scientific
American* (November, 1986), 114b–125.

49. Hypotheses about the neural basis of the searchlight are advanced in
Francis Crick, "Function of the Thalamic Reticular Complex: The Searchlight
Hypothesis," *Proceedings of the National Academy of Sciences*, 81 (1984),
4586–90.

50. Kitcher, *Kant's Transcendental Psychology*, p. 85.

51. Simon Blackburn, "Moral Realism," in *Morality and Moral Reasoning*,
edited by J. Casey (London: Methuen, 1971), pp. 101–24, and *Spreading the
Word* (Oxford: Oxford University Press, 1984), pp. 182–89.

52. In the alternative terminology of Jaegwon Kim, we could also put
Blackburn's premise by saying that moral properties supervene weakly but not
strongly on natural properties. See Kim's "Concepts of Supervenience,"
Philosophy and Phenomenological Research, 45 (1984), 153–76; reprinted in
his *Supervenience and Mind* (Cambridge: Cambridge University Press, 1993),
pp. 53–78.

53. Is a world in which there are no repetitions of states therefore vacuously deterministic? We could avoid having to say yes by counterfactualizing,
stipulating that if any state *were* to recur, so would all the states that followed
it before. But then matters would get messy if we tried to give the truth conditions of counterfactuals in terms of what happens in other worlds.

54. James Dreier, "The Supervenience Argument Against Moral Realism,"
The Southern Journal of Philosophy, 30 (1992), 13–38. Dreier puts the point
in terms of dates and the property of yesterday-occurrence, and he uses it
against a somewhat differently construed version of Blackburn's argument.

55. I have passed from 'necessarily, every event has a cause' to 'every event
is such that it necessarily has a cause', which is all right given that events are
essentially events.

56. David Lewis, *On the Plurality of Worlds* (Oxford: Blackwell, 1986), p. 200.

57. Ibid., p. 204.

58. James Van Cleve, "Mereological Essentialism, Mereological Conjunctivism, and Identity Through Time," *Midwest Studies in Philosophy*, vol. 11, edited by Peter A. French, Theodore E. Uehling, Jr., and Howard K. Wettstein (Minneapolis: University of Minnesota Press, 1986), pp. 141–56.

59. A.N. Prior, *Time and Modality* (Oxford: Clarendon Press, 1957), pp. 8–12.

60. A.N. Prior, "The Notion of the Present," *Studium Generale*, 23 (1970), 245–48, at p. 247.

61. John Foster, *The Case for Idealism* (London: Routledge & Kegan Paul, 1982), ch. 15.

62. Ibid., p. 245.

63. Ibid., p. 244.

64. To see this, let the "it is physically true that" operator be replaced by "Ralph believes that" and let the proposition h be 'someone believes something'; the resulting versions of (a) and (b) are both true.

65. We may take for granted in the derivation that Pp, if it holds at all, holds necessarily, and that phenomenalism, if true at all, is true necessarily.

66. Given the way Foster defines sustainment on page 5, it is also questionable whether the modal portion of (a) is sustained by the experiential constraints. It is logically implied by them, but not mediated by them.

67. Foster mentions the possibility of a phenomenalism that grounds physical reality in a "causal field" defined by the constraints it would impose on minds *if* they existed (*Case for Idealism*, p. 240). Such a field would be similar, perhaps, to Mill's "permanent possibilities of sensation." But Foster does not avail himself of this option, and it is not in any case a pure phenomenalism.

68. It is said by some Wittgensteinians that from within the practice of mathematics, we acknowledge that even if our conventions or habits of mind were different, it would still be true that $7 + 5 = 12$, whereas when we reflect on this practice from the outside, we see that if our conventions or habits of mind were different, it would no longer be true that $7 + 5 = 12$. One might attempt to cash out this internal/external distinction in Foster's way, in terms of the placement of operators. Letting 'MT' mean 'it is true within our mathematical framework that', we would have the internal 'MT(if our conventions were different, it would still be true that $7 + 5 = 12$)' and the external 'if our conventions were different, it would no longer be the case that MT($7 + 5 = 12$)'. But I believe that this distinction collapses just as Foster's does.

69. See especially Davidson's articles "Causal Relations" and "Mental Events" in his *Essays on Actions and Events* (Oxford: Clarendon Press, 1980), pp. 149–62 and 207–25, and "Thinking Causes" in *Mental Causation*, edited by John Heil and Alfred Mele (Oxford: Clarendon Press, 1995), pp. 3–17. The phrase "under a description" apparently originated in Elizabeth Anscombe's *Intention* (Oxford: Blackwell, 1957), p. 11. In her "Under a Description" [*The Collected Papers of G. E. M. Anscombe* (Minneapolis: University of Minnesota Press, 1981), vol. 2, pp. 208–19) she rejects the use of the phrase that is my target in this appendix.

70. If events were conceived of more abstractly as having just a single constitutive property [as in Jaegwon Kim, "Events as Property Exemplifications," in his *Supervenience and Mind*, pp. 33–52], we could say that events by themselves enter into laws by virtue of having the constitutive properties they do. For Davidson, on the other hand, it is only one or another property or description of an event that can enter into laws.

71. I am in wholehearted agreement with Quine on the following point: the law of substitutivity and the permissibility of "quantifying in" go together, so if it is not permissible to substitute co-referring terms within a given context,

then neither is it permissible to existentially quantify regarding terms in that context. [See W.V. Quine, "Reference and Modality," in *From a Logical Point of View* (New York: Harper Torchbooks, 1963), pp. 139–59.] If this point is accepted, those who refuse to allow the inference 'e1 caused f; e1 = e2; therefore, e2 caused f' must also refuse to say that there is *something* that caused f. But double-aspect interpreters of Kant certainly do not wish to deny that *something* caused me to have a certain representation or that *something* caused me to perform a certain action.

72. The key to appreciating this point is to note that 'e1 causes e2' is defined by an existential generalization, so if e1 and e2 have *some* descriptions that are linked by law, then it is true absolutely that e1 causes e2. Compare David Wiggins's views on identity in *Sameness and Substance* (Cambridge, Mass.: Harvard University Press, 1980), ch. 1. He thinks no items x and y are ever identical unless for *some* sortal concept F, x and y are the same F, but consistent with this, he denies that x and y can be the same thing under the sortal F and different things under the sortal G. Although dependent on a covering sortal, identity for Wiggins is absolute, not relative. In analogous fashion, although causation for Davidson is dependent on covering descriptions and laws, it is absolute, not relative. He is quite explicit about this matter in "Thinking Causes."

73. Compare Allison: "It is still meaningful to ask whether Kant's statements about objects affecting the mind and producing sensations involve a reference to objects considered in their empirical character as appearances, or, rather, to these same objects considered in abstraction from their empirical character, and thus as they are in themselves" [*Kant's Transcendental Idealism: An Interpretation and Defense* (New Haven, Conn.: Yale University Press, 1983), p. 248].

74. One could put what I just said by saying that if e1 and e2 are causally related under some of their descriptions, then they are causally related under all of them. Thus, Terence Irwin says that if an event is determined, it is true of it under all its true descriptions that it is determined ["Morality and Personality: Kant and Green," in *Self and Nature in Kant's Philosophy*, edited by Allen W. Wood (Ithaca, N.Y.: Cornell University Press, 1984), p. 38]. *Pace* Allison, what Irwin says should not be taken to imply "that being causally determined is a necessary or essential property of any occurrence of which it is predicated" [*Kant's Theory of Freedom* (Cambridge: Cambridge University Press, 1990), pp. 43–44].

75. Ralf Meerbote, "Kant on Freedom and the Rational and Morally Good Will," in *Self and Nature in Kant's Philosophy*, edited by Allen W. Wood (Ithaca, N.Y.: Cornell University Press, 1984), pp. 57–72.

76. To say that e2 is undetermined (uncaused, anomalous) under H can only mean this: (i) e2 has H and (ii) there is no event e1 and no property F such that e1 has F and it is a law that F-events are followed by H-events. This status, which is perhaps better represented as 'un(determined under H)' than as 'undetermined under H', is quite compatible with an event's being determined, period.

77. Blackburn, *Spreading the Word*, pp. 233–35.

78. Ibid., p. 234.

79. Ibid., p. 235.

80. That is, we could never know concerning any of our beliefs that *it* is true, even if (as some maintain) we could be sure that our total set of beliefs must contain many truths.

81. Blackburn, *Spreading the Word*, p. 235.

82. For discussion relevant to premise 1, see my "Epistemic Supervenience and the Circle of Belief," *The Monist*, 68 (1985), 90–104.

83. The plausibility of premise 2 is further diminished if we adopt a minimalist theory of truth, which in my opinion is capable of capturing the central insights of the correspondence theory. For minimalism, to say that the belief that snow is white corresponds with the facts is merely to say that snow *is* white (and, of course, that the belief to this effect exists). What considerations about the concept-ladenness of all cognition are supposed to keep us from knowing that snow is white? For more on these issues, see Paul Horwich, *Truth* (Cambridge, Mass.: MIT Press, 1990); Matthew McGrath, *Between Deflationism and the Correspondence Theory: A Theory of Truth* (Ph.D. dissertation, Brown University, 1998); and James Van Cleve, "Minimal Truth Is Realist Truth," *Philosophy and Phenomenological Research*, 56 (1996), 869–75.

84. For more on Lichtenberg's dictum, see Guenter Zoeller, "Lichtenberg and Kant on the Subject of Thinking," *Journal of the History of Philosophy*, 30 (1992), 417–41. Zoeller argues that Lichtenberg's real point was not to advocate a "no subject" view, but rather to demote the subject from its status as agent to status as mere observer.

85. Bernard Williams, *Descartes: The Project of Pure Inquiry* (New York: Humanities Press, 1978), pp. 95–101. I have tried to eliminate features of Williams's exposition that I find confusing, especially on his page 97.

References

Ackerman, Felicia. "How Does Ontology Supervene on What There Is?" In Savellos and Yalçin (1995), 264–72.

Adams, Robert M. *The Virtue of Faith*. Oxford: Oxford University Press, 1987.

Adickes, Erich. *Kants Lehre von der doppelten Affektion unseres Ich*. Tübingen: Mohr, 1929.

Allison, Henry E. *The Kant-Eberhard Controversy*. Baltimore: Johns Hopkins University Press, 1973.

_____. "The Non-spatiality of Things in Themselves for Kant." *Journal of the History of Philosophy*, 14 (1976), 313–21.

_____. *Kant's Transcendental Idealism: An Interpretation and Defense*. New Haven, Conn.: Yale University Press, 1983.

_____. *Kant's Theory of Freedom*. Cambridge: Cambridge University Press, 1990.

Ameriks, Karl. "Kant's Transcendental Deduction as a Regressive Argument." *Kant-Studien*, 69 (1978), 273–87.

_____. "Recent Work on Kant's Theoretical Philosophy." *American Philosophical Quarterly*, 19 (1982), 1–24.

_____. *Kant's Theory of Mind*. Oxford: Clarendon Press, 1987.

Anscombe, Elizabeth. *Intention*. Oxford: Blackwell, 1957.

_____. "Under a Description." In *The Collected Papers of G.E.M. Anscombe*, vol. 2, pp. 208–19. Minneapolis: University of Minnesota Press, 1981.

Aquila, Richard. "Things in Themselves: Intentionality and Reality in Kant." *Archiv Für Geschichte der Philosophie*, 61 (1979), 293–307.

_____. *Representational Mind: A Study of Kant's Theory of Knowledge*. Bloomington, Ind.: Indiana University Press, 1983.

Aristotle. *Aristotle's Categories and De Interpretatione*. Edited with notes by J. L. Ackrill. Oxford: Clarendon Press, 1963.

Armstrong, D. M. *Perception and the Physical World*. London: Routledge & Kegan Paul, 1961.

Ayer, Alfred J. *Language, Truth, and Logic*. New York: Dover, 1952; reprint of 1946 edition.

_____. *The Origins of Pragmatism*. San Francisco: Freeman, Cooper, 1968.

Bayle, Pierre. *Historical and Critical Dictionary*. Translated by Richard Popkin. Indianapolis, Ind.: Bobbs-Merrill, 1965.

Beck, Lewis White. "Can Kant's Synthetic Judgements Be Made Analytic?" *Kant-Studien*, 46 (1955), 168–81; reprinted in Gram (1967), 228–46.

_____. *A Commentary on Kant's Critique of Practical Reason*. Chicago: University of Chicago Press, 1960.

_____. "Kant's Theory of Definition." In *Studies in the Philosophy of Kant*. Indianapolis, Ind.: Bobbs-Merrill, 1965; reprinted in Gram (1967), 215–27.

_____. *Essays on Kant and Hume*. New Haven, Conn.: Yale University Press, 1978.

Beckermann, A., H. Flohr, and J. Kim, eds. *Emergence of Reduction?* Berlin: De Gruyter, 1992.

Benacerraf, Paul. "Tasks, Super-Tasks, and the Modern Eleatics." *The Journal of Philosophy,* 59 (1962), 765–84.

_____. "What Numbers Could Not Be." *The Philosophical Review*, 74 (1965), 47–73.

Bencivenga, Ermanno. *Kant's Copernican Revolution*. Oxford: Oxford University Press, 1987.

Bennett, Jonathan. *Kant's Analytic*. Cambridge: Cambridge University Press, 1966.

_____. *Kant's Dialectic*. Cambridge: Cambridge University Press, 1974.

_____. "The Age and Size of the World." *Synthese*, 23 (1971), 127–46; reprinted in Walker (1982), 176–94.

_____. *A Study of Spinoza's Ethics*. Indianapolis, Ind.: Hackett, 1984.

Berkeley, George. *Three Dialogues Between Hylas and Philonous*. Edited by Robert M. Adams. Indianapolis, Ind.: Hackett, 1979.

_____. *Principles of Human Knowledge*. Edited by Kenneth Winkler. Indianapolis, Ind.: Hackett, 1982.

Bird, Graham. *Kant's Theory of Knowledge*. London: Routledge & Kegan Paul, 1962.

Blackburn, Simon. "Moral Realism." In *Morality and Moral Reasoning*, edited by J. Casey. London: Methuen, 1971.

_____. *Spreading the Word*. Oxford: Clarendon Press, 1984.

_____. "Morals and Modals." In *Truth, Fact, and Value*, edited by Graham MacDonald and Crispin Wright, pp. 119–41. Oxford: Oxford University Press, 1986.

BonJour, Laurence. "Can Empirical Knowledge Have a Foundation?" *American Philosophical Quarterly*, 15 (1978), 1–13.

Borges, Jorge Luis. "The Circular Ruins." In *A Personal Anthology*, edited by Anthony Kerrigan, pp. 68–74. New York: Grove, 1967.

Born, Max. "Physical Reality." *Philosophical Quarterly*, 3 (1953), 139–49.

Boscovich, Roger. *A Theory of Natural Philosophy*. Cambridge, Mass.: MIT Press, 1966; English translation of the 1763 edition.

Brentano, Franz. *The True and the Evident*. Edited and translated by Roderick M. Chisholm et al. New York: Humanities Press, 1966.

_____. *Psychology from an Empirical Standpoint*. Edited and translated by Linda L. McAlister et al. New York: Humanities Press, 1973; first published in 1874.

Broad, C.D. *Mind and Its Place in Nature*. London: Routledge & Kegan Paul, 1925.

_____. "Kant's Mathematical Antinomies." *Proceedings of the Aristotelian Society*, 55 (1954–55), 1–22.

_____. *An Examination of McTaggart's Philosophy*, 2 vols. New York: Octagon Books, 1976; reprint of the 1938 Cambridge edition.

_____. *Kant: An Introduction.* Cambridge: Cambridge University Press, 1978.

Brown, Curtis. "Internal Realism: Transcendental Idealism." In *Midwest Studies in Philosophy*, vol. 12, edited by Peter A. French, Theodore E. Uehling, Jr., and Howard K. Wettstein, pp. 145–55. Minneapolis: University of Minnesota Press, 1988.

Buroker, Jill Vance. *Space and Incongruence.* Dordrecht: Reidel, 1981.

Carnap, Rudolf. *The Logical Structure of the World.* Translated by Rolf A. George. Berkeley: University of California Press, 1967.

Cartwright, Richard. "Negative Existentials." *The Journal of Philosophy*, 57 (1960), 629–39.

Castañeda, Hector-Neri. "'He': A Study in the Logic of Self-Consciousness." *Ratio*, 8 (1966), 130–57.

Chisholm, Roderick M. "'Appear,' 'Take,' and 'Evident.'" *The Journal of Philosophy*, 53 (1956); reprinted in *Perceiving, Sensing, and Knowing*, edited by Robert J. Swartz, pp. 473–85. Berkeley: University of California Press, 1976.

_____. *Perceiving: A Philosophical Study.* Ithaca, N.Y.: Cornell University Press, 1957.

_____. "Intentionality." In *The Encyclopedia of Philosophy*, edited by Paul Edwards, vol. 4, pp. 201–4. New York: Macmillan, 1967.

_____. "On the Observability of the Self." *Philosophy and Phenomenological Research*, 30 (1969), 7–21.

_____. *Person and Object.* La Salle, Ill.: Open Court, 1976.

_____. *Theory of Knowledge.* Englewood Cliffs, N.J.: Prentice-Hall, 1977; 2nd edition.

_____. "The Self and the World." In *Wittgenstein and His Impact on Contemporary Thought: Proceedings of the Second International Wittgenstein Symposium*, pp. 407–10. Vienna: Hoelder Pichler Tempsky, 1978.

_____. *The First Person.* Minneapolis: University of Minnesota Press, 1981.

Crick, Francis. "Function of the Thalamic Reticular Complex: The Searchlight Hypothesis." *Proceedings of the National Academy of Sciences*, 81 (1984), 4586–90.

Cummins, Phillip. "Kant on Outer and Inner Intuition." *Nous*, 2 (1968), 271–92.

Curley, E.M. "Descartes on the Creation of the Eternal Truths." *The Philosophical Review*, 93 (1984), 569–97.

Davidson, Donald. *Essays on Action and Events.* Oxford: Clarendon Press, 1980.

_____. *Inquiries into Truth and Interpretation.* Oxford: Clarendon Press, 1984.

_____. "A Coherence Theory of Truth and Knowledge." In *Truth and Interpretation: Perspectives on the Philosophy of Donald Davidson*, edited by Ernest LePore, pp. 307–19. Oxford: Blackwell, 1986.

_____. "Thinking Causes." In *Mental Causation*, edited by John Heil and Alfred Mele, pp. 3–17. Oxford: Clarendon Press, 1995.

Demopoulos, William, and Michael Friedman. "The Concept of Structure in *The Analysis of Matter*." In *Minnesota Studies in the Philosophy of Science*, vol. 12, edited by C. Wade Savage and C. Anthony Anderson, pp. 183–89. Minneapolis: University of Minnesota Press, 1989.

Dennett, Daniel. *Consciousness Explained.* Boston: Little, Brown, 1991.

Descartes, René. *The Philosophical Works of Descartes*, 2 vols. Translated by Elizabeth S. Haldane and G.R.T. Ross. Cambridge: Cambridge University Press, 1931.

_____. *Philosophical Letters.* Edited and Translated by Anthony Kenny. Minneapolis: University of Minnesota Press, 1981.

_____. *The Philosophical Writings of Descartes*, 3 vols. Translated by John

Cottingham, Robert Stoothoff, and Dugald Murdoch. Cambridge: Cambridge University Press, 1984.

Deutsch, Harry. "Logic for Contingent Beings." *Journal of Philosophical Research*, 19 (1994), 273–329.

Devitt, Michael. *Realism and Truth*. Princeton, N.J.: Princeton University Press, 1984.

Dewey, John. "Propositions, Warranted Assertibility, and Truth." In *Problems of Men*, pp. 331–53. New York: Philosophical Library, 1946.

Dicker, Georges. "Hume's Fork Revisited." *History of Philosophy Quarterly*, 8 (1991), 327–42.

_____. *Descartes: An Analytical and Historical Introduction*. Oxford: Oxford University Press, 1993.

Dodge, Jeffery. "Uniformity in Empirical Cause-Effect Relations in the Second Analogy." *Kant-Studien*, 73 (1982), 47–54.

Dreier, James. "The Supervenience Argument Against Moral Realism." *The Southern Journal of Philosophy*, 30 (1992), 13–38.

Dretske, Fred. "Counting to Infinity." *Analysis*, 25 (1965), 99–101.

Dryer, D.P. *Kant's Solution for Verification in Metaphysics*. London: Allen and Unwin, 1966.

Ducasse, C.J. *Nature, Mind, and Death*. La Salle, Ill.: Open Court, 1951.

Dummett, Michael. *Truth and Other Enigmas*. Cambridge, Mass.: Harvard University Press, 1978.

_____. "Realism." *Synthese*, 52 (1982), 55–112.

_____. *The Logical Basis of Metaphysics*. Cambridge, Mass.: Harvard University Press, 1991.

Earman, John. "Kant, Incongruous Counterparts, and the Nature of Space and Space-Time." *Ratio*, 13 (1971), 1–18; reprinted in Van Cleve and Frederick (1991), 131–49.

_____. *A Primer of Determinism*. Dordrecht: Reidel, 1986.

Edwards, Paul. "The Cosmological Argument." *The Rationalist Annual*, 1959; reprinted in Rowe and Wainwright (1973), 136–48.

Edwards, Paul, and Arthur Pap. *A Modern Introduction to Philosophy*. New York: Free Press, 1965.

Ewing, A.C. *Kant's Treatment of Causality*. London: Kegan Paul, 1924.

_____. *The Fundamental Questions of Philosophy*. London: Routledge & Kegan Paul, 1951.

Falkenstein, Lorne. "Kant, Mendelssohn, Lambert, and the Subjectivity of Time." *Journal of the History of Philosophy*, 29 (1991), 227–51.

Feldman, Richard, and Earl Conee. "Evidentialism." *Philosophical Studies*, 48 (1985), 15–34.

Findlay, J.N. "Can God's Existence Be Disproved?" *Mind*, 52 (1948). Reprinted in Plantinga (1965), 111–22.

_____. *Kant and the Transcendental Object*. Oxford: Clarendon Press, 1981.

Fodor, Jerry. *A Theory of Content*. Cambridge, Mass.: MIT Press, 1990.

Forgie, J. William. "Kant on the Relation Between the Cosmological and Ontological Arguments." *International Journal for Philosophy of Religion*, 34 (1993), 1–12.

Foster, John. *The Case for Idealism*. London: Routledge & Kegan Paul, 1982.

Frankfurt, Harry. "Descartes on the Creation of the Eternal Truths." *The Philosophical Review*, 86 (1977), 36–57.

Frege, Gottlob. *The Foundations of Arithmetic*. Translated by J.L. Austin. Evanston, Ill.: Northwestern University Press, 1980.

Gardner, Martin. *The Ambidextrous Universe*. San Francisco: Freeman, 1989; 3rd edition.

Geach, P.T. "Omnipotence." *Philosophy*, 48 (1973), 7–20.

_____. *Truth, Love, and Immortality: An Introduction to McTaggart's Philosophy.* Berkeley: University of California Press, 1979.

George, Rolf. "Kant's Sensationism." *Synthese*, 47 (1981), 229–55.

Goodman, Nelson. *Ways of Worldmaking.* Indianapolis, Ind.: Bobbs-Merrill, 1978.

Gram, Moltke S., ed. *Kant: Disputed Questions.* Chicago: Quadrangle Books, 1967.

_____. *The Transcendental Turn.* Gainesville: University of Florida Press, 1984.

Green, T.H. *Prologomena to Ethics.* Oxford: Clarendon Press, 1883.

Grice, H.P. "Personal Identity." *Mind*, 50 (1941); reprinted in Perry (1975), 73–95.

Grice, H.P., and P.F. Strawson. "In Defense of a Dogma." *Philosophical Review*, 65 (1956), 141–58.

Grünbaum, Adolf. *Modern Science and Zeno's Paradoxes.* Middletown, Conn.: Wesleyan University Press, 1967.

Guyer, Paul. *Kant and the Claims of Knowledge.* Cambridge: Cambridge University Press, 1987.

Hartshorne, Charles. "The Necessarily Existent." In Plantinga (1965), 123–35.

_____. "The Logic of the Ontological Argument." In Rowe and Wainwright (1973), 108–10.

Hempel, Carl. "On the Logical Positivists' Theory of Truth." *Analysis*, 2 (1935), 49–59.

Hilbert, D., and S. Cohn-Vossen. *Geometry and the Imagination.* Translated by P. Nemenyi. New York: Chelsea, 1956; from the 1932 German edition.

Hintikka, Jaakko. "On Kant's Notion of Intuition (*Anschauung*)." In *The First Critique: Reflections on Kant's Critique of Pure Reason*, edited by T. Penelhum and J. McIntosh, pp. 38–53. Belmont, Calif.: Wadsworth, 1969.

Hinton, G.E., J.L. McClelland, and D.E. Rumelhart. "Distributed Representations." In *Parallel Distributed Processing: Explorations in the Microstructure of Cognition*, edited by David E. Rumelhart and James L. McClelland, pp. 77–109. Cambridge, Mass.: MIT Press, 1986.

Hirsch, Eli. *Dividing Reality.* Oxford: Oxford University Press, 1993.

Hirst, R.J. "Realism." In *The Encyclopedia of Philosophy*, edited by Paul Edwards, vol. 7, p. 77. New York: Macmillan, Inc., 1967.

Horwich, Paul. *Truth.* Cambridge, Mass.: MIT Press, 1990.

Howell, Robert. "Intuition, Synthesis, and Individuation in the *Critique of Pure Reason*," *Nous*, 7 (1973), 207–32.

Hume, David. *Dialogues Concerning Natural Religion.* Edited by Nelson Pike. Indianapolis, Ind.: Bobbs-Merrill, 1970.

_____. *A Treatise of Human Nature.* Edited by L.A. Selby-Bigge. Oxford: Oxford University Press, 1978; 2nd edition.

Hylton, Peter. *Russell, Idealism, and the Emergence of Analytical Philosophy.* Oxford: Clarendon Press, 1990.

Irwin, Terence. "Morality and Personality: Kant and Green." In Wood (1984), 31–56.

Jackson, Reginald. "Locke's Distinction Between Primary and Secondary Qualities." *Mind*, 38 (1929); reprinted in *Locke and Berkeley*, edited by C.B. Martin and D.M. Armstrong, pp. 53–77. Notre Dame, Ind.: University of Notre Dame Press, 1968.

James, William. *The Principles of Psychology*, 2 vols. New York: Dover, 1950; reprint of the 1890 edition.

Joseph, H.W.B. "A Comparison of Kant's Idealism with That of Berkeley." *Proceedings of the British Academy*, (1929), 213–34; reprinted in *The*

Real and The Ideal, edited by R.C.S. Walker, pp. 47–68. New York: Garland, 1989.

Kant, Immanuel. *Kant's Inaugural Dissertation and Early Writings on Space*. Translated by John Handyside. Chicago: Open Court, 1929.

_____. *Prologomena to Any Future Metaphysics*. Translated by Lewis White Beck. Indianapolis, Ind.: Bobbs-Merrill, 1950.

_____. *Critique of Pure Reason*. Translated by Norman Kemp Smith. New York: St. Martin's Press, 1965.

_____. *Metaphysical Foundations of Natural Science*. Translated by James Ellington. Indianapolis, Ind.: Bobbs-Merrill, 1970.

_____. *Logic*. Translated by Robert S. Hartman and Wolfgang Schwarz. Indianapolis, Ind.: Bobbs-Merrill, 1974.

_____. "The Use in Natural Philosophy of Metaphysics Combined with Geometry." In *Kant's Latin Writings*, edited by Lewis White Beck, pp. 111–34. New York: Peter Lang, 1986.

_____. *Lectures on Logic*. Translated by J. Michael Young. Cambridge: Cambridge University Press, 1992.

_____. *Theoretical Philosophy, 1755–1770*. Edited and translated by David Walford in collaboration with Ralf Meerbote. Cambridge Edition of the Works of Immanuel Kant, vol. 1. Cambridge: Cambridge University Press, 1992.

_____. *The One Possible Basis for a Demonstration of the Existence of God*. Translated by Gordon Treash. Lincoln: University of Nebraska Press, 1994; reprint of the 1979 Abaris Books edition.

Kemp Smith, Norman. *A Commentary to Kant's 'Critique of Pure Reason'*. New York: Humanities Press, 1962; reprint of the 1923 edition.

Kenny, Anthony. *Descartes: A Study of His Philosophy*. New York: Random House, 1968.

Kim, Jaegwon. "Concepts of Supervenience." *Philosophy and Phenomenological Research*, 45 (1984), 153–76; reprinted in Kim (1993), 53–78.

_____. "Epiphenomenal and Supervenient Causation." In *Midwest Studies in Philosophy*, edited by Peter A. French, Theodore E. Uehling, Jr., and Howard K. Wettstein, vol. 9, pp. 257–70. Minneapolis: University of Minnesota Press, 1984; reprinted in Kim (1993), 92–108.

_____. *Supervenience and Mind*. Cambridge: Cambridge University Press, 1993.

Kitcher, Patricia. *Kant's Transcendental Psychology*. Oxford: Oxford University Press, 1990.

Konyndyk, Kenneth. *Introductory Modal Logic*. Notre Dame, Ind.: University of Notre Dame Press, 1986.

Körner, S. *Kant*. Baltimore: Penguin Books, 1955.

Kripke, Saul. "Semantical Considerations on Modal Logic." *Acta Philosophica Fennica*, fasc. XVI, pp. 83–94; reprinted in *Reference and Modality*, edited by Leonard Linsky, pp. 63–72. Oxford: Oxford University Press, 1971.

_____. "Outline of a Theory of Truth." *The Journal of Philosophy*, 72 (1975), 690–716.

_____. *Naming and Necessity*. Cambridge, Mass.: Harvard University Press, 1980.

Lakatos, Imre. *Proofs and Refutations*. Cambridge: Cambridge University Press, 1976.

Lambert, Karel, and Gordon Brittan. *An Introduction to the Philosophy of Science*. Englewood Cliffs, N.J.: Prentice-Hall, 1970.

Lambert, Karel, and Bas C. van Fraassen. "Meaning Relations, Possible

Objects, and Possible Worlds." In *Philosophical Problems in Logic*, edited by Karel Lambert, pp. 1–19. Dordrecht: Reidel, 1970.

Langford, C.H. "A Proof That Synthetic *A Priori* Propositions Exist." *The Journal of Philosophy*, 46 (1949), 20–24.

Leibniz, Gottfried Wilhelm. *Philosophical Papers and Letters*. Edited and translated by Leroy E. Loemker. Dordrecht: Riedel, 1969; 2nd edition.

_____. *Philosophical Writings*. Edited by G.H.R. Parkinson. London: Everyman's Library, 1973.

_____. *New Essays on Human Understanding*. Translated by Peter Remnant and Jonathan Bennett. Cambridge: Cambridge University Press, 1981.

Lewis, C.I. *An Analysis of Knowledge and Valuation*. La Salle, Ill.: Open Court, 1946.

_____. *Mind and the World Order*. New York: Dover, 1956; reprint of 1929 edition by Scribner's.

Lewis, David. *On the Plurality of Worlds*. Oxford: Blackwell, 1986.

Locke, John. *Essay Concerning Human Understanding*. Edited by Peter H. Nidditch. Oxford: Oxford University Press, 1975.

Lovejoy, Arthur. "Kant's Classification of the Forms of Judgment." *The Philosophical Review*, 16 (1907), 588–603; reprinted in Gram (1967), 269–83.

_____. "On Kant's Reply to Hume." *Archiv für Geschichte der Philosophie*, (1906); reprinted in Gram (1967), 284–308.

Mackie, J.L. *The Cement of the Universe*. Oxford: Clarendon Press, 1974.

Malcolm, Norman. "Anselm's Ontological Arguments." *The Philosophical Review*, 69 (1960); reprinted in Plantinga (1965), 136–59.

Marks, Charles E. *Commissurotomy, Consciousness, and Unity of Mind*. Montgomery, Vt.: Bradford Books, 1980.

Matthews, H.E. "Strawson on Transcendental Idealism." *Philosophical Quarterly*, 19 (1969), 204–20; reprinted in Walker (1982), 132–49.

McCann, Edwin. "Skepticism and Kant's B Deduction." *History of Philosophy Quarterly*, 2 (1985), 71–89.

McDermid, Douglas. *Is Pragmatism Coherent?* Ph.D. dissertation, Brown University, 1997.

McGrath, Matthew. *Between Deflationism and the Correspondence Theory: An Account of Truth*. Ph.D. dissertation, Brown University, 1998.

McLendon, Hiram J. "Uses of Similarity of Structure in Contemporary Philosophy." *Mind*, 64 (1955), 79–95.

McTaggart, J.M.E. *The Nature of Existence*, 2 vols. Cambridge: Cambridge University Press, 1927.

Meerbote, Ralf. "Kant on Freedom and the Rational and Morally Good Will." In Wood (1984), 57–72.

_____. "Kant's Functionalism." In *Historical Foundations of Cognitive Science*, edited by J.C. Smith, pp. 161–87. Dordrecht: Kluwer, 1990.

Meinong, Alexius. "The Theory of Objects." In *Realism and the Background of Phenomenology*, edited by R.M. Chisholm, pp. 76–117. New York: Free Press, 1960.

Mellor, D.H. *Real Time*. Cambridge: Cambridge University Press, 1981.

Melnick, Arthur. *Kant's Analogies of Experience*. Chicago: University of Chicago Press, 1973.

Mill, John Stuart. *An Examination of Sir William Hamilton's Philosophy*, 2 vols. Boston: Spencer, 1865.

Moore, G.E. "Refutation of Idealism." *Mind*, 12 (1903), 433–53.

_____. *Some Main Problems of Philosophy*. New York: Collier Books, 1962; first published by Macmillan in 1953.

_____. "The Conception of Intrinsic Value." In *Philosophical Studies*. Totowa,

N.J.: Littlefield, Adams, 1968; first published in London by Routledge & Kegan Paul in 1922.

Mortensen, Chris, and Graham Nerlich. "Physical Topology." *Journal of Philosophical Logic*, 7 (1978), 209–23.

Murphy, Arthur. *Reason and the Common Good: Selected Essays of Arthur E. Murphy*. Edited by W.H. Hay and M.G. Singer. Englewood Cliffs, N.J.: Prentice-Hall, 1963.

Nerlich, Graham. *The Shape of Space*. Cambridge: Cambridge University Press, 1976.

Newman, M.H.A. "Mr. Russell's 'Causal Theory of Perception.'" *Mind*, 37 (1928), 138–48.

Nozick, Robert. *Philosophical Explanations*. Cambridge, Mass.: Harvard University Press, 1981.

Pap, Arthur. "Once More: Colors and the Synthetic *A Priori*." *The Philosophical Review*, 66 (1957), 94–99.

_____. *Semantics and Necessary Truth*. New Haven, Conn.: Yale University Press, 1958.

Parfit, Derek. *Reasons and Persons*. Oxford: Clarendon Press, 1984.

Parsons, Charles. "Kant's Philosophy of Arithmetic." In Walker (1982), 13–40.

Paton, H.J. *Kant's Metaphysic of Experience*, 2 vols. London: Allen & Unwin, 1970; first published in 1936.

Perry, John. "The Same F." *The Philosophical Review*, 79 (1970), 181–200.

_____, ed. *Personal Identity*. Berkeley: University of California Press, 1975.

Pettit, Philip. "Realism and Response-Dependence." *Mind*, 100 (1991), 587–626.

Plantinga, Alvin, ed. *The Ontological Argument*. Garden City, N.Y.: Anchor Books, 1965.

_____. *God, Freedom, and Evil*. New York: Harper Torchbooks, 1974.

_____. *The Nature of Necessity*. Oxford: Oxford University Press, 1974.

Pollock, John L. *Knowledge and Justification*. Princeton, N.J.: Princeton University Press, 1974.

Posy, Carl. "Dancing to the Antinomy: A Proposal for Transcendental Idealism." *American Philosophical Quarterly*, 20 (1983), 81–94.

_____. "Kant's Mathematical Realism." *The Monist*, 67 (1984), 115–34.

_____. "Kant and Conceptual Semantics." *Topoi*, 10 (1991), 67–78.

Powell, C. Thomas. *Kant's Theory of Self-Consciousness*. Oxford: Oxford University Press, 1990.

Prauss, Gerold. *Kant und das Problem der Dinge an Sich*. Bonn: Grundmann, 1974.

Price, H.H. *Perception*. London: Methuen, 1973; reprint of the 1932 edition.

Prichard, H.A. *Kant's Theory of Knowledge*. Oxford: Clarendon Press, 1909.

Prior, A.N. "Berkeley in Logical Form." *Theoria*, 21 (1955), 117–22.

_____. "The Notion of the Present." *Studium Generale*, 23 (1970), 245–48.

_____. *Time and Modality*. Oxford: Clarendon Press, 1957.

Putnam, Hilary. "Reds, Greens, and Logical Analysis." *The Philosophical Review*, 65 (1956), 206–17.

_____. "Red and Green All Over Again: A Rejoinder to Arthur Pap." *The Philosophical Review*, 66 (1957), 100–3.

_____. *Meaning and the Moral Sciences*. London: Routledge & Kegan Paul, 1978.

_____. "Analyticity and Apriority: Wittgenstein and Quine." In *Midwest Studies in Philosophy*, vol. 4, edited by P. French, Theodore E. Uehling, Jr., and Howard K. Wettstein, pp. 423–41. Minneapolis: University of Minnesota Press, 1979.

_____. *Reason, Truth, and History*. Cambridge: Cambridge University Press, 1981.

_____. *Realism and Reason*. Cambridge: Cambridge University Press, 1983.

_____. *The Many Faces of Realism*. La Salle, Ill.: Open Court, 1987.

_____. *Representation and Reality*. Cambridge, Mass.: MIT Press, 1988.

Quine, W.V. *Word and Object*. Cambridge, Mass.: MIT Press, 1960.

_____. *From A Logical Point of View*. New York: Harper Torchbooks, 1963.

_____. *Set Theory and Its Logic*. Cambridge, Mass.: Harvard University Press, 1969; revised edition.

_____. *Philosophy of Logic*. Englewood Cliffs, N.J.: Prentice-Hall, 1970.

Quinton, Anthony. "The *A Priori* and the Analytic." *Proceedings of the Aristotelian Society*, 64 (1963–64), 31–54; reprinted in *Philosophical Logic*, edited by P.F. Strawson, pp. 107–28. Oxford: Oxford University Press, 1967.

Ramsey, F.P. "Critical Notice of L. Wittgenstein's *Tractatus Logico-Philosophicus*." *Mind*, 32 (1923), 465–78.

Reid, Thomas. *Essays on the Intellectual Powers of Man*. Edited by Baruch Brody. Cambridge, Mass.: MIT Press, 1969; originally published in 1785.

Remnant, Peter. "Kant and the Cosmological Argument." *The Australasian Journal of Philosophy*, 37 (1959), 152–55.

Rescher, Nicholas. "Kant and the 'Special Constitution' of Man's Mind: The Ultimately Factual Basis of the Necessity and Universality of *A Priori* Synthetic Truths in Kant's Critical Philosophy." In *Studies in Modality*. American Philosophical Quarterly Monograph Series, no. 8 pp. 71–83. Oxford: Oxford University Press, 1974.

Robinson, Hoke. "Two Perspectives on Kant's Appearances and Things in Themselves." *Journal of the History of Philosophy*, 32 (1994), 411–41.

Rorty, Richard. "Strawson's Objectivity Argument." *The Review of Metaphysics*, 24 (1970), 207–44.

_____. *Consequences of Pragmatism*. Minneapolis: University of Minnesota Press, 1982.

Rosenberg, Jay. "'I Think': Some Reflections on Kant's Paralogisms." In *Midwest Studies in Philosophy*, vol. 10, edited by Peter A. French, Theodore E. Uehling, Jr., and Howard K. Wettstein, pp. 503–31. Minneapolis: University of Minnesota Press, 1986.

Rosenkrantz, Gary. "The Nature of Geometry." *American Philosophical Quarterly*, 18 (1981), 101–10.

Rowe, William L. *The Cosmological Argument*. Princeton, N.J.: Princeton University Press, 1975.

Rowe, William L., and William J. Wainwright, eds. *The Philosophy of Religion*. New York: Harcourt Brace Jovanovich, 1973.

Rucker, Rudolf. *Geometry, Relativity, and the Fourth Dimension*. New York: Dover, 1977.

Russell, Bertrand. *The Problems of Philosophy*. London: Oxford University Press, 1912.

_____. *The Analysis of Matter*. London: Kegan Paul, Trench, Trubner, 1927.

_____. *A History of Western Philosophy*. New York: Simon & Schuster, 1945.

_____. *Human Knowledge: Its Scope and Limits*. New York: Simon & Schuster, 1948.

_____. *Logic and Knowledge*. Edited by Robert C. Marsh. London: Allen & Unwin, 1956.

_____. *An Inquiry into Meaning and Truth*. Baltimore: Penguin Books, 1962; first published by Allen & Unwin in 1940.

Savellos, Elias E., and Umit D. Yalçin, eds. *Supervenience: New Essays*. Cambridge: Cambridge University Press, 1995.

Schopenhauer, Arthur. *On the Fourfold Root of the Principle of Sufficient Reason.* Translated by E.F.J. Payne. La Salle, Ill.: Open Court, 1974.

Sellars, Wilfrid. "Empiricism and the Philosophy of Mind." In *Science, Perception, and Reality*, pp. 127–96. London: Routledge & Kegan Paul, 1963.

_____. *Science and Metaphysics: Variations on Kantian Themes.* London: Routledge & Kegan Paul, 1968.

_____. "Metaphysics and the Concept of a Person." In *Essays in Philosophy and Its History*, pp. 214–43. Dordrecht: Reidel, 1974.

_____. "Kant's Transcendental Idealism." In *Proceedings of the Ottawa Congress on Kant*, edited by P. Laberge, F. Duchesneau, and B.E. Morrisey, pp. 165–81. Ottawa: University of Ottawa Press, 1976.

Shaffer, Jerome. "Existence, Predication, and the Ontological Argument." *Mind*, 71 (1962), 307–25.

Simons, Peter. "On What There Isn't: The Meinong-Russell Dispute." In *Philosophy and Logic in Central Europe from Bolzano to Tarski*, pp. 159–91. Dordrecht: Kluwer, 1992.

Sklar, Lawrence. *Space, Time, and Spacetime.* Berkeley, Calif.: University of California Press, 1974.

Smart, J.J.C. *Philosophy and Scientific Realism.* New York: Humanities Press, 1963.

Smith, Michael, and Daniel Stoljar. "Global Response-Dependence and Noumenal Realism." Manuscript in preparation.

Sosa, Ernest. "Subjects among Other Things." In *Philosophical Perspectives*, edited by James Tomberlin, vol. 1, pp. 155–87. Atascadero, Calif.: Ridgeview, 1987.

Stevenson, Leslie. "Wittgenstein's Transcendental Deduction and Kant's Private Language Argument." *Kant-Studien*, 73 (1982), 321–37.

Stevenson, Leslie, and Ralph C.S. Walker. "Empirical Realism and Transcendental Anti-Realism." *Proceedings of the Aristotelian Society* (1983), 131–77.

Strawson, P.F. "Propositions, Concepts, and Logical Truths." *Philosophical Quarterly*, 7 (1957), 15–25.

_____. *The Bounds of Sense.* London: Methuen, 1966.

Stroud, Barry. "Transcendental Arguments." *The Journal of Philosophy*, 65 (1968), 241–56; reprinted in Walker (1982), 117–31.

Sumner, L.W., and John Woods, eds. *Necessary Truth.* New York: Random House, 1969.

Thompson, Manley. "Singular Terms and Intuitions in Kant's Epistemology." *The Review of Metaphysics*, 26 (1972), 314–43.

Thomson, James. "Tasks and Super-Tasks." *Analysis*, 15 (1954–55), 1–13.

Treisman, Ann. "Features and Objects in Visual Processing." *Scientific American*, November 1986, 114b–125.

Van Cleve, James. "Four Recent Interpretations of Kant's Second Analogy." *Kant-Studien*, 64 (1973), 71–87.

_____. "Foundationalism, Epistemic Principles, and the Cartesian Circle." *The Philosophical Review*, 88 (1979), 55–91.

_____. "Substance, Matter, and the First Analogy." *Kant-Studien*, 70 (1979), 149–61.

_____. "Epistemic Supervenience and the Circle of Belief," *The Monist*, 68 (1985), 90–104.

_____. "Three Versions of the Bundle Theory," *Philosophical Studies*, 47 (1985), 95–107.

_____. "Mereological Essentialism, Mereological Conjunctivism, and Identity Through Time." In *Midwest Studies in Philosophy*, vol. 11, edited by Peter

A. French, Theodore E. Uehling, Jr., and Howard K. Wettstein, pp. 141–56. Minneapolis: University of Minnesota Press, 1986.

_____. "Right, Left, and the Fourth Dimension." *The Philosophical Review*, 96 (1987), 33–68; reprinted in Van Cleve and Frederick (1991), 203–34.

_____. "Inner States and Outer Relations: Kant and the Case for Monadism." In *Doing Philosophy Historically*, edited by Peter H. Hare, pp. 231–47. Buffalo, N.Y.: Prometheus Books, 1988.

_____. "Mind-Dust or Magic? Panpsychism Versus Emergence." In *Philosophical Perspectives*, edited by James Tomberlin, vol. 4, pp. 215–26. Atascadero, Calif.: Ridgeview, 1990.

_____. "Introduction to the Arguments of 1770 and 1783." In Van Cleve and Frederick (1991), 15–26.

_____. "Analyticity, Undeniability, and Truth." *Canadian Journal of Philosophy*, 18 suppl. (1992), 89–111.

_____. "Semantic Supervenience and Referential Indeterminacy." *The Journal of Philosophy*, 89 (1992), 344–61.

_____. "Descartes and the Destruction of the Eternal Truths." *Ratio*, 7 (1994), 58–62.

_____. "Does Truth Supervene on Evidence?" In Savellos and Yalçin (1995), 306–15.

_____. "Putnam, Kant, and Secondary Qualities." *Philosophical Papers*, 24 (1995), 83–109.

_____. "If Meinong Is Wrong, Is McTaggart Right?" *Philosophical Topics*, 24 (1996), 231–54.

_____. "Minimal Truth Is Realist Truth." *Philosophy and Phenomenological Research*, 56 (1996), 869–75.

_____. "The Manifestation Argument Against Realism." Forthcoming in *Realism: Responses and Reactions (Essays in Honour of Pranab Kumar Sen)*, edited by D.P. Chattopadhyaya et al.

Van Cleve, James, and Robert E. Frederick, eds. *The Philosophy of Right and Left*. Dordrecht: Kluwer, 1991.

Van Fraassen, Bas C. "Presuppositions, Supervaluations, and Free Logic." In *The Logical Way of Doing Things*, edited by Karel Lambert, pp. 67–91. New Haven, Conn.: Yale University Press, 1969.

Van Inwagen, Peter. *Material Beings*. Ithaca, N.Y.: Cornell University Press, 1990.

_____. *Metaphysics*. Boulder, Co.: Westview Press, 1993.

Vesey, G.N.A. "Seeing and Seeing As." *Proceedings of the Aristotelian Society*, 56 (1955–56), 109–24; reprinted in *Perceiving, Sensing, and Knowing*, edited by Robert J. Swartz, pp. 68–83. Berkeley: University of California Press, 1976.

Walker, Ralph C.S. *Kant*. London: Routledge & Kegan Paul, 1978.

_____, ed. *Kant on Pure Reason*. Oxford: Oxford University Press, 1982.

Walsh, W.H. *Kant's Criticism of Metaphysics*. Chicago: University of Chicago Press, 1975.

Warren, Daniel. "Things in Themselves and in Relation to Others." Paper presented at Brown University, 1992.

Weldon, T.D. *Kant's Critique of Pure Reason*. Oxford: Clarendon Press, 1958; 2nd edition.

Wiggins, David. *Sameness and Substance*. Cambridge, Mass.: Harvard University Press, 1980.

Williams, Bernard. *Descartes: The Project of Pure Inquiry*. New York: Humanities Press, 1978.

Wilson, Margaret. "The Phenomenalisms of Berkeley and Kant." In Wood (1984), 157–73.

Winkler, Kenneth. "The New Hume." *The Philosophical Review*, 100 (1991), 541–79.

Wittgenstein, Ludwig. "Some Remarks on Logical Form." *Proceedings of the Aristotelian Society*, 9 suppl. (1929), 162–71.

_____. *Tractatus Logico-Philosophicus*. Translated by D.F. Pears and B.F. McGuinness. London: Routledge & Kegan Paul, 1961.

Wolff, Robert Paul. *Kant's Theory of Mental Activity*. Cambridge, Mass.: Harvard University Press, 1963.

Wood, Allen W. *Kant's Rational Theology*. Ithaca, N.Y.: Cornell University Press, 1978.

_____, ed. *Self and Nature in Kant's Philosophy*. Ithaca, N.Y.: Cornell University Press, 1984.

Wright, Crispin. *Truth and Objectivity*. Cambridge, Mass.: Harvard University Press, 1992.

Zoeller, Guenter. "Lichtenberg and Kant on the Subject of Thinking." *Journal of the History of Philosophy*, 30 (1992), 417–41.

Zweig, Arnulf, ed. and trans. *Kant: Philosophical Correspondence, 1759–99*. Chicago: University of Chicago Press, 1967.

Index

Ackerman, Felicia, 114
Adams, Robert M., 303 n. 34
Adickes, Erich, 163
Adverbial theories of sensation, 9,
    260 n. 13
Allison, Henry, 144, 293 n. 48
    on backdrop argument, 107–108
    on one-world interpretation, 4, 8,
        146–149, 259 n. 6, 291 nn. 29, 39
Alteration
    and carving substances as we like,
        113–115, 286 nn. 28–29
    and change, 53, 109, 115–117, 284 n. 8
    events as, 123, 130
    and logical form, 115–117
    of substance, 106–107, 108–111, 115, 117,
        173–174, 284 nn. 8–9, 13, 285 nn.
        14–15, 18
    and temporal order of appearances, 53–61
    and verificationism, 111–113
    See also Change; Substance
Ameriks, Karl, 120
Amphiboly of Concepts of Reflection, 149,
    155, 292 n. 41
Analogies of Experience
    First, 53, 105–121, 173
    Second, 11, 60, 93, 106, 122–133, 162,
        230–231, 234, 246, 286 n. 28
    Third, 129, 234
    See Also Causation; Substance
Analytic truth. See Truth, analytic
Anomalous monism, 253
Anselm, Saint, 187, 191
Anticipations of Perception, 162, 297 n. 105
Antinomies of Pure Reason
    First, 60, 220–223, 310 n. 39
    Second, 62–72, 110, 220
    Third, 121, 136, 253

Fourth, 204, 306 n. 59
    See also Infinity; Freedom; God; Matter
Antirealism
    and bivalence, 219, 222
    epistemic, 222, 223–225
    and evidence-dependence, 12–14, 113,
        142–143, 212, 218, 223–225, 261 n. 30
    and excluded middle, 218–219,
        309 n. 26
    self-refuting, 142–143
    and two assertive frameworks, 249–252
    verificationism of, 142, 218
Appearance
    cause of, 135, 137–138, 162–167
    ground of, 163–164
    in inner sense, 58, 59–60
    as intentional object, 8, 50–51, 91, 93,
        164–165, 281 n60
    isomorphism of, with thing in itself,
        155–162, 294 n. 71, 295 nn. 77, 84
    as logical construction, 11, 50–51, 58–59,
        60, 127, 260 nn. 21, 22
    material object as, 123–125
    matter as, 69–70 , 120–121, 155
    in one-world interpetation, 4, 6–8,
        153–154, 291 nn. 29, 39
    and representation, 7–8, 124, 163–164
    and rules, 94–95, 281 n. 69
    as supervenient object, 11–12, 58–59, 260
        n. 24
    temporal ordering of, 53–61
    and thing in itself, 3, 6–8, 35, 36–37, 48,
        49–50, 51, 59–60, 92, 136–137,
        146–147, 150, 162–167, 170–171
    and transcendental ideality of time,
        53–61
    in two-worlds interpetation, 8–12,
        154–155

Appearance (*continued*)
and unity of apperception, 238–241, 313 n. 33
unperceived, 233–235
as virtual object, 8–12, 50–51, 58–60, 120, 136–137, 139, 150, 163–167, 271 nn. 23–24
See also Representation
Apperception. *See* Transcendental Unity of Apperception; Unity of apperception
A priori. See Knowledge, *a priori*; Truth, synthetic *a priori*
Aquila, Richard, 12
Aristotle, 105
Arithmetic. *See* Mathematics
Armstrong, David, 170
Ayer, A. J., 11, 93, 123, 260 n. 21

Barcan formula, 197
Bare particular, 139–140
Baumgarten, A., 120
Bayle, Pierre, 62, 65, 170, 174–175
Beck, Lewis White, 144, 264 n. 33
on Second Analogy of Experience, 122, 125–128, 130–131, 287 nn. 5, 14, 21
on Transcendental Deduction, 97–98
Beck, J.S., 163
Behaviorism, 166
Bennett, Jonathan, 76, 194, 275 n. 19
on alteration in substance, 113–116, 117, 118, 119
on change in substance, 108, 284 n. 13
on cosmological argument, 305 n 53, 306 n. 59
on necessity and contingency, 208, 209, 210–211
Berkeley, George, 123, 165
on idealism, 136, 137, 140, 145
on primary properties, 168, 169, 170
on secondary properties, 167, 168, 297 n. 103
Bernstein, Jeremy, 264 n. 34
Binding problem, 243–244
Bird, Graham, 143
Bivalence, 219, 222
Blackburn, Simon, 42–43, 244–245, 254–255
BonJour, Lawrence, 216
Borges, Jorge Luis, 184
Born, Max, 142
Boscovich, R.J., 66
Bradley, F. H., 89
Brentano, Franz, 8–9, 10, 241
Broad, C. D., 83, 274 n. 4, 291 n. 34
on isomorphism, 159, 160
on tense of copula, 199–200
on two-worlds interpretation, 156, 294 n. 68
Brouwer, L. E. J., 222–223
Buddhism, 115, 163, 183, 240
Buroker, Jill Vance, 47–48, 159–160, 295 n. 82

Cantor, Georg, 29
Carnap, Rudolf, 21

Castañeda, Hector-Neri, 83
Categories
application of, to thing in itself, 137–139, 140–141
and consciousness, 74–75, 78–79, 79–84
and experience, 16, 74–76, 78–79, 98–99, 101–103
and judgment, 87–90, 279 nn. 49, 52, 54
knowledge of, 6, 32–33, 161–162
objective validity of, 73, 76–79, 94
pure, 120–121, 137, 138, 139, 163–164, 173
schematized, 120–121, 138, 139, 163–164
See also Causation; Concept; Substance
Caterus, 191, 193
Causal law, particular
contingency of, 3–4, 30–31, 229–231, 244, 246
necessity of, 266 n. 55
Causal maxim, general
contingency of, 267 n. 63
necessity of, 3–4, 30–31, 229–231, 244, 246, 266 n. 55
Causation
derivative, 166–167
and description, 252–253, 316 nn. 72, 74, 76
downward, 166
and freedom, 252–253
and irreversibility, 124–128, 287 n. 12
knowledge of, 128–133, 289 nn. 32–34
and necessity, 229–231
noumenal, 133, 137–139
phenomenal, 162–167
as regular succession, 164–165, 166
relativity of, 252, 253
schematized, 127, 163–164, 165
simultaneous, 129, 288 n. 22
and substance, 128–130
supervenient, 165, 166
transeunt, 129, 288 n. 23
See also Causal law, particular; Causal maxim, general
Change
and alteration, 53, 109, 115–117, 284 n. 8
of substance, 106–107, 108–111, 115, 117, 284 nn. 8–9, 285 nn. 14–15, 17
and temporal order of appearances, 53–61
and verificationism, 111–113
See also Alteration; Substance
Chisholm, Roderick, 9, 82, 181, 183
on *a priori* truths, 29, 266 n. 51
Clarke, Samuel, 204–205
Class, virtual, 9
Coherence theory of truth, 215–216, 255–256
Color, 24–25, 226–229, 311 n. 3–4
Comparison argument, 215–216
Complexes, 149, 62–72, 160–161
Concept
a priori, 6, 16, 32–33
in analytic propositions, 18–20
and consciousness, 16, 74–75, 78–79, 79–84, 276 n. 7
and experience, 16, 74–76, 77, 78–79, 96, 98–99, 101–104

and intuition, 74–76, 77, 78–79, 96
non-containment of, in synthetic proposi-
    tions, 16, 22
non-singularity of, 119
    See also Categories
Condillac, E. B., 95
Congruence, 23–24
    See also Incongruent counterparts
Consciousness
    and concepts, 16, 74–75, 78–79, 79–84,
        276 n. 7
    disunified, 242
    as emergent property, 178–180
    and intuition, 75–76, 78–79
    memory, 181–182
    self-, 75–76
    temporality of, 55
    unity of, 79–84, 100–103, 178, 238–243,
        278 nn. 27, 30–31, 299 n. 17, 313 n. 4
    veridical, 180–181
    See also Transcendental Unity of
        Apperception; Unity of apperception;
        Unity of mind
Contingency, 207, 208–211, 307 n. 66
    See also Necessity
Converse Barcan formula, 197
Copernican revolution, 5–6, 11, 34, 37, 93,
    254
Correspondence theory of truth, 215–216,
    254–256, 308 n. 10
Cosmological argument for God
    contradiction of, 203–204, 306 n. 58
    and ontological argument, 201–204
    first stage of, 204–207
    Principle of Sufficient Reason in, 207–208
    second stage of, 200–204
Cummins, Phillip, 12, 273 n. 26
Curley, E. M., 39
Cusmariu, Arnold, 300 n. 29

Davidson, Donald, 29, 215–216, 252–253,
    266 n. 50
Demopoulos, William, 294 n. 73
Dennett, Daniel, 56
Dependence, evidence-, 12–14, 113,
    142–143, 212, 218, 223–225, 261 n. 30
    See also Antirealism; Realism, internal
Dependence, knowledge-, 12–14, 113
    See also Dependence, evidence-;
        Dependence, mind-
Dependence, mind-, 12–14, 113, 167, 168,
    169, 249–252
    See also Antirealism; Realism, internal
Descartes, René, 25, 91, 98, 184, 239
    on eternal truths, 39–40, 41–42
    on immanent and transcendent objects,
        91
    on inner sense, 57–58, 273 n. 20
    on ontological argument for God,
        187–189, 191
    on primary properties, 169
    on substance, 105, 121
Description,, 252–253, 316 n. 72, 74, 76
Determinism, 230, 244–246, 314 n. 53
Devitt, Michael, 143, 146–147
Dewey, John, 216

Diallelus, problem of, 215–216
Dicker, Georges, 266 n. 61
Dispositional properties, 178
Dodge, Jeffery, 230
Double affection theory, 163, 167–171
Double aspect theory. *See* Transcendental
    Idealism, one-world interpetation of
Dreier, James, 245, 314 n. 54
Dryer, D.P., 143
    on categories and experience, 76, 88
    on change in substance, 108, 112, 285 n.
        14
Ducasse, C.J., 9
Dummett, Michael, 14, 212, 217–225,
    268 n. 10, 309 n. 27, 31

Earman, John, 233
Eberhard, J. A,, 236
Eccles, J. J., 242
Edwards, Jonathan, 165
Ego, transcendental, 163
Einstein, Alfred, 142
Emergence. *See* Property
Empirical object. *See* Object, material
Empiricism, concept, 267 n. 68
Enantiomorphism, 232–233. *See also*
    Incongruent counterparts
Essence, 115–117, 118–120
Event, 123, 130, 132, 289 nn. 32–34
Evidence-dependence. *See* Dependence, ev-
    idence-
Evidence-independence. *See* Independence,
    evidence-
Evidentialism, 13–14, 142–143, 218, 222,
    223–225
    See also Antirealism; Transcendental
        Idealism
Excluded middle, 218–219, 309 n. 26
Existence
    dependence of, on characteristics, 5, 37,
        198, 268 n. 10
    God's necessary, 192–198, 200–204, 303
        nn. 27, 34
    not a real predicate, 116, 188–189,
        190–191, 200, 301 nn. 3, 6, 302 n. 22
    and predication, 191–192, 199–200, 302
        nn. 19, 22, 304 n. 45
    and quantification, 115–117, 189–190,
        198–199
    and subsistence, 190
    See also Quantification
Experience
    and concept, 16, 74–76, 77, 78–79, 96,
        98–99, 101–104
    and judgment, 74, 76, 276 n. 12
    and knowledge, 16–17, 77–78, 277 n. 19
    and self-consciousness, 75–76
    and sensation, 74, 75, 100–103, 282 n. 84
    temporal sequencing of, 55–57, 98,
        272 nn. 17–18, 273 n. 21
    of temporal sequencing, 55–57
    thick, 74–76
    thin, 74–76, 78, 100
    and thing in itself, 135, 137–139, 162–167
Extension, 297 n. 105
Extensionalism, 227, 228

Faith, 136
Falkenstein, Lorne, 53, 272 n. 5–6
Fallibilism, 29
Findlay, J. N. 136, 155, 156, 159, 160, 161, 296 n. 86
First Analogy of Experience, 53, 105–121, 173
  See also Substance
First Antinomy of Pure Reason, 60, 221–222
  See also Infinity
First Paralogism of Pure Reason, 173–178, 184, 197–198
  See also Self
Fodor, Jerry, 33
Forgie, J. William, 305 n. 50–51, 306 n. 54
Foster, John, 56, 249–251, 272 n. 17–18
  The Case For Idealism, 249
Fourth dimension, 46, 231–233, 312 n. 16
Fourth Antinomy of Pure Reason, 204, 306 n. 59
  See also God
Frankfurt, Harry, 39
Freedom, 121, 252–253
Frege, Gottlob
  on analytic truths, 21, 22
  on a priori knowledge, 16–17
  on existence changes, 115–117, 119
  on logicism, 22
  on quantification, 115–117, 189–190, 196–198, 301 nn. 8–9, 302 nn. 12–13
  on relational instantiation, 119
Friedman, Michael, 294 n. 73
Function, 279 n. 45
Future, 247

Galileo Galilei, 169
Gardner, Martin, 232
Gassendi, Pierre, 191
Gaunilo, 191
Geach, P.T., 39
Geometry
  epistemology of, 25–27, 35–36, 265 n. 37
  Euclidean, 3–4, 23–24, 25, 36, 41, 214
  necessary truth in, 38–41
  non-Euclidean, 22, 23, 25, 26, 36, 41
  synthetic a priori truths in, 23–24, 25–27, 36, 40, 263 nn. 22–23, 26–27
  and thing in itself, 35–37
  and transcendental ideality of space, 3–4, 7–8, 11, 34–41, 44–48, 50–51, 120, 135, 136, 146–150, 168, 170, 225, 267 nn. 3–4, 6–7, 269 n. 22
George, Rolf, 76, 282 n. 77
God
  cosmological argument for, 187, 200–211
  impossibility of, 194–198
  Meinongian ontological argument for, 198–200
  modal ontological argument for, 192–198
  modes of, 158
  necessary existence of, 192–198, 200–204, 303 nn. 27, 34
  ontological argument for, 187–192
  as substance, 121
Gödel, Kurt, 22
Goldbach's hypothesis, 219

Goodman, Nelson, 140, 141, 158–159
Green, T.H., 95
Grice, H.P., 28, 240
Grünbaum, Adolf, 66
Guyer, Paul, 76, 268 n. 8, 277 n. 14

Haecceities. See Individual essence
Hamilton, William, 3
Hartshorne, Charles, 192
Hegel, G. W. F., 214
Heraclitus, 115
Herz, Marcus, 32–33, 55, 93
Hilbert, David, 222
Hintikka, Jaakko, 236, 237
Homomorphism, 232–233. See also Incongruent counterparts
Howell, Robert, 313 n. 28
Hume, David, 10, 260 n. 14
  on causation, 30–32, 33, 74, 122, 123, 127–128, 151, 229, 239
  on cosmological argument, 203, 205–206, 208, 303 n. 35
  on projectivism, 245–246
  on self, 182, 183, 239
  An Inquiry Concerning Human Understanding, 230
  A Treatise of Human Nature, 31, 32, 230

Idealism
  absolute, 163
  constructive, 162
  defined, 12
  dogmatic, 104
  ontological, 222
  problematic, 104
  pure, 3
  See also Antirealism; Internal Realism; Irrealism; Transcendental Idealism
Identity of indiscernibles, 149, 160–161, 292 nn. 41–42, 44
Identity, relative, 292 nn. 43–44, 300 n. 26
Incongruent counterparts
  and absolute space, 44–48, 231–233
  absolutism about, 231–232, 233
  argument from intelligibility, 45, 270 n. 7
  argument from interchangeability, 45–46, 270 n. 11
  argument from reducibility, 47–48, 270 nn. 13–14
  defined, 44
  externalism about, 231–233
  internalism about, 231–233
  and thing in itself, 45–46, 48
  and transcendental ideality of space, 44–48, 50–51, 136, 159, 225
Independence, evidence-, 12–13
  See also Realism, metaphysical
Independence, mind-, 13, 213, 214, 216–217, 249–252, 315 n. 68
  See also Realism, metaphysical
Individual essence, 118–119
Induction, 131
Infinity, 63–65, 68–70, 100, 275 n. 23
Inaugural Dissertation, 32, 44, 52, 161, 231, 237

Inner sense, 55, 57–58, 59–60, 273 n. 20
Instantiation, 119
Intentional inexistence.See Appearance;
    Object, intentional; Object, virtual
Intentional object. See Object, intentional
Internal realism. See Realism, internal
Intuition
    in argument from geometry, 37, 40–41
    and concepts, 74–76, 77, 78–79, 96
    and consciousness, 75–76, 78–79
    contingency of forms of, 40–41,
        269 n. 19
    immediacy of, 235–238, 313 n. 29
    and knowledge, 135
    pure, 25
    singularity of, 119, 235–238, 286 n. 38,
        313 n. 28
Intuitionism, mathematical, 218, 219,
    222–223, 268 n. 7, 309 n. 32
Irrealism
    antirealism as, 212, 217–225
    internal realism as, 212–217
    See also Antirealism; Internal Realism;
        Transcendental Idealism
Irreversibility, 124–128, 287 n. 12, 288
    n. 15
Irwin, Terence, 316 n. 74
Isomorphism
    of appearances and thing in itself,
        155–162, 294 n. 71, 295 nn. 77, 84
    concepts of, 253–254
    of equinumerous sets, 157
    too strong, 159–161
    too weak, 156–159

Jacobi, F. H., 134, 135, 137
James, William, 81, 86, 176, 240, 273 n. 19
Joseph, H. W. B., 162
Judgment
    and concept, 87–90, 279 nn. 49, 52, 54
    defined, 87
    and experience, 74, 76, 276 n. 12
    in Metaphysical Deduction, 88,
        279 n. 49
    synthetic a priori, 16, 226–229
    See also Knowledge; Knowledge, a priori;
        Knowledge, empirical

Kemp Smith, Norman, 45, 95, 215,
    236–237
    on categories and experience, 76, 78
    on causal maxim, 30, 31
Kenny, Anthony, 198–200
Kim, Jaegwon, 165, 315 n. 70
Kitcher, Patricia, 241, 243–244, 298 n. 7,
    313 n. 39
Knowledge
    and experience, 16–17, 74, 76, 77–78,
        95–96, 277 n. 19
    and intuition, 96, 135
    relativity of, 151, 155, 293 n. 56
    See also Judgment; Knowledge, a priori;
        Knowledge, empirical
Knowledge, a priori
    of categories, 6, 32–33, 161–162

defined, 15–17, 31–32
    of thing in itself, 136, 146, 150–155
    of time, 52, 271 n. 1
    See also Truth, analytic; Truth, synthetic
        a priori
Knowledge, empirical
    of causation, 128–133, 289 n. 32–34
    defined, 15–17
    source and ground of, 269 n. 22
    of time, 52, 271 n. 1
    and verification, 111–113
Körner, S., 76
Kripke, Saul, 228

Lambert, J. H., 52, 53, 54, 57, 59, 60,
    272 n. 6
Lambert, Karel, 226, 227–228
Langford, C. H., 264 n. 32
LaPlace, Pierre, 230, 311 n. 9
Laws. See Causal laws, particular
Leibniz, G. W., 54, 105, 152, 177, 179, 226
    on cosmological argument for God,
        204–205
    on experience, 74–75
    on metaphysical principles, 149, 207, 292
        n. 41
    on modal ontological argument for God,
        193
    on monads, 137, 158
    on space, 44, 47, 48, 114, 209
    on truths of reason, 17
Lewis, C. I., 21, 76, 142
    on analytical phenomenalism, 92, 93,
        123
    on intrinsic properties, 150–151
    on thin and thick experience, 73–74
    Mind and the World Order, 150–151
Lewis, David, 180, 228, 293 n. 55,
    307 n. 66
    on modifiers and contradiction, 147, 148,
        247, 291 n. 33
Lichtenberg, Georg, 256–257
Liu, Quanhua, 300 n. 36
Locke, John, 3, 144
    on personal identity, 180, 181–182
    on primary qualities, 135, 169
    on secondary qualities, 152, 167, 168,
        170–171
Logic
    Aristotelian, 214
    free, 197
    intuitionist, 219
    modal, 38–41, 193–194, 197
    quantified modal, 197, 303 n. 33
Logical construction
    appearance as, 11, 50–51, 58–59, 60, 127,
        260 nn. 21–22
    intentional object as, 50–51, 93, 164–165
    material object as, 91–94, 120, 123, 164
    matter as, 71–72
    modes as, 110, 286 n. 20
    phenomenal object as, 9, 11, 50–51, 91,
        93, 164
    virtual object as, 9, 11, 50–51, 164
Logicism, 22

Logic, laws of
  bivalence, 219, 222
  excluded middle, 218–219, 309 n. 26
  non-contradiction, 20–21, 30, 31–32
  See also Truth, analytic; Truth, necessary
Lovejoy, Arthur, 127, 130, 131, 288 n. 15

Maass, J. G., 18–19, 36
Malcolm, Norman, 193
Manifold, 82, 86
  See also Concept; Intuition;
    Representation
Marks, Charles E., 241–242
Material object. *See* Object, material
Mathematics
  intuitionism about, 218, 219, 222–223,
    309 n. 32
  necessary truth in, 38–41
  Platonism about, 218, 309 n. 32
  synthetic *a priori* truth in, 22, 23–24,
    25–27, 263 nn. 19, 22–23, 26–27
  See also Geometry
Matter
  as appearance, 69–70, 120–121, 155
  infinite complexity of, 63–65
  as logical construction, 71–72
  primary properties of, 168–169
  transcendental ideality of, 62, 67–72
  ultimate simplicity of, 65–66, 274 n. 4
Matthews, H. E., 4, 139–140, 143
McGilvary, E. B., 147–148
McGrath, Matthew, 307 n. 75
McTaggart, J. M. E., 58, 245, 284 n. 3
  on unreality of time, 199–200, 272 n. 10
Meerbote, Ralf, 253, 294 n. 60
Meinong, Alexis, 10, 304 n. 46
  on independence principle, 198,
    304 n. 42
  on quantification and existence, 198–199
Meinongian ontological argument for God,
    198–200
Mellor, D. H., 55–56, 57, 272 n. 13
Melnick, Arthur, 112–113
Memory, 57, 181–182
Mendelssohn, Moses, 52, 53, 54, 57, 59, 60
Mental states. *See* Appearance; Conscious-
    ness; Object, intentional;
    Representation
Metaphysical Deduction of The Categories,
    77, 78, 88–90, 138,
    279 n.49
  See also Transcendental Deduction of the
    Categories
Metaphysical Exposition of Space, 237
*Metaphysical Foundations of Natural
    Science*, 70, 106, 284 n. 7
Metaphysical realism. *See* Realism, meta-
    physical
Mill, James, 151
Mill, John Stuart
  on intrinsic properties, 151, 152,
    153–154, 155
  on relativity of knowledge, 151, 155, 293
    n. 56
Mind-dependence. *See* Dependence, mind-
Möbius, Wolfgang, 232, 264 n. 35

Modal ontological argument for God,
    192–198
Modes, 105, 109–110, 120, 179–180, 197,
    286 n. 20
Monadism, 137, 294 n. 60
Monism, cheap, 114–115, 285 n. 15
Moore, G.E., 8, 38, 41, 60
Morality, 136
Murphy, A. E., 130–131

Necessary truths. *See* Truth, necessary
Necessity, 17
  and contingency, 207, 208–211, 307 n. 66
  de re and *de dicto*, 89, 190, 194, 303 nn.
    25, 29, 30
  of general causal maxim, 3–4, 30–31,
    229–231, 244, 246, 266 n. 55
  of particular causal laws, 266 n. 55
  and supervenience, 244–245, 314 n. 52
Neglected alternative argument, 36, 267 n. 1
Nerlich, Graham, 232–233
Neurath, Otto, 216
Newman, M. H. A., 156–158, 294 n. 73
Newton, Isaac, 44, 54, 114, 209
Non-extensionality, 252–253
Noumenalism, 11, 151. *See also*
    Transcendental Idealism
Noumenon, 3, 134. *See also* Thing in itself
Nozick, Robert, 208–209

O'Shea, James, 285 n. 17
Object, empirical. *See* Object, material
Object, intentional (object₁), 8, 91, 281 n. 60
  as logical construction, 50–51, 93,
    164–165
Object, material (object₂)
  in one-world interpretation, 146–150
  as logical construction, 91–94, 120, 123,
    164
  mind-dependence of, 5, 216, 308 n. 10
  as sequence of appearances, 8–9, 92–95,
    123–125
  as virtual object, 91–94, 120, 123–125,
    280 n. 57, 281 nn. 65–66
Object, phenomenal
  and adverbial theory of sensation, 9
  as cause of representation, 162–167
  as logical construction, 9, 11, 50–51, 91,
    93, 164
  See also Object, virtual
Object, physical. *See* Object, material
Object, supervenient, 11–12, 58–59, 260 n.
    24, 295 n. 83
Object, virtual
  appearance as, 8–12, 50–51, 58–59, 120,
    136–137, 139, 150, 163–167, 271 nn.
    23–24
  intentional object as, 8, 50–51, 91, 93,
    164–165, 281 n. 60
  as logical construction, 9, 11, 50–51, 164
  material object as, 91–94, 120, 123–125,
    280 n. 57, 281 nn. 65–66
  mind-dependence of, 261 n. 28
  as supervenient object, 11–12, 260 n. 24,
    295 n. 83
  and virtual classes, 9

One-world interpretation. *See*
   Transcendental Idealism, one-world
   interpretation of
Ontological argument for God, 187–192
   and cosmological argument, 201–204
   modal, 192–198
   See also Existence

Pap, Arthur, 24, 226, 227, 267 n. 62
Paralogisms of Pure Reason
   First, 173–175, 184, 197–198
   Second, 175–179, 185, 197, 198
   Third, 180–182
   See also Self
Parfit, Derek, 181–182
Parity, fall of, 233, 312 n. 16
Parsons, Charles, 236, 237, 312 n. 27
Past, 247
Paton, H. J., 76, 144, 155–156, 159, 160
Perception, 77, 86, 112, 123, 156–162
   See also Appearance; Intuition; Sensation
Perfections, God's, 188, 189, 301 n. 6
Personal identity, 181–182
Phenomenalism
   analytical, 71, 92, 93, 99, 123–125,
      127–128
   ontological, 11, 68, 71–72, 93, 123–124,
      151
   reductive, 249–52
   transcendental idealism as, 11, 68, 71–72,
      123
   See also Antirealism; Realism, internal;
      Transcendental Idealism
Phenomenon, 3, 134. *See also* Appearance;
   Representation
Physics, Newtonian, 148, 214
Pistorius, 36
Plantinga, Alvin, 192
Platonism, 119–120, 218, 309 n. 32
Pollock, John, 29, 266 n. 52
Positivism, 143
Possibility, 249–251
Postulates of Empirical Thought, 234–235
Posy, Carl, 220–223, 225, 275 n. 18, 310 nn.
   37–38
Prauss, Gerold, 144
Predicate
   as property, 188
   relational, 246–248
   relative, 246–248
   tautological, 189
Predication, 191–192, 199–200, 302 nn. 19,
   22, 304 n. 45
   See also Existence
Price, H. H., 276 n. 7, 282 n. 84
Prichard, H. A., 163
Primary qualities. *See* Property (quality),
   primary
Principle of Complete Determination, 225
Principle of Fecundity, 208–211, 307 n. 70
   limited, 209–210, 307 n. 74
Principle of Independence, 198, 304 n. 42
Principle of Mereological Reducibility,
   175–179
Principle of Relational Reducibility, 47–51
   See also relation, reducibility of

Principle of Sufficient Reason, 207–208,
   223–224
Prior, A. N., 248
Prolegomena to Any Future Metaphysics, 6,
   34, 44, 45, 136, 154, 159, 167–168
Property
   dispositional, 152, 178, 294 n. 62
   emergent, 177–180
   extensional identity criterion of, 227, 228
   as predicate, 188
   whole- and part-, 177–179
Property, extrinsic, 151, 152, 293 nn. 52–53,
   55–56
Property, intrinsic, 148, 151–155, 292 nn.
   45, 48, 293 nn. 52–53
Property (quality), primary, 3, 135, 168–171
Property (quality), secondary
   categorical basis of, 152, 293 n. 57
   dispositional criterion of, 167, 168
   inferiority of, 3, 169–170
   and intrinsic properties, 151, 293 nn.
      52–53
   mind-dependence criterion of, 167, 168
Propositions
   a priori/empirical, 15–17
   necessary/contingent, 17
   analytic/synthetic, 17–21, 26–27, 27–30
   See also Truth, analytic; Truth, necessary;
      Truth, synthetic *a priori*
Putnam, Hilary, 33, 294 n. 62
   on indeterminacy of thing in itself,
      141–143, 290 n. 15
   on internal realism, 14, 212–217
   on secondary properties, 151–153,
      167–168, 293 n. 56
   on synthetic *a priori* judgments, 226–229
   Reason, Truth, And History, 213
Pythagorean Theorem, 40

Qualities. *See* Property; Property (quality),
   primary; Property (quality), secondary
Quantification
   and existence, 115–117, 189–190,
      198–199
   Kant-Frege view, 115–117, 189–190,
      196–198, 301 nn. 8–10, 302 nn. 12–13
   over possible individuals, 228
   Quinean view, 189, 301 n. 9, 302 n. 12
   See also Existence
Quine, W. V., 9, 13, 75, 315 n. 71
   on analyticity, 17, 21, 27–30, 265 nn. 40,
      47, 266 n. 50
   on necessity, 42, 269 n. 27
   on quantification, 189, 301 n. 9, 302 n. 12
Quinton, Anthony, 265 n. 39

Ramsey, F. P., 25
Rationalism, 32, 33
Realism
   defined, 12
   and evidence-independence, 12–13
   hard-core, 142–143
   internal, 14, 212–217
   metaphysical, 3, 142, 212–217, 308 n. 13
   and mind-independence, 13, 213, 214,
      216–217, 249–252

Realism (*continued*)
  soft-core, 141–142
  transcendental, 220, 222–223
  See also Realism, internal; Realism, meta-
    physical
Realism, internal
  coherence truth criterion of, 213, 214–217
  mind-dependence criterion of, 213, 214,
    216–217
  two theories criterion of, 213, 214, 217
Realism, metaphysical
  correspondence truth criterion of, 213,
    214–17, 308 n. 13
  mind-independence criterion of, 213,
    214, 216–217
  one true theory criterion, 142, 213, 214,
    217
Refutation of Idealism, 60
Reid, Thomas, 95, 153, 181, 281 n. 60, 291
  n. 40, 311 n. 9
Relation
  grounded and ungrounded, 160
  natural and unnatural, 158–159
  reducibility of, 47–48, 149, 155–156
  self-contained, 159, 295 n. 80
  See also Causation; Irreversibility;
    Isomorphism; Knowledge; Space; Time
Relativism, 147–148
Relativity, 52, 142, 166
Representation
  alteration in, 53–61
  and appearance, 7–8, 124, 163–164
  caused by phenomenal, 162–167
  change in, 53–61
  irreversibility of, 124–128, 287 n. 12
  as logical construction, 127
  sequences of, as material object, 8–9,
    92–95, 123–125
  synthesis of, 84–87, 92–95, 279 nn.
    40–41, 43
  and transcendental ideality of space, 7
  and transcendental ideality of time, 7,
    53–61
  unity of, 79–84, 88
  See also Appearance
Rescher, Nicholas, 268 n. 13
Robinson, Hoke, 296 n. 92
Rorty, Richard, 102, 141, 216
Rosenberg, Jay, 282 n. 70
Rosenkrantz, Gary, 32
Rowe, William L., 307 n.65
Rules, 94–95
Russell, Bertrand, 9, 22, 29, 93, 304 n. 16
  on isomorphism of percept and object,
    156–158
  on argument from geometry, 37–41
  on logical construction, 11, 239, 260 n.
    21
  on arguments for God, 198, 201
  on negative empirical propositions, 112
Russell's paradox, 29

Schematism, 106, 120–121, 138, 139,
  163–164
  See also Categories; Causation
Schopenhauer, Arthur, 129

Schulze, J. G., 19
Second Analogy of Experience, 60, 93, 106,
  162, 230–231, 234, 246
  Beck's version, 122, 125–128, 130–131,
    287 nn. 5, 14, 21
  See also Causation
Second Antinomy of Pure Reason, 62–72,
  110, 120
  See also Matter
Second Paralogism of Pure Reason,
  175–179, 185, 299 n. 15
  See also Self
Secondary qualities. *See* Property (quality),
  secondary
Self
  as absolute subject, 175, 298 n. 9
  bundle, 53
  empirical, 182, 185, 186
  as enduring, 172, 180–182
  identity of empirical and noumenal, 184,
    300 n. 34
  identity of empirical and transcencenden-
    tal, 184
  identity of transcendental and noumenal,
    184–185
  immateriality of, 176–177, 298 n. 14
  as mode, 179–180
  no self view of, 183, 256–257, 317 n. 84
  noumenal, 83, 182, 185–186
  simplicity of, 172, 175–179
  as substance, 172, 173–175, 180,
    197–198, 298 n. 5
  transcendental, 182–186
Self-consciousness, 75–76
Sellars, Wilfrid, 49, 178, 299 n. 15
  on appearances, 12, 261 n. 25
  on experience, 276 n. 7, 12
Sensation, 74, 75, 100–103, 276 nn. 5–6,
  282 n. 84
  See also Experience; Intuition; Percep-
    tion
Sensationism, 95
Shape, 148–149
Simples, 65–66, 225, 310 n. 32
Skepticism, 73, 104, 135, 255–256
Smart, J. J. C., 170
Sosa, Ernest, 11–12
Soul. *See* Self
Space
  absolute, 44–48, 114, 231–233
  epistemology of, 45
  and geometry, 34–37
  and incongruent counterparts, 44–48,
    231–233
  neglected alternative argument and, 36
  relational, 114
  transcendental ideality of, 3–4, 7–8, 11,
    34–41, 44–48, 50–51, 120, 135, 136,
    146–150, 168, 170, 225, 267 nn. 3–4,
    6–7, 269 n. 22
Spencer, Herbert, 151
Spinoza, Baruch, 105, 114, 158, 197, 208,
  306 n. 62
Split brain cases, 241–243, 313 n. 40
Strawson, P.F., 28, 75, 76, 273 n. 29, 288 n.
  15, 298 n. 14

on conceptualizability of experience, 98, 101–104
on objectivity, 98, 99, 100–101, 103–104, 282 n. 83
on unity of consciousness, 98, 100–101, 103–104, 282 n. 83
on verificationism, 68, 69
The Bounds of Sense, 98–104
Stroud, Barry, 104
Subsistence, 190
Substance
alteration in, 106–107, 108–111, 115, 117, 173–174, 284 nn. 9, 13, 285 nn. 14, 18
anchoring argument for, 109–111
backdrop argument for, 107–108
carving of, as we like, 113–115
and causation, 128–130
change in, 106–107, 108–111, 115, 117, 284 nn. 8–9, 285 nn. 14, 17
as mode, 120
noumenal, 120–121
as permanent (substance$_2$), 106–111, 173
phenomenal, 120–121
self as, 172, 173–175, 180, 197–198, 298 n. 5
as subject (substance$_1$), 105–106, 108–111, 115, 117, 121, 173–175, 298 n. 5
and thing in itself, 138–139
verificationist argument for, 111–113, 286 n. 28
Supervenience
causal, 165, 166
no difference formulation of, 143
dispositional, 152, 293 n. 57
and necessity, 244–245, 314 n. 52
truth value, 210, 307 n. 75
Supervenient object. *See* Object, supervenient
Synthesis
and binding problem, 243–244
defined, 85
and judgment, 87, 222
of representations, 84–87, 92–95, 279 nn. 40–41, 43
in Transcendental Deduction, 84–87, 90, 94–97
Synthesis of Apprehension in Intuition, 85
Synthesis of Recognition in a Concept, 85, 87
Synthesis of Reproduction in Imagination, 85
Synthetic *a priori* truth. *See* Truth, synthetic *a priori*

Temporary intrinsics, 247
Temporal parts, 247, 248
Tense, 248
Thing in itself
and appearance, 3, 6–8, 35, 36–37, 49–50, 51, 59–60, 92, 136–137, 146–147, 150, 162–167, 170–171
application of categories to, 137–139, 140–141
as bare particular, 139–140
as cause of experience, 135, 137–138, 162–167

composition of complex, 160–161
disposability of, 140–141, 290 n. 13
distinct from noumenon, 134, 259 n. 1
double affection of, 163, 167–171
and geometry, 35–37
as ground of experience, 135, 138–139, 163–164
and identity of indiscernibles, 149, 160–161, 292 nn. 41–42, 44
and incongruent counterparts, 45–46, 48
indeterminacy of, 141–143
as intrinsic, 49, 148, 150–155, 292 nn. 45, 48
isomorphism of, with appearances, 155–162, 294 n. 71, 295 nn. 77, 84
knowledge of, 136, 146, 150–155
nonspatiality of, 4, 7, 135, 136, 138, 146–150, 164
nontemporality of, 4, 7, 135, 136, 138, 146–150, 164
in one world interpretation, 7–8
pre-Critical sense of, 45, 48
relations between, 152–153, 156–162
senselessness of, 136
in two-worlds interpretation, 146–150, 154–155
unknowability of, 49, 134, 135–137, 138–143, 150
Third Analogy of Experience, 129, 234
See also Causation
Third Antinomy of Pure Reason, 121, 136, 253
See also Freedom
Third Paralogism of Pure Reason, 180–182
See also Self
Thompson, Manley, 236–237, 238
Time
and appearance, 53–61
knowledge of, 52, 271 n. 1
rupture in unity of, 107–108
transcendental ideality of, 3, 4, 7–8, 11, 52–61, 120, 135, 146–150, 170
Transcendental Aesthetic, 34–37, 52–54, 60, 144, 162
Transcendental argument, 35, 104
Transcendental Deduction of the Categories
category premise in, 87–90
George's version, 96–97
objective, 76–79
Strawson's version, 98–104
subjective, 76, 79–90, 96–97
synthesis premise in, 84–87
unity premise in, 79–84
Transcendental ego, 163
Transcendental Idealism
as analytical phenomenalism, 124–125, 127–128
as epistemic antirealism, 222, 223–225
as evidentialism, 14, 222, 223–225
as ontological phenomenalism, 68, 71–72, 123, 124
as tautology, 4, 8
as verificationism, 68–69, 104, 274 n. 17, 275 n. 18
See also Appearance; Categories; Consciousness; Experience; Geometry;

Transcendental Idealism (*continued*)
Incongruent counterparts; Intuition; Judgment; Representation; Space; Thing in itself; Time; Transcendental Idealism, one-world interpretation of; Transcendental Idealism, two-worlds interpretation of
Transcendental Idealism, one-world interpretation of
appearance in, 4, 6–8, 153–154, 291 nn. 29, 39
and descriptions, 252–253, 315 n. 70
and intrinsic properties, 150–155
problems with, 146–150
textual evidence for, 144–146
thing in itself in, 7–8, 150–155
Transcendental Idealism, two-worlds interpretation of
appearance in, 8–12, 154–155
qualified, 150
relation in, 155–156
textual evidence for, 146
thing in itself in, 154–155
Transcendental Realism, 220, 223
Transcendental Unity of Apperception
as principle, 79, 83–84
as property, 79–83, 278 nn. 27, 30–31
See also Unity of apperception
Treisman, Ann, 243–244
Truth
coherence theory of, 255–256
correspondence theory of, 215–216, 254–256, 308 n. 10
minimalist theory of, 317 n. 83
physical, 249–251, 315 n. 64
supervenience of, 210, 307 n. 75
Truth, analytic
containment characterization of, 18–20, 22, 262 nn. 9–10
contradiction characterization of, 20, 22, 31–32, 262 nn. 11–12
definition characterization of, 20–21, 26–27
and thing in itself, 136
Truth, necessary
alleged circularity of, 42–43, 269 n. 27
alleged triviality of, 42, 269 n. 25
conventionality of, 42, 269 n. 23
in geometry, 17, 38–41
in logic, 17, 20–21, 27–30, 218–219
in mathematics, 38–41
Truth, synthetic *a priori*
in color judgment, 24–25, 226–229
framework proposition, 24–27

in geometry, 23–24, 25–27, 36, 40, 263 nn. 22–23, 26–27
in mathematics, 22, 23–24, 25–27, 263 nn. 19, 22–23, 26–27
possibility of, 31, 33
Two-worlds interpretation. *See* Transcendental Idealism, two-worlds interpretation of

Unity
defined, 80
of representations, 81–84, 85
in Transcendental Deduction, 79–84, 88
Unity of apperception
defined, 80
and object constitution, 94–97
and split brain cases, 241–243, 313 n. 40
subjectless models of, 240
and unity of mind, 238–241
Unity of mind
center theories of, 83, 239, 283 n. 85
synchronic and diachronic, 182, 240
system theories of, 83, 239, 283 n. 85
and unity of apperception, 238–241
U-relatedness, 81–84, 87–88
See also Unity of apperception

Van Fraassen, Bas, 226, 227–228
Verificationism
antirealism as, 104, 142, 218
and substance, 111–115, 286 n. 28
and thing in itself, 136
and transcendental idealism, 68–69, 104, 274 n. 17, 275 n. 18
Vesey, G. N. A., 276 n. 12

Walker, Ralph, 4
Walsh, W. H., 107–108, 285 n. 15
Warren, Daniel, 293 n. 48
Weight, 148
Weyl, Hermann, 232
Whitehead, Alfred North, 22, 141, 147–148
Wiggins, David, 316 n. 72
Williams, Bernard, 256–257
Wilson, Margaret, 171
Wittgenstein, Ludwig, 24, 25, 156, 197, 226, 264 n. 31
Wolff, R. P., 76, 78, 81, 277 n. 13
Wolff, Christian, 131
Wood, Allen, 305 n. 52

Zeno, 62